St Peter-on-the-Wall

St Peter-on-the-Wall

Landscape and heritage on the Essex coast

Edited by

Johanna Dale

First published in 2023 by
UCL Press
University College London
Gower Street
London WC1E 6BT

Available to download free: www.uclpress.co.uk

Collection © Editor, 2023
Text © Contributors, 2023
Images © Contributors and copyright holders named in captions, 2023

The authors have asserted their rights under the Copyright, Designs and Patents Act 1988 to be identified as the authors of this work.

A CIP catalogue record for this book is available from The British Library.

Any third-party material in this book is not covered by the book's Creative Commons licence. Details of the copyright ownership and permitted use of third-party material is given in the image (or extract) credit lines. If you would like to reuse any third-party material not covered by the book's Creative Commons licence, you will need to obtain permission directly from the copyright owner.

This book is published under a Creative Commons Attribution-Non-commercial Non-derivative 4.0 International licence (CC BY-NC-ND 4.0). This licence allows you to share, copy, distribute and transmit the work for personal and non-commercial use provided author and publisher attribution is clearly stated. Attribution should include the following information:

Dale, J. (ed). 2023. *St Peter-on-the-Wall: Landscape and heritage on the Essex coast*. London: UCL Press. https://doi.org/10.14324/111.9781800084353

Further details about Creative Commons licences are available at https://creativecommons.org/licenses/

ISBN: 978-1-80008-437-7 (Hbk.)
ISBN: 978-1-80008-436-0 (Pbk.)
ISBN: 978-1-80008-435-3 (PDF)
ISBN: 978-1-80008-438-4 (epub)
DOI: https://doi.org/10.14324/111.9781800084353

Contents

List of figures vii
List of tables xi
List of abbreviations xiii
List of contributors xv
Acknowledgements xix

Introduction: A contested landscape 1
Johanna Dale

Part I: St Peter's Chapel and its pre-modern contexts

1 St Peter's Chapel: What the building has to tell us 27
   David Andrews

   Appendix: The 1978 survey of St Peter's Chapel 41

2 The Roman fort of Othona 53
   Andrew Pearson

3 Dengie, *Ythancæstir* and Othona: The early medieval landscape context of St Peter-on-the-Wall 78
   Stephen Rippon

4 Cedd, Bradwell and the conversion of Anglo-Saxon England 110
   Barbara Yorke

5 Put to good use: The religious afterlife of the Saxon Shore Forts 130
   Richard Hoggett

6 Early medieval monasteries on the North Sea coast of Anglo-Saxon England 159
   David Petts

7 Land, marsh and sea: Transformations in landscape and
  farming at Bradwell on Sea, c. 1086–c. 1650   177
  Kevin Bruce and Christopher Thornton, assisted by Neil Wiffen

Part II: St Peter's Chapel and its modern contexts

8 'A building of altogether exceptional interest': The
  rediscovery of St Peter's Chapel in the nineteenth century,
  and its restoration in the twentieth   217
  James Bettley

9 'And withal a great silence': The spiritual landscape
  of the Othona Community and St Peter-on-the-Wall   239
  Ken Worpole

10 A case study in vulnerability: Bradwell A, a trial
   environment for nuclear power   257
   Gillian Darley

11 The St Peter's Way: Leisure, heritage and pilgrimage   286
   Johanna Dale

12 Maldon and the Blackwater Estuary: Literature, culture
   and practice where river meets sea   308
   Beth Whalley

13 The last of Essex: Contemporary architecture and
   cultural landscape   332
   Charles Holland

14 Care and maintenance in perpetuity? The nuclear
   landscape of the Blackwater Estuary   355
   Warren Harper and Nastassja Simensky

Index   380

List of figures

0.1	Aerial view of Bradwell Bay Airfield.	9
0.2	The former flower meadow.	13
0.3	Pilgrims approaching the chapel in the mid-1950s.	16
0.4	*The Chapel*, 2022, by Nabil Ali.	18
1.1	The chapel from the south-west.	27
1.2	Plan of the Roman fort and St Peter's Chapel as revealed by the nineteenth-century excavations.	28
1.3	Plan of Bradwell based on a map of 1583.	29
1.4	Plan of St Peter's Chapel.	31
1.5	Plan of the church at Reculver as originally built.	32
1.6	Elevation of the east wall seen from outside, showing the original masonry only, and reconstructing the two arches of the screen.	33
1.7	Fragment of plaster with red paint probably of thirteenth-century date (arrowed) in the soffit of a probable blocked window arch in the north-east corner of the nave.	36
1.8	Interior of the chapel, showing the blocked screen wall and the butt purlin roof.	39
1.9	Reconstruction of St Peter's Chapel.	40
1.10	West elevation of St Peter's Chapel.	43
1.11	West wall of St Peter's Chapel.	44
1.12	North elevation of St Peter's Chapel.	45
1.13	North wall of St Peter's Chapel.	46
1.14	East elevation of St Peter's Chapel.	47
1.15	East wall of St Peter's Chapel.	48
1.16	South elevation of St Peter's Chapel.	49
1.17	South wall of St Peter's Chapel.	50
2.1	Bradwell Chapel, from a drawing by the Rev. H. Milligan.	56
2.2	The upstanding Roman defences in 1907.	57
2.3	The Roman landscape around Othona.	58

2.4	Reconstruction of the Roman fort at Pevensey (Anderita).	60
2.5	Field investigations of Othona: 1990–present.	62
2.6	Othona: plan of identified Roman features and surface artefact distribution.	62
2.7	Military metalwork recovered during the 1864 investigations of Othona.	73
3.1	The Anglo-Saxon kingdoms of eastern England and the boundary zones between them, and the postulated boundaries of the *regio* called *Deningei* and its major geology/soil types.	79
3.2	The landscape context of Othona and *Ythancæstir*.	80
3.3	Evidence used in reconstructing the extent of the *regio* of *Deningei*.	84
3.4	The possible extent of the 70 *cassati* in the *regio* called *Deningei* that King Swæfred of the East Saxons granted to Ingwald, bishop of London.	95
3.5	The eighth-century fish weir at Sales Point, near Othona, in the Blackwater Estuary, Essex, and reconstruction drawing by Nick Nethercoat.	96
4.1	The remains of the medieval church of Lindisfarne, on the site of the church founded by Aidan.	112
4.2	The medieval church of Lastingham, probably on the site of the church founded by Cedd.	114
4.3	Aerial view of Lastingham showing its position between Ryedale and the North York Moors.	119
4.4	Statue on Lindisfarne of St Aidan by Kathleen Parbury (1958).	121
4.5	Lastingham 07 and Lastingham 08: two fragments from a possible shrine of Cedd at Lastingham.	125
5.1	The locations of the Saxon Shore Forts, spanning the coast of Britain from The Wash to the Solent.	132
5.2	A map identifying the Saxon Shore Forts, from a fifteenth-century Swiss copy of the *Notitia Dignitatum*.	133
5.3	Watercolour view of the ruins of Walton Castle, painted by Francis Grose in 1766.	137
5.4	Aerial view of Burgh Castle from the south-west, showing the walls of the Roman fort and the parish church.	140
5.5	'Interior ruins of Reculver's church, Kent', by I. Baynes.	144
6.1	View across the Alde Estuary towards Iken.	162

6.2	Reconstruction of the Saxon settlement at Barber's Point by David Gillingwater.	171
7.1	Reconstruction of probable boundaries of Domesday Estates (1086) in north-east Bradwell on Sea.	178
7.2	Reconstruction of boundaries and location of medieval and Tudor estates (to *c.* 1650) in north-east Bradwell on Sea.	179
7.3	Map of East Hall Farm in 1768, an estate belonging to New College, Oxford, from 1391 to 1865.	183
7.4	Map of Down Hall and Gardiners Farm in 1753.	187
7.5	Map of Wymarks Farm in 1714.	189
8.1	Interior of St Peter's Chapel, looking west, 1907.	218
8.2	Visit by the Essex Field Club, 6 August 1910.	221
8.3	Survey drawing of St Peter's Chapel by HM Office of Works.	222
8.4	St Peter's Chapel under restoration, *c.* 1919–20, showing the north and west walls.	223
8.5	St Peter's Chapel from the south, 1925.	224
8.6	St Peter's Chapel from the south, 1942, showing damage to the roof, and barbed wire and other military debris.	226
8.7	Interior of St Peter's Chapel, looking east, 1947.	228
8.8	Laurence King's proposals for restoring St Peter's Chapel to its presumed Saxon appearance, 1948.	230
8.9	Interior of St Peter's Chapel, 2020, showing the hanging crucifix by Francis Stephens, 1949, and altar by Gerald Shenstone, 1985.	234
9.1	Medlar Cottage, the Othona Community.	241
9.2	One of the original wartime Nissen huts, first home of the Othona community.	244
9.3	The permanent sleeping yurts at Othona.	245
9.4	The Solar Building at Othona, made out of compacted clay dug from the ground below and elevated above flood level.	246
10.1	The model of Calder Hall displayed at Bradwell Village Hall, photograph originally published in the *Maldon and Burnham Standard*, 2 February 1956.	266
10.2	Voting at the Bradwell Parish Council meeting, photograph originally published in the *Maldon and Burnham Standard*, 22 March 1956.	268
10.3	View of the power station from the west in 1969.	279

11.1	First view of the chapel across the Tillingham and Bradwell marshes.	288
11.2	St Mary's Mundon before and after coming into the care of the Friends of Friendless Churches.	302
12.1	Viking longship at the 1991 millennium celebrations.	317
12.2	Panel 1 of the Maldon Embroidery.	318
12.3	Panel 2 of the Maldon Embroidery.	319
12.4	*Byrhtnoth*, by John Doubleday, 2006.	321
13.1	*A House for Essex*, by FAT/ Grayson Perry, external view.	333
13.2	*A House for Essex map,* by Grayson Perry.	335
13.3	Blackmore Church.	345
13.4	*A House for Essex* exterior and interior sketches.	347
13.5	*A House for Essex* by FAT/ Grayson Perry, interior of living room.	349
14.1	Thomson & Craighead, *Temporary Index*, 2016.	361
14.2	Goldin+Senneby, *Spruce Time*.	365
14.3	Inas Halabi, WE HAVE ALWAYS KNOWN THE WIND'S DIRECTION, 2019–2020.	369
14.4	*Rosa floribunda* 'Atom Bomb' displayed in Gabriella Hirst's *An English Garden*, 2021.	371

List of tables

3.1	Data used in reconstructing the 'greater Tillingham' estate (King Swæfred's grant of 70 *cassati* in the *regio* called *Deningei*).	86
3.2	Concordance of the various references to coins having been found at Othona or Bradwell on Sea.	98
4.1	Timeline for the life of Cedd.	111
7.1	Domesday manors in Bradwell, tenants-in-chief and sub-tenants, 1066 and (1086).	180
7.2	Domesday economic statistics: population, ploughs and value, 1066 and (1086).	190
7.3	Domesday economic statistics: pasture, woodland, animals and fisheries, 1066 and (1086).	195
7.4	Bradwell occupations as indicated by 63 wills, 1565–1604.	205
7.5	Major exports of produce from Bradwell, 1565–1703.	207

List of abbreviations

BL	British Library
BRB	Bradwell Power Generation Company Limited
Cal. Inq. p.m.	*Calendar of Inquisitions Post Mortem preserved in the Public Record Office* (HMSO, 1904–2004)
Cal. Pat.	*Calendar of the Patent Rolls preserved in the Public Record Office* (HMSO, 1891–1986)
DB Ess.	*Domesday Book: Essex* (Rumble 1983)
ERO	Essex Record Office
Feet of Fines, Essex	*Feet of Fines for Essex*, Volumes 1–4. Colchester: Essex Archaeological Society, 1899–1910; Volumes 5–6. Oxford: Leopard's Head Press, 1991, 1993.
HMSO	Her (His) Majesty's Stationery Office. London.
NCA	New College Archives (Oxford).
NHLE	National Heritage List England: https://historicengland.org.uk/listing/the-list
ODNB	*Oxford Dictionary of National Biography*
RCHME	Royal Commission on the Historical Monuments of England
Rot. Hund.	*Rotuli Hundredorum* (Record Commission, 1812).
TNA	The National Archives
VCH	*Victoria History of the Counties of England*

List of contributors

David Andrews is an independent researcher and consultant who spent 17 years running archaeological projects in Italy and England, and over 20 years working as an archaeologist and conservation officer at Essex County Council, eventually in the role of Historic Buildings Manager.

James Bettley is an architectural historian whose publications include new editions of the Pevsner Architectural Guides to *Essex* (2007), *Suffolk* (2015) and *Hertfordshire* (2019). He has also contributed to successive volumes of the *Victoria County History of Essex*. He was awarded his PhD by the Courtauld Institute of Art in 1999 and was elected a Fellow of the Society of Antiquaries in 2002. He has lived in Essex since 1991.

Kevin Bruce is a local historian who has researched diverse aspects of the local history of the Dengie Hundred area for over 50 years, with particular attention to Bradwell and Tillingham and the coastal marshlands. He shares his knowledge of local and natural history with visiting school groups to the Othona Community at Bradwell and gives talks to local groups and societies. He worked at Bradwell power station for 35 years and produced the booklet celebrating its 40th anniversary. Current projects include researching the impressive, newly discovered medieval walls of what is believed to be one of the bishops of London's palaces in Southminster and the land activities around the Essex coast by the Royal Navy during the Napoleonic Wars.

Johanna Dale is a research fellow in the Department of History at UCL, where she previously held a British Academy Postdoctoral Fellowship. Her research is focused on the political and cultural history of the medieval period, and her first book, *Inauguration and Liturgical Kingship in the Long Twelfth Century: Male and female accession rituals in England, France and the Empire*, was shortlisted for the Royal Historical Society's Whitfield Prize in 2020. As a resident of Essex, she has a long-standing interest in the medieval heritage of the county.

Gillian Darley was President of the Twentieth Century Society from 2014 to 2021 and a Trustee of the Society for the Protection of Ancient Buildings (SPAB) until 2015. She is a widely published author and biographer, broadcaster and journalist. Her first book was *Villages of Vision* (1975) and the most recent *Excellent Essex* (2019). She co-authored *Ian Nairn: Words in place* (2013) with David McKie.

Warren Harper is a curator and researcher based between Toronto, Canada, and Southend-on-Sea, Essex, UK, where he is Co-Director at The Old Waterworks (TOW), an artist-led charity that provides studios, facilities and research and development opportunities for artists. He is a PhD candidate at Goldsmiths, University of London, where his practice-based curatorial research project investigates the nuclear landscapes of the Blackwater Estuary and Foulness Island, and Essex's role in the UK's nuclear story. Warren has worked with various galleries and institutions, including Arts Catalyst, Focal Point Gallery, South London Gallery, Cement Fields and Goldsmiths, University of London.

Richard Hoggett is a freelance heritage consultant, lecturer and writer with over 20 years' experience in the academic, commercial and local authority heritage sectors. His doctoral research, completed at the University of East Anglia, focused on the historical and archaeological evidence for Christianisation in the Anglo-Saxon kingdom of East Anglia, and was subsequently published as *The Archaeology of the East Anglian Conversion* (Boydell, 2010). Since then, he has published extensively on heritage-related subjects in numerous books and journals, and recently authored the *Middle to Late Anglo-Saxon Resource Assessment* for the East of England Regional Research Framework. He is an elected Fellow of the Society of Antiquaries of London and a member of the Chartered Institute for Archaeologists.

Charles Holland is an architect and a Professor of Architecture at the University of Brighton. He is the principal of Charles Holland Architects, an architecture, design and research practice based in the UK. He is a former director of the architecture and art practice FAT and a Visiting Professor at Yale University and the ABK Stuttgart. Charles writes regularly about architecture- and design-related issues and is currently writing a book – *How to Enjoy Architecture* – for Yale University Press.

Andrew Pearson is Post-Excavation Manager at Cotswold Archaeology. He holds a PhD from the University of Reading, is a Fellow of the Society of Antiquaries of London and has research associate status at Brunel

University. He is the author of six books, which include *The Roman Shore Forts* (Tempus, 2002) and *The Construction of the Saxon Shore Forts* (BAR, 2003).

David Petts is Associate Professor in the Department of Archaeology, Durham University. He specialises in the archaeology of early medieval Britain, with a particular interest in early Christianity and monasticism. He has been carrying out collaborative fieldwork on the early medieval monastery of Lindisfarne (Holy Island) since 2016, which has led to a wider interest in the early medieval engagement with the islands and maritime cultural landscapes from both an economic and a social perspective. He is also working on the archaeology of the later medieval and post-medieval coast of eastern England.

Stephen Rippon is Professor of Landscape Archaeology at the University of Exeter and a former President of the Society for Medieval Archaeology. His recent books include *The Fields of Britannia* (with Chris Smart and Ben Pears, 2015), *Kingdom, Civitas and County* (2018), *Planning in the Early Medieval Landscape* (with John Blair and Chris Smart, 2020) and *Territoriality and the Early Medieval Landscape: The countryside of the East Saxon kingdom* (2022).

Nastassja Simensky is an artist and lecturer who often works collaboratively with artists and non-artists including fishermen, archaeologists, ham radio operators, composers and musicians to make writings, place-specific performances, events, sound works and videos as a form of ongoing fieldwork. Commissions and residencies include: *SHERDS*, Nottingham Contemporary, 2020; *Zu Gast bei den KunstVereinenRuhr*, Urbane Künste Ruhr, 2019; *Brightspot*, Diaspore Project Space, 2018; *Material Culture Unearthed*, In-situ Brierfield, 2018; *Radiophrenia*, Centre for Contemporary Art Glasgow, 2017; Estuary Festival: Points of Departure, 2016; and *Fictive Dreams*, ICA Singapore, 2016.

Christopher Thornton recently retired as County Editor of the *Victoria County History of Essex*. He remains a volunteer researcher with that project and an Associate Fellow of the Institute of Historical Research, University of London. He received his doctorate from the Centre for English Local History, University of Leicester. After holding research posts at the University of Leicester and Hertford College, Oxford, he joined the *Victoria County History* in 1992. He has contributed articles to five volumes in the *VCH Essex* series, and edited three volumes, as well as publishing many articles and edited books on local history and medieval history. He is a Fellow of the Society of Antiquaries of London, Chairman of the Friends of Historic Essex and a vice-president of the Essex Society for Archaeology and History.

Beth Whalley holds a PhD from King's College London and works at the intersection of early English studies, political ecology and contemporary creative-critical practice. She has authored articles for *Of Mud and Flame: A Penda's Fen sourcebook* (Strange Attractor, 2019), *Yearbook of English Studies* (2022) and *Lost Artefacts from Medieval England and France: Representation, reimagination, recovery* (York Medieval Press, 2022). She is also a project coordinator for two of Historic England's Cultural Programmes in Somerset.

Neil Wiffen is a Broomfield-based historian who has worked at the Essex Record Office since 2000. He was the Honorary Editor of the *Essex Journal* between 2007 and 2020, and he is currently studying for a PhD in Landscape History at the University of East Anglia. His main areas of interest are agricultural and military history.

Ken Worpole is a writer and social historian, whose work includes books on architecture, landscape and public policy. In recent years he has focused on recovering the social history of communitarian experiments in town and country, writing extensively about the Essex landscape and its twentieth-century social history, in such books as *350 Miles: An Essex journey* and *The New English Landscape*. His most recent book, *No Matter How Many Skies Have Fallen* (2021), is a study of a wartime Christian pacifist community in Frating, Essex. He was a founder member of the Demos think-tank and of openDemocracy, and has served on the Expert Panel of the Heritage Lottery Fund, the UK government's Green Spaces Task Force, and as an adviser to the Commission for Architecture and the Built Environment.

Barbara Yorke is Professor Emeritus of Early Medieval History at the University of Winchester and Honorary Professor of the Institute of Archaeology, University College London. Major publications include *Kings and Kingdoms in Early Anglo-Saxon England* (1990), *Wessex in the Early Middle Ages* (1995), *Nunneries and the Anglo-Saxon Royal Houses* (2003), *The Conversion of Britain, 600–800* (2006) and *Power and Place in Early Medieval Europe* (edited with Jayne Carroll and Andrew Reynolds, 2019). She is currently historical adviser to the Winchester Cathedral Mortuary Chest project and to the Leverhulme-funded 'Lordship and Landscape in East Anglia AD 400–800'.

Acknowledgements

This book is a response to the public consultation launched by BRB in early 2020. Although Bradwell had long been designated a potential site for nuclear development, many local people, me included, were shocked by the plans that came through our letterboxes, as they significantly exceed, indeed practically double, the scale of development envisaged in the government's appraisal of sustainability site report (2010). BRB also intend to extend the proposed development site eastwards so that it would come to within 150m of the seventh-century chapel of St Peter-on-the-Wall, which, as the front cover shows, currently sits in splendid isolation close to the shore. As a medieval historian living in the area, I felt a responsibility to highlight the inevitable detrimental impact such an enormous development would have on this wonderfully atmospheric early medieval survival.

My greatest thanks go to the contributors to this volume, who answered my pleas for help and produced outstanding essays in the challenging conditions of the COVID-19 pandemic. In the early months of the pandemic, as I began to think about putting together a book, I sent lots of unsolicited emails, many to people I did not yet know. All were met with supportive and positive responses. It should be mentioned that while all contributors agree on the academic interest and importance of the Roman fort and chapel at Bradwell, the inclusion of their work in this volume does not imply an opinion on the merits of nuclear power in general, or the Bradwell B plans in particular. I am also very grateful to those who reviewed essays for me, including Tim Howson, Eric Cambridge, Andrew Gardner, Maria Medlycott, Adam Chapman, Bob Mills, Clare Price, Rebecca Pinner, Len Scales, Katrina Navickas, Linda Ross and Catherine Clarke. My own chapter on the St Peter's Way would have been much less enjoyable to research without the company of my friend Chesca Douglas, who uncomplainingly tramped through the autumnal mud with me as I droned on about medieval landscapes. Many thanks are also due to Jane Wadham, who kindly agreed that the previously unpublished drawings from her 1978 thesis on the chapel could be included in the volume. The wonderful cover image was supplied by Jim Pullen of Mersea Island, just across the Blackwater from Bradwell.

Many thanks are also due to Chris Penfold and all the team at UCL Press and Bourchier for guiding this book from its conception to its birth. The Essex Heritage Trust generously provided a grant to cover the cost of indexing. I thank them for supporting this volume and also all the excellent local history and heritage projects their funding makes possible across the county every year.

Essex is a hugely underrated county, which doubtless contributes to its unselfconscious and unpretentious charm. Its rural coast is bewitching. It has certainly bewitched me. We came to Essex purely for the pragmatic reason that it was a cheap place to keep a sailing boat, never expecting to stay long. That was 13½ years ago. I am still amazed by what we found here. The understated beauty of the vast expanses of grazing marsh, saltmarsh, mud, sea and sky, ever shifting with the weather and the rhythm of the tide. The sense of timelessness that obscures a complex historic environment that continually intrigues. The outstanding natural environment, in which it is routine to encounter curlew, avocet, kestrel, marsh harrier, owl, hare, stoat and seal, amongst many other wonders. I have spent so much time on muddy sea walls and up muddy creeks that I have come, to borrow the words of J. A. Baker, to feel 'like a wading bird, happy only at the edges of the world where land and water meet'. For all that I really could have done without the extra pressure of taking on an additional project during the pandemic, my work on this book has been done in gratitude for the happiness, release and friendship we have found on this coast, on land, in the mud and on the water. It is dedicated to my fledgling wading bird, Sebastian, and to all the other children of the Dengie Peninsula, in hope for their futures on this edge of the world.

North Fambridge
December 2022

Introduction

A contested landscape
Johanna Dale

In spring 2020 a Stage One public consultation was held by the Bradwell Power Generation Company Limited (BRB), a partnership between China General Nuclear Power Group (CGN) and Électricité de France (EDF), about their plans for the development of a new nuclear power station at Bradwell on Sea on the Essex coast. In the foreword of the consultation summary document, CEO Alan Raymant wrote that the proposed power station 'would build on the long-established history of nuclear power in the area'.[1] As part of their public-facing work BRB have created a local history website called 'My Bradwell', charting the history of the area from 1901 until 2002.[2] While it is reasonable for a history project to be chronologically limited, it seems clear that these terminal dates have been chosen for particular reasons, to present a positive narrative of the history of nuclear power at Bradwell and to justify future development. The first entry in the 'My Bradwell' timeline is 1901, with this start date chosen because it was apparently in 1901 that 'plans for a power station in the area were hatched'.[3] It is clear that this is being presented as the precedent for the later development of Bradwell A, but in reality, a small 'generation station' for a proposed light railway hardly 'shows the ambition for a power plant in Essex' at the opening of the twentieth century, as the website goes on to claim.[4] The chronological end of the project is 2002, when Bradwell A ceased to produce electricity, thereby conveniently avoiding the complications of the decommissioning period.

While one might expect a corporate history project to emphasise positive aspects of history that support the corporation's aims and objectives, it is also necessary to challenge such a one-dimensional presentation of history to the public. The aim of this book is to place the 65 years of nuclear activity at Bradwell in the context of much longer-established histories of human activity in the area. It has as its focus the seventh-century chapel of St Peter-on-the-Wall, a unique and atmospheric early medieval survival, which would be significantly impacted by both the construction and the operation of a power station of the magnitude proposed.[5] The book aims to establish an academic baseline around the monument and the landscape surrounding it and to inform debate and policy around Bradwell B. While geopolitical considerations have injected a degree of uncertainty into the nuclear permissions process, even if deteriorating Anglo-Sino relations were to spell the end of plans for Bradwell B in its current incarnation, the site remains designated for possible future nuclear development, meaning this book can also inform possible future policy debates. The chapters in this book highlight the multiple ways in which the chapel and landscape around Bradwell are historically and archaeologically significant, while also drawing attention to the modern importance of Bradwell as a place of Christian worship, of sanctuary and of cultural production. As the chapters have been written under time pressure, due to the nuclear permissions process, and also during a period when the pandemic led to libraries and archives being closed for extended periods, this book is not intended to be the last word on the chapel. Instead, its contributors seek to draw attention to the manifest historical and archaeological importance of the building and surrounding landscape and, it is hoped, to be the catalyst for subsequent research leading to a more comprehensive understanding and appreciation of the chapel and its setting.

St Peter-on-the-Wall stands at the eastern end of a narrow strip of higher ground at the north-eastern corner of the Dengie Peninsula, which is bounded to the north by the River Blackwater, to the south by the River Crouch and to the east by the Greater Thames Estuary, into which the Crouch and Blackwater both flow. This stretch of the Essex coast evokes a sense of timelessness; however, this is an illusion and belies the changes, both natural and man-made, that have formed and transformed the landscape.[6] The boundary between land and sea has historically been rather more fluid and blurred than the sharp rigid lines of sea walls on modern maps suggest. The area has seen Roman colonisers, Christian missionaries and Viking incursions, and has been defended against possible Dutch, French and German invasions. Since the mid-nineteenth century this stretch of the Essex coast has also been subject to a number of large-scale external interventions, some of which have come to pass and others of which have failed to make the leap from plan to reality. From the stalled land reclamation works, during which the walls of the Roman fort were rediscovered in 1864, through the use of the extensive mudflats by the military and the purchase of nearby Foulness Island by the War Office, a planned light railway from Southend to Colchester, the development of an airfield at the start of the Second World War and the building of Bradwell A, to the plans for a major new airport on the Maplin Sands in the 1970s, the low-lying and rural coast around Bradwell has been seen as ripe for major developments. The lower reaches of the Thames Estuary, in which Bradwell lies, have often been treated as marginal.[7] A place for unwanted things, for London's sewage and aeroplane noise, for nuclear power and for weapons testing.[8] Whereas the countryside, villages and towns on the Thames above London have long been appreciated and preserved for their historic significance and for the story they tell of England's past, the tidal Thames Estuary has, since the demise of the excursion industry, following the sinking of the *Princess Alice* in 1878, seldom been valued for its past.[9] Instead the lower reaches of the Thames have come to stand for present and future, a place of industry, trade and commerce, for the benefit of the metropolis and the nation. The proposed Bradwell B nuclear power station should thus be considered in this wider context of planned large-scale external intervention and exploitation of the outer reaches of the estuary, which raises all sorts of questions about place, spatial conflicts and 'power geometries'.[10]

The failure of the land reclamation works, the demise of the proposed light railway and the abandonment of plans to build an airport on the Maplin Sands are indicative of the fact that taming this stretch of coast has not always been as straightforward a proposition as it seems from London and elsewhere. While on modern maps the Dengie Peninsula appears to have hard boundaries, defined by the straight lines of its sea walls, the reality is that these barriers have always been and remain permeable. Since the initial moves to 'in' the marsh during the Middle Ages, high tides have on occasion overwhelmed sea walls and set back the process of land reclamation.[11] In recent years, a number of managed realignment schemes have begun to reverse the 'inning' process, returning reclaimed land to salt marsh, and the South Suffolk and Essex Shoreline Management Plan envisages further managed realignment around the peninsula.[12] The underlying topography continues to characterise the landscape; it has been obscured but not erased through the establishment of coastal grazing marsh. The ghostly tendrils of former tidal creeks lie dormant but ready to reassert themselves, should the sea walls fail or be deliberately breached.[13]

The physical reality of the peninsula, bounded by tidal rivers and fringed by coastal grazing marsh, much of which lies below mean high-water level, helps to explain the failure of some of the more grandiose plans, such as the planned light railway from Southend to Colchester, which included the small 'generation station' at Bradwell. An application was made in November 1901 for permission to construct the Southend (and District), Bradwell on Sea and Colchester Light Railways. The proposed route of the railways crossed three bodies of water: the Crouch between Wallasea Island and Creeksea, the Blackwater between Bradwell and Mersea, and the Strood channel, which separates Mersea Island from the mainland.[14] While a railway bridge was a viable option for crossing the Strood, bridges were not suitable on the Crouch, where one would have prevented navigation upstream, or on the Blackwater, which additionally was far too wide and deep, so the railways terminated at the riverbanks and alternative intermediate onward transport was proposed. An early iteration of the plan from May 1901 included a cable car crossing of the Crouch, at an estimated cost of £16,000.[15] By August 1902 this had been replaced by a ferry, presumably a money-saving modification, at £8,000 being half the estimated cost of the cable car.[16] At both Bradwell and West Mersea the railway was planned to run out on substantial piers, extending to below the line of low-water springs so that the connecting ferry could run at all states of the tide. The sum of £20,000 was earmarked for a pier at Bradwell, where the deep-water channel to Maldon lies relatively close to the shore. Double that amount was estimated for West Mersea, where shallow mudflats extend far out into the Blackwater. Of a total cost estimate of £294,282 in August 1902, over £80,000 was earmarked to enable the crossing of the Crouch and Blackwater rivers by ferry and for works on the Strood channel.[17] The expense and complexity of the scheme meant that it never got off the drawing board, but even if it had, it seems unlikely that demand would have justified it. Only a few years earlier, in 1895, a through route from Southend to Colchester via Wickford, Maldon and Witham had closed to passengers due to low usage after only five years of operation.[18] Far from demonstrating the 'ambition for a power plant', plans for the light railway exhibited a distinct lack of understanding of the realities of the area's geographical and economic topography.

The extent of the mudflats on the Dengie Peninsula coast has made it attractive to speculative large-scale attempts at land reclamation, often in the face of significant opposition from local landowners.[19] The South Essex Estuary and Reclamation Act was passed on 17 June 1852 to enable the reclaiming of 'marshes, mud banks, and waste lands of considerable extent'; however, this ambitious plan had already met with some scepticism.[20] Lewis D. B. Gordon, who inspected the scheme for the

Admiralty and authored a report that was presented to parliament in March 1852, wrote that, while the proposal claimed it would bring into cultivation 30,420 acres of land, his view was that there was 'not 1,000 acres along the whole foreshore' that were fit for reclamation, especially within the 21-year time frame envisaged by the Act, given the slow rate of accretion along the coast.[21] The Admiralty were understandably particularly concerned about the impact the scheme would have on navigation, given that what was proposed would profoundly alter approaches to the Colne, Blackwater and Crouch rivers. Gordon's conclusion was that, once what was prejudicial to the public from a navigational perspective had been removed from the plans, the project would probably not be viable. The Admiralty's warnings were not heeded, yet they were shown to be prescient: by 1868 the South Essex Estuary and Reclamation Company had been wound up, precipitating a legal case in Chancery.[22] By then, of course, the initial work on the project had led to the discovery of Roman walls near St Peter's Chapel, precipitating a flurry of antiquarian archaeological activity, as James Bettley's chapter in this volume describes.

Interest in reclaiming large areas of land on the Essex coast did not disappear with the winding up of the South Essex Estuary and Reclamation Company. The Metropolis Sewage and Essex Reclamation Company aimed to reclaim the flats around Foulness Island and along the coast of the Dengie Peninsula by constructing pipelines from London to carry the capital's sewage on to the areas to be reclaimed.[23] This too came to nothing, and after 1880 the agricultural depression meant that plans for large-scale land reclamation faded away until the 1960s, when the Thames Estuary Development Company proposed a joint airport–seaport on the Maplin Sands south of Foulness Island, involving the reclamation of 18,000 acres.[24] The Foulness airport proposal was accepted by the Roskill Commission as one of four plausible sites for a third airport serving London, from an initial longlist of 78 sites, the other three being Thurleigh near Bedford, Cublington in Buckinghamshire and Nuthampstead in Hertfordshire.[25] In January 1971 the Commission revealed Cublington as the preferred option of all but one commissioner, but when the government formally responded to the Roskill report in April, it announced that the site of the airport would be Foulness rather than Cublington.[26] In this decision they followed the view of the dissenting commissioner, Professor Colin Buchanan, who had refused to endorse most of the report and instead had produced his own 11-page note of dissent, in which he rejected the cost-benefit approach taken by the commission and invoked what he saw as central planning principles, the protection of the rural background around London and the preservation of national heritage. Buchanan had no doubt that 'the things I find of interest in the open background of London are things that will interest many generations to come. I am profoundly certain they are *good* things.'[27] In his assertion that Foulness was therefore the only acceptable site, he stood in a long tradition that viewed the Thames Estuary and the Essex coast as being of less interest and value than the Thames Valley and the Chilterns.[28] As Derrick Wood, of opposition group Defenders of Essex, put it, 'It was clear where political pressures were driving the Government. Environment, defined as the preservation at all costs of one's own present way of life, was the great god and all things inland were beautiful, anything to do with the coastal regions ugly and expendable.'[29] The fact that in 1971 some 25 MPs from constituencies representing inland sites had come together to form an 'Inland Group' to promote Foulness, demonstrates the truth of Wood's assertion.[30]

The oil crisis of 1973–4 precipitated by the Arab–Israeli War and a change to a Labour government saw the cancellation of the project in July 1974. By then projected costs had spiralled, weakening the economic case, and the idea that an airport at Foulness would have minimal environmental impact had been exposed as an illusion, once the ancillary development of transport links and a new town housing 600,000 people was taken into account.[31] Alongside local grassroots organisation the Defenders of Essex, the RSPB had emerged as an opponent. In an impassioned essay published in the RSPB's autumn 1971 magazine, Essex-based naturalist J. A. Baker argued for the importance of the Essex coast while alluding to outsiders' dismissal of its value:

> An austere place perhaps, withdrawn, some might say desolate ... When strangers come here, many will say, 'Its flat. There is nothing here'. And they will go away again. But there is something here, something more than the thousands of birds and insects, than the millions of marine creatures. The wilderness is here ... Man is killing the wilderness, hunting it down. On the east coast of England, this is perhaps its last home.[32]

In Baker's view, when the airport went ahead, 'this last home of the wilderness will be imprisoned in a cage of insensate noise. Cordoned by motorways, overshadowed by the huge airport city, the uniqueness of this place will be destroyed as completely as though it has been blown to pieces by bombs.'[33]

Baker's invocation of military destruction referenced another type of large-scale government intervention in his coastal birdwatching territory: military use. The Shoeburyness firing range and Atomic Weapons Research Establishment (AWRE) on Foulness Island had been added complications to the airport plans, and both were part of a longer history of military involvement on the Essex coast.[34] Taking an extended perspective, this includes the Saxon Shore Fort of Othona, on whose walls St Peter's Chapel was built. Although, as Andrew Pearson's chapter makes explicit, the exact functions of the Shore Forts remain disputed, Othona can be seen as the first major infrastructure project on this stretch of coast. Following the departure of Roman forces, the dilapidated fort then became the base for a new wave of Christian colonisation from the mid-seventh century, before the advent of the Vikings brought violence to coastal communities across northern Europe, including along the Greater Thames Estuary. The defeat of Byrhtnoth, Ealdorman of Essex, at the hands of Vikings at the Battle of Maldon in August 991 was commemorated in an Old English poem, which still influences the culture of the Blackwater Estuary, as Beth Whalley's chapter in this volume makes clear. Another pivotal battle between Danish and English forces was probably fought at Ashingdon, on the south bank of the River Crouch, in 1016, at which Canute triumphed over Edmund Ironside.[35] The low-lying, marshy Essex coast with its myriad tidal creeks, was vulnerable to attack from the sea, and in the late eighteenth century plans were made to defend the coast against the French. In April 1798 a naval signal station was set up by St Peter's Chapel as part of a chain of stations stretching from the Nore up to Yarmouth; Linnets Cottage, planned as a temporary building, but which still stands to the south-east of the chapel, was constructed at this time to house the signal station personnel. Shortly after the threat of invasion rose again with the resumption of hostilities in 1803, plans were put forward for a chain of Martello towers along the Essex coast.[36] Three were proposed for Bradwell at Sales Point, Wymarks and New Wick, and two either side of the Crouch Estuary. The huge cost of the whole scheme caused the withdrawal of the first ten proposed towers, with the chain instead beginning across the Blackwater Estuary at St Osyth.[37]

From the mid-nineteenth century military use of the Essex coast intensified. In 1855 the War Department had established an artillery practice and testing range at South Shoebury, overlooking the Shoebury Sands (a continuation of the Maplin Sands).[38] By the end of the century the government had determined that Foulness and the Maplin Sands should be used as a weapons research and development centre, and thus began the slow acquisition of the island by the War Department. Starting in 1900, the War Department bought up land farm by farm on the island, but the lord of the manor of Foulness, Alan G. Finch, refused to sell, and as he leased large portions of the sands to copyhold tenants for fishing kiddles, negotiations in 1912 to secure shooting rights over the sands failed.[39] Following Finch's death in 1914, the department was able to purchase the lordship and its ancient demesne lands, which comprised about two-thirds of the island.[40] In his history of Foulness Island, published in 1970 in the context of the airport plans, J. R. Smith speculated on the possibility of the kiddle fishing industry being resurrected 'when the Ministry leaves Foulness and firing across the sands ceases'.[41] Fifty years later the Ministry itself has left Foulness, but the weapons development industry has not. Qinetiq, a public limited company created out of the now-defunct government organisation Defence Evaluation and Research Agency (DERA), which floated on the London Stock Exchange in 2006, now manages the site for the MOD and regularly tests weapons on the island and sands, precluding kiddle fishing for the foreseeable future.[42]

The twentieth century also saw the intensification of military activity on the other side of the Crouch on the Dengie Peninsula. During the First World War troops camped around the peninsula for training and St Peter's Chapel was commandeered as a base for members of the signal corps.[43] Some of the sailing barges operating out of Bradwell Creek were employed in transporting coke over to France for use by troops, in addition to their usual crop-carrying work. Between the wars the area became increasingly popular for recreation, but most recreational features were swept away in the run-up to the Second World War. In 1937 'hundred acre' field on Down Hall Farm was commandeered for the laying out of a grass airstrip and a bombing range was constructed on the Dengie Flats.[44] Targets were built off Sandbeach Farm and three towers were built to monitor bombing activity. The northern tower still just about stands to the east of the chapel and some of the targets partially survive on the mudflats, where navigational markers warn sailors taking the short route between the Crouch and Blackwater of their existence. As elsewhere in England, pillboxes were constructed around the peninsula, with a particular concentration of boxes (11 in total) between the chapel and Bradwell Waterside. In 1941 the Air Ministry expanded the grass airstrip of the bombing range to create a full-scale airfield, known as Bradwell Bay. With a main runway aligned roughly east–west, two secondary runways and the full suite of ancillary buildings, the construction of Bradwell Bay, covering much of Down Hall, New Wick and Wymarks farms, transformed the landscape of Bradwell on Sea, which became a

Figure 0.1 Aerial view of Bradwell Bay Airfield. Kevin Bruce Collection.

military zone.[45] With the end of the war, the zone was scaled back, but the bombing range continued to be used by the United States Air Force.

The history of all these plans, hatched predominantly by outsiders, for large-scale land reclamation and infrastructure projects, both civil and military, culminating with the proposed Bradwell B nuclear power station, raises all sorts of questions about place, space and power relations.[46] While answering all these questions is beyond the scope of this book, by championing the importance of Bradwell's historic environment it aims to draw attention to some of the issues at stake. The planning system is, as Kirby put it, 'responsible for locating on the landscape major negative externalities'.[47] There can be no doubt that a development of the size and kind proposed would be a major negative externality, and it is important to recognise the level of damage that would be done to Bradwell's historic environment should it go ahead. It is possible to see the South Essex Estuary and Reclamation Company as being part of a longer lineage of reclaiming land in the area for agricultural use, as outlined in Kevin Bruce, Chris Thornton and Neil Wiffen's contribution to this book, albeit on a far larger scale and initiated by outsiders rather than local landowners. Some of the military activities can also be understood as part of an extended history of defending a coastline that could provide an enemy with easy access to the capital. The establishment of a military complex based around Foulness Island and the siting of a nuclear power station at Bradwell, however, were both radical breaks from past human activities in the area and wider region. The requirements of military weapons development and training, as well as the generation of nuclear power, ruptured existing patterns of human activity by introducing large military–industrial complexes into predominantly rural areas.[48]

Internal colonisation by the military from the late nineteenth century, the context in which Foulness came under military control, saw significant areas of heath and farmland acquired throughout England and Wales, as well as areas of the Scottish Highlands. This wave of internal colonisation was accelerated by withdrawal from the colonies and the mass mobilisations during the world wars of the early twentieth century.[49] The increasing range of rifled artillery and the introduction of mechanised mobile weapons necessitated the use of large tracts of land, from which the public were excluded by military by-laws, and aerial warfare also irrevocably transformed the rural landscape.[50] Sites were ideally relatively remote, both due to potential danger to civilians and for reasons of secrecy. Major acquisitions, alongside Foulness, included Salisbury Plain (Wiltshire), Otterburn (Northumberland) and Dartmoor (Devon).[51] Foulness, an isolated island with a small population engaged exclusively in agriculture and fishing, was transformed into a militarised space. Matthew Flintham has explored how, over time, military space has developed on the island, where a dwindling civilian population still lives.[52] Following the initial acquisition, a network of military roads, infrastructures and facilities spread across the island, military by-laws were imposed, restrictions were imposed on shipping due to artillery firing out to sea, and airspace above and around the island is also restricted, creating what Flintham has termed 'an invisible carapace'.[53] The military presence is not therefore confined to the island, because the controlled space extends both vertically and horizontally. Moreover, the sound impact of military activity extends further, with explosions heard all across the Thames Estuary and particularly in areas of Southend-on-Sea and across the flat coastal grazing marshes of the Dengie Peninsula.[54]

The selection of Bradwell in the 1950s as a site for a nuclear power station had a similarly transformative impact on a rural area just as the wartime military presence around the village was being scaled back. Indeed, as Gillian Darley points out in her chapter, some villagers even hoped that the development of the power station would put an end to the surrounding mudflats and sands being used by the military for bombing practice, thereby removing a source of noise that regularly punctured the tranquillity of the local area.[55] As nuclear power stations need significant quantities of water, coastal locations are necessary. However, the potential danger of civil nuclear power meant that existing industrialised coastal locations were deemed unsuitable, and it is striking how, on the East Coast, the development of nuclear power stations took place in close proximity to the development of atomic weapons – Bradwell and Sizewell are less than 15km from Foulness and Orford Ness respectively, both of the latter sites being part of the AWRE at the time the power stations were constructed.[56] The requirements of nuclear power fundamentally altered the existing industrial map, and the power stations transformed the places where they were built by introducing enormous industrial buildings, towering pylons and associated additional development into remote rural areas. At Bradwell, the first-generation nuclear power station now sits as a redundant hulk encased in aluminium, a state in which it must remain until at least 2083, when it is assumed that it will be safe to finally demolish.[57] Twenty years after it ceased generating electricity, what remains is an enormous, bulky vertical intrusion into an otherwise predominantly horizontal coastal landscape.[58]

Places are double constructs – they are made physically, and they are also imbued with meaning by people.[59] The Essex coast has been made and remade by natural and human forces.[60] Alongside the incremental altering of the landscape by those who lived and worked in it, through the 'inning' of the marshes and the construction of sea walls, Bradwell has seen waves of change precipitated by external intervention, Roman and Saxon, military and nuclear. Tim Ingold has written of landscape as being 'history congealed', and the chapters in this book aim to make the layers of congealed history at Bradwell more readily visible, so that they are not eclipsed by the redundant hulk of Bradwell A, or erased by the possible advent of Bradwell B.[61] At Bradwell the combination of the natural and historic environments works powerfully on inhabitants and visitors alike to suggest connections across time. Children's author Michael Morpurgo lived in Bradwell as a young boy, and the departure of his family from the village, precipitated by the construction of Bradwell A, was a defining rupture in his childhood.[62] In a short story based around the coming of the power station, Morpurgo described a visit he made to Bradwell as an adult, which exemplifies the combination of history and nature out of which the sense of place of St Peter's Chapel and the landscape surrounding it is constructed:

> When I reached the chapel, no one was there. I had the place to myself, which was how I had always liked it. After I had been inside, I came out and sat down with my back against the sun-warmed brick and rested. The sea murmured. I remembered again my

childhood thoughts, how the Romans had been there, the Saxons, the Normans, and now me. A lark rose then from the grass below the sea wall, rising, rising, singing, singing.[63]

The outstanding natural environment at Bradwell, as Morpurgo's reminiscence makes apparent, is a key element in people's interaction with the historic environment here, with St Peter's being the key site. It is also indicative of the synergy between conservation of the historic and natural environments, which is often overlooked by bodies set up to deal with one or another rather than both. Agricultural intensification from the beginning of the Second World War eroded 'the complexity and intricate nature of the ancient countryside that characterises rural Essex' while also destroying important habitats.[64] The environmental impact of the removal of hedgerows, ploughing up of heath and common land and draining of wetlands on native and migrating species has long been recognised, but that this was also a loss in terms of the historic environment is less well understood. In a report about conservation management of the rural historic environment in Essex, Adrian Gascoyne drew attention to some examples of the positive management of significant rural archaeological sites, one of which was St Peter's Chapel and Othona fort.[65] In 2000 an English Heritage report had highlighted the ongoing damage being suffered by the fort, principally as a result of arable cultivation, and in 2003, after some negotiation, it was agreed with the farm manager of East Hall Farm that, as part of an amendment to an existing Countryside Stewardship agreement, the 1 hectare of cultivated land within the interior of the fort would be reverted to grassland and wild flowers and opened up for public access. As Gascoyne commented, this not only helped to protect the remains of the fort and improve the setting of St Peter's Chapel, but also benefited wildlife, including ground-nesting birds and rare species of bee.[66]

The fragility of this scheme was, however, revealed in 2020. In August of the previous year the Essex-based Strutt & Parker Farms business had been sold.[67] At roughly the same time, East Hall Farm, which had been managed by Strutt & Parker but owned separately, also came under new ownership. Unfortunately, this change of ownership saw the by then well-established wild flower meadow had been placed back under arable cultivation, in the words of Nigel Brown 'destroying instantly its value for nature conservation and renewing the process of erosion of the archaeological deposits'.[68] The success of the scheme had demonstrated the potential of historic and conservation bodies to work together to mutual advantage, its demise the precarious nature of many of the schemes

Figure 0.2 The former flower meadow. Kevin Bruce.

in place to protect the natural and historic environments. Despite historic scheduling and listing of the fort and chapel building on one hand and environmental protections on the other, the historic and natural environments at Bradwell can be impacted by the whims of new owners making a simple decision about the value of a grant for delivering 'public benefit' being smaller than the value of an arable crop.[69] The threat to the natural and historic setting of St Peter's from the proposed new nuclear power station is far greater than that visited by this arable cultivation, but the demise of the stewardship scheme does raise the question of how well the chapel and its setting are actually protected by existing legislation and stewardship schemes. The chapters in this book set out many of the ways in which the chapel and its setting are historically and archaeologically significant and it is hoped that by raising the profile of the building the book will both generate further research and also more durable schemes to protect the historic and natural environments in the area surrounding it.

The two parts of the book reflect the history of the chapel, with the first part placing the chapel in its pre-modern context and the second exploring responses to it in the modern world. The chronological gap between the two sections mirrors the chapel's own history. The first part explores the importance of the site under the Romans and in the early medieval period, before the beginning of a gradual decline throughout the high Middle Ages, which saw the chapel eventually fall out of ecclesiastical use entirely and become an agricultural building by the late seventeenth century. The second part explores the reawakening of interest in the building from the mid-nineteenth century, which led to its refurbishment and reconsecration, drawing attention to some of the many ways the chapel has inspired social and cultural initiatives, which resonate well beyond Bradwell itself.

The opening chapter, by David Andrews, examines the surviving fabric of the chapel, uncovering what this can tell us about the use of the building through time. As Andrews points out, the chapel is a remarkable building in that it preserves much of its early medieval fabric – unlike a typical parish church, it lacks the layers of history of an ecclesiastical building that has been in continuous use and as a result has not been expanded and altered through the centuries. In an Appendix, Andrews reproduces drawings from a stone-by-stone survey carried out by Jane Wadham in 1978 and hitherto unpublished, to inform future studies of the building. In Chapter 2 Andrew Pearson reconsiders the history and potential function of the Roman fort of Othona, in the context of other sites that belonged to the Saxon Shore Fort network. He synthesises existing scholarship to provide an outline of the form of the fort and its extramural area, before a comprehensive discussion of the likely uses of the site. The idea that the Shore Forts were a defensive anti-piracy network dates back to the sixteenth century, but recent scholarship has debated this point, suggesting that perhaps there was no overarching defensive plan to the scheme. Tantalising evidence provided by finds of animal bones, along with the proximity to numerous Roman red hills, raises the possibility that meat production was an important function of Othona, with its position in coastal networks stretching across the North Sea meaning it was well placed to supply the needs of Roman soldiers from the northern British forts and those on the lower Rhine.

Stephen Rippon provides an analysis of the early medieval landscape context of St Peter's, both within Bradwell and the Dengie Peninsula and within the larger *regio* or folk territory of *Deningei*, from which the peninsula takes it name. Rippon argues that *Deningei* encompassed not only the peninsula itself but also extended across the Danbury Hills and down into the Sandon Valley. He discusses the relationship between the minster at Bradwell and other central places within the landscape, furthering our understanding of the role of the ecclesiastical site in early medieval society. In Chapter 4, Barbara Yorke places Cedd's foundation of Bradwell within the wider context the conversion of Anglo-Saxon England. In doing so, she draws together various scraps of evidence to build up a fuller picture of Cedd's life and career. As Yorke points out, narratives of the conversion tend to focus on the foreign missionaries from Italy and Ireland who established the first mission stations, but the work of second-generation missionaries like Cedd, promoting Christianity among their own people, was crucial to the consolidation of Christianity in the Anglo-Saxon kingdoms.

Richard Hoggett and David Petts both consider Bradwell's coastal position. Hoggett discusses the evidence from Bradwell and from other Shore Forts on the East Anglian and Kent coasts for the construction of churches within the abandoned remains of these Roman structures. As he argues, while the dilapidated Roman forts provided building materials, we should see this phenomenon not as one of purely practical opportunism but also as a symbolic act imbued with religious significance. Petts also places Bradwell within wider coastal networks, arguing that we need to move away from seeing coastal locations as evidence of an ecclesiastical urge towards isolation and remoteness. Certainly such sites resonated with symbolism, but they were also enmeshed in complex coastal networks, which included ecclesiastical and secular sites. Indeed, as Petts demonstrates, it is often difficult to distinguish between the two. The turn to the coast in the seventh century was not just a spiritual urge, but also had social and economic drivers.

The final chapter of the first part of the book returns the focus to Bradwell itself. Chris Thornton, Kevin Bruce and Neil Wiffen place the site of the chapel within the evolving economy and landscape of Bradwell between the late eleventh and early seventeenth centuries. They outline the area's complex landowning structure and investigate the changing nature of the marshlands as a result of agricultural activities, which led to the gradual reclamation of the marshes. As they show, pastoral and arable modes of production existed together throughout the period under examination, though the balance between them shifted in response to demand. This chapter, focused on the north-eastern parts of Bradwell parish, closest to the chapel, evidences the rich range of historical sources that can shed light on the parishes of the Dengie Peninsula, and it is to be hoped that it provides the impetus for further research on the area.

The second part of the book examines some of the ways in which the chapel has been approached in the modern era and how this historic building acts as an anchor, holding fast in a rapidly changing environment and being fundamental to Bradwell's sense of place. It opens with James Bettley's comprehensive study of the rediscovery, rededication and refurbishment of St Peter's in the late nineteenth and early twentieth centuries. Bettley's chapter makes apparent the vast symbolic and

Figure 0.3 Pilgrims approaching the chapel in the mid-1950s. Courtesy of Katherine Weaver.

religious importance the chapel had, and still has, for the diocese of Chelmsford. While this book approaches the chapel predominantly as an historical monument, its significance as a place of Christian worship should also be recognised. Ken Worpole's chapter also makes this point, charting the history of the Othona Community, founded in 1946 by RAF padre Norman Motley, who was drawn to Bradwell by the presence of St Peter-on-the-Wall. The continued flourishing of the Othona Community, who regularly use the chapel for services and act as custodians of the building, ensures that St Peter's remains a living religious building within a spiritual landscape.

In Chapter 10 Gillian Darley considers the original decision to site a nuclear power station at Bradwell, exploring the embryonic frameworks of environmental and heritage designations, which offered little protection to the chapel's landscape setting. To those of us used to modern planning inquiries, the speed with which the original nuclear programme was driven through comes as quite a surprise, as does the lack of consideration given to the historic environment. Darley's contribution certainly raises the question as to whether the sites chosen in the 1950s, and subject to cursory scrutiny without a robust framework of heritage or environmental protections, remain suitable or acceptable for nuclear developments on a vastly more substantial scale today.

The remaining chapters explore some modern responses to the chapel and Maldon District's medieval heritage. In Chapter 11 Johanna Dale discusses the establishment of a long-distance walking route to the chapel from Chipping Ongar, demonstrating that the resonances of Bradwell's historic and natural environments extend across the county, inspiring walkers from West Essex as well as those living closer to the area. In the context of a growth of long-distance walking routes with medieval themes nationally, Dale argues that more use could and should be made of this established green infrastructure to stimulate the rural economy of Essex and to promote other medieval sites in the county, which are linked to St Peter's thanks to the existence of the St Peter's Way. In Chapter 12 Beth Whalley discusses the way in which the public arts and heritage industries have responded to Maldon District's medieval past and why particular narratives have dominated. Although St Peter's is an integral part of the district's heritage ecosystem, it is the intangible heritage of the Old English poem *The Battle of Maldon* that dominates local discourse, with important tangible and material medieval heritage in the district, such as St Peter's Chapel and the ruins of the medieval hospital on Spital Road in Maldon, barely featuring in the wider narrative. As Whalley argues, the choices made about which elements of medieval heritage we prioritise and celebrate have a real impact on communities today.

Charles Holland's contribution also analyses a narrative, this time about the social and economic landscape of Essex and how this is encapsulated in Grayson Perry's *A House for Essex*, for which Holland acted as architect. Holland's chapter discusses this complex work, related to the life of the fictional Julie Cope, whose trajectory from Canvey Island to Basildon, South Woodham Ferrers, Maldon, Colchester and finally Wrabness acts as a kind of pilgrimage through the built landscape of Essex, with all its social and economic implications. St Peter's was one of a number of buildings that informed the conceptual and design development of *A House for Essex*, demonstrating the huge diversity of responses to this early medieval chapel. In the final chapter curator Warren Harper and artist Nastassja Simensky discuss their own creative approach to the nuclear landscape of the Blackwater Estuary, exploring how existing art works inform their practice and how St Peter's and the Othona Community stand in relationship to the nuclear legacy of Bradwell A. This second part of the book is in no way exhaustive, but it does make apparent the variety of ways in which people have responded to the building and landscape in the modern age, and to the chapel's potential to inspire social, economic and cultural activities in the future.

The dialogue between people, the chapel and the landscape at Bradwell is continually evolving. In late summer 2022, as I finished work on the final manuscript of this book, a new collection of landscape paintings entitled 'Along the Saltmarsh' by artist Nabil Ali depicting the Bradwell coastline was exhibited in the chapel.[70] The collection was the result of an arts residency, supported by Essex Cultural Diversity Project, Cultural Engine and Arts Council England, and comprises a series of viewpoints from the pillboxes along the sea wall. These images of the environment and nature are not simply depictions of the land- and seascapes but are also made of them. Ali collected materials from the beach and processed them into pigments, which he mixed with a natural gum to form a workable paint. London Clay was used to create shades of grey, crushed chalk stones to produce an off-white and roman red bricks to create an orange hue. Ali's work, which alludes to 'a hidden darkness which shadows' the area, thus encapsulates the relationship between the chapel and its natural and historic environments.

Figure 0.4 *The Chapel*, 2022. Courtesy of Nabil Ali.

To those who know them, the chapel and the landscape surrounding it are imbued with value, but to those who are not familiar with them the historic grazing marshes of the Essex coast most often seem to be considered as a blank space rather than as a meaningful place. Baker's characterisation of outsiders thinking it a flat landscape containing nothing of value often rings true. In 2014 Essex County Council published a substantial report about historic grazing marshes. The report was precipitated by the development of the second Shoreline Management Plan, in which surviving grazing marsh seems to have been considered a target for managed realignment schemes, demonstrating that the historic environment significance of the marshes was not remotely appreciated by those drawing up the plan.[71] As discussed above, the lesser value outsiders placed on coastal Essex compared with the inland rural areas around London was made explicit in the arguments around the proposed third London airport in the 1960s and 1970s. The Wing Airport Resistance Association (WARA), which fought to prevent airports first at Cublington and subsequently at nearby Hoggeston in 1979, actively promoted Foulness as an alternative and their protesters shouted the catchy slogan 'Don't foul Bucks, Foulness', with the implication that while Buckinghamshire would be ruined by an airport, coastal Essex would not be – it was already foul.[72]

Writing in the eighth century in Northumbria, a centre of early medieval Christianity and royal power, the Venerable Bede commented that Cedd had gathered a number of people from the East Saxon kingdom into his communities at Bradwell and Tilbury and taught them the monastic rule, 'so far as these rough people were capable of receiving it'.[73] Bede's rather dismissive attitude to the inhabitants of the East Saxon kingdom is echoed in modern derogatory caricatures about those living in Essex – Essex man and his even more reviled companion, Essex girl – whose home county is deemed flat and uninteresting.[74] In his fervent essay opposing the proposed Maplin Sands airport, J. A. Baker, who was the antithesis of the Essex man caricature, wrote with evident pain about the transformation of the countryside of his home county in the post-war period: 'Essex has suffered so much; the new towns, the vast growth and overspill of London, the lancing through of motorways.' Raging against the incessant noise that the proposed airport would produce, he continued, 'we could at least have been allowed to keep the best of our county, the peace of its ancient bird-haunted coast that is the only peace that is left'.[75] The collapse of the Maplin Sands airport plans meant that Baker's worst fears were not realised. Yet, 50 years after Baker wrote, large-scale nuclear development on the one hand and rising sea levels on the other mean that the ribbon-like sea walls and the patchwork blankets of saltmarsh and coastal grazing marsh on the Dengie Peninsula are again under threat. As is the enigmatic figure of St Peter-on-the-Wall, which stands guardian over this peaceful, eerie and atmospheric landscape, its 'grey loafshape' visible for miles and miles over marsh, mudflat and sea.[76] The landscape may be flat, but this book rails against the assumption that there is nothing of interest here. St Peter's embodies many centuries of human history on the Dengie Peninsula; in comparison, the nuclear presence is not 'long-established' but is merely a recent brief episode.

Notes

1. Bradwell B 2020, 3.
2. https://mybradwell.bradwellb.co.uk [accessed 16 May 2022].
3. https://mybradwell.bradwellb.co.uk [accessed 16 May 2022].
4. On the proposed light railway see below.
5. The boundary of the proposed main development site would be less than 150m from the chapel.
6. Murphy and Brown 1999, 11.
7. See Whalley, in this volume, for examples.
8. For example, Burrows 2016. Coastal historic landfills, such as those along the Essex Thames Estuary shoreline, are now recognised as being at risk from tidal flooding or coastal erosion, which could have major damaging effects on environmentally sensitive areas. See Brand 2017.
9. Readman 2018, 263.
10. Massey 1994, 149.
11. The history of sea wall construction and coastal flooding on the Dengie Peninsula has not been systematically studied. Thornton 2020, 28–31, gives an outline of coastal erosion and flooding for the coast between St Osyth and the Naze, to the north-east of Bradwell. Smith 1970, 25–37, details episodes of flooding on Foulness Island to the south. Galloway 2012 provides a detailed studied of the impact of flooding higher up the tidal Thames at Barking. In her classic account of the 1953 North Sea flood in Essex, Grieve 1959 gives an overview of the history of flooding in the county.
12. On managed realignment see Oliver 2021. The 2010 South Suffolk and Essex Shoreline Management Plan is available here: http://www.eacg.org.uk/docs/smp8/essex&southsuffolk%20smp%20final%202.4.pdf. [accessed 16 May 2022].
13. A former tidal creek is visible on the front cover, lying to the left of the chapel. As the ground is slightly lower where the creek formerly ran, water collects along its course during winter.
14. ERO C/P 125.
15. ERO C/P 125.
16. ERO C/P 125.
17. ERO C/P 125.
18. Mitchell 2010.
19. Smith 1970, 44.
20. The South Essex Estuary and Reclamation Act 1852.
21. Gordon 1852, 4.
22. Hemming 1869, 215–17.
23. Smith 1970, 44.
24. Smith 1970, 44.
25. Hall 1982, 29.
26. Helsey and Codd 2014, 24.
27. Hall 1982, 36.
28. On the marginality of the lower reaches of the Thames Estuary see Whalley, in this volume.

29 Wood 1974, 248.
30 Pepper 1980, 180.
31 Hall 1982, 38.
32 Baker 1971.
33 Baker 1971.
34 On 29 July 1971 Lord Beswick asked a question in the House of Lords about the number of missiles that had been fired into the Maplin Sands, how many were likely to be unexploded and what the estimated cost of clearing unexploded ordinance would be. Hansard HL Deb (29 July 1971), vol. 323, cols 615–16. Available online: https://hansard.parliament.uk/Lords/1971-07-29/debates/b966878d-6700-4ac7-a459-4c330bcd1706/FoulnessAirportSiteAndUnexplodedMissiles [accessed 16 May 2022].
35 On the site of the Battle of Assandun see Rodwell 1993.
36 TNA WO/55/1548/2 and MR 1/1388. I am grateful to Kevin Bruce for supplying this reference and for sharing his research on the modern history of Bradwell with me.
37 TNA WO/55/1548/2 and MR 1/1388.
38 Smith 1970, 21.
39 Smith 1970, 21.
40 Smith 1970, 21.
41 Smith 1970, 22.
42 https://www.qinetiq.com/en/shoeburyness [accessed 16 May 2022].
43 This account of modern military activities on the Dengie Peninsula is based on research by Kevin Bruce.
44 TNA CRES 37/334.
45 The construction of airfields during the Second World War transformed East Anglia, whose relatively flat fields within easy reach of the continent were ideal for creating airstrips, which 'fractured the landscape of trees, hedges and fields created by enclosure'. This transformation was accelerated by the entry of America into the war in 1941. See Edwards 2010, 211.
46 There is a vast literature on place and space. Good starting points include Tuan 1977 and Massey 1994. Kirby 1982, 99–129, specifically considers the case of the third London airport and the siting of nuclear power stations.
47 Kirby 1982, 108.
48 See Darley, in this volume.
49 Flintham 2014, 57.
50 Flintham 2014, 57.
51 Flintham 2014, 57.
52 Flintham 2010.
53 Flintham 2014, 58.
54 It is 14.5km as the crow flies from the military complex on the north-eastern tip of the island to my house. I frequently hear explosions while working in my study.
55 See Darley, in this volume.
56 On Sizewell see Wall 2019. On Orford Ness, now a National Trust reserve, see Cocroft and Alexander 2009 and Wainwright 2009.
57 Details about decommissioning and the care and maintenance phase can be found on the Office for Nuclear Regulation website: https://www.onr.org.uk/sites/bradwell.htm [accessed 17 May 2022].
58 The redundant Bradwell A can be clearly seen, for example, from Maldon's Promenade Park (14.5km away as the crow flies).
59 Gieryn 2000, 465.
60 Murphy and Brown 1999, 11.
61 Ingold 2000, 150. As places are constructed it follows that they can also be deconstructed: 'Space is what place becomes when the unique gathering of things, meaning, and values are sucked out'. Gieryn 2000, 465.
62 Morpurgo 2018.
63 Morpurgo 2006, 268.
64 Gascoyne 2006, 1.
65 Gascoyne 2006, 15–17.
66 Gascoyne 2006.
67 https://www.fwi.co.uk/business/strutt-parker-farms-business-sold-to-investment-company [accessed 3 May 2022].

68 Brown 2020, 2.
69 Brown 2020, 2.
70 Ali 2022.
71 Gascoyne and Medlycott 2014, 5.
72 Pepper 1980, 180.
73 Colgrave and Mynors 1969, 284–5 (III, 22).
74 Nixon 2017, 214. On Essex stereotypes see Biressi and Nunn 2013, 23–43.
75 Baker 1971.
76 Baker 1971.

Bibliography

Ali, N. 2022. *Along the Saltmarsh*. https://0201b58c-a41d-4b16-888c-6e6648e93297.filesusr.com/ugd/4e37d7_f47de614563a475fb515210ad271a27a.pdf [accessed 5 September 2022].
Baker, J. A. 1971. 'On the Essex coast'. *RSPB Birds Magazine* 3: 281–3.
Biressi, A., and H. Nunn. 2013. *Class and Contemporary British Culture*. London: Palgrave Macmillan.
Bradwell B. 2020. *Stage One – Consultation Summary Document*. https://bradwellb.co.uk/wp-content/uploads/2020/03/Summary-document.pdf [accessed 16 May 2022].
Brand, J. H. 2017. 'Assessing the risk of pollution from historic coastal landfills'. Unpublished PhD thesis, Queen Mary University of London.
Brown, N. 2020. 'From the President'. *The Essex Society for Archaeology and History Newsletter*. https://www.esah1852.org.uk/library/files/newsletter-192-autumn-2020-21510114531.pdf [accessed 27 February 2023].
Burrows, T. 2016, 'The only grave is Essex: how the county became London's dumping ground'. *The Guardian*. 25 October. https://www.theguardian.com/cities/2016/oct/25/london-dumping-ground-essex-skeleton-crossrail-closet [accessed 16 May 2022].
Cocroft, W. D., and M. Alexander. 2009. *Atomic Weapons Research Establishment, Orford Ness, Suffolk: Cold War research and development site*. Portsmouth: English Heritage.
Colgrave, B., and R. A. B. Mynors (ed. and trans.). 1969. *Bede's Ecclesiastical History of the English People*. Oxford: Clarendon Press.
Edwards, S. 2010. 'Ruins, relics and restoration: the afterlife of World War Two airfields in England, 1945–2005'. In *Militarized Landscapes: From Gettysburg to Salisbury Plain*, edited by C. Pearson, P. Coates and T. Cole. 209–28. London: Continuum.
Flintham, M. 2010. 'The Shoeburyness complex: military spatial production and the problem of the civilian body'. In *Militarized Landscapes: From Gettysburg to Salisbury Plain*, edited by C. Pearson, P. Coates and T. Cole. 81–94. London: Continuum.
Flintham, M. 2014. 'The military spatial complex: interpreting the emerging spaces of British militarism'. In *Emerging Landscapes: Between production and representation*, edited by D. Deriu, K. Kamvasinou and E. Shinkle. 55–65. Farnham: Ashgate.
Galloway, J. A. 2012. '"Tempests of weather and great abundance of water": the flooding of the Barking marshes in the later middle ages'. In *London and Beyond. Essays in honour of Derek Keene*, edited by M. Davies and J. A. Galloway. 67–83. London: Institute of Historic Research.
Gascoyne, A. 2006. *Conservation Management of the Rural Historic Environment in Essex*. Chelmsford: Essex County Council.
Gascoyne, A., and M. Medlycott. 2014. *Essex Historic Grazing Marsh Project*. Chelmsford: Essex County Council.
Gieryn, T. F. 2000. 'A space for place in sociology'. *Annual Review of Sociology* 26: 463–96.
Gordon, L. D. B. 1852. 'Report on the project for the South Essex Estuary reclamation and improvement of navigation of River Blackwater'. In *Reports from Commissioners. Session 3 February–1 July 1852*, vol. 26. London: Houses of Parliament.
Grieve, H. 1959. *The Great Tide: The story of the 1953 flood disaster in Essex*. Chelmsford: Essex County Council.
Hall, P. 1982. *Great Planning Disasters*. Berkley and Los Angeles: University of California Press.
Helsey, M., and F. Codd. 2014. 'Aviation: proposals for an airport in the Thames Estuary, 1945–2014'. House of Commons Library Note SN/BT/4920.

Hemming, G. W. 1869. *The Law Reports including Bankruptcy and Lunacy Cases, before the Lord Chancellor and the Court of Appeal in Chancery*, vol. 4. London: The Council of Law Reporting.

Ingold, T. 2000. *The Perception of Environment: Essays in livelihood, dwelling and skill*. London: Routledge.

Kirby, A. 1982. *The Politics of Location: An introduction*. London: Methuen.

Massey, D. 1994. *Space, Place and Gender*. Minneapolis, MN: University of Minnesota Press.

Mitchell, V. 2010. *Branch Lines to Southend and Southminster*. Midhurst: Middleton Press.

Morpurgo, M. 2006. *Singing for Mrs Pettigrew*. London: Walker Books.

Morpurgo, M. 2018. 'Michael Morpurgo on Bradwell on Sea: "The exhilaration of infinite beauty"'. *The Guardian*. 6 October. https://www.theguardian.com/books/2018/oct/06/michael-morpurgo-bradwell-sea-essex-village-home [accessed 17 May 2022].

Murphy, P., and N. Brown. 1999, 'Archaeology of the coastal landscape'. In *The Essex Landscape: In search of its history*, edited by L. S. Green. 11–19. Chelmsford: Essex County Council.

Nixon, S. J. 2017. 'Vanishing peregrines: J. A. Baker, environmental crisis and bird-centred cultures of nature, 1954–73', *Rural History* 28: 205–26.

Oliver, S. 2021. *Land Abandoned to the Sea: The managed realignment of coastal areas*. London: Bloomsbury.

Pepper, D. 1980. 'Environmentalism, the "lifeboat ethic" and anti-airport protest'. *Area* 12(3): 177–82.

Readman, P. 2018. *Storied Ground: Landscape and the shaping of English national identity*. Cambridge: Cambridge University Press.

Rodwell, W. J. 1993. 'The battle of *Assandun* and its memorial church: a reappraisal'. In *The Battle of Maldon: Fact and fiction*, edited by J. Cooper. 127–58. London: Hambledon.

Smith, J. R. 1970. *Foulness: A history of an Essex island parish*. Chelmsford: Essex County Council.

Thornton, C. C. 2020. 'Introduction: St Osyth to the Naze'. In *VCH Essex*, XII (part 1), edited by C. C. Thornton and H. Eiden. 1–58. Woodbridge: Boydell & Brewer.

Tuan, Y.-F. 1977. *Space and Place: The perspective of experience*. Minneapolis, MN: University of Minnesota Press.

Wainwright, A. 2009. 'Orford Ness – A landscape in conflict?' In *Europe's Deadly Century: Perspectives on 20th century conflict heritage*, edited by N. Forbes, R. Page and G. Pérez. 134–42. Swindon: English Heritage.

Wall, C. 2019. '"Nuclear prospects": the siting and construction of Sizewell A power station, 1957–1966'. *Contemporary British History* 33(2): 246–73.

Wood, D. 1974. 'Maplin: a campaign concluded'. *New Statesman*. 23 August.

Part I
St Peter's Chapel and its pre-modern contexts

1
St Peter's Chapel: What the building has to tell us

David Andrews

Figure 1.1 The chapel from the south-west. N. Hallett.

St Peter's Chapel is as remote in its coastal isolation as are its origins at the beginning of the Christian era in this country. It was founded by St Cedd in 654 in the course of his mission to re-establish Christianity in the kingdom of the East Saxons.[1] Cedd had chosen the site of a Roman Shore Fort for his monastery, which had by his time developed into what Bede called the *civitas* of *Ythancæstir*.[2] The Roman fort wall, but little else, was rediscovered in the mid-nineteenth century in the course of earth-moving for coastal defences.³ The landowner sponsored excavations in 1864, which made it possible to establish the plan of the western half of the fort, which had not been consumed by the sea. It was roughly square with round towers. The chapel was shown to straddle its west wall, aligned on the road of Roman origin which leads to the site, and hence thought to be on the position of the main landward gate. It was revealed to have lost an apsidal chancel, a porch, and a *porticus* or small rectangular side chapel on its north side. The uncovering of a similar *porticus* on the south side had to await the removal of an adjacent shed.

Although there must have been a settlement and monastery in Saxon times, its fortunes and fate are almost entirely lost to history. It presumably functioned as a minster and then a parish church, and later as a chapel of ease. By 1086, *Ythancæstir* is identifiable with two Domesday manors known as *Effecestra* and later in the Middle Ages as *La Waule*.⁴ These, together possibly with as many as five other mostly small manors in the area, probably represent a landholding associated with the monastic site which had become fragmented by 1086. Two of these manors had fisheries. Fish traps exposed in the Blackwater Estuary intertidal zone, including two at Sales Point and Pewet Island near

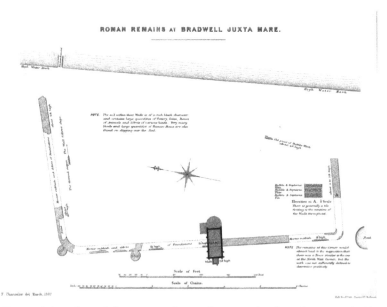

Figure 1.2 Plan of the Roman fort and St Peter's Chapel as revealed by the nineteenth-century excavations (from Lewin 1867).

St Peter's, have been broadly dated to the seventh to tenth centuries.[5] The existence of the monastery could explain these large complex structures. A copy of a sixteenth-century map shows a series of mostly unoccupied empty plots along the straight road between the St Peter's and Bradwell on Sea, evidence of a shrunken settlement to the west of the chapel.[6] However, the origins of the chapel, and why and by whom it was founded, were unknown to the jurors who appeared before an ecclesiastical inquisition of 1442 which was intended to establish its legal status and relationship to the parish church of St Thomas.[7] One said it consisted of a nave, chancel and small bell tower with two bells. Another said there had been a fire, and the rector had repaired the chancel and the parishioners the nave. An examination of the fabric does not provide much evidence for a fire, though inside some stones and plaster look pinkish and possibly

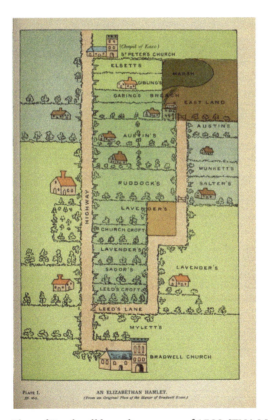

Figure 1.3 Plan of Bradwell based on a map of 1583 (TNA MPC 1/259). The original was thought to be lost but has recently been rediscovered at The National Archives, where it was incorrectly catalogued as being of Bradwell in Lancashire.

scorched, as do a few around the doorway. Stones could, however, have been burnt in a previous use. It was generally agreed that, though there was no obligation to do so, the rectors had provided a chaplain to say Mass three days a week, though this custom had lapsed for the last 15 years or so. The sixteenth-century surveyor and map-maker Norden recognised it as a chapel of ease, but by 1686 it was leased as a barn.[8] It was described as a barn by the eighteenth-century county historian Philip Morant, and identified as such on the 1777 county map by Chapman and André. It remained an agricultural building until restoration in 1920.

In view of the silence of the documentary sources, there is little more than its fabric that can be used to trace the history of the chapel. Interest in this was awakened after the excavations, though no detailed record seems to have been made of its foundations. Speculation as to its age was resolved in favour of it being seventh-century. Research on the chapel and other seventh-century churches by Sir Charles Peers informed his careful restoration in 1920 for the Ministry of Public Buildings and Works.[9] A short but thorough monograph was published by H. M. Carter in 1966, and a detailed study carried out by Jane Wadham in 1978.[10] The latter included a stone-by-stone external survey from a tower scaffold. Although a considerable achievement, this did not shed much new light on the chapel, which is a strikingly one-dimensional building for its age, lacking the obvious layers of history presented by the typical parish church, its fabric not telling any very clear story between the seventh century and the seventeenth or eighteenth, when it became a barn.

The plan of the chapel is significant. It was unlike the churches of 'Celtic' and Northern Christianity, despite Cedd's origins in that part of the country, which were plain long narrow rectangular buildings. Instead, it resembles the Kentish churches associated with Augustine's mission of 596. These include St Peter and St Paul, St Pancras and St Martin in Canterbury and the church at Reculver. Their distinctive features are relatively short naves, walls with shallow buttresses, arched screens between nave and chancel, apses, and *porticus* or side chapels. There is thus the conundrum of a Kentish-style church in the fashion of those established by the Christian mission sent from Rome, being built by a northern evangelist coming from the 'Celtic' tradition. The chapel could therefore be seen, though it would be simplistic, as anticipating the success of the Roman Christian tradition over the 'Celtic' at the Synod of Whitby ten years later, in 664.[11] Since the conclusion of antiquarian debates about the age of the building, Wadham has dared raise the question of whether the chapel is a replacement of that founded by Cedd, in which case its design could be seen as less remarkable. Inasmuch as

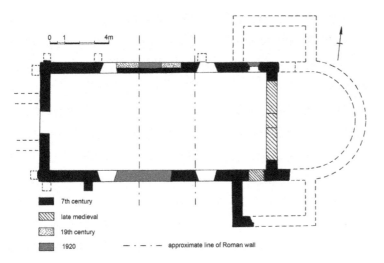

Figure 1.4 Plan of St Peter's Chapel (after Wadham and the RCHME). Drawn by the author.

monastic foundations are often seen as starting with short-lived buildings, for instance in timber, before more permanent reconstruction, this is a question worth bearing in mind. However, the ten years between the establishment of Cedd's mission and his death of plague in 664, just after the Synod of Whitby, could have left enough time for two phases of construction. In a sequence of events such as this, a church built at a later date would be expected by the followers of the Augustinian mission to conform to a Kentish plan, which was derived from the buildings of Christian Rome and carried important symbolic and political messages.[12]

From having been seen as a homogeneous group, the Kentish churches have been re-interpreted as a developmental sequence, reflecting the phases of the Augustinian mission from 596 and architectural influences initially from Gaul or France, and later in the seventh century from Italy, particularly from the area of Ravenna.[13] Bradwell has not figured much in the discussion of these early churches, lacking their historical and archaeological context, though the historical and archaeological sources for them are so threadbare and ambiguous as to make meaningful discussion very challenging. It is one of the later churches in the group, so it is perhaps unsurprising that it most closely parallels Reculver St Mary, which King Egbert of Kent gave to the priest Bassa for a minster in 669. Although largely demolished in the nineteenth century, Reculver is well recorded as having the full quotient of wall buttresses, arched screen, apse, in this case polygonal, and *porticus*.[14]

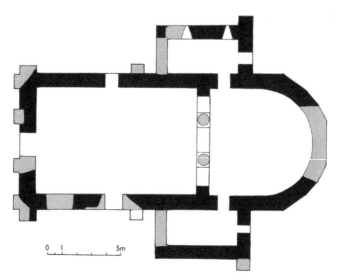

Figure 1.5 Plan of the church at Reculver as originally built (after English Heritage). The apse is polygonal. Drawn by the author.

There are differences between Bradwell and the Kentish churches. The proportions of its nave plan are different, being rather more than two squares, measuring about 21ft 4in × 48ft (6.5 × 14.7m) internally, the others having a length to breadth ratio of about 1:1½. It is thus less wide and quite significantly longer than, for instance, Reculver (37 × 24ft, 11.3 × 7.3m).[15] The proportions of St Peter's, which relate better to later Anglo-Saxon churches, could have been influenced by underlying Roman foundations. Carter pointed out that there were only two arches, not three, in the screen between nave and apse, as had previously been thought. This conclusion was confirmed by Wadham's careful measuring of the truncated arch springings.[16] The porch at Bradwell is also a feature not found in the Kentish churches, but this may not be original to the chapel (see below).

It is interesting, if not very profitable, to contrast the masonry of St Peter's with that of the Kentish churches. The oldest of these are the chancel of St Martin's, St Pancras, St Peter and St Paul, and St Mary, which lie beneath the remains of St Augustine's Abbey, Canterbury. These were all well built with thin walls of roughly coursed Roman brick, bonded with good-quality mortar with coarse aggregate. The later buildings, still dating from the seventh century however, the nave of St Martin's and Reculver, were built of a mixture of stones, roughly shaped of medium size, with levelling courses of Roman tile. Their masonry is

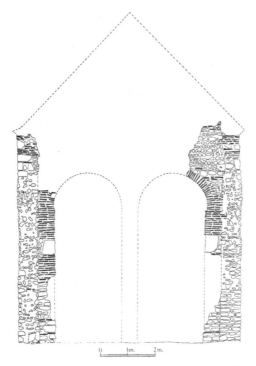

Figure 1.6 Elevation of the east wall seen from outside, showing the original masonry only, and reconstructing the two arches of the screen. The radius of the circles may in fact have been slightly smaller, in which case the space between the arches would have been wider. They were presumably separated by a masonry pier, not a column as at Reculver. J. Wadham.

comparable to St Peter's, but at St Peter's it is superior, with the use of stone more uniform in type and size, and no tile courses. Because in all cases the building materials were largely if not totally reused, little can be concluded from this except that they presumably reflect availability, and that there was definitely a preference for using Roman tile where possible. It is probable that the walls would have been rendered, in which case the character of the masonry would have been irrelevant to their appearance.

There must be at least half a dozen different types of stone in St Peter's, including tufa, septaria, ironstone and a variety of limestones. However, for the most part, its original masonry is fairly consistent, consisting of roughly shaped blocks of relatively uniform size, varying within a range of 4–5in (100–130mm) high and up to 1ft (300mm) long. Weathering and lichen make identification of the stone types difficult. Much of what can be seen externally seems to be an oolitic limestone, from the belt of Jurassic stones that extend from Dorset in the south-west through Northamptonshire into Lincolnshire. It can be difficult to identify the source of these limestones. That at Bradwell resembles the products of the Barnack quarries. The chapel has been said, however, to be built of Kentish Rag.[17] Rag was much used by the Romans. A Roman ship loaded with it has been found in London. In Roman London, the main source of building stone seems to have been Kent, supplying Rag and also tufa, but stone also came from the Cotswolds, Lincolnshire and the Paris basin.[18] It would be reasonable to expect to find Rag at Bradwell. There may be a small amount of it in the fabric, but it mainly occurs in the modern blocking in the north wall.

The immediate provenance of the stone must have been the Roman fort. This had a defensive wall 12ft (3.7m) thick, built mainly of septaria, with tile or brick levelling courses at intervals of about four courses (see Figure 2.2). The septaria blocks were regular in shape with dressed faces, which implies they were quarried, not obtained from the foreshore. The chapel, as has been seen, stands on the wall, on what must have been the site of a gatehouse. Nothing is known of the buildings within the fort, though many artefacts were found, including Roman military equipment and some late Saxon objects, the latter virtually the only known evidence for the continuing life of the settlement.[19] The limestone would seem to have come from the *principia* or other buildings that no longer served a useful purpose. Large blocks of a different oolitic limestone, a better freestone, were used for the quoins and the window and door surrounds, some with mortices and lifting holes, and hence clearly reused from relatively grand or monumental buildings.

Traditionally built masonry walls are raised so much at once, allowing time for the mortar to go off, and working only in the summer months. This process leaves horizontal lines or 'lifts' visible in the stonework, some of which correspond to the heights of the scaffold platforms. In medieval Essex churches, these lifts might be typically 6–18in high. At Bradwell, they are much higher, about 5ft, indicating that the walls were built in five stages.[20] Putlog holes capped with Roman tile, representing the stages of the scaffolding, are the clearest evidence for some of the lifts. They can be seen to correspond to the bottom of the windows, for it is logical to make lifts and openings relate to each other. There is a difference between the masonry in the bottom of the walls, in the lowest two lifts, and the upper parts, the stones being longer and more rectangular, those above smaller and squarer. This change could represent a seasonal break in construction over a winter. The chapel would have taken at least two years to build.

In Essex churches of the eleventh and twelfth centuries, the mortar was often very weak, little more than earth, which explains why the lifts are so shallow. At Bradwell the mortar is excellent, which explains why the chapel is so well preserved and the lifts relatively high. The original mortar is evident in much of the north and south walls, apparently never repointed. It is pale yellow-brown, coarse with pebbles, pieces of flint and occasionally *opus signinum*, reused Roman mortar or flooring characterised by crushed brick. It seems to contain no shell, one of the obvious sources of lime in a coastal situation. Instead, it is possible that it was made by burning septaria. These clay nodules were used in the nineteenth century for making so-called Roman cement and the stucco of Regency buildings and terraces. Good mortar, with a rapid 'set', would have made the deep lifts in the masonry possible. Even if the limestone and other blocks were reused, they were competently laid to courses, much more regular than the Kentish churches and some of the early medieval work in Europe. There is thus clear evidence of the ability of the builders, something striking in view of the often presumed loss of technical skill from the fifth century. As noted previously, it is probable that the chapel walls were plastered, as was invariably true of Essex rubble-built medieval churches.

It is surprising that the chapel is not built mainly of septaria, the locally occurring stone of Essex coastal districts, used by the Romans for the walls of Colchester and available in the walls of the fort. Septaria are hardened clay nodules which form in London Clay. The stone can be variable in colour and shape and, although very hard, can be shaped. It is present in the wall core and the interior elevations, and it may be that many of the smaller stones in the top of the walls are septaria. Its limited use could imply that the fort walls were still extant, presumably forming an enclosure to Cedd's monastery. However, this may not be the case. The chapel is a breach in the fort walls, coinciding, it seems, with a gateway. Churches were often incorporated in medieval defensive walls, but not with their entrances facing outwards. The gaps in its north and south walls, apparently made for barn doors, coincide with the line of the fort ramparts. At the base of the inside of the south wall there is a course of Roman tile which could correspond to a levelling course in the fort wall. Excavation in 1985 for the foundation of a new altar revealed an earlier floor level at a depth of about 2ft (600mm). Excavation in 1947 to the north of the chapel found a shallow recut to the approximately 25ft (7.6m) wide and 13ft (4m) deep infilled ditch outside the walls. Ipswich Ware found in the fill of the recut could indicate the ditch had been filled, and by implication the walls partially removed, by the eighth century or even, it has been suggested, by the seventh century, before the construction of the chapel.[21] The possibility that such substantial defences had been slighted on this scale in a period of about 150 years is striking.

The chapel has four windows in the nave, two high up in the north and south walls. These are rectangular, about 3ft (0.9m) wide and 4ft (1.2m) high, with a single splayed embrasure. Their jambs, where original, are made of long blocks of reused good-quality limestone set vertically. They apparently had flat lintels, not arches made of Roman brick or tile, as might be expected. Indeed, the limited use of Roman brick in the fabric is a striking contrast with Essex eleventh- and twelfth-century churches, as well as the Kentish group of churches. An exception is the springing of the arches for the screen between the nave and apse. The interior of the chapel would have been plastered; indeed, some of this remains, particularly high up on the south wall, and so the brickwork of these arches would have been concealed. The window high up in the west wall has been considered a later insertion. It is not at the same level as the other windows, or the same width, and its almost pointed arch is formed in Roman brick. However, its jamb on the south side includes a long vertical limestone block, an argument for it being original but adapted with a rebuilt head when work was done to the west gable, dating probably to the twelfth or thirteenth centuries.

Figure 1.7 Fragment of plaster with red paint probably of thirteenth-century date (arrowed) in the soffit of a probable blocked window arch in the north-east corner of the nave. David Andrews.

In the absence of an old roof line, and in view of their small size and low height, the *porticus* may have had lean-to roofs. They differ either side of the chapel. That on the north side had a door into the apse. That on the south side communicated with the nave. A vertical jamb stone survives at the side of the patch where the door was. Inside, it is possible to make out the springing formed in Roman brick of the arch for the doorway. Of the other Kentish churches, only Reculver and Canterbury St Martin have *porticus*, the latter only one on the south side. The *porticus* at Reculver are different to Bradwell in that they communicated only with the apse. *Porticus* could function as side chapels or be used for burial. A row of them alongside a nave resemble an aisle. Bede records that St Augustine was buried in a *porticus* on the north side of Sts Peter and Paul in Canterbury. *Porticus* flanking a chancel correspond to the prothesis and diaconicon of the Greek Church, the former on the north side serving for the preparation of the sacraments, the latter functioning more as a vestry.

At the east end of the north wall, east of the wall scar for the *porticus*, there was a brick patch or blocking which was removed in the 1920 restoration and made good with limestone blocks so that it is almost invisible. Inside the chapel, this corresponds to an embrasure apparently for a window about 2ft (600m) wide, which has traces of painting in red in the soffit of its almost pointed arch. The painting looks twelfth- or thirteenth-century. If correctly interpreted as a window of this date, located where the *porticus* overlapped the nave and chancel, then it implies that the *porticus* had been demolished by this time. Since the *porticus* was entered only from the apse, it could imply that the apse had also been demolished. However, the reference in the 1442 inquisition to a nave and chancel could suggest the apse was still there at that time. It is also the case that the removal of the apse has previously been regarded as occurring when the chapel became a barn; however, the apse was hardly incompatible with the changed use. The rather irregular masonry of the blocked arched screen wall, and its mortar, seem more likely to be medieval than seventeenth-century. The lower half of the blocking of the door into the south *porticus* is bonded with a bright yellow-brown mortar which certainly looks medieval.

There may have been structural reasons for the disappearance of the chancel, arising from the relationship of the chapel to Roman foundations beneath it, which could have led to differential settlement. Churches have often lost aisles, but the loss of a chancel, the most important sacramental space, is more significant. That the chapel was superseded in the role of parish church by St Thomas in the village is clear, but less clear is when that happened. The oldest part of St Thomas that has been recognised is fourteenth-century. However, it is recorded as 'Bradewell with the chapel of la Vale' in the register of Fulk Basset, bishop of London, of c. 1254.[22] That this register, and the taxation of Nicholas IV, shows that the priory of Hatfield Peverel had rights to a portion of the tithes owed by St Thomas suggests a link to Ranulf de Peverel, lord of the manor of Down Hall in 1086, which could imply the church existed by the late eleventh century. The much-refaced chancel of St Thomas contains some well-coursed masonry, including a little stone that may have been taken from the fort, which looks twelfth-century or earlier. The loss of any parochial function at an early date could well have removed any impetus to maintain or rebuild the chancel.

As has been noted, porches are not typical of the Kentish group of churches. Wadham thought the porch might not be original. The foundations of the porch shown on the excavation plan are irregular in shape and width. A comparison might be made with St Pancras, Canterbury. It is very evident from the surviving foundations there that the west door had buttresses either side of it, onto which a porch in Roman tile was later built. There may have been a similar sequence at St Peter's. It is notable at St Peter's that the door does not have monolithic jambs like the doors for the *porticus* or the nave windows. If this feature is taken as a criterion of originality, it raises the question of where the entrance was. Were there doors in the north and south walls, or other features such as buttresses, then the later agricultural use of the building would have obliterated them. The porch is seen as the base for the tower recorded in 1442. There are scars for its walls either side of the west door. Since these do not extend into the upper part of the wall, there may have been a timber belfry. An improbable-looking tower is indicated on a copy of a seventeenth-century map.[23]

The roof is of butt purlin construction stiffened with wind braces, in which the purlins butt against the principal rafters, and short rafters are laid between and over the purlins. Roofs of this sort in Essex are typically sixteenth- or seventeenth-century. Curiously, the roof is in two parts, having an adjacent pair of principal rafters about halfway along the nave. The eaves are probably at about their original height, as any raising or rebuilding would probably have been in brick or tile. The original roof covering could have been thatch, shingles or reused Roman tile. If the latter, the roof would have had a slack pitch, as Roman tiles are heavy and designed for low pitch roofs, usually of king post design. When roof repairs were made in 1993, it was noted that brick patches at the wall tops seem to mark the positions of former trusses. There seem to have been eight of these, about 5–6ft (1.5–1.8m) apart. If correct, they could represent an archaic roof datable to the twelfth century or earlier with closely set principal trusses.

Evidence for the existing roof pitch exists in the west gable, which is of masonry resembling the main building, but with brick and

Figure 1.8 Interior of the chapel, showing the blocked screen wall, and the butt purlin roof. N. Hallett.

tile courses suggesting shallow lifts. This is unfortunately undatable, but looks medieval. The east gable is in neat brickwork which could be seventeenth- or early eighteenth-century. As such, it could be contemporary with the butt purlin roof. A significant repair to the chancel was the insertion of a lower tie-beam presumably to strengthen the rather badly built east wall where the arched screen was taken down and the gap filled with rubble. This timber, probably elm, is strapped at each end and connected to tie bars in the north and south walls. The use of forelock bolts suggests a seventeenth- or eighteenth-century date.

It has been seen that the scars in the north and south walls, apparently representing the site of barn doors, correspond to the line of the fort walls. That in the north wall is full height. Lewin in his account of the excavations published in 1868 said that there had been a square extension here 'within the memory of man'.[24] The excavation plan shows what look like foundations in this position. This was presumably a porch or midstrey added for the use of the chapel as a barn. The blocking is mainly in Kentish

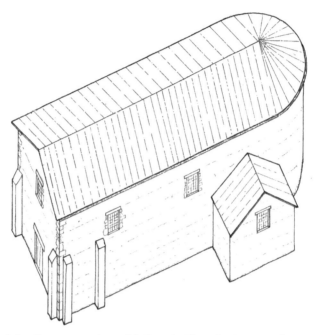

Figure 1.9 Reconstruction of St Peter's Chapel. The west door may not have been an original feature. If so, the entrance would have been in the long sides, where large barn doors were later opened. Drawn by the author.

rag, a stone that blends quite well with the original masonry of the chapel, though it comprises large, irregular-shaped blocks laid in a rather random way. A small door was left in it for access to the barn. In the south wall there is no evidence for a porch, only a wide doorway below a brick segmental arch, which looks nineteenth-century. This remained open until 1920. Leap boards at the bottom of this door show that the chapel was used for threshing, but old photographs suggest the final chapters in its agricultural history saw it mainly used for livestock and storage.

The 1920 Ministry of Public Buildings and Works restoration was informed by Sir Charles Peers's careful assessment of the building in his account of the Kentish churches.[25] The barn doors in the south wall were blocked using blocks of Clipsham, an oolitic limestone, and roughly squared septaria, of the same shape as those which are predominant in the fabric of the chapel. This would be an almost invisible restoration, had the new masonry not been laid leaving the original slightly proud of it. This is interesting in view of Peers's opinions on the restoration of monuments. Similar stonework was used to make good the east end of this wall where the *porticus* and a shed had been removed, as well for blocking the small door in the north side. The latter shows how skilful this work was. The blocking looks like a small patch of original masonry floating within the much larger older blocking in Kentish Rag. The mortar used in this restoration is also an excellent match for the original, clearly designed to resemble it, though possibly gauged with some cement. It contains shell, a common inclusion in better-quality medieval mortars, but not obviously present in the original chapel mortar. The windows were reinstated with wooden frames and leaded lights. The west door was reopened and given a new frame and oak door. In the roof, a repair was carried out to the north wall plate.

Repairs were later carried out after a landmine damaged the roof and wall tops in 1942. This was followed by a further restoration in 1948 by Laurence King as surveyor to Chelmsford Diocese. This saw a major rebuild of the roof, the west half completely renewed. King recommended 'cleaning down the internal face of stonework' and reinstatement of lime plaster to the walls, but this was not done. The west elevation was repointed in 1970 with a shelly, greyish cementitious mortar, not a particularly happy intervention, typical of the disregard for the original which has characterised much repair work to historic buildings in the later twentieth century.[26]

Acknowledgements

I am grateful to Kevin Bruce for sharing his local knowledge and providing copies of Jane Wadham's survey, to Eric Cambridge for comments on the text and to Nicolette Hallett for her photographs.

Appendix: The 1978 survey of St Peter's Chapel

The only detailed record of the chapel is a stone-by-stone hand-drawn survey at 1:20 by Jane Wadham in 1978 for a University of London Institute of Archaeology thesis. Because of the very limited circulation of this record and its potential value for the understanding and curation of the chapel, it has seemed appropriate to publish the drawings in this appendix and make scanned images of them more widely available. The drawings have been annotated with the approximate levels of the lifts.

The masonry of the west elevation has been rather obscured by repointing in the late twentieth century in a cementitious mortar. Either side of the door are scars left by the removal of the porch or tower. The door lacks the vertical jamb stones typical of other apertures and the quoins at the angles of the chapel, raising a question over whether the door is an original feature. The existence of such jambs suggests that the window is original, but at some point, perhaps in the thirteenth century, it has been rebuilt with a pointed head in brick. The roof pitch would have been much like the existing if it was thatched or shingled, but much slacker if covered with Roman tiles.

The wide breach in the north elevation dates from the use of the chapel as a barn, when a porch seems to have been added to it. It was blocked except at the top in Kentish Ragstone, leaving a small doorway which was itself later blocked by the Ministry of Public Buildings and Works in 1920. The eastern of the two original windows is recognisable from its vertical jamb stone. It seems to have been blocked when the breach was made in the wall. The other windows were boarded over during the agricultural use of the chapel, and restored in 1920. At the east end of the wall, the window thought to date from the thirteenth century had been blocked in brick, but in 1920 this was replaced with limestone to match the original masonry.

The east wall consists of the blocked-up arches of the screen that once divided the nave and apse. A medieval date can be argued for this blocking. It was roughly built and seems to comprise two phases, the lower including blocks of stone presumably from the apse or other ruins surviving at the time. The neat small bricks at the top of the wall look seventeenth- or early eighteenth-century. Two beam holes either side of the top of the wall could be for the wall plates of the apse; if so, they would have been about 3ft (0.9m) below the top of the nave wall.

The original masonry is best preserved in the south wall. Putlog holes capped with Roman tile reveal stages in the scaffolding. The difference is clear between the larger stonework of the bottom two lifts and the smaller blocks in the upper part of the wall, which could mark a winter break in the construction of the chapel. At the east end is the scar left by the removal of the *porticus* and the blocking of the door between it and the nave. In the middle of the wall is the blocking of barn doors removed in 1920.

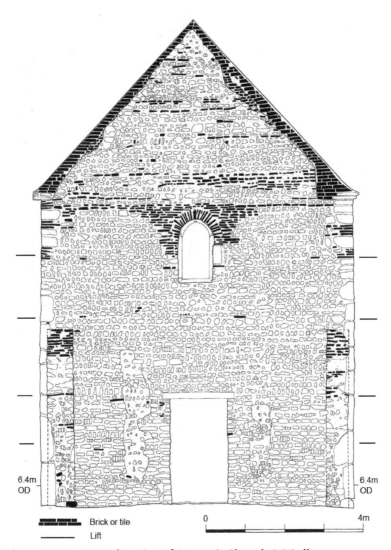

Figure 1.10 West elevation of St Peter's Chapel. J. Wadham.

WHAT THE BUILDING HAS TO TELL US

Figure 1.11 West wall of St Peter's Chapel. N. Hallett.

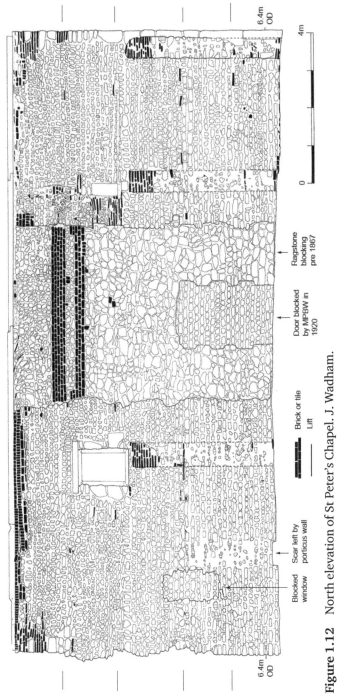

Figure 1.12 North elevation of St Peter's Chapel. J. Wadham.

Figure 1.13 North wall of St Peter's Chapel. N. Hallett.

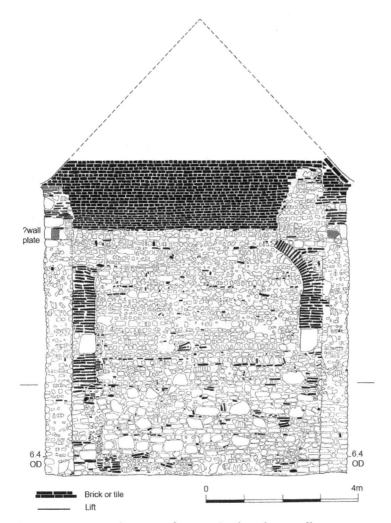

Figure 1.14 East elevation of St Peter's Chapel. J. Wadham.

Figure 1.15 East wall of St Peter's Chapel. N. Hallett.

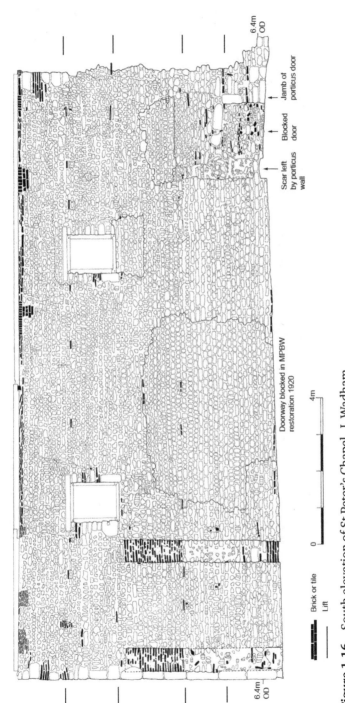

Figure 1.16 South elevation of St Peter's Chapel. J. Wadham.

Figure 1.17 South wall of St Peter's Chapel. N. Hallett.

Notes

1. On Cedd's mission see Yorke, in this volume.
2. On the reuse of Saxon Shore Forts for monastic foundations see Hoggett, in this volume. On the Roman fort see Pearson, in this volume.
3. Lewin 1868.
4. See Bruce and Thornton, in this volume.
5. Heppell 2011.
6. Hall 1888, plate I. This is described as being 'From an Original Plan of the Manor of Bradwell'. The map dating from 1583 has recently been rediscovered in The National Archives (TNA MPC 1/259) by Kevin Bruce, whose previous identification of the plot names in the court rolls had showed the copy to be based on an authentic original.
7. London Metropolitan Archives DL/A/A/005/MS09531/006, fol. 196r. Relevant extract from the bishop's register in ERO D/P 96/28/47.
8. ERO D/DC 21/5–6. 'All that Barne commonly called or known by the name of St. Peter's Chappell together with ten Acres of Land thereto adjoyning.'
9. Peers 1901. Also see Bettley, in this volume.
10. Carter 1966. I am grateful to Kevin Bruce for making available a copy of Wadham's dissertation, as well as other information. See Appendix for Wadham's survey drawings.
11. On the Synod see Yorke, in this volume.
12. See Barnwell 2015.
13. Cambridge 1999.
14. Peers 1928; Taylor and Taylor 1980, 503–9.
15. Thomas 1981, 189.
16. Carter 1966; Wadham 1978.
17. For example, Carter 1966, 12.
18. Hayward and Roberts 2019.
19. On continued settlement after Cedd's death see Rippon, in this volume.
20. A diagram of the south wall showing the lifts has been published in Rodwell 1986, 162.
21. Rodwell 1976; Walker 2001.
22. Fowler 1928, 25.
23. Hall 1888, plate I. See above, note 6.
24. Lewin 1867.
25. Peers 1901.
26. Wadham 1978, 9.

Bibliography

Barnwell, P. S. (ed.) 2015. *Places of Worship in Britain and Ireland, 300–950*. Donington: Shaun Tyas.

Cambridge, E. 1999. 'The architecture of the Augustinian mission'. In *St Augustine and the Conversion of England*, edited by Richard Gameson. 202–36. Stroud: Sutton Publishing.

Carter, H. M. 1966. *The Fort of Othona and the Chapel of St Peter-on-the-Wall, Bradwell-on-Sea, Essex*. Hunstanton: Witley Press (2nd ed. 2000).

Fowler, R. C. 1928. 'Fulk Basset's register and the Norwich taxation'. *Transactions of the Essex Archaeological Society*, n.s. XVIII: 15–26, 119–34.

Hall, H. 1888. *Society in the Elizabethan Age*, 3rd ed. London: Swan Sonnenschein & Co.

Hayward, K. M. J., and G. W. Roberts. 2019. 'Defending Londinium and the Tower of London: the raw materials. A petrological re-evaluation of the fabric of the Wardrobe Tower and adjoining Roman defensive structures at the Tower of London'. *Transactions of the London and Middlesex Archaeological Society* 70: 105–28.

Heppell, E. M. 2011. 'Saxon fishtraps in the Blackwater Estuary, Essex: monitoring survey at Collin's Creek, Pewet Island and the Nass 2003–2007'. *Transactions of the Essex Society for Archaeology and History* (4th series) 2: 76–97.

Lewin, T. 1868. 'On the castra of the litus Saxonicum, and particularly the castrum of Othona'. *Archaeologia* 41: 421–52.

Peers, C. R. 1901. 'On Saxon churches of the St Pancras type'. *Archaeological Journal* 58: 402–34.
Peers, C. R. 1928. 'Reculver: its Saxon church and cross'. *Archaeologia* 77: 241–56.
Rodwell, W. J. 1976. 'Some unrecorded archaeological discoveries in Essex, 1946–75'. *Essex Archaeology and History* 8: 234–48.
Rodwell, W. J. 1986. 'Anglo-Saxon church building: aspects of design and construction'. In *The Anglo-Saxon Church: Papers on history, architecture, and archaeology in honour of Dr H. M. Taylor*, edited by L. A. S. Butler and R. K. Morris. 156–75. London: Council for British Archaeology Research Report 60.
Taylor, H., and J. Taylor. 1980. *Anglo-Saxon Architecture*, vol. II. Cambridge: Cambridge University Press.
Thomas, C. 1981. *Christianity in Roman Britain to AD 500*. London: Batsford.
Wadham, J. 1978. 'The Church of St. Peter, Bradwell-on-Sea, Essex: An Analysis of the Surviving Fabric'. Unpublished dissertation, University of London Institute of Archaeology.
Walker, H. 2001. 'An Ipswich-type ware vessel from Althorne Creek'. *Essex Archaeology and History* 32: 243–6.

2
The Roman fort of Othona

Andrew Pearson

The construction of a Roman military base at the end of the Dengie Peninsula during the late third century represented the first, and indeed only, intensive occupation at Bradwell. Part of the coastal system of 'Saxon Shore Forts', Othona was home to a substantial garrison and was a key part of the maritime link between southern England, the British northern frontier and the continental north-west empire. Perhaps due to the poor survival of the Roman remains at Bradwell, Othona has received little attention compared with other elements of the Saxon Shore. This chapter synthesises what is known of the fort at Bradwell, and reconsiders its history and potential functions in the context of the other sites which belonged to this coastal network.

The rediscovery of Othona

The Roman remains at Bradwell appear to have been viewed by William Camden, probably during his itinerary through East Anglia in 1578. In *Britannia*, Camden correctly made the connection between the ruins at Bradwell, the Anglo-Saxon place name of *Ythancæstir* and the lost Roman fort of Othona. The first English-language edition of *Britannia*, translated by Philemon Holland, appeared in 1610, with some additional content supplied by Camden and probably translated under Camden's direction. This presented Camden's observations at Bradwell and his reasoning for the association with Othona:

> Doubtlesse this Ithancester was situate upon the utmost Promontorie of this Dengy Hundred, where in these daies standeth Saint Peters upon the Wall ... And I my selfe am partly of this minde, that this

> Ithancester was that Othona where a Band of the Fortenses with their Captaine, in the declination of the Romane Empire, kept their station or Guard under the comes or Lieutenant of the Saxon shore, against the depredations of the Saxon Rovers for the altering of Othona to Ithana is not hard straining, and the situation thereof upon a Creeke into which many rivers are discharged was for this purpose very fit and commodious, and yet heere remaineth a huge ruin of a thicke wall, whereby many Romane coines have beene found.[1]

Evidently, from the description of a 'huge ruin', and despite having been quarried for the building of St Peter's Chapel and other churches on the Dengie Peninsula during the Saxon and later medieval periods, the standing Roman remains at Bradwell continued to be substantial in the late sixteenth century.[2] However, over the following century stone robbing must have occurred on a major scale, perhaps accompanied by coastal erosion and sediment accretion, such that by the time that the antiquarian Cromwell Mortimer (d. 1752) wrote of the site, nothing of the defences stood above ground:

> I found here, at low water, several ragged pieces of free-stone, of which there is none naturally on this shore, and a great many pieces of Roman brick: upon the sea wall stands an old Roman building, now a barn, but commonly called St. Peter's Chapel. This seems to have been the place, where stood the Othona of the Romans, or Ithanchester of the Saxons ... The fishermen told me they often drudge up pieces of broken earthen ware, and sometimes, though rarely, copper or brass money.[3]

Other key antiquarian figures of the eighteenth century overlooked the site entirely, including William Stukeley, whose *Iter V* of his *Itinerarium Curiosum* took in Richborough, Lympne, Burgh Castle and the Dover Lighthouse, recognising these as Roman works, but bypassed the Dengie Peninsula. Othona was also absent from Herman Moll's map of 1724, based on information by Stukeley, which attempted to chart the Roman sites mentioned on the Antonine Itinerary, and which could also have drawn on other texts that were available to eighteenth-century scholars, among which was the *Notitia Dignitatum*.[4]

The physical remains of the Roman fort came back to light in 1864, as the result of works undertaken by the South Essex Sewage and Reclamation Company, which had purchased marginal coastal land on the Dengie Peninsula with a view to enclosing it for agriculture.

The circumstances of the discovery were narrated in an article by the eminent antiquarian Charles Roach Smith in *The Gentleman's Magazine*.[5] In this text, Roach Smith described a meeting on the site involving himself, the landowner Oxley Parker and several other interested parties. At the time of the meeting the defences were exposed, while Oxley Parker was also able to display the numerous finds that had been recovered. As catalogued in the 1940s, these included several hundred Roman coins, pottery and numerous objects of bronze, iron, glass, stone and bone. Quite typically of finds from Roman forts, the artefact assemblage was not overtly military in character, although some undated spear heads were identified and three bronze brooches (including one crossbow type) were present, the latter often being associated with Roman Army officers or bureaucrats (see Figure 2.6). The remainder of the assemblage comprised a wide variety of domestic objects, including other brooches, a ring, a stylus, pins, combs, a spoon, knife handle and spindle whorls. A very large quantity of animal bone and oyster shell was also present.[6]

A significant number of inhumation burials had also been revealed by the excavations, described by one observer, a Mr Spurrell, as being 'close to the wall, buried only about 2 ft deep'. Spurrell noted how, 'in every case a Roman coin lies close to the ribs, as if it had been placed at the burial within the hands, or under the tongue of the deceased'. These burials, not unreasonably given the presence of the coins, Spurrell thought to be Roman. Distinct from these were more bodies: 'five perfect skeletons, all laid out at full length, but somewhat in confusion, and with the faces downwards'. Spurrell suggested these to be the bodies of persons killed in fighting, 'most likely Saxon, or Danish aggressors', but in fact none is likely to belong to the Roman period. Their location within the fort makes a Roman date improbable, and it is much more likely that they relate to the Saxon phase of the site and are associated with the use of the chapel.[7]

Roach Smith's account is interesting not only for the discoveries it described but also for the fact that they related to a site about which neither Roach Smith nor his colleagues had a clear understanding. Despite the writings of Camden almost three centuries earlier, Oxley Parker begged the question of these visiting experts 'whether we now stand on the site of Othona of the Romans, the *Ithancester* of the Saxons …?',[8] while the opinions of those present were divided about whether St Peter's Chapel was of Saxon, Norman or even later date.[9]

Despite his familiarity with the Kent Shore Forts of Reculver, Richborough and Lympne, Roach Smith did not express a firm opinion on the identification of Bradwell as Othona. This was left to Thomas Lewin,

Professor of Ancient History at Oxford University, in a paper read at the Society of Antiquaries in 1867.[10] In his lecture, Lewin led his audience through a historical account of the *Litus Saxonicum*, before describing the physical remains at the known sites, from Brancaster round to Portchester. Lewin then turned his attention to the discoveries at Bradwell. To some extent he reiterated the chance findings as described by Roach Smith, but Lewin was also able to draw on somewhat more formal investigations made subsequent to the 1864 antiquarian meeting at the site, noting that 'Oxley Parker ... has with the most laudable zeal laid open the foundations of all that is left of the outer wall, and in the interior has cut a series of trenches parallel to each other, only a few feet apart from east to west, so that he may be said to have exhausted the area' (Figure 2.1).[11] In discussing the findings from these investigations, Lewin made a clear connection between the site at Bradwell and Othona, which has remained unquestioned since.

Nothing more was reported about the site for the remainder of the nineteenth century or the first decade of the twentieth, before military works during the First World War once again revealed archaeological finds. These were recorded by the Count de la Chapelle, who watched the works and scoured the site for artefacts. In his papers the count recorded that 'off the castrum in the tidal creeks, various objects have been found,

Figure 2.1 Bradwell Chapel, from a drawing by the Rev. H. Milligan entitled 'Land trenched [in 1864 by Oxley Parker] for the discovery of walls' (from Chancellor 1877, 216).

large blocks of stone grouped together suggest a building ... the tide covers the site ... close to the stones a cinerary urn in situ in the gravel, but broken ... many fragments of pottery and tiles'. He also noted that several cinerary urns were found by the troops, at an unspecified location in or around the fort, about three feet below the surface.[12]

The Count de la Chapelle's opportunistic discoveries were followed shortly after by more systematic, albeit small-scale, excavations by Charles Peers on behalf of the Ministry of Works in the early 1920s. These were carried out around the chapel and do not appear to have shed any light on the Roman period of the site. Peers's trenching was not followed by any further investigations until 1947, when Major J. Brinson cut a single trench across the western defences, about 20m north of the chapel. This trench provides the most precise evidence for the dimensions and make-up of the perimeter wall and its foundations, as well as for the rampart and probable external ditch. It did not, however, extend to the fort interior.[13]

Another lengthy interlude followed until the early 1990s. Since then, various investigations have taken place, principally within the fort's extramural area. These comprise limited development-led evaluation trenching to the north of the fort, on the Othona Community site,[14] complemented by broader geophysical survey, fieldwalking and aerial

Figure 2.2 The upstanding Roman defences in 1907. The person depicted is John Chillingworth, who farmed Bradwell Hall. Kevin Bruce Collection.

photographic analysis (see Figure 2.5 below). Collectively, these projects give a partial insight into the Roman phase at Bradwell, principally in respect of the extramural area, although the geophysics did also cover the ground within the defences.

The form of the fort

As Stephen Rippon describes in Chapter 3, topographical survey of the Dengie Peninsula has demonstrated that the late Roman fort was established on a low promontory, with estuarine alluvium and creeks to both north and south (Figure 2.3).

From the antiquarian accounts described above, it is obvious that practically nothing of the fort has survived above ground for many centuries. What can be surmised about the form of the defences and the fort interior is limited. Coastal erosion has entirely destroyed the eastern half of the defences, while the archaeology has been disturbed by the land reclamation works of the 1860s and by the cutting of an anti-tank ditch across the western defences during the Second World War. At some point between 1927 and 1954 the farmer also bulldozed the site level.[15]

Below ground, the only side of the perimeter defences to survive for their entire length is the western wall, which the 1860s excavations show to be c. 160m long. The northern wall can be traced for c. 88m, and the

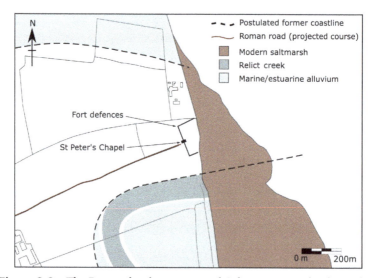

Figure 2.3 The Roman landscape around Othona. Drawn by the author.

southern wall for *c.* 45m, before each terminates at the edge of the saltings. The eastern defences have been entirely destroyed by erosion, but early theories that the fort was open-sided (as once also thought for Richborough) are now discounted. The north and south walls are not quite parallel, and thus the fort could not have conformed to the standard square or rectangular layout of 'traditional' Roman forts of the first and second centuries. Othona therefore shared the irregular plan form of others of the Shore Forts, being most closely comparable to Burgh Castle, whose north and south walls are slightly off-parallel. A roughly square fort would have had a total perimeter of around 640m, enclosing 2.5ha – but without evidence such dimensions are merely supposition. The fort's western gate has been identified as the aperture now occupied by St Peter's Chapel; while there are gaps in the north and south walls, these appear to be the result of destruction of the wall, rather than gateways. Two semicircular bastions have been proved by excavation, at the north-west angle and on the west wall.

The perimeter walls, as revealed in Brinson's section across the western defences, were ashlar-faced with a rubble-mortar core. They were 4.2m thick at the base, stepping in on the exterior face above the lowest three courses to 3.8m.[16] The exposed sections displayed the characteristic banding of the outer wall face that is seen elsewhere in Shore Forts and other contemporary defensive architecture from Britain and the north-west empire. In Bradwell's case, a single tile course was overlain by four courses of local septarian cementstone, then three of tile and three of septaria alternately. These appear to be the dominant materials employed for the defences, although, as discussed below, Lincolnshire Limestone was also present in limited quantities, most plausibly used in the west gate; these blocks were subsequently reused as quoins in St Peter's Chapel.[17]

The defensive wall superstructure rests on foundations of 4.2m width, within a vertical-sided trench that extended to at least a depth of 1.1m. Evidence for a rampart against the inner face is provided by the mass of yellow clay behind the west wall, while its presence on the north and south walls is indicated by a roll in the ground behind the line of the defences. An outer ditch has been harder to prove, but it may have been identified on the north side of the fort, separated from the wall by a berm of 9–14m.[18]

The 1963 the *VCH* observed that after nearly a century of exposure the stub of the defences that stood above ground was in need of conservation.[19] This never occurred, and in the modern day a fragment of the south wall, less than 2m in length and overgrown, is all that remains visible. This unimpressive ruin, however, belies the very substantial scale of the defences. The walls of Othona are markedly thicker than those of the earlier members of the Shore Fort series, namely Brancaster, Caister and Reculver. Indeed, they are comparable to those of Pevensey, whose massive perimeter defences, still standing above 8m, are some of the most impressive Roman remains in Britain (Figure 2.4).

The layout of the fort's interior is far more enigmatic. Oxley Parker's trenches recovered a significant amount of artefactual material but found little evidence for internal structures. The plan of his excavations shows the interior as a blank area, other than an 'old piece of rubble work about 4ft high' in its south-eastern part (see Figure 1.2 in previous chapter): this roughly corresponds to a possible fragment of wall footing identified more recently from aerial photographs.[20]

A geophysical survey conducted in 1999 has augmented this picture.[21] Only partial coverage of the fort interior was achieved, due to the extent of unsurveyable ground and areas of magnetic disturbance.

Figure 2.4 Reconstruction of the Roman fort at Pevensey (Anderita). The width of the defences' foundations and base of the superstructure are similar to those at Bradwell, and it can be assumed that the two forts were similarly imposing. The marshland setting shown here may also have been quite similar. © Historic England Archive; image reference IC078_003 (illustration by Peter Urmston).

Nevertheless, the west wall of the defences was apparent, together with the line of the north wall, although in the case of the latter the masonry was suggested to have been robbed away.[22] Potential evidence of internal structures was identified, primarily in the northern part of the fort, around its perimeter. The most prominent of these is aligned with, and appears to extend along the full length of, the west wall. The survey report suggested this to be characteristic of a barrack block. Other fragmentary ditch features were also detected within the fort, perhaps indicative of structures, these being more apparent in the northerly portion of the site and much less in the southern part. Evidence for a central east–west road was also identified.

In the account of the discoveries given by Oxley Parker to Roach Smith, Parker also described having seen 'sectional views of pits or holes' containing animal bone and other refuse, but whether these related to Roman or later activity is not known. Regardless, an annotation on the site plan accompanying Lewin's article attests to the general archaeological potential of the site, stating that 'The soil within these walls [is] of a rich black character and contains large quantities of pottery, coins, bones of animals and debris of various kinds. Very many skulls and large quantities of human bones are also found in digging over the soil.'[23]

The dearth of structural evidence from the interior of Othona, and the general vagaries of the findings, represent a common Shore Fort problem. The Victorian excavations at Othona could reasonably be expected not to have recovered the full suite of data, with a consequent lack of detail about the interior layout. However, more recent and rigorous investigations, for example those spanning the 1920s to 1960s at Richborough and at Portchester between 1961 and 1979, have yielded similarly partial and enigmatic internal plans. Only the earlier-constructed members of the Shore Fort group appear to exhibit a regimented plan typical of forts of the Principate. The layout of those with a later third-century construction date is more of a mystery, but what seems clear is that there was a use of space that was far less intensive.[24]

The extramural area

Beyond the defences, evidence has emerged in recent decades for Roman extramural activity in the area surrounding the Bradwell fort. The picture is again incomplete, based on limited geophysical and fieldwalking surveys, while ground truthing through trenching has been restricted to a small area north of the fort (Figures 2.5 and 2.6). Meanwhile, aerial

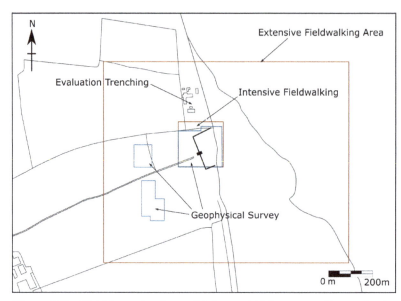

Figure 2.5 Field investigations of Othona: 1990–present. Drawn by the author.

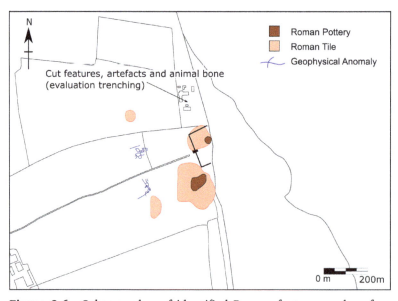

Figure 2.6 Othona: plan of identified Roman features and surface artefact distribution. Drawn by the author.

photography – a technique that has proved successful in identifying extramural features outside certain others of the Shore Fort – has not been productive in the case of Bradwell.[25]

The present road and track leading to St Peter's Chapel are possibly of Roman origin. This route follows a completely straight course for c. 2.4km, on an east–north-east alignment between Bradwell East End and the fort's west gate. A landward route to the fort must have existed and would surely have been close to this alignment, but no archaeological section has yet been cut across the track to confirm this point.

Close to the fort, at the end of the Dengie Peninsula in the area known to have been dryland during the Roman period, geophysics has identified further evidence for field systems. These lie both to the north and south of the presumed Roman road, at distances of c. 200m from the defences. On the north side of the road, the anomalies comprised a discrete group of features characteristic of a settlement, the anomalies here containing a large proportion of material that has been significantly magnetically enhanced. This suggests a close association between the features and human occupation and/or industrial activity. The function of the features to the south of the road is less obvious, though they appear to form part of an enclosure or boundary system. Importantly, the geophysics only sampled two small parts of the extramural area, but archaeological features were abundant in both.[26] The implication is that a more extensive survey would reveal numerous other features.

Transect-based fieldwalking has been undertaken on the land on the western, northern and southern sides of the fort.[27] An informal walkover has also been carried out on the mudflats beyond the surviving limits of the fort. Within the fort's perimeter and in its immediate vicinity, a thin scatter of undiagnostic and late Roman pottery and a heavy scatter of Roman brick and tile was found. Other finds included one tessera made from tile, one tessera made from sandstone, several fragments of mortar and one fragment of tufa. Beyond the defences, several concentrations of Roman material were identified. A heavy scatter of undiagnostic and late Roman pottery was discovered to the immediate south-west of the fort. Pieces of undiagnostic and late Roman pottery were also found to the north-west and the far south-west. A small concentration of pottery was found c. 150m to the south of the chapel. Pieces of Roman brick and tile, including box-flue tile, were present in all the field walked areas. A very large concentration of material was found to the immediate south of the fort, and smaller assemblages to the south-west and north-west. Single pieces of tesserae made from tile were found in nine locations; these were all fairly large and as such are unlikely to be from a tessellated pavement of any quality.

The coastal erosion to the east of the defences has erased any evidence of what lay on the seaward side of the fort. However, during the Second World War a bomb fell into the intertidal mud a quarter of a mile from the fort, its crater revealing a solid mass of masonry which was regarded as Roman.[28] This must have lain a considerable distance from the defences and, given its placement between the fort and the sea, seems unlikely to relate to a *vicus*. It could have been a building or structure related to a harbour, though its form and purpose must remain a mystery.[29]

To the north of the defences, on the Othona Community site, evaluation trenching in 1991 and 2009 has provided a limited archaeological insight into the extramural area.[30] Located about 120m outside the fort walls, the trenching has revealed post-holes, gullies, pits and ditches. Although the trenches were too narrow for any firm idea of a site plan to emerge, it appears that certain of the ditches intersected to form at least two enclosures. A short length of a late fourth-century rubble foundation was also present, suggested to be part of an outbuilding. The majority of the archaeological evidence represents late third- to late fourth-century activity, thus clearly related to the Roman fort. Both the 1991 and 2009 trenching recovered pottery of mid/late third- and fourth-century date, in which local wares were dominant, although some regional fabrics such as Oxford ware (OXRC) and late shell-tempered ware (LSH) were also present.[31] This is consistent with the pottery recovered from fieldwalking elsewhere in the extramural area. This was again of late third- and fourth-century date and with a range of fabric types that is typical of late Roman sites in the region.[32] A sample of the Roman brick and tile from the fieldwalking was also analysed, the fabrics including one with inclusions of pale clay, also found at Elms Farm, Heybridge, and shelly tile made at Harrold in Bedfordshire. Other examples of Harrold tile have been recovered previously from the land around the Bradwell fort. At excavated sites, Harrold tile occurs almost exclusively in fourth-century contexts, with production perhaps starting in the late third century. It has a wide geographical distribution and has been found in excavations from at least one other Saxon Shore Fort, Lympne.[33]

The ecofactual evidence from the 2009 trenching complemented that from the 1991 investigations, but with a larger animal bone assemblage, which contained evidence for primary butchery of cattle. A large assemblage of shells also indicates that oysters, with smaller amounts of whelks, cockles, mussels and clams, formed part of the Othona diet. This evidence dovetails with the large quantities of animal bone and oyster shells reported from the investigations of the fort interior during the 1860s.

Up to the present, the only archaeological evaluation at Bradwell has been within the Othona Community site. Consequently, neither the features identified by the geophysical survey, nor the areas where fieldwalking encountered higher densities of surface artefacts, have been examined archaeologically. It is also notable that the features found by the geophysics did not correlate with the areas where the higher concentrations of Roman surface artefacts were found. The relationship between the road, geophysical features and concentrations of Roman artefacts on the ground surface is therefore still unclear. Nevertheless, the present data demonstrate that there was Roman extramural activity across most, if not all, of the end of the Othona peninsula. On the north side of the fort, fieldwalking between the Roman defences and the Othona Community buildings has revealed a distinct spread of pottery sherds and tile fragments. This was densest in concentration in the immediate vicinity of the fort, but did extend out as far as the evaluation trenches.[34] It seems clear, therefore, that the extra-mural activity extended up to the limits of the salt marsh on the fort's northern side. Meanwhile, on the south side of the fort, the large concentration of tile found by fieldwalking perhaps suggests that another focus of settlement lay here. How far the extramural activity extended westwards, on the landward side of the fort, is presently unclear.

The exact character of activity within the *vicus* has yet to be established, but at least one substantial building must have been present. The Community Site excavations recovered tile, including box-flue tile, the most likely context for a hypocausted building being a bathhouse. Such a structure would be expected to be situated outside the defences, but exactly where this lay in relation to Othona is unclear. This issue is somewhat confused by the fact that box-flue tile has been found both to the north of the fort, on the Community Site, and on the opposite side of the fort entirely, near the creek to the south. One possibility, of course, is that this tile derives from two completely separate buildings. The bathhouse or another higher-status building must have had a mosaic floor, as evidenced by the tesserae recovered by fieldwalking.

Looking further afield, across the Dengie Peninsula as a whole, there is evidence for activity which is probably Roman and logically would be contemporary with Othona's occupation. Cropmarks near to East End, c. 1.8km west of the fort, are immediately next to the presumed Roman road and seem to share their orientation with this feature. Although unexcavated, these cropmarks are likely to relate to a small Roman farmstead and its surrounding field system. Assuming late Roman occupation here, then this farm was too distant to be part of any *vicus*, so would have been an attendant but separate settlement.[35] Elsewhere on the peninsula there a number of other cropmark complexes which have been identified from aerial photographs. Once again, these have not been formally dated, but they are comparable with similar cropmarks elsewhere in the region which excavation has proved to belong to the Late Iron Age and/or Roman periods. It is reasonable to interpret these as small individual farmsteads with associated field systems. Further archaeological work on these sites could resolve the question of their date, while doubtless other settlement and activity sites on the Dengie Peninsula still await discovery.

Discussion

The archaeological evidence gathered from the site since the 1860s allows for a reasonable impression to be gained of the Shore Fort, and of the area of extramural activity that occupied this part of the Dengie Peninsula from the later third century onwards.

The creation of this fort was a major undertaking. It is estimated that the defensive perimeter alone required over 23,000m³ of stone, mortar and timber, while its construction needed of the order of 78,000 man-days' labour. Assuming a working year of 280 days (which takes account of the practicality of working in winter), this equates to a labour force of nearly 300 people across the course of a single season. This is a scenario we might contemplate if Othona's construction was a rapid project (perhaps under Carausius, as discussed below), but a more drawn-out timescale would clearly have required a smaller annual labour force. Most of the building stone came from the coast; its transport equated to the order of 870 boatloads of a vessel of comparable size to Blackfriars I.[36] These figures are a bare minimum, since one has to consider the additional raw materials and labour needed for the construction of any internal or external buildings, and for the logistical support of the labour force.[37] To give one example, it is estimated that a Roman soldier would eat half a tonne of wheat per year, and this was just one component of the diet.[38] None of this was beyond the capacity of the Roman authorities, but it nonetheless demonstrates the scale of what was undertaken at Bradwell, which would have become a hive of industrial activity during the construction phase.

In terms of the fort's building date and occupation sequence, the principal evidence is provided by the coins recovered from within and immediately outside the defences (some 322 coins in total). The coin sequence is dominated by late third- and fourth-century issues, with Carausian and Allectan coins very well represented. Also present are a very few late fourth- or early fifth-century coins of Arcadius (reigned 393–423) and Honorius (383–408).[39] An analysis of the third-century coin assemblages from the Shore Forts has dated Othona's construction to Carausius (286–93), but its author acknowledged various methodological difficulties.[40] The excavators of the Othona Community site preferred a date perhaps several decades earlier, on the basis of their recovery of mid third-century pottery,[41] although securely dated contexts were all of the late third century onwards. At present, the most that can be said with any certainty is that the fort belongs to an undefined date in the late third century, and is thus separate from the initial group comprising Brancaster, Caister-on-Sea and Reculver, which originated in the early third century and are notable for their 'traditional' defensive architecture.[42]

The coins prove occupation of Othona during the fourth century, although whether this occupation was continuous or sporadic (the latter being demonstrably the case at Portchester) cannot be established from the coinage alone. The presence of coins of Honorius and Arcadius indicates that the fort had some form of occupation until close to the end of formal Roman rule in Britain. The other artefactual evidence from the site bears out this general picture, being of late third- and fourth-century date. Of the garrison itself, little is known. The *Notitia Dignitatum* records it as being the *numerus Fortensium*, a light cavalry unit. This began life as a vexillation (detachment) from *Legio II Traiana*, which was honoured on coins of the Gallic emperor Victorinus alongside other continental legions. Gallienus is thought to have created two other cavalry units stationed at the Shore Fort, the *equites Dalmatae Brandodunenses* (Brancaster) and *equites Stablesiani Garionnonenses* (Burgh Castle), which he moved to Britain after the collapse of the Gallic Empire in 274. It is quite possible, therefore, that the *numerus Fortenses* was also deployed to Britain from the continent at a similar time and was the original garrison at Bradwell. Writing on Othona in the 1860s, Lewin suggested that its garrison numbered between 500 and 1000, which is to say a full-size auxillary *millenaria* regiment. More recently, however, suggestions have been made that some of the northern frontier forts were garrisoned by no more than 100 men, and although this idea is now questioned, we should nevertheless be open to the possibility that a similar 'caretaker' force may have occupied Othona, at least at times.[43]

Othona was a formidable site, as imposing as any of its counterparts around the Saxon Shore, however, its function (or functions) remain speculation. The precise nature of the *litus Saxonicum* as listed in the

Notitia Dignitatum, and thus the role of the Shore Forts, has been a subject of discussion since the sixteenth century. In the introduction to Panciroli's 1593 edition of the *Notitia*, the *litus Saxonicum* was envisaged as a coastline settled by the Saxons, as opposed to one invaded by them. However, the prevailing view quickly changed to that of the Shore Forts as a defence against barbarian piracy. This was first given expression by Camden, who wrote of the 'depredations and robberies of Barbarians, but of Saxons especially, who grievously infested Britaine'.[44] Camden never gave the reasoning behind his interpretation, but although historic and modern scholarship have offered alternative theories, the idea of a British coast under barbarian attack endures as the most popular explanation of the Saxon Shore. The sixteenth-century scholarship which identified the physical remains at Bradwell as belonging to Othona is, therefore, inextricably linked to the popular interpretation of its function which prevails to this day. In the nineteenth century, the publications by Roach Smith and Lewin about the rediscovery of Othona show unqualified acceptance of the anti-piracy theme, their reading of the evidence being laced through by this idea.

The anti-piracy interpretation has been given its fullest expression in Stephen Johnson's *Roman Forts of the Saxon Shore*. Although published in 1976 and thus now over two generations old, this text remains highly influential. There are, however, multiple problems with this theory.[45] Most fundamentally, the evidence for barbarian coastal raiding – both historical and archaeological – is very slight. There is nothing that proves large-scale or persistent coastal attacks in the late Roman period, while many scholars now posit that the Germanic 'conquest' of England from the fifth century onwards did not involve mass migrations but instead was achieved by small numbers and a relatively acquiescent native population.[46] The capacity of barbarian peoples to mount seaborne attacks on Britannia and Gaul has also been questioned,[47] while the geographic positioning of the Shore Forts lacks logic as a defensive scheme, especially when their piecemeal abandonment from the mid-fourth century onwards is considered.[48]

The revisionist position is that much of the coastal network around Britain was never intended to combat piracy from the outset – if indeed at any point in its operation. Such theories take two principal forms. Some scholars envisage the Shore Forts as defences against Rome, originating as a Carausian–Allectan project designed to safeguard their breakaway regime of 286–96.[49] Others see no connection to defence at all, regarding them instead as links in a military logistical network, connecting southern Britain with the northern frontier and the Rhineland provinces.[50] Such ideas are not mutually exclusive. It is quite possible, for example, that a defensive scheme created by Carausius and Allectus was put to a different use by Constantius and his successors, after their recapture of the British province. Over the course of the fourth century, a hybrid or changing role seems quite plausible, while individual sites may have had distinct functions.

This fundamental question is far from settled, nor in fact is it ever likely to be definitively answered. The historical sources are as ambiguous to us as they were to the early antiquarians, while archaeology cannot conclusively resolve the issue. Recent research into the Shore Forts certainly offers little that would advance the present discussion. At Richborough, excavations have examined the fallen east wall,[51] while a geophysical survey inside Pevensey's Roman defences has revealed a number of features, though whether these are of Roman, Saxon or later date is presently unclear.[52] At Burgh Castle a community project has investigated the *vicus* through geophysics, the results indicating a planned layout with no occupation phases preceding the Shore Fort.[53] Elsewhere, excavations at the church of St John the Baptist, Reedham, have confirmed the presence of Roman structures, reinforcing its interpretation as a lighthouse or watchtower on the Great Estuary, contemporary with Burgh Castle and Caister-on-Sea.[54] Meanwhile, the published synthesis on the Roman town of Great Chesterford indicates that it developed a significant regional role in the mid- to late fourth century, with the construction of massive masonry walls around the urban core. The authors argue that these were defensive in nature (as opposed to the alternative, an expression of civic pride), and may have enabled the town to act as a military base and a supply depot. As such, along with Cambridge (also provided with defences in the fourth century), Great Chesterford could have been an inland component of the Saxon Shore, guarding the East Anglian interior.[55] Once again this idea is open to debate, but it certainly emphasises the necessity of considering the Shore Forts within wider geographical contexts.

While the Shore Forts' primary function must remain opaque, it is more feasible to make comment about other aspects of these sites, in particular about their economic role. The forts were mainly positioned in marginal, isolated places, often with little existing settlement. Othona is a case in point, illustrating the way that a new fort stimulated activity in its environs and linked the district into wider trade and logistical networks. Prior to the late third century, there is little evidence for anything more than a background level of Roman activity on the Dengie Peninsula as a whole, with small dispersed occupation sites present on the drier land.[56] Such settlement existed alongside exploitation of the intertidal margins for salt production, this being part of a regional industry which extended across much of the East Anglian coastal zone.[57] Its presence is attested by numerous 'red hills' or salterns, comprising low, often extensive, mounds or surface spreads of red burnt soils. At a regional level, this industry was of long standing, spanning late prehistory to the end of the Roman period. At the present time it is not known exactly how salt production on the Dengie Peninsula related chronologically to Othona, though the assumption is that it coincided. However, at least some of the salterns pre-dated Othona by several centuries, as demonstrated by excavation of one example to the south-west of the fort; this proved to be a relatively short-lived site of Late Iron Age date (for the location of red hills see Figure 3.2 in following chapter).[58]

The coins and other material culture from the fort and its immediate environs strongly indicate that there was no significant occupation of the site prior to the building of Othona. Its construction was therefore a step-change, transforming an area of marginal coastal land into a major building site. Critically, too, over the longer term it introduced a sizeable military presence into a region that lay firmly within Britannia's 'Civilian Zone', having been demilitarised since the later first century. Exactly how this influenced the wider pattern of settlement and industry on the peninsula must await further archaeological research, but it is already clear that it brought considerable change within the fort's immediate extramural zone.

The character of this zone is not yet fully understood, so it remains an open question as to how much of what went on there was settlement and how much was simply 'activity' associated with the functioning of the fort. Nevertheless, what evidence has been recovered so far points strongly towards a focus on butchery and meat production. The abundance of animal bone unearthed during the 1860s was initially commented upon by Roach Smith and Lewin, the latter painting a picture of a garrison living handsomely off the products of hunting in the Essex forests. The recent evaluation trenches on the Othona Community site have also produced large quantity of animal bone, with evidence for primary butchery, mainly of cattle. The enclosures that have been detected by these trenches, and more widely by geophysics in the extramural area, could potentially have been animal corrals.[59] As such, a rather less romantic conclusion to that of Lewin needs to be preferred, namely that the garrison was engaged with large-scale meat production.

Such evidence has parallels at some of the other Shore Forts. Large assemblages of animal bones have been recovered from Brancaster,

Caister-on-Sea and Burgh Castle, with specific areas for butchery having been identified within the *vicus* at first of these sites.[60] At Caister-on-Sea, 'Building 1' inside the fort is suggested as the place of butchery, while the adjacent 'Building 2' had a series of small 'rooms' lined with waterproof *opus signinum* plaster which may have served as tannery tanks. At all three forts there is a bias towards the non-meat-bearing bones, suggesting that the product of the butchery (in other words, the main joints) was going elsewhere.[61] When coupled with the evidence for salt production in their environs, there is a clear case to be made for the East Anglian Shore Forts having an important – and perhaps even a primary – role in the production and trans-shipment of meat. The Roman army had a vast requirement for meat, as well as for other animal products such as hides and gut. Sites such as Othona would have been ideally placed to serve as collecting and processing points, supplying the northern British forts and those on the Lower Rhine frontier. Similarly, large butchery assemblages have been found at other military sites with access to Britain's east coast: for example, from the late fourth-century phase at Binchester (County Durham) on the River Wear.[62] These too may have contributed to a widely dispersed, long-distance military supply network.

Whether meat production was Othona's principal function, one of several specialisms at the site, or simply an activity that was ancillary to a defensive coastal fort, requires greater archaeological research.[63] Similarly, more data is required to better understand the economic connections of the site, which was not only a producer but also a consumer. Some hints of these connections are already provided by the construction materials used in the fort defences and other buildings. Most of the stone for the defences was locally sourced, but the large blocks of Lincolnshire Limestone that were rebuilt into St Peter's Chapel are clearly of Roman date, and are a good match with Ketton Stone from Rutland. Meanwhile, as discussed above, some of the tile present on the site was from Bedfordshire. These long-distance connections may have been short-lived, confined only to the construction period. Nevertheless, their existence, along with evidence from elsewhere in Roman Britain for the long-distance movement of other commodities – for example BB1 pottery – is indicative of the complex and widespread networks into which coastal sites were integrated.[64]

Given the relatively slight archaeological evidence from the site, it is difficult to reach any detailed conclusion about its abandonment. As noted above, the coin sequence points towards a presence at the fort until at least the end of the fourth century, though only a small proportion of the coin assemblage is made up of such late issues and none comes from a stratified archaeological context. The date of the pottery supports this to an extent, six contexts from the 2009 excavation of the Othona Community site containing pottery of the second half of the fourth century.[65] It is logical to assume that if there was activity in the extramural area, then the fort itself was occupied and active.

The decommissioning of the Shore Fort group as a whole was a piecemeal affair. Large-scale occupation at Lympne ended shortly after 350, while the garrison at Reculver was withdrawn c. 360. Caister-on-Sea and Burgh Castle were both abandoned about the year 380. The use of other sites such as Brancaster, Richborough and Portchester extended at least to the end of the fourth century and perhaps beyond. The evidence from Bradwell suggests that it was one of the latest of the coastal sites on the south and east coast of Britain to be occupied, and thus presumably was deemed one of the more significant or useful parts of the group. Of the final date of Othona's abandonment, and any continued occupation into the early Saxon period, nothing is known. There are no signs of any violent destruction of the fort, and the Victorian interpretation of some of the burials within the fort as resulting from conflict can almost certainly be dismissed. A deliberate decommissioning seems far more likely, involving a substantial reduction, or complete removal, of the garrison. This event would presumably have been accompanied by cessation of activity in the extramural area and the demise of any reliant settlement. The Colchester Museum catalogue dates two brooches to the late fifth century but identified no objects that would bridge the gap from the early parts of the century. Similarly, the excavated pottery assemblage also lacks late Roman imports, and thus does not evidence any continuity into the fifth century.

Numerous questions remain about Roman Bradwell, but the research for this chapter indicates that there is great potential to answer them. In terms of sources of data that are already accessible, re-examination of the coins may perhaps refine our understanding of the site's construction and occupation, while a modern analysis of the other artefacts in the Colchester Museum collection would doubtless enhance the existing commentary. The current catalogue was created in the 1940s, and artefact typologies have advanced significantly since that time. The military brooches (see Figure 2.7) are of particular interest, given that they have the potential to inform us about the higher-status occupants of the fort, and perhaps even about the presence of Germanic mercenaries.[66] The 1940s catalogue also did not attempt to distinguish between iron objects of Roman, Saxon and later periods; this too might now be possible.

In archaeological terms, and despite the above-ground destruction of the defences, it is also evident that this is a landscape that is ripe for further investigation. Inside the fort, there is a good prospect for

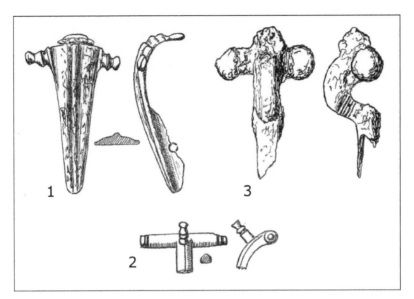

Figure 2.7   Military metalwork recovered during the 1864 investigations of Othona: (1) brooch with broad fluted bow and strong central rib; (2) head of brooch of 'light crossbow pattern'; (3) corroded brooch of 'heavy crossbow type'. Not to scale. Descriptions taken from the Colchester Museum catalogue (Borough of Colchester 1947/48).

undisturbed archaeology to survive in the gaps between Oxley Parker's trenches.[67] Modern excavations elsewhere – for example those of Insula IX at Silchester – demonstrate how much archaeology survives within sites that had supposedly been completely 'dug out' by the Victorians. Meanwhile, the extramural area seems comparatively undisturbed, the archaeological work undertaken here from the 1990s demonstrating that fieldwalking, geophysics and field excavation are all extremely productive. An integrated research project, looking inside and outside the defences, and encompassing both archaeology and artefacts, therefore has great potential to increase our understanding of the nature of the fort and its occupation, as well as about subsequent phases of this highly significant site.

Notes

1   Camden 1610.
2   On the reuse of Roman stone from Othona within religious and secular buildings on the Dengie Peninsula see Allen and Fulford 1999.
3   Cited in Walford 1812, 149.

4   Stukeley 1776, 126–33; Moll 1724. See also Hoggett, in this volume.
5   Roach Smith 1865, vol. 1 (for January–June inclusive), 67–71. The report submitted by Roach Smith referred to a meeting on the site on 26 October 1864.
6   The small finds recovered during the excavations were lent by Mr Christopher Parker to the Colchester Museum in 1905. These were returned to the Parker family again in 1917, before being permanently bequeathed to the same museum in 1947, where they still remain. This acquisition complemented a collection of 29 coins from the Bradwell fort which the museum had purchased from the Count de la Chapelle in 1937. A description and illustration of the principal artefacts is given in the annual report for the museum: Borough of Colchester 1947/48, 20–30.
7   For Spurrell's comments see Roach Smith 1865, vol. 1, 70.
8   Roach Smith 1865, vol. 1, 68.
9   This is slightly surprising, as some local publications of the mid-nineteenth century (for example, *White's Directory of Essex*, 1848; https://historyhouse.co.uk/placeB/essexb24a.html [accessed 8 March 2022]) still cited Camden and Holland's assertions about Othona being at Bradwell. The identification of St Peter's Chapel appears to have been more durable. It is marked on maps of Essex including those by Saxton (1576), Moll (1724) and Cary (1798). Even so, its date was clearly uncertain: Chancellor (1877) published his conclusion that the building dated to the latter end of the twelfth century and was built for ecclesiastical purposes. See Bettley, in this volume.
10 Lewin 1867.
11 Lewin 1867, 440.
12 Twenty-nine more coins were bought from the count by the museum, ranging from Claudius II to Arcadius. The count's records were acquired by the museum within the papers of the noted Colchester archaeologist Philip Laver: Borough of Colchester 1947/48, 29.
13 Powell 1963, 54 and fig. 14; Rodwell 1976.
14 Medlycott 1991, 1994; Sparrow 2009, 2011.
15 Wartime contravention work involved the construction of anti-tank ditches and pillboxes. The location of many of these works is not known, although anti-tank ditches were identified at the Othona Community site (Medlycott 1994) and by the geophysical survey (Wardill 2000). The levelling of the site by the farmer is noted by Lavender (2000, 5).
16 Powell 1963, fig. 14; Lewin 1867, 442, records the thickness of the superstructure as 'about 12 feet' (3.6m).
17 Pearson 2003, Appendix 1. On the fabric of the chapel see Andrews, in this volume.
18 Powell 1963, fig. 13.
19 Powell 1963, 53. The details about Othona are given in the entry for Bradwell on Sea.
20 Air Photo Services 1999, Fig. 2.
21 Wardell 2000.
22 These conclusions do not entirely agree with the 1867 plan, which depicts at least some surviving masonry around the north-east angle, and at the east end of the north wall.
23 Roach Smith 1865, vol. 1, 69.
24 Pearson 2002a, Chapter 7.
25 Air Photo Services 1999. Other than in the area within the Roman fort, all recorded features were natural.
26 The geophysical of the fort comprised an area of 3.6ha; Area 'A' comprised 0.8ha and Area 'B' 1.4ha.
27 Germany 2000; Lavender 2000, fig. 1, for survey areas. An intensive fieldwalking survey of 16 hectares (20 per cent coverage by area) took place over the scheduled area of the fort and its immediate environs. Some 35ha of arable land to the west of the chapel and fort were also investigated by transect, but at a lower (10 per cent) coverage by area. The mudflats to the east of the fort were examined by a cursory walkover.
28 Rodwell 1976, 238.
29 See Rippon, in this volume, for the suggestion this may have been material tipped there during the construction of a new sea wall.
30 Medlycott 1991, 1994; Sparrow 2009, 2011.
31 The assemblage, though a small sample, suggests that activity on the site commenced 'in the mid third century': Sparrow 2009, 12. This potentially draws the construction date of the fort somewhat earlier than the Carausian period.

32 The Colchester Museum catalogue of the Oxley Parker collection notes that most of the pottery was of fourth-century date.
33 Charge 1995, 56–9; Germany 2000, 11.
34 Medlycott 1991.
35 These features are recorded in the Essex Historic Environment Record as EHER 2027 (road), EHER 2069 (field system immediately adjacent to the road) and EHER 2068 (field system further to the north).
36 The Blackfriars I vessel was a second-century ship discovered on the Thames foreshore during the construction of a new riverside wall in the City of London in 1962. It belongs to the Romano-Celtic (or Gallo-Roman) tradition of boat-building. It was a small single-masted sailing vessel, able to operate both in rivers and on coastal voyages, and capable of carrying a maximum cargo of about 50 tonnes (Marsden 1994).
37 Pearson 2003, 94–9 and Appendix 2.
38 Breeze 1984, 269.
39 The list of coins is summarised in Powell 1963 and given in somewhat more detail in the Colchester Museum catalogue: Borough of Colchester 1947/48, 25–6.
40 Casey 1994, Chapter 9. Casey's caution was justified, as his analysis suggested Pevensey as a pre-Carausian project, when subsequent excavations have dated the southern defences' construction to 293: Fulford and Tyers 1995.
41 Sparrow 2009, 11.
42 Johnson's (1976) articulation of the Shore Fort scheme saw the building of the forts as sequential, beginning with Brancaster and Reculver, whose construction is proven in the early third century, and whose defensive architecture continued in the traditions of second-century fort-building. The second phase of Shore Fort construction followed a typological progression, and was seen to begin with Burgh Castle and Dover, built no earlier than the reign of Gallienus (253–68). These rather imperfectly incorporate external bastions and were seen as a transitional phase in fort design. It was then suggested that the remaining forts were built in close succession, beginning with Richborough from c. 275. Johnson considered Bradwell to fall within this group of architecturally advanced fortifications.
43 The idea of very light garrisoning of the northern frontier is found in James 1984. For subsequent counter arguments see Hodgson and Bidwell 2004.
44 Camden 1586.
45 For recent summaries of the debate, see Pearson 2002a, Chapter 6, and Pearson 2005, 2006.
46 Esmonde Cleary 1989, 204; Higham 1992.
47 Wood 1990.
48 For a summary of the recent debate on the Shore Forts, see Pearson 2005, 2006.
49 This is an idea first proposed by White (1961), whose rather unfashionable theory has been revived and refined by Fulford and Tyers (1995), in the light of their determination of Pevensey's construction date as c. 293.
50 For example, Cotterill 1993.
51 Wilmott and Smither 2020.
52 Chaussée 2019.
53 Bescoby 2016.
54 Lyons 2019.
55 Medlycott 2011, 115–16 and fig. 7.9.
56 Cropmark evidence suggests that there are at least three or four Roman farms within the proposed Bradwell B land-take. Archaeological evaluation of these has yet to commence (Maria Medlycott, personal communication).
57 Fawn et al. 1990; see also Jones and Mattingly 1990, map 6:43.
58 Ennis and Atkinson 2013.
59 Sparrow 2009.
60 Hinchcliffe and Sparey-Green 1985, 176–7.
61 Pearson 2002a, 160.
62 Petts 2013.
63 The excavations at Caister-on-Sea, for example, have not only revealed evidence for industrial-scale butchery but have also recovered evidence for the production of grey mortaria.
64 On the distribution of BB1 pottery see Allen and Fulford 1996. The Colchester Museum catalogue of Oxley Parker's finds describes, among other objects, three spindle whorls of

Kimmeridge shale, a fragment from the edge of a moulded slab or tablet of Purbeck marble and two pieces of white marble sheathing from a building.
65 Sparrow 2009, 11.
66 See, for example, the work of Swift 2000, which employs military badges of office (brooches and belt sets) as a means of tracing the movement of personnel on the Roman frontiers. This study demonstrates the increasing importance of Germanic-style culture even in the fourth century.
67 Oxley Parker's trenches in the fort interior were never drawn on plan, but it is known that they were set out in parallel on an east–west alignment and '10 to 20 ft apart' (Chancellor 1877).

Bibliography

Air Photo Services. 1999. 'Bradwell on Sea, Area Centred TM0308, Essex. Aerial Photographic Interpretation.' Report No. 1999/15.

Allen, J. R. L., and M. G. Fulford. 1996. 'The distribution of south-east Dorset black burnished ware category 1 pottery in south-west Britain'. *Britannia* 27: 223–90.

Allen, J. R. L., and M. G. Fulford. 1999. 'Fort building and military supply along Britain's eastern Channel and North Sea coasts: The later second and third centuries'. *Britannia* 30: 163–84.

Barford, P. n.d. 'Bradwell-on-Sea, Essex: The Roman Shore Fort, Saxon Monastery and Church.' Unpublished monograph.

Bescoby, D. 2016. 'Burgh Castle Roman Fort: Life outside the walls – the geophysical survey'. Unpublished report for the Norfolk Archaeology Society.

Borough of Colchester. 1947/48. *Report of the Museum and Muniment Committee for the Period April 1st 1947 to March 31st 1948*, 20–31.

Breeze, D. 1984. 'Demand and supply on the northern frontier'. In *Between and beyond the Walls: Essays in honour of George Dobey*, edited by R. Miket and C. Burgess. 265–76. Edinburgh: John Donald.

Camden, W. 1586. *Britannia, sive Florentissimorum Regnorum Angliæ, Scotiæ, Hiberniæ, et Insularem adiacentium ex intima antiquate*. London: Bishop and Norton.

Casey, P. 1994. *Carausius and Allectus: The British usurpers*. London: Batsford.

Chancellor, F. 1877. 'St Peters on the Wall, Bradwell juxta Mare'. *Archaeological Journal* 34(1): 212–18.

Charge, B. 1995. 'Field survey of sites at Yen Hall, West Wickham, Cambs'. *Journal of the Haverhill and District Group* 6(1): 6–55.

Chaussée, S. 2019. *Report on a Geophysical Survey at Pevensey Roman Fortress and Medieval Castle, March 2019*. GeoTechnê Prospection Report SREP 01/2019.

Cotterill, J. 1993. 'Saxon raiding and the role of the late Roman coastal forts of Britain'. *Britannia* 24: 227–41.

Cunliffe, B. 1975. *Excavations at Portchester Castle III: The outer bailey and its defences*. Research Report of the Society of Antiquaries 34. London: Society of Antiquaries.

Cunliffe, B. 1977. 'The Saxon Shore: some problems and misconceptions'. In *The Saxon Shore*, edited by D. Johnson. 1–6. York: Council for British Archaeology Research Report 18.

Ennis, T., and M. Atkinson. 2013. *Bradwell Wind Farm, Hockley Lane, Bradwell-on-Sea, Essex: Archaeological excavation*. Essex County Council Field Archaeology Unit Report No. 2353.

Esmonde Cleary, A. 1989. *The Ending of Roman Britain*. London: Routledge.

Fawn, A., K. Evans, G. Davies and I. McMaster. 1990. *The Red Hills of Essex: Salt making in antiquity*. Colchester: Colchester Archaeological Group.

Fulford, M., and I. Tyers. 1995. 'The date of Pevensey and the defence of an "Imperium Britanniarum"'. *Antiquity* 69: 1009–14.

Germany, M. 2000. 'Othona, Bradwell-on-Sea, Essex: Archaeological survey by field walking'. Unpublished report, Essex County Council Field Archaeology Unit.

Higham, N. 1992. *Rome, Britain and the Anglo-Saxons*. London: Routledge.

Hinchliffe, J., and C. Sparey-Green. 1985. *Excavations at Brancaster, 1974 and 1977*. Dereham: East Anglian Archaeology Report no. 23.

Hodgson, N., and P. Bidwell. 2004. 'Auxiliary barracks in a new light: recent discoveries on Hadrian's Wall'. *Britannia* 35: 121–57.

James, S. 1984. 'Britain and the late Roman army'. In *Military and Civilian in Roman Britain: Cultural relationships in a frontier province*, edited by T. Blagg and A. King. 161–83. Oxford: British Archaeological Report No. 136.

Johnson, S. 1976. *The Roman Forts of the Saxon Shore*. London: Harper Collins.

Jones, B., and D. Mattingly. 1990. *An Atlas of Roman Britain*. Oxford: Blackwell.

Lavender, N. 2000. 'Othona, Bradwell-on-Sea, Essex. Archaeological survey: synthesis of results'. Unpublished report, Essex County Council Field Archaeology Unit.

Lewin, T. 1867. 'On the Castra of the Littus Saxonicum, and particularly the Castrum of Othona'. *Archaeologia* xli: 421–52.

Lyons, A. 2019. 'Roman Britain in 2018: Sites explored - 6. East Anglia'. *Britannia* 50: 442–4.

Marsden, P. 1994. *Ships of the Port of London: First to eleventh centuries AD*. English Heritage Archaeological Report 3. London: English Heritage.

Medlycott, M. 1991. 'The Othona Community Site, Bradwell-on-Sea'. Unpublished report, Essex County Council Field Archaeology Unit.

Medlycott, M. 1994. 'The Othona Community site, Bradwell-on-Sea, Essex: the extra-mural settlement'. *Essex Archaeology and History* 25: 60–71.

Medlycott, M. 2011. *The Roman Town of Great Chesterford*. Chelmsford: East Anglian Archaeology Report no. 137.

Moll, H. 1724, *In gratiam Itinerantium Curiosorum Antonini Aug. Itinerarium per Britanniam*. London: Thomas Bowles.

O'Connor, T. 2006. 'Bradwell-on-Sea, Historic Settlement Assessment Report'. Unpublished report by the Historic Environment Branch of Essex County Council.

Panciroli, G. 1593. *Notitia utraque Dignitatum cum orientis tum occidentis*. Venice.

Pearson, A. 2002a. *The Roman Shore Forts: Coastal defences of southern Britain*. Stroud: Tempus.

Pearson, A. 2002b. 'Stone supply to the Saxon Shore Forts at Reculver, Richborough, Dover and Lympne'. *Archaeologia Cantiana* 122: 197–220.

Pearson, A. 2003. *The Construction of the Saxon Shore Forts*. British Archaeological Report, British Series 349. Oxford: Archaeopress.

Pearson, A. 2005. 'Barbarian piracy and the Saxon Shore: a reappraisal'. *Oxford Journal of Archaeology* 24(1): 73–88.

Pearson, A. 2006. 'Piracy in late Roman Britain: a perspective from the Viking Age'. *Britannia* 37: 337–53.

Petts, D. 2013. 'Military and civilian: reconfiguring the end of Roman Britain in the north'. *European Journal of Archaeology* 16(2): 314–35.

Powell, W. (ed.) 1963. *Victoria County History of the County of Essex*, vol. 3, *Roman Essex*. London: University of London.

Roach Smith, C. 1865. 'Essex Archaeological Society'. *The Gentleman's Magazine* 218: 67–71.

Rodwell, W. 1976. 'Some unrecorded archaeological discoveries in Essex, 1946–75'. *Essex Archaeology and History* 8: 234–48.

Sparrow, P. 2009. *Othona Community Site, Eastend Road, Bradwell-on-Sea, Essex: Archaeological excavation*. Essex County Council Field Archaeology Unit. Report No. 2073.

Sparrow, P. 2011. 'Othona: Roman extra-mural activity at the Othona Community site, Bradwell-on-Sea'. *Essex Archaeology and History* 2 (4th series): 69–75.

Stukeley, W. 1776. *Itinerarium Curiosum; Or, an account of the antiquities, and remarkable curiosities in nature or art, observed in travels through Great Britain: Centuria I*. London: Baker and Leigh.

Swift, E. 2000. *The End of the Western Roman Empire: An archaeological investigation*. Stroud: History Press.

Walford, T. 1812. 'Observations on the situation of Camulodunum'. *Archaeologia* 16: 145–50.

Wardill, R. 2000. 'Othona, Bradwell-on-Sea, Essex: Geophysical survey report'. Unpublished report, Essex County Council Field Archaeology Unit.

White, D. A. 1961. *Litus Saxonicum: The British Saxon shore in scholarship and history*. Madison: University of Wisconsin Press.

Wilmott, T., and P. Smither. 2020. 'The plan of the Saxon Shore Fort at Richborough'. *Britannia* 51: 147–74.

Wood, I. 1990. 'The Channel from the fourth to the seventh centuries AD'. In *Maritime Celts, Frisians and Saxons*, edited by S. McGrail. 93–8. York: Council for British Archaeology Research Report No. 71.

3
Dengie, *Ythancæstir* and Othona: The early medieval landscape context of St Peter-on-the-Wall

Stephen Rippon

Introduction

Bede's account of St Cedd's foundation of a church at *Ythancæstir* in 653 records how it lay on the banks of the River *Pant* – the Old English (OE) name for the Blackwater – but tells us nothing else about the landscape within which it lay.[1] We know that *Ythancæstir*, in the later parish of Bradwell on Sea, lay at the eastern tip of a long peninsula of dryland that extended far out into former saltmarshes on what today is a particularly remote part of the Essex coast. In addition to St Peter's Chapel itself, this landscape is of particular interest because of two relatively early Anglo-Saxon charters. The first is clearly a forgery that purports to record that King Æthelbert of Kent gave Tillingham (immediately south of Bradwell on Sea) to Mellitus, bishop of London, in 604x616.[2] The second – clearly genuine – charter records that a hundred years later King Swæfred of the East Saxons granted 70 *cassati* [hides] in the *regio* called *Deningei* to Ingwald, who was bishop of London some time between 705 and 745 (the date probably being towards the start of that period).[3] Together, these charters are the starting point for reconstructing the landscape context of *Ythancæstir*, which appears to have been part of an early folk territory covering around 340km².

The landscape context of *Ythancæstir*

We can say something about the landscape around *Ythancæstir* by mapping its topography, geology and soils, as well as the results of archaeological surveys.[4] These show that the fort of Othona and church at *Ythancæstir* lay close to the eastern end of a long, narrow peninsula of sand and gravel overlying London Clay, the eastern end of which has been lost to later erosion (Figures 3.1 and 3.2). It is reported that when a Second World War bomb fell into the intertidal

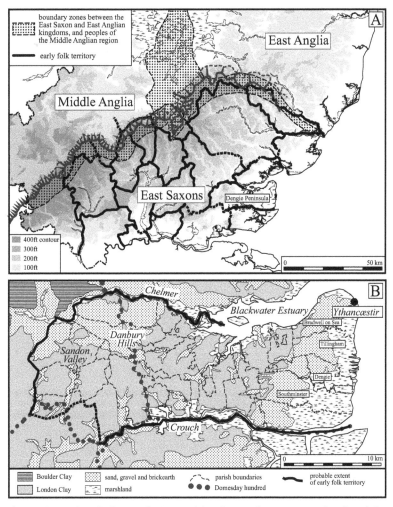

Figure 3.1 (Top) the Anglo-Saxon kingdoms of eastern England and the boundary zones between them, with the possible early folk territories within the East Saxon kingdom (after Rippon 2018a); and (bottom) the postulated boundaries of the *regio* called *Deningei* and its major geology/soil types, with places referred to in the early part of this chapter. Drawn by the author.

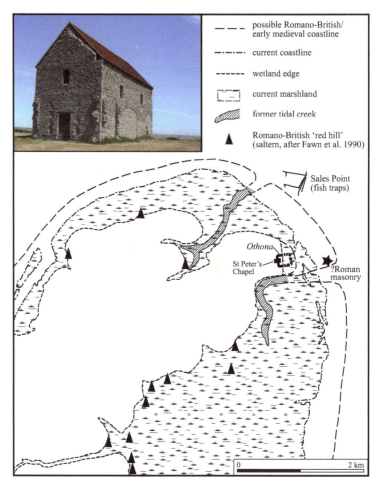

Figure 3.2 The landscape context of Othona and *Ythancæstir*. Drawn by the author.

mud a quarter of a mile east of the fort, the crater revealed a solid mass of masonry which was regarded as Roman. This structure lies too far east to have been the eastern wall of the fort, and it has been suggested that it was a harbour-related structure.[5] Kevin Bruce, however, suggests (personal communication) that it could be material tipped there during the construction of a new sea wall. The contractors apparently approached Oxley Parker – the owner of Eastlands Farm – for permission to dig soil from his land around St Peter's Chapel, and this is what led to the discovery of the Roman fort and Oxley Parker's subsequent excavations. The reclamation scheme was abandoned, but this may explain why the Ordnance Survey first-edition six-inch maps of the 1880s show an east–west linear spread of debris at this location called Tip Head.

The peninsula was surrounded by intertidal saltmarshes and mudflats, with substantial tidal creeks both to the north (between East Hall and Weymarks Farm) and directly south of the fort at Othona, which could have provided sheltered landing places for small boats.[6] These wetlands either side of the peninsula could not have been cultivated – as they would have been regularly flooded by the sea – but will have afforded rich grazing land and the opportunity to extract salt from seawater, while areas lower down the intertidal zone provided the ideal environment for the construction of fish-traps (see below).

The derivation of the name *Ythancæstir* is well known, the OE *Ythan* being derived from the Roman Othona with the OE *cæster* being a common suffix used for Roman sites.[7] Othona, however, 'is a very problematic name',[8] although Breeze has recently suggested that *Oth-* may be a corruption of *oct-*, derived from the British *oeth*, which means 'what is difficult to achieve or obtain; something that is hard to find'; if this were extended to 'a place hard to reach' then it fits the seventh-century experience of the location of Othona/*Ythancæstir* perfectly, as that was a period when virtually all travel will have been on foot.[9]

The wider context of *Ythancæstir*: the East Saxon kingdom and its *regiones*

The context of Cedd's foundation of a church at *Ythancæstir* was an East Saxon kingdom that first converted to Christianity under King Sæbert in 604 (when London was chosen as the location for Bishop Mellitus's church of St Paul), but which then apostatised in 616–17, when Sæbert died and his three sons expelled Mellitus.[10] In 653 the East Saxon King Sigebert appointed Cedd as bishop, who, Bede tells us, 'established churches in several places', especially in the city called *Ythancæstir* and also *Tilaburg* (Tilbury, on the north bank of the Thames).[11] While Cedd was bishop of the East Saxons he often revisited his home kingdom of Northumbria, where he founded a church at Lastingham in Yorkshire, where he died of the plague in 664.[12] Bede tells us that when the brothers of Cedd's monastery in the kingdom of the East Saxons heard that their founder had died and been buried in Northumbria, about 30 of them left their monastery and went to Lastingham, where they too died of plague. Note that Bede does not actually say which of Cedd's churches the

30 brethren came from, or that the entire community of that unnamed church left for Lastingham (an important point when considering whether *Ythancæstir* was deserted in 664: see below).

The extent of the East Saxon kingdom is far from clear, but based upon a wide range of archaeological and documentary evidence it appears to have embraced the later counties of Essex, Middlesex, southern Suffolk and most of Hertfordshire (Figure 3.1).[13] It was bounded by water on two sides – the North Sea to the east, and the Thames Estuary to the south – and had extensively wooded high ground to the west (the Chiltern Hills) and north (the high Boulder Clay plateau of north-west Essex and south-west Suffolk). Charters such as King Swæfred's gift of 70 *cassati* in the *regio* called *Deningei* show how Anglo-Saxon kingdoms were divided up into smaller districts sometimes referred to as *regiones* or *pagi*. In 704x709, for example, King Offa of the East Saxons granted Wealdhere, bishop of London, land in the *pagus* of *Hæmele* (Hemel Hempstead, in the Vale of St Albans, Hertfordshire: S.1784).[14] *Pagus* was a term used in the Roman period to refer to small districts (within larger administrative regions known as *civitates*), of which there is a single documented example from Roman Britain: a wooden writing tablet from London referring to an area of woodland in 'the *pagus Dibussu* in the *civitas* of the *Cantiaci*'.[15]

These *regiones* were folk-based territories as is reflected in the small number of examples where we know their original names. The *pagus* of *Hæmele*, for example, is derived from the Old English district name **hamol**, 'the broken country',[16] while the two other East Saxon early folk territory names for which we have contemporary references contain place names containing **ingas**: the *regiones* of *Deningei* and *Geddinges* (Yeading, in Middlesex).[17] Of the 22 early folk territories that can be reconstructed in the East Saxon kingdom fifteen have evidence in later sources for folk names containing -*ingas* (such as the Rodings), while another has a cluster of place names that include the personal name element Tolla.[18]

In a seminal study Steven Bassett attempted to reconstruct one of these districts whose name survives in the group of eight parishes and sixteen Domesday manors named Roding (OE *Rodinges*, derived from OE personal name *Hrōtha* + **ingas**, giving **Hrōthingas*, 'the people of Hrotha').[19] Bassett skilfully used a wide range of documentary sources to show how these parishes once formed a single early medieval territory, but he made a mistake in assuming that its extent was limited to that group of parishes. In contrast, a study of the wider landscape that looked beyond the cluster of Roding place names reveals a web of territorial connections that extended well to the south and embraced the whole river valley. The result is an early folk territory covering *in the region of* 285km² that was bounded by interfluvial areas with poorly drained soils that as late as the eighteenth century included large areas of unenclosed common land.[20]

Across the East Saxon kingdom, the 22 early folk territories that can be reconstructed have an average area of around 350km² (the range being 104–692km²).[21] This suggests that in the average-sized early folk territory most people will have lived no more than around 20 km (12 miles) from its central point. Although it is difficult to know how far someone in the past could have travelled in a day – due to variations in topography, road conditions, what they were carrying and whether they were on foot, on horseback or accompanied by a packhorse, ox- or horse-drawn cart – various strands of evidence suggest a figure of *c.* 20km. The Antonine Itinerary, for example, suggests that many Romano-British *mansiones* – official buildings whose roles included providing overnight accommodation for Imperial officials – were around 12 to 15 Roman miles apart (18–22km), although they will have been linked by well-made roads that were relatively easy to walk on.[22] In the nineteenth century it was said that people would travel up to 6 or 7 miles to get to a market town in a day (in other words, a round trip of 12–14 miles [19–23km]).[23] It seems likely, therefore, that in an average-sized early folk territory of around 350km² most people could have walked to a communal gathering at the centre of the territory in one day, although not all would have been able to go home the same day.

Reconstructing the *regio* of *Deningei*

Reconstructing the extent of the *regio* of *Deningei* (Figure 3.3) involves the integration of a wide range of sources within a spatial framework provided by historical maps. We do not know how large the *regio* was, although it was clearly greater than the 70 *cassati* that King Swæfred of the East Saxons granted to Ingwald in the early eighth century. The name *Deningei* is formed from the OE personal name *Dæni* and the place-name element **ēġ** ('island') suggesting that it meant 'the island named after Dæni'.[24] *Deningei* must have referred to the peninsula of land – which went on to become Dengie Hundred – that was surrounded by water on three sides, with the Blackwater Estuary to the north, the North Sea to the east and the Crouch Estuary to the south. To the west (in Chelmsford Hundred) lay the high ground of Danbury, whose place name also includes the OE personal name *Dæni*. The earliest form of Danbury is its spelling in Domesday Book – *Danengeberiam* – which is derived from *Dæni* + **ingas** (giving the OE folk name *Dænningas*) and OE **byriġ** (burh, meaning a defended enclosure,

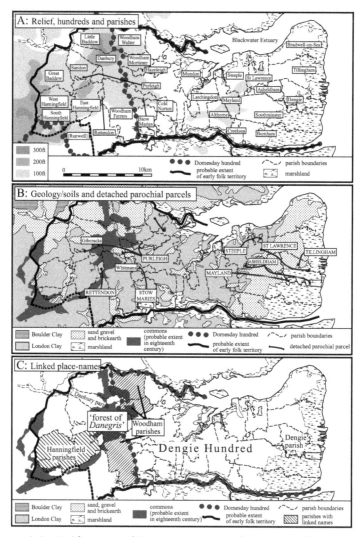

Figure 3.3 Evidence used in reconstructing the extent of the *regio* of *Deningei*. Drawn by the author.

here referring to an Iron Age hill fort), giving 'the stronghold occupied by the *Dænningas*'.[25] In the thirteenth century the Danbury Hills were known as the forest of Danegris, derived from *Dænningas* + OE **hrīs** (shrubs, brushwood).[26] Taken altogether, this group of closely related place names suggest that the *regio* (district) called *Deningei* corresponded to the modern Dengie Peninsula at least as far west as the Danbury Hills (the forest of Danegris), was named after someone called *Dæni*, and was occupied by a community known as the *Dænningas*.

Although this area was known as the *Danesie*, *Denegeia* and finally Dengie Hundred from the late twelfth century, in Domesday it was described as *Witbrictesherna* Hundred. This may be derived from the OE personal name *Wihtbeorht* + -**hyrne**, hence 'Wihtbeorht's corner', although Anderson suggests the second part is derived from the OE -**þyrne** (hence 'Wihtbeorht's thorn bush').[27] Presumably, the late twelfth-century name was a reversion to its pre-Domesday form. In addition to the personal name *Dæni*, commemorated in the names of the *regio* and Danbury, a complex web of territorial links connected the lowlands of the Dengie Peninsula with both the coastal marshland to the east and the wooded heaths to the west (Figure 3.3). Asheldham, Dengie, Mayland and St Lawrence parishes, as well as Stansgate manor in Steeple,[28] and Bacons manor in Bradwell,[29] all had detached parcels down on the coastal marshes. Looking westwards, Purleigh had several detached parcels up on the Danbury Hills (including Gibcracks). These detached parochial parcels presumably resulted from the dividing up of what had been common land, with each community holding rights in the common receiving a parcel of land following its enclosure. Domesday Book makes an oblique reference to this intercommoning of the coastal marshes through a unique feature of the Essex folios: inclusion of 'pasture for X sheep'.[30] The extent of these pastures must have been vast, as Southminster, for example, had 'pasture for 1,300 sheep'.[31] It is curious that several manors in eastern parts of the Dengie Peninsula had 'woodland for pigs' (Table 3.1). It seems highly unlikely that there was extensive woodland on the light, easily cultivated soils of Bradwell on Sea – an area that was almost devoid of woodland by 1777 – and it is tempting to see this 'woodland for pigs' as lying up on the Danbury Hills (a remnant of when lowland parishes held grazing rights in the communal wood-pasture there).

Another feature of the landscape suggesting that the various parishes within the Dengie Peninsula were once part of a single

Table 3.1 Data used in reconstructing the 'greater Tillingham' estate (King Swæfred's grant of 70 *cassati* in the *regio* called *Deningei*). Identifications in square brackets are from Round 1903, 391–2.

Domesday vill [and later ecclesiastical parish]	Domesday			Vill hidage		Notes
	DB Ess.	1066 land-holder	hide assessment	DB	originally	
[TILLINGHAM]						
Tillingham	5,5	St. Paul's	20 hides + 6 acres	20 hides + 6 acres	20 hides	The additional 6 acres is probably the 6 acres removed from *Donā* [Bradwell Hall, in Bradwell on Sea]
[BRADWELL on SEA]						
Hacflet [previously identified as Bradwell Quay, but Bruce et al. (this volume) argues it was Hockley Manor]	18,23	Alfward, a freeman	2 hides + 30 acres	2 hides + 30 acres	30 hides + 40 acres = 30 hides	The entry also states that there was '1 freeman with 30 acres and he was outlawed': Bruce et al. (this volume) argue this is the 30 acres in the main entry
Donā [Down Hall]	25,8	Moding	2 hides + 20 acres			Next entry after Down Hall and logically in Bradwell
Landuna [tentatively identified as Eastlands Farm]	25,9	4 freemen	½ hide + 20 acres	4 hides + 50 acres		
Acleta	25,10	Moding	1½ hides + 10 acres			Next entry after *Landuna* and held by Moding, so logically in Bradwell
Donā [Bradwell Hall]	34,23	Siward	14 hides	19 hides less 6 acres		
	34,25	Siward (8 freemen sub-tenants)	5 hides less 6 acres			woodland for 50 pigs
Effcestra [East Hall in eastern Bradwell on Sea]	14,6	Thorkell, a freeman	1½ hides + 20 acres	4 hides + 80 acres [5 hides?]		Nearly identical land-holdings that presumably represent the division of an earlier estate into three (Bruce et al. (this volume) argue that all three may actually have been 1½ hides + 20 acres, giving a 5-hide estate)
		3 freemen	1½ hides			
	27,12	Ingulf, a freeman [can be identified as the later manor of Battails]	1½ hides			

[DENGIE]					
Dengie	14,7	Thorkell, a freeman	2½ hides	5 hides	5 hides	
	18,22	Siric	2½ hides			
[ASHELDHAM]						
Haintuna [Asheldham; had a detached parcel in Steeple]	24,43	Godric, a freeman	½ hide + 37 acres	1 hide + 74 acres	2 hides	Identical land-holdings that presumably represent the division in two of an earlier estate
	24,55	1 freeman	½ hide + 37 acres			
[ST. LAWRENCE]						
Niuuelanda [Newland in St Lawrence; had a detached parcel in the marshes of Dengie parish]	2,6	Holy Trinity, Canterbury	3 hides	4 hides + 95 acres	5 hides	
Niuuelanda [East Newland in St Lawrence]	37,14	Ingvar	1½ hides + 35 acres			
[STEEPLE]						
Steeple [which had two detached parcels in St Lawrence]	1,15	Aelfric, a freeman	1 hide	7 hides + 111 acres	8 hides	woodland for 10 pigs
	25,7	Norman	3 hides + 35 acres			
	29,3	Bondi, a freeman	3½ hides			
	90,81		16 acres			
Stansgate (in Steeple)	34,26	Siward	9½ hides	10 hides + 90 acres	10 hides	woodland for 60 pigs
	90,12	2 freemen	1 hide + 30 acres			
Total hide assessment			**80 hides + 50 acres**		**80 hides**	

Source: Compiled by the author.

territory is the way that their boundaries zigzag through fields, suggesting that they were created after the fieldscape. This is in sharp contrast to the long, sinuous watershed boundaries that mark the postulated southern and western edges of the *regio* of *Deningei* (see below) as well as other early folk territories such as the Rodings (see above). The western boundary of Dengie/*Witbrictesherna* Hundred – which lay to the east of the Danbury Hills – also zigzags through the historic landscape, and in some places even cuts diagonally across fields in a way that suggests it was a relatively recent creation.[32] The hundred boundary also divides a group of parishes called Woodham, while another curiosity is the way that lowland Purleigh (in Dengie Hundred) had detached parcels up on the Danbury Hills (in the neighbouring Chelmsford Hundred). Along with the sharing of the personal name *Dæni* in *Deningei* and Danbury, this clearly establishes that the *regio* of *Deningei* extended at least as far as the Danbury Hills (embracing part of what in Domesday had become Chelmsford Hundred).

In addition to thirteenth- to sixteenth-century references to the 'forest of *Danegris*',[33] there are various indications that the Danbury Hills were covered in extensive woodland, wood pasture and heathland. The 1777 map of Essex, for example, shows extensive woodland and unenclosed common stretching across the Danbury Hills from Woodham Walter, in the north, through Danbury, Woodham Mortimer, Hazeleigh and Purleigh to Woodham Ferris, to the south. To this concentration of woodland-related place names can be added the OE **lēah** in Rugley Green in Purleigh, Colickey Green in Woodham Walter [*Curlai* in Domesday] and Studly in Woodham Ferris [*Estolleia* in Domesday]. The OE **wuda** in these Woodham parish names is clearly associated with woodland. *Wudaham* is documented in two charters of 962x991 and 1000x1002,[34] and the three vills in Domesday are simply called *Odeham/ Udeham/Wdeham*.[35] Birchwood Farm in Purleigh was probably the home of Saier atte Birchwode in 1342,[36] birch being a typical heathland tree in this region. The name Gibcrack – one of the detached parcels of Purleigh, which lies immediately west of Bicknacre and Danbury Commons – suggests a 'flimsily built house'[37] as might be expected in a woodland assart.

The earliest maps showing the field boundary patterns across this entire area date to the nineteenth century, by which time some areas that had been common in 1777 were enclosed, with the resulting field boundaries being characterised by long straight lines and exact right-angled corners. Other areas with these carefully planned field boundary patterns are probably former commons enclosed in the seventeenth and eighteenth centuries. Even today, the Danbury Hills are cloaked with extensive areas of woodland, wood pasture and heathland, and this makes them a prominent feature looming up above the surrounding low-lying claylands.

The south-western limit of the *regio* of *Deningei* probably lay along a remarkably long, sinuous field boundary between Rettendon and Runwell that clearly pre-dates the adjacent fields. (Rettendon also has a detached parcel between East Hanningfield and Woodham Ferrers to the north.) Although Kemble made a case for the western limit of the *regio* of *Deningei* running across the Danbury Hills, there are a number of territorial links that extend across the Danbury Hills and down into the Sandon Valley.[38] Purleigh, to the east of the Danbury Hills, for example, had a large detached parcel in Sandon, while Danbury parish – whose church lay up on the Danbury Hills – extended across the Sandon Brook as far as the River Chelmer (and this large detached parcel divided Little Baddow from Great Baddow).

The Sandon Valley contained seven parishes: Little Baddow, Great Baddow, Sandon and Danbury, as well as East, South and West Hanningfield. The place name Hanningfield – 'open country of the *Haningas*, the people called after Hana'[39] – is consciously drawing a very sharp contrast with the woodland-dominated Danbury Hills to the east. The boundaries between these Sandon Valley parishes all zigzag through the historic landscape and are clearly relatively recent, while the way that Great and Little Baddow are separated by Danbury also suggests these parishes were all once part of the same territory. In contrast to the zigzagging boundaries within this block of parishes, the western edges of Great Baddow, West Hanningfield and South Hanningfield follow a long, sinuous, watershed boundary that runs along a range of hills south of Chelmsford. These hills represent some of the highest ground in southern Essex, which in 1777 was still relatively well wooded and partly unenclosed.[40]

The high ground marking the southern watershed of the Sandon Valley was also covered by a series of commons in 1777.[41] There were also stretches of long, sinuous parish boundary that appear to be relatively early features within the landscape, including the southern boundary of East Hanningfield that ran along the edge of Rettendon Great and Little Commons. Where other parish boundaries zigzag through the landscape it is because they post-date the enclosure of former commons (for example, the southern edge of South Hanningfield). As late as 1777 these hills were also more wooded than the adjacent lower-lying areas, and an analysis of the field boundary patterns suggests that there was once an almost continuous belt of unenclosed common and woodland stretching from the Danbury Hills across the high ground south of the Hanningfields and then over the hills south of Chelmsford. Overall, while the Sandon Valley was a compact and clearly defined territory – probably occupied by a group identifying themselves as the *Haningas* – it appears to have been part of the *regio* of the *Deningei*. This gives an early folk territory of around 340km², making it very close to the average for the East Saxon kingdom.

Central places within the landscape

Across the East Saxon kingdom, early folk territories contained places with central place functions such as a royal vill, early church and communal meeting place. The development of towns from the tenth century onwards saw these central place functions consolidated into single places, before which they were often in separate locations.[42] The only excavated royal vill in the East Saxon kingdom is at Bonhunt Farm in Wicken Bonhunt.[43] This was part of a polyfocal cluster of central places in the Granta Valley with the meeting place of Uttlesford Hundred being at Mutlow Hill overlooking 'Uda's ford' (now Uttlesford Bridge, in Wendens Ambo), 3km north of Bonhunt Farm.[44] Nearby Newport – the 'new town', 1km north-east of Bonhunt Farm – was a royal manor in Domesday that paid two knights' service.[45] Although Newport was once thought to have been the Edwardian *burh* of *Wiginamere*, this has now been rejected,[46] but it may have been Edward the Confessor's mint of *Nipeport*.[47] Although the present structure of Newport church is thirteenth-century, its cruciform plan is suggestive of an early medieval minster,[48] and a fragment of Late Anglo-Saxon cross-shaft was reused in the north aisle.[49] A thirteenth-century judgement stated that the chapel at Wicken Bonhunt formerly belonged to the church at Newport.[50] Overall, there appears to have been a polyfocal royal centre whose various functions were spread across Wicken Bonhunt (the royal vill), Wendens Ambo (the assembly place) and Newport (the minster, and later market town and mint), which were all within 3km of each other.

In the case of the *regio* of *Deningei*, however, it is difficult to identify either the royal vill or the communal meeting place. The only royal landholdings in *Witbrictesherna* Hundred at the time of Domesday Book were several small parcels of land, not all of which had been held by the king in 1066.[51] There was probably an early church at Southminster – presumably so named in relation to the church at

Bradwell to the north – which in Domesday was held by the bishop of London: at 30 hides this was a sizeable estate,[52] but there is no evidence for a royal vill there.

One contender for an early medieval central place is Maldon. The Half Hundred of Maldon consisted simply of Maldon itself, where Domesday records that the king had a hall, 180 houses held by burgesses and 18 that were derelict.[53] The configuration of the boundaries of Maldon Half Hundred and the wider historic landscape suggests that it was carved out of Dengie Hundred, and in Domesday two freemen in Maldon are described as being in Dengie Hundred.[54] In 1056 Edward the Confessor's chaplain Ingelric granted the church at Maldon (with two hides of land and their tithes) to the church at St Martin le Grand (in London), and a land-holding of this size is suggestive of a minster.[55] This importance of Maldon could, however, be no older than the early tenth century. King Edward the Elder camped there in 912 as part of his reconquest of Essex from the Danes, and then ordered the construction of a burh in 916. The location of the temporary camp and later burh has seen much discussion, but both appear to lie on the high ground to the west of the later medieval town.[56] This was a strategic location, at the head of the Blackwater Estuary and mouth of the River Chelmer.

The question is whether the early tenth-century burh was founded close to an existing royal vill. There certainly is some evidence for a high-status settlement in the eighth century on the lower ground at the head of the Blackwater Estuary. Ipswich Ware has been found in various places, with stratified Middle Saxon occupation excavated at the former Croxley Works on Church Street in an area known as the Hythe, on the banks of the Blackwater Estuary just north of St Mary's Church.[57] The presence of Ipswich Ware – an extremely rare find in Essex – suggests a site of relatively high status, while other finds suggest textile production and iron smithing. Although very little metalwork has been found in the area – a single Series S *sceatta* (a silver penny) of East Saxon manufacture from Maldon itself, and a Series D *sceatta* from nearby Heybridge[58] – this can be accounted for by extensive urban development leading to few opportunities for metal detecting. Overall, it would appear that Maldon was an important coastal settlement in the eighth century, and the way in which it was chosen as Edward the Elder's camp in 912 might suggest an existing royal vill, as does the way that it was subsequently developed as a burh and town.

Another possibility, however, is that the royal vill within the *regio* of *Deningei* was closer to *Ythancæstir*, which was just 7½km north-east of the parish of Dengie, which is assumed to have been the hundred meeting place.[59] That *Ythancæstir* housed priests who ministered to the wider community, as well as contemplative monks, is suggested by Bede's statement that Bishop Cedd:

> established churches in various places and ordained priests and deacons to assist him in preaching the word of faith and in the administration of baptism, especially in the city called *Ythancæstir* in the Saxon tongue and also in the place called Tilbury ... In these places he gathered together a multitude of Christ's servants [in other words, monks] and taught them to observe the discipline of a Rule.[60]

It is easy to assume that the apparently remote location of *Ythancæstir* – about as far from the geographical centre of the *regio* as it was possible to go – makes it an unlikely location for a minster church let alone a royal vill, but this need not have been the case. It is in fact very common for early churches to have been located in places that were relatively remote from where the vast majority of the population – who will have been subsistence-level farmers – lived, including coastal locations and peninsulas within wetlands.[61] There are various reasons why so many early churches were located in such geographically marginal places. The first is that there was a strong desire to place early churches within sites associated with Britain's Roman – and therefore Christian – past (in this case the ruins of the late Roman fort of Othona that Bede refers to as a *civitas*, or 'city').[62] This link with *Romanitas* is seen, for example, at St Augustine's Church, which was built immediately outside the Roman walls of Canterbury, and Mellitus's church, which was constructed within the ruins of the former Roman town at London. St Augustine's Church at Canterbury – dedicated to Sts Peter and Paul – was the first of three early seventh-century churches built there in a line, an arrangement that may reflect that seen at Old St Peter's in Rome (this layout being another link with *Romanitas*).[63] The reuse of geographically remote Roman forts was also common practice.[64] King Sigebert of East Anglia, for example, gave *Dommoc* (probably the Roman coastal fort at Walton[65]) to Felix, and the same king gave *Cnobheresburg* (probably the coastal fort at Burgh Castle) to Fursa, both in the 630s. King Ecgberht of Kent gifted Reculver to Bassa in 669.[66] This desire on the part of the early Church and Anglo-Saxon kings to connect with *Romanitas* is also seen in the use of sophisticated grid-based planning in many early churches and the reuse of Roman building material.[67]

While *Ythancæstir* is in a very remote location in terms of how we lead our current lives, we should also remember that, in a time when roads will have been little more than muddy tracks, a location on the coast may have meant that it was potentially more accessible for the higher echelons of society who had access to ships. The medieval period has generally been seen as a period when relatively little use was made of water for transport;[68] however, it has been shown that there was rather more innovation in the period 950–1250 than previously thought. Before the tenth century we have little information as to the extent to which people moved around by boat.[69] Graveney (*grafon eah*: 'ditch stream or 'dug river'), on the northern coast of Kent, is first mentioned in a charter dated 812 and hints that improvements were being made to the navigability of waterways.[70] It is striking that in addition to the major eighth-century coastal/estuarine emporia – including Southampton, London and Ipswich – there were a number of smaller landing places where eighth-century coinage and pottery imported from outside of the East Saxon Kingdom has been found (for example, Barking, Tilbury and Canvey Island in the Thames Estuary, and Fingringhoe on the Colne Estuary).[71] There are also several Old English place-name elements indicative of the use of inland waterways,[72] although it is unclear whether these places existed in the seventh century. All in all, while *Ythancæstir* certainly was in a very remote location from the perspective of the vast majority of the population living within its *regio* – who lived inland, well away from navigable watercourses, and will not have had the wealth to access seagoing vessels – for the elite within society it was much easier to reach.

So, could a royal vill have lain somewhere in the vicinity of *Ythancæstir* and the presumed later hundredal meeting place at nearby Dengie? Dengie parish lay within an area of light, sandy soil at the eastern end of the Dengie Peninsula that will have been easier to cultivate than the heavy London Clay further west (Figure 3.1). These light, sandy soils extended from Bradwell on Sea in the north through Tillingham, Dengie and Southminster to Burnham-on-Crouch in the south, and this good agricultural land would have been an obvious choice for a royal vill even though it was not centrally located within the *regio*. With the church at *Ythancæstir* and the probable hundredal meeting place at Dengie, the obvious location for a royal vill is Tillingham, midway between them, which is the name given in the forged charter of 604x616; Tillingham was still an episcopal manor in Domesday. Although the distance between Tillingham and *Ythancæstir* (6km) is further than that between the royal vill at Wicken and the church at Newport, it was comparable to the distance between the minster at Great Wakering, the presumed royal vill at Prittlewell, and the hundred meeting place at Rochford (c. 7–8km) in the Rochford peninsula early folk territory immediately south of *Deningei*.[73]

The Tillingham estate and fragmentation of the *regio* called *Deningei*

From the late seventh century onwards early folk territories such as *Deningei* started to fragment as increasingly powerful Anglo-Saxon kings created discrete estates and gifted them to the Church. The charter purporting to record the grant of 'Tillingham' by King Æthelbert of Kent to Mellitus, bishop of London between 604 and 616,[74] is clearly a forgery for three reasons: the tradition of writing such documents did not start until the late seventh century; Tillingham was not within the kingdom of Kent; and the witness list is late seventh-century.[75] It may have been written to explain how the Dean and Chapter of St Paul's came to hold Tillingham, and reflects Bede's account of how King Æthelbert of Kent founded Mellitus's church in London and bestowed gifts of land upon it for the maintenance of the bishop's household.[76] We know that St Paul's held Tillingham in c. 1000, when Bishop Theodred granted it to the church of St Paul's, which still held it at Domesday.[77] It is, however, unclear whether the estate was already the property of St Paul's and had been held by Theodred *ex officio*, or was his personal property.[78]

Rather than King Æthelbert of Kent giving Tillingham to St Paul's in 604, it is possible that it was included in King Swæfred's grant of 70 *cassati* in the *regio* called *Deningei* to Bishop Ingwald in the early eighth century. The block of parishes in the north-eastern part of the Dengie Peninsula – to the west of Mayland Creek and north of Asheldham Brook – would appear to have once been a single territory. This is reflected in the way that Steeple had two detached parcels in the neighbouring parish of St Lawrence (which were part of Stansgate manor), and Asheldham had a detached parcel in Steeple. The total Domesday hidage for all of these Domesday landholdings is 80 hides and 50 acres (Table 3.1; Figure 3.4).[79]

To the south we can be confident that there was a separate estate, as the bishop of London held Southminster – while the Dean and Chapter held Tillingham – from at least c. 1000,[80] which in Domesday was assessed as 30 hides.[81] While it is tempting to assume that St Paul's initial endowment in Dengie included Southminster,[82] and we should not take the 70 *cassati* as being a very precise measure, it is strange that there are no earlier charters referring to Southminster. Including both Steeple and the 30 hides of Southminster in the 70 *cassati* in *Deningei* would bring its assessment in Domesday up to 108 hides, which is far too high. It is therefore suggested here that Southminster was not part of the 70 *cassati* in the *regio* called

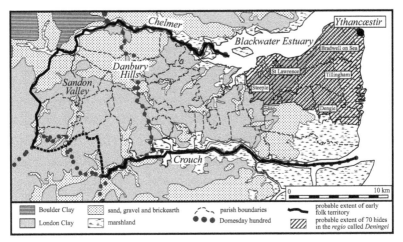

Figure 3.4 The possible extent of the 70 *cassati* in the *regio* called *Deningei* that King Swæfred of the East Saxons granted to Ingwald, Bishop of London in AD 706x709 (S. 1787). Drawn by the author.

Deningei, and that St Paul's held two ancient estates in the Dengie Peninsula: 70 *cassati* at Tillingham (including *Ythancæstir*, which – although not named as such in contemporary sources – was the 'north minster'), and another 30-or-more-hide estate at Southminster.

Seventh-century and later life at *Ythancæstir*

Soon after he founded the church at *Ythancæstir* Cedd left to establish a monastery at Lastingham in Northumbria, where he died in 664.[83] Mirrington has argued that 664 marks the abandonment of the monastery at *Ythancæstir*,[84] but this is not necessarily the case as the 30 or so brethren that left were not necessarily the entire community, and they could have included members of Cedd's other monastery at Tilbury.

There are, in fact, various strands of evidence suggesting that some form of occupation continued at *Ythancæstir*. Sherds of at least two Ipswich Ware vessels from a midden deposit in the upper fill of the fort ditch point to occupation in the eighth century,[85] since Blinkhorn now argues that its production started *c.* 720.[86] Half an Ipswich Ware jar was also found by Kevin Bruce wedged against one of the posts of the east wall of Sales Point fish trap in the 1970s. Ipswich Ware is extremely rare in Essex, being largely restricted to high-status sites such as Barking Abbey, the royal vill at Wicken Bonhunt and the coastal settlement at Maldon. More recent excavations to the north of the Roman fort – at the Othona Community site – produced four sherds of sand-tempered pottery that can only be dated as fifth- to ninth-century, and two sherds of shell-tempered ware that are probably tenth-century.[87] The collection of artefacts from excavations at Othona in 1864–5 by J. Oxley Parker included various finds accessioned into Colchester Museum as 'Saxon'.[88] These include two styli (one bronze, the other iron) and a circular bronze reliquary mount framing a cross and inlaid with millefiori, which are undated but which are exactly the sort of artefacts we would expect to be associated with an early medieval church.[89] Crucially, three ninth-century strap-ends, one with Trewhiddle style plant ornament,[90] and

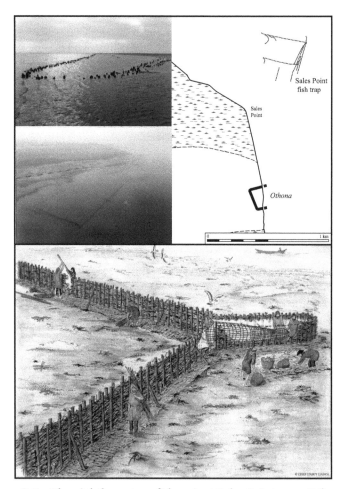

Figure 3.5 The eighth-century fish weir at Sales Point, near Othona, in the Blackwater Estuary, and reconstruction drawing by Nick Nethercoat. Aerial photos © Kevin Bruce; reconstruction © Essex County Council.

a small group of coins (discussed below) point to occupation of the site after 664.

Another strand of evidence that the monastery at Othona – or at least some form of settlement there – continued into the eighth and ninth centuries is the intertidal fish weir constructed off the coast at Sales Point (Figure 3.5).[91] Four radiocarbon determinations suggest that the earliest phase of use was in the mid-seventh to eighth centuries, and that the weirs were maintained into the ninth century.[92]

There is also numismatic evidence that occupation at *Ythancæstir* continued in some form into the eighth and ninth centuries, although some confusion has been created over the size of this coin assemblage. There are four sources of information on the early medieval coins found in and around *Ythancæstir* (Table 3.2). Colchester Museum's accession records of the Oxley Parker collection refer to seven Anglo-Saxon coins. Two can be identified from their descriptions: a 'silver sceatta on which one side depicts a mythical winged creature, the other an anthropomorphic spiral design' is probably Series S, and the 'silver sceatta depicting a saint or other figure flanked by crosses' is probably a Series U. Two others are listed as having dates in the first half of the eighth century, while another is described as a sceatta on which 'one side bears early crosses'. The remaining two are described as 'penny or sceattas' and are presumably the coins of King Coenwulf of (796–821) and King Æthelwulf of Wessex (839–56) that are described in a contemporary account of the excavations but are now lost.[93]

The 'Corpus of Early Medieval Coin Finds' (EMC) lists two silver sceattas of Series E (found in 1865) and S (found by 1986).[94] The Portable Antiquities Scheme Database[95] contains two coins: a silver sceatta of Series N (c. 710–60; PAS ESS-B5EB76) and a bronze styca of Æethelred II of Northumbria (c. 858–62: PAS ESS-B5A2F7): as these are recorded as having been found in 2001 and 2000 respectively, they are clearly different from the coins in Colchester Museum and the EMC. As the EMC's Series S sceatta is probably the one in Colchester Museum, we know of nine identifiable coins from *Ythancæstir*: one continental issue of c. 695–c. 740 (Series E), five 'secondary sceattas dating to c. 710–60 (Series N; Series S; Series U; and two other sceattas in the Oxley Parker Collection dated in the catalogue to this period); and three later pennies (King Coenwulf, 796–821; King Æthelwulf of Wessex, 839–56; King Æthelred II, c. 858–62).

A far more problematic source is a thesis by Alexander Mirrington, whose Graphs 12 and 13 suggest there are 14 coins from Bradwell on Sea parish.[96] His acknowledgements reference the use of Historic Environment Records (HERs), the Corpus of Early Medieval Coins, and the Portable

Table 3.2 Concordance of the various references to coins having been found at Othona or Bradwell on Sea.

No. in this paper	Source	Coin (including description and date in primary source)	Found	Date
1 = 19?	EMC 1977.0003	silver sceatta, Series E	1865	c. 695–c. 740
2 = 13 = 8?	EMC 1986.0418	silver sceatta, Series S (Type 47)	1986	c. 710–c. 760
3	COLEM1905.1009.1	silver sceatta, dating from c. 730–c. 740	1865	c. 710–c. 760
4	COLEM:1905.1009.2	silver sceatta	1865	
5	COLEM:1905.1009.3	silver sceatta	1865	
6	COLEM:1905.1009.4	silver sceatta, dating from c. 710–720	1865	c. 710–c. 760
7	COLEM:1905.1009.11	silver sceatta: one side bears early crosses	1865	
8 = 2? = 13?	COLEM:1905.1009.13	silver sceatta: one side depicts mythical winged creature, the other an anthropomorphic spiral design [Series S: John Naylor pers. comm.].	1865	c. 710–c. 760
9 – 18?	COLEM:1905.1009.14	silver sceatta: depicting a saint or other figure flanked by crosses [Series U?: John Naylor pers. comm.]	1865	c. 710–c. 760
10	Mirrington 2013, Graph 12 shows three coins dating to 650–99		[Southminster, 1980–5?]	650–99
11				650–99
12				650–99
13 = 2 = 8?	Mirrington 2013, NB map 19 and page 188 say one Series S sceatta has been found at Bradwell, but Graph 13 shows two	silver secondary sceatta, Series S (East Saxon)	[Mirrington's second Series S sceatta = Southminster, 1980–5?]	c. 710–c. 760

14	Mirrington 2013, Graph 13 shows two Series S sceattas		[Southminster, 1980–5?]	
15	Mirrington 2013, Graphs 12 and 13	silver secondary sceatta, Series C (Kentish)	[Southminster, 1980–5?]	c. 710–c. 760
16	Mirrington 2013, Graph 13 says that there are single examples of Series L/N and N, but map 21 shows only one	silver secondary sceatta, London (Series L, O/N, K33, K32a, K20/18, N)	[Southminster, 1980–5?]	c. 710–760
17 = 24?		silver secondary sceatta, Series N		
18 = 9?	Mirrington 2013, Graphs 12 and 13 (203 references Challis 1992, 216)	silver secondary sceatta, Series U/23b (Mercian)		c. 710–c. 760
19 = 1	Mirrington 2013, Graphs 12 and 13, 207; NB Graph 13 claims two Series E sceattas have been found	silver secondary sceatta, Series E (Frisian)		c. 710–760
20	Hull 1963, 54; Mirrington 2013, Graph 13 shows two pennies of Coenwulf (which along with the Aethelwulf penny [No. 21 below] accounts for the three coins dating to 800–49 in Graph 12.	penny of Coenwulf (796–821)		800–49
21	Hull 1963, 54; Mirrington 2013, Graphs 12 and 13	penny of King Aethelwulf of Wessex (839–56)		900–49
22 = 24	Mirrington 2013, Graphs 12 and 13	Northumbrian styca, Æethelred c. 760–c. 850		c. 760–c. 850
23 = 16?	PAS ESS-B5EB76	silver sceatta, Series N	2001	c. 710–c. 760
24 = 22	PAS ESS-B5A2F7	bronze 'styca' of Æethelred II of Northumbria	2000	c. 858–862

Source: Compiled by the author.

Antiquities Scheme (PAS), but crucially he does not provide a list of the coins with their primary database numbers (and only six are referred to in the text of the thesis). Graph 12 simply shows there being three coins from 650–99, seven from 700–49, three from 800–49 and one from 850–99. Graph 13 says that there are two Series B and one Series C [presumably the three coins from 650–99], two Series E, one Series L/N, one Series N, two Series S and one Series U [presumably the seven coins from 700–49], pennies of Coenwulf (796–821) and Æthelwulf (839–56) [two of the three coins dating to 800–49] and a styca of Æthelred [the one from 850–99].

Four of these coins can be accounted for in the specimens in the Colchester Museum Collection, EMC and PAS,[97] while the pennies of Coenwulf (796–821) and Æthelwulf (839–56) are described in a contemporary account of the excavations (see above). This leaves six sceattas that cannot be accounted for in any other sources (three Series B,[98] one Series C, one Series L/N, one Series S). It is striking that this list of sceattas is identical to a group in the EMC said to have been found in Southminster in 1980–5 – along with a Merovingian gold tremissis (EMC 1986.0201-0207) – which raises the possibility that Mirrington has erroneously attributed this 'Southminster' group to Bradwell on Sea. In fact, David Andrews (personal communication) reports Joe Bispham – who was the author of the entry in the *British Numismatic Journal* registering the coins found at 'Southminster' – has been able to contact two of the people who found them, and the Merovingian tremissis and the class C sceatta were actually found at Asheldham. We are still left, however, with the question of where the other 'Southminster' coins came from!

Overall, we must reject Mirrington's listing of 14 early medieval coins, leaving the seven identifiable coins from *Ythancæstir* – one continental issue of *c.* 695–*c.* 740 (Series E), five 'secondary sceattas dating to *c.* 710–60 (Series N, Series S, Series U, and two other sceattas in the Oxley Parker Collection dated in the catalogue to this period) and the 'styca' of Æthelred II (*c.* 858–62). Even this small group, however, establishes occupation after 664.

That the later medieval parish church of Bradwell on Sea is located 3km inland from *Ythancæstir* suggests that, when it came to establishing the network of parochial churches across Essex, the old site within the remote ruins of Othona was no longer regarded as fit for purpose. The earliest surviving fabric in the parish church is fourteenth-century, although a church at Bradwell with its chapel of ease [at Othona] is referred to in the mid-thirteenth century.[99] Kevin Bruce has suggested that a possible context for the construction of the new parish church was the period when the lord of the manor, John de la Mare, was investing in other aspects of the landscape, including obtaining a licence for a new deer park,[100] establishing a weekly market and annual fair (granted in 1283) and possibly building 'New Hall' (distinct from the existing farms at Bradwell Hall, East Hall, Hockley and Down Hall).[101]

Anglo-Saxon settlement?

There has been much debate over the nature and scale of Anglo-Saxon immigration into south-east England, with suggestions varying between mass folk migration and almost complete displacement of the Romano-British population through to the hypothesis that it amounted to little more than an elite takeover by a small group of warriors with their immediate families and retinues. Recent detailed analysis of the distribution of settlements that are most obviously associated with immigrant communities (that is, those containing *Grubenhäuser*), as well as of cemeteries in the Anglo-Saxon tradition (that is, cremations, and burials with Germanic grave goods), shows that they were not evenly distributed across the landscape.[102] Within the East Saxon kingdom, for example, the vast majority of Anglo-Saxon settlements and cemeteries are found in coastal and estuarine districts, with particular concentrations on the gravel terraces overlooking the Thames and Blackwater/Chelmer estuaries.[103]

It is striking, therefore, that the only evidence for fifth- to sixth-century Anglo-Saxon settlement within the putative *regio* of *Deningei* (beyond the immediate hinterland of the Roman settlement at Heybridge) is from the light, sandy soils in the far east of the peninsula. The Oxley Parker Collection of artefacts from excavations at Othona in 1865 includes a range of material whose character suggests a fifth- to sixth-century pagan cemetery. This includes at least two cruciform brooches and an S-shaped brooch, which are illustrated, as well as two buckles – at least one of which was D-shaped – and an iron socketed spearhead that are said to be Saxon, while fragments of a copper alloy handle made of twisted wire cannot be closely dated.[104] 'Tags to a girdle (Saxon)' referred to in a list of the finds are likely to be fifth- to sixth-century.[105] Oxley Parker apparently found many east–west-oriented skeletons, and while these were 'especially around the chapel',[106] it is possible that some are early Anglo-Saxon and were the source of these probable grave goods. It is curious that the early general overviews of Anglo-Saxon archaeology in Essex (for example, Smith 1903; Jones 1980) overlooked these important finds, as they conform to the well-known pattern of early Anglo-Saxon immigrants having been attracted to the extramural areas of major Roman sites seen so clearly at places such as

Caistor St Edmund and Colchester.[107] It is also striking how all four pieces of fifth- to sixth-century metalwork reported to the PAS more recently are from the far east of the Dengie Peninsula: a small-long brooch and button brooch from Tillingham (PAS ESS-D1E6A7 and ES-830F62), a saucer brooch from 'the Bradwell-on-Sea area' (PAS ESS-D02382) and a gold bead from St Lawrence (ESS-01B025). Laver found fragments of an urn within the Iron Age hill fort at Asheldham that he thought 'correspond very closely with the class of pottery usual in this district of Saxon date', but there was no reference to decoration or form and so the identification must be regarded as uncertain.[108]

In part, the absence of evidence for fifth- to sixth-century Anglo-Saxon *Grubenhäuser* across the central Dengie Peninsula, the Danbury Hills and the Sandon Valley is because these other areas have seen relatively little archaeological survey and excavation, the only major project being the construction of the new A130 through the Sandon Valley. This revealed what was suggested as a single 'possible' *Grubenhaus* at Downhouse Farm in West Hanningfield, but no further details are published.[109] Sherds of 'Saxon' pottery were also recovered at several of the sites, although this was usually found within the upper fills of late Roman features.[110] 'Saxon' pottery was also recovered through field-walking at various other sites, but no features datable to this period were found during the subsequent excavations.[111]

These 'Saxon' sherds, from simple, hand-made, globular, undecorated vessels with simple everted rims, are of a type that have been identified on a growing number of sites across Essex, including Asheldham Church and more recently in a ditch at the nearby Dengie Crops Ltd site in Asheldham.[112] The ethnic tag these sherds have been given may, however, be misleading. These sherds are from simple, handmade, globular, undecorated 'simple pots' that lack distinctive Anglo-Saxon features such as biconical and carinated forms, decoration such as incised lines and stamped motifs, and the application of a gritty slip known as *Schlickung*. In contrast, the universal characteristic of these 'simple pots' is that they would have been easy to make, which probably accounts for them being so similar to vessels made during the Iron Age, with the simple globular forms being exactly what we would have expected if farming communities – and unskilled potters – had to make their own vessels. As such we should stop describing these vessels as 'Saxon', regard them instead as 'early medieval' and have an open mind as to whether they were produced and used by native British or immigrant Anglo-Saxon communities.

Conclusions

Cedd's church at *Ythancæstir* was one of the most remote locations in the East Saxon kingdom. This windswept place was chosen because the ruins of the Roman fort at Othona provided a link with *Romanitas*, a very common factor in determining where early churches were located. We know that *Ythancæstir* lay within the *regio* of *Deningei*, and it is suggested that this covered around 340km^2, being bounded by the River Chelmer and the Blackwater Estuary (the *Pant*) to the north, the North Sea to the east, the Crouch Estuary to the south and the high ground south of the Chelmsford hills to the west. This appears to have been the territory of a community known as the *Dænningas*, whose name is commemorated in the parish and hundred of Dengie, and the parish and forest of Danbury.

We would expect a *regio* of this type to have had a royal vill, a communal meeting place and a minster church, and while the former cannot be located with certainty there are two possibilities. It may have lain close to the later hundredal centre (also unlocated, though probably in Dengie parish) and church at *Ythancæstir*, or at Maldon (which may have been a royal vill from at least the eighth century). We must remember that the charter purporting to record King Æthelbert of Kent giving Tillingham to Mellitus in 604x616 is clearly a forgery, but the fact that it named Tillingham may reflect a folk memory that this was the most important place in the area whenever the charter was actually written (perhaps in the late seventh century). The clearly genuine charter in which King Swæfred granted 70 *cassati* in the *regio* called *Deningei* to Ingwald, bishop of London, in the early eighth century dates, in contrast, to during the period when the early folk territories were starting to fragment. As such, it comes at a time when the East Saxon kings may well have been disposing of some of their property, particularly in more remote locations. Indeed, this may have been the context for the growth of Maldon as a small port by the sheltered waters at the head of the Blackwater Estuary, in a far more central location within the East Saxon kingdom. If this hypothesis is right, then during the seventh century the *regio* called *Deningei* may have had a royal vill at Tillingham, a church at *Ythancæstir* and a communal meeting place at Dengie. It seems highly likely that some form of occupation continued at *Ythancæstir* into the eighth and possibly the ninth centuries, by which time it was part of an estate belonging to the church of St Paul's in London.

Acknowledgements

I would like to thank: Maria Medlycott of Essex County Council Historic Environment Service for supplying various unpublished reports, and for giving permission to reproduce the photographs and reconstruction drawing used in Figure 3.5; Glynn Davies of Colchester Museum for supplying information on the Oxley Parker Collection; and John Naylor of the Ashmolean Museum/Portable Antiquities Scheme for discussing the early medieval coins. I would also like to thank Kevin Bruce and Chris Thornton for discussing some of the medieval documentary sources.

Notes

1. Colgrave and Mynors 1969, 282–5 (III, 22).
2. Sawyer 1968, no. 5.
3. Sawyer 1968, no. 1787; Hart 1971, no. 7; Kelly 2004, no. 6.
4. Wilkinson and Murphy 1995, 195, fig. 119.
5. Rodwell 1976, 238.
6. Wilkinson and Murphy 1987, 1995, fig. 119.
7. Watts 2004, 109.
8. Rivet and Smith 1979, 434.
9. Breeze 2020.
10. Colgrave and Mynors 1969, 142–3, 150–1 (II, 3,5); see Yorke 1990, 45–57, for a general history of the East Saxon kingdom.
11. Colgrave and Mynors 1969, 282–5 (III, 22); see Yorke, in this volume, for Cedd's life and career.
12. Colgrave and Mynors 1969, 288–9 (III, 23).
13. Rippon 2018a.
14. Sawyer 1968, no. 1784; Gelling 1979, no. 160; Kelly 2004, no. 4.
15. Tomlin 1996.
16. Watts 2004, 296.
17. Sawyer 1968, no. 100; Gelling 1979, no. 198; Brooks and Kelly 2013, no. 13.
18. Rippon 2022.
19. Bassett 1989b, 1997; Watts 2004, 505.
20. Rippon 2018b, 2022.
21. Rippon 2022.
22. Jones and Mattingly 1990, map 2.8.
23. Kowaleski 1995, 49, 54–5.
24. Watts 2004, 183.
25. Watts 2004, 178, 183.
26. Reaney 1935, 249.
27. Reaney 1935, 207–8, 213; Anderson 1939, 48.
28. The manor of Stansgate owned the southern portion of Tillingham marshes at Midlands and Tillingham Grange, though this was never regarded as part of the parish of Steeple. It is not known if this ownership existed before Domesday, or exactly when Stansgate Abbey acquired the land (rental of the manor of Stansgate, 1540–41 (ERO D/DC fol. M 32); rental of the manor of Stansgate, 1525-6 (TNA E36/164 fols 69–72)); I would like to thank Kevin Bruce for this information.
29. The manor of Bacons in Dengie parish owned two parcels of land in Bradwell which contained marshes. Bacons was given to the abbey of St Valery along with East Hall in Bradwell and one of their marshes lay beside the Bacons' portion (Inquisition relating to the Manor of Bacons,

30 1598 (TNA E 367/1193), and dispute re access to Buxsey Marsh, 1583–4 (TNA DL 4/26/75)); I would like to thank Kevin Bruce for this information.
30 Darby 1952, 242–4.
31 *DB Ess*. 3,9. Althorne and at least the southern part of Mayland were included in the Domesday manor of Southminster Hall. The detached portion of Mayland lies immediately north of Southminster and appears to have been carved out from it. It is curious that of the parishes with detached parcels Asheldham (*DB Ess*. 23,43; 23,55) and St Lawrence (*DB Ess*. 2,6; 37,14) did not have 'pasture for sheep' listed.
32 This boundary also marked the western edge of Stow Maris, Cold Norton, Whitmans (a detached parcel of Stow Maris), Purleigh and Woodham Mortimer parishes.
33 Reaney 1935, 249.
34 Hart 1971, nos 18 and 34.
35 *DB Ess*. 29,4 (Woodham Ferris), 33,4 (Woodham Walter) and 34,11 (Woodham Mortimer).
36 Reaney 1935, 223.
37 Reaney 1935, 248–9.
38 Kemble 2019.
39 Watts 2004, 277.
40 Galleywood, Calves, Stock, and Kiln and Ramsden Back Commons.
41 Ramsden Heath, Crowsheath, Downham Green, Hanningfield Tye, and Rettendon Great and Little Commons, the latter lying just a short distance south-west of Bicknacre Common up on the Danbury Hills.
42 For example, see Reynolds 2013 for how this manifested itself in the administration of justice, and Rippon 2022 for examples across the East Saxon kingdom.
43 Wade 1980.
44 Christy 1926, 188; Reaney 1935, 516, 543.
45 *DB Ess*. 1,28; Watts 2004, 435.
46 Haslam 1988, 29.
47 Freeman 1985, 214–15.
48 RCHME 1916, 198–210; Rodwell and Rodwell 1977, 114; Secker 2013.
49 Secker 2013.
50 Davis 1974, 17–18.
51 For example, half a hide and 30 acres, and another 30 acres, both in Latchingdon that were held by freeman in 1066 (*DB Ess*. 1,6; 1,7).
52 *DB Ess*. 3,9.
53 *DB Ess*. 1,25.
54 *DB Ess*. 1,17.
55 Hart 1957, no. 84.
56 Haslam 2015; Ennis 2016.
57 Ennis 2016.
58 Corpus of Early Medieval Coin Finds CR 1991.100; 1984.0105.
59 For example, Anderson 1939, 48; cf. Christy 1926, 183–4, which argued that the hundredal meeting place was at Lawling in Latchingdon simply because of its physical centrality within the Hundred.
60 Colgrave and Mynors 1969, 282–5 (III, 22); Blair 2005, 68.
61 For example, Blair 2005, 193.
62 Pearson this volume; RCHME 1923, 13–16; Rivet and Smith 1979, 435; *VCH Essex* III, 52–5.
63 Gittos 2013, 75–6.
64 Hoggett, in this volume.
65 Pestell 2004, 20; Hoggett 2010, 35–8.
66 Blair 2005, 188; Hoggett 2010, 44–5.
67 For example, Blair et al. 2020.
68 Blair 2007b, 1.
69 Blair 2007a.
70 Watts 2004, 260; Blair 2007b, 4.
71 Mirrington 2013, 308–12, 314, 324.
72 Cole 2007, 61.
73 Rippon 2022.
74 Sawyer 1968, no. 5.
75 Sawyer 1968, no. 5; Hart 1971, no. 1; Kelly 2004, no. 1.

76 Colgrave and Mynors 1969, 142–3 (II, 3).
77 Hart 1971, no. 11; Kelley 2004, appendix 2; *DB Ess.* 5,5.
78 Thornton 2020b, 119.
79 The vills of *Hacflet* [Hockley manor], St Peter's Chapel, Down Hall, Tillingham, Dengie, Asheldham, Steeple and Stansgate, and the later parishes of Bradwell on Sea, Tillingham, Dengie, Asheldham, Steeple and St Lawrence.
80 Kelly 2004, no. 25.
81 *DB Ess.* 3,9.
82 For example, Thornton 2020a, 9.
86 For Cedd's life and career see Yorke, in this volume.
87 Mirrington 2013, 322.
88 Rodwell 1976, 236.
89 Blinkhorn 2012.
87 Medlycott 1994, 67; further excavations in 2009 produced no further early medieval material: Sparrow 2011.
88 Colchester Museum Accession Number COLEM:1905.1009. The title of the collection as originally accessioned was 'The Oxley Parker collection of Roman and Saxon remains found within the Roman Fort of Othona, including the Bradwell mount, inlaid with millefiori' (COLEM:1947.328), but unfortunately the mount is now unlocatable. The surviving collection appears to have been re-accessioned in 1947 as COLEM:1905.1009. Also see: Essex HER Site no. 32; Roach Smith 1865; Chancellor 1877; Borough of Colchester 1947/48; Hull 1963, 53.
89 This accounts of the finds is from Mirrington 2013, 355, which cites two unpublished sources (a 1992 MPhil dissertation by K. D. Challis and a typescript report by Paul Barford for which no source is given).
90 COLEM:1905.1009.7–8; Borough of Colchester 1947/48, plate IX nos 4–6.
91 Hall and Clarke 2000; Heppell 2011; Ingle and Saunders 2011.
92 Hall and Clarke 2000, fig. 9.
93 Anon. 1878; Hull 1963, 54; presumably these are the two ninth-century coins mentioned in Smith 1903, 328.
94 EMC 1977.0003; EMC 1986.0418; https://emc.fitzmuseum.cam.ac.uk/ [accessed 8 March 2022].
95 https://finds.org.uk [accessed 8 March 2022].
96 Mirrington 2013.
97 Presumably his Series E sceatta is EMC 1977.0003; his S sceatta is EMC 1986.0418; his Series N sceatta is PAS ESS-B5EB76 (although he claims that this is Series B); and the Northumbrian styca is PAS ESS-B5A2F7. Mirrington 2013, 188.
98 That Graph 12 shows three coins from 650–99 contrasts with Graph 13, which shows only two: this might be accounted for by Mirrington (2013, 187) saying that PAS ESS-B5EB76 is a Series B sceatta whereas in fact it is Series N.
99 RCHME 1923, 14. The Register of Fulk Basset, bishop of London (1244–59), refers to Bradewelle with the chapel of la Vale. The prior of St Valery holds in the same parish one acre of land and a certain marsh, from which he retains all the tithes. The prior of Hatfield Peverel receives *alias(? duas) partes* of all tithes from the demesne which was of Roger de Hakeny to an estimate of 40s. (Kevin Bruce personal communication).
100 *Cal. Pat.* 1292–1301, 145; Cantor 1983, 29.
101 *Cal. Pat.* 1257–1300, 265; Letter 2013; Howson 2014, 67.
102 Rippon 2018a.
103 For the Thames, examples include Mucking (Hamerow 1993; Hirst and Clark 2009), North Shoebury (Wymer and Brown 1995) and Orsett Cock (Carter 1998).
For the Blackwater/Chelmer, examples are Heybridge (Drury and Wickenden 1982) and Springfield Lyons (Tyler and Major 2005).
104 COLEM:1905.1009.15–16; COLEM:1947.328 photographs; Borough of Colchester 1947/48, 28, Plate IX, nos 1–3.
105 Anon. 1878.
106 Hull 1963, 54.
107 Myres and Green 1973; Crummy 1981.

108 Laver 1928, 181.
109 Dale et al. 2005, 19.
110 Shotgate Farm, Windmill Hill, Monument Borrow Pit: Dale et al. 2005.
111 Shangri-La Culvert and Bonvilles Farm: Dale et al. 2005.
112 For Asheldham Church see Drury and Rodwell 1978; Andrews and Smoothey 1990. For Dengie Crops Ltd see Hanson 2013.

Bibliography

Anderson, O. S. 1939. *The Hundred Names of the South-Eastern Counties*. Lund: Lunds Universitets årsskrift.
Andrews, D. and Smoothey, M. 1990. 'Asheldam Church revisited'. *Essex Archaeology and History* 21, 146–51.
Anon. 1878. 'Annual general meeting at Maldon, 1st August, 1878'. *Transactions of the Essex Archaeological Society*, V, 318–19.
Bassett, S. (ed.) 1989a. *The Origins of Anglo-Saxon Kingdoms*. London: Leicester University Press.
Bassett, S. 1989b. 'In search of the origins of Anglo-Saxon kingdoms'. In *The Origins of Anglo-Saxon Kingdoms*, edited by S. Bassett. 1–27. London: Leicester University Press.
Bassett, S. 1997. 'Continuity and fission in the Anglo-Saxon landscape: the origins of the Rodings (Essex)'. *Landscape History* 19: 24–42.
Blair, J. 2005. *The Church in Anglo-Saxon Society*. Oxford: Oxford University Press.
Blair, J. 2007a. *Waterways and Canal Building in Medieval England*. Oxford: Oxford University Press.
Blair, J. 2007b. 'Introduction'. In *Waterways and Canal Building in Medieval England*, edited by J. Blair. 1–18. Oxford: Oxford University Press.
Blair, J., S. Rippon and C. Smart. 2020. *Planning in the Early Medieval Landscape*. Liverpool: Liverpool University Press.
Blinkhorn, P. 2012. *The Ipswich Ware Project: Ceramics, trade and society in middle Saxon England*. Medieval Pottery Research Group Occasional Paper 7.
Borough of Colchester 1947/48. *Report of the Museum and Muniment Committee for the Period April 1st 1947 to March 31st 1948*. 20–31. Colchester: Colchester Borough Council.
Breeze, A. 2020. 'A Celtic-Roman mystery: the name Othona'. *Essex Journal* 55(1): 11–15.
Cantor, L. 1983. *The Medieval Parks of England: A gazetteer*. Loughborough: Department of Education, Loughborough University of Technology.
Carter, G. 1998. *Excavations at the Orsett 'Cock' Enclosure, Essex, 1976*. East Anglian Archaeology 86.
Chancellor, F. 1877. 'St Peter's on the Wall, Bradwell Juxta Mare'. *Archaeological Journal* 34: 212–18.
Christy, M. 1926. 'The Essex hundred moots: an attempt to identify their meeting-places'. *Transactions of the Essex Archaeological Society* (new ser.) 18(3): 172–97.
Cole, A. 2007. 'The place-name evidence for water transport in early medieval England'. In *Waterways and Canal Building in Medieval England*, edited by J. Blair. 55–84. Oxford: Oxford University Press.
Colgrave, B., and R. A. B. Mynors (ed. and trans.). 1969. *Bede's Ecclesiastical History of the English People*. Oxford: Clarendon Press.
Crummy, P. 1981. *Aspects of Anglo-Saxon and Norman Colchester*. Colchester: Colchester Archaeological Report 1.
Dale, R., D. Maynard and J. Compton. 2005. 'Archaeology on the mid-Essex clay. Investigations on the A130 by-pass: A12 Chelmsford by-pass to the A127 Southend Arterial Road, 1991–4 and 1999–2002'. *Essex Archaeology and History* 36: 10–54.
Darby, H. C. 1952. *The Domesday Geography of Eastern England*. Cambridge: Cambridge University Press.
Davis, R. H. C. 1974. 'The college of St Martin-le-Grand and the anarchy, 1135–54'. *London Topographical Record* 23: 9–26.
Drury, P. J., and W. J. Rodwell. 1978. 'Investigations at Asheldham, Essex: an interim report on the church and the historic landscape'. *Antiquaries Journal* 58(1): 133–51.

Drury, P., and N. Wickenden. 1982. 'An early Saxon settlement within the Romano-British small town at Heybridge, Essex'. *Medieval Archaeology* 26: 1–40.

Ennis, T. 2016. 'Middle Saxon and later occupation at the former Croxley Works, Church Street, Maldon'. *Transactions of the Essex Archaeological Society* (4th ser.) 7: 163–78.

Fawn, A. J., K. A. Evans, I. McMaster and G. M. R. Davies. 1990. *The Red Hills of Essex: Salt-making in antiquity*. Colchester: Colchester Archaeological Group.

Freeman, A. 1985. *The Moneyer and the Mint in the Reign of Edward the Confessor*. Oxford: BAR (British Series), 145.

Gelling, M. 1979. *The Early Charters of the Thames Valley*. Leicester: Leicester University Press

Gittos, H. 2013. *Liturgy, Architecture, and Sacred Places in Anglo-Saxon England*. Oxford: Oxford University Press.

Hall, R. L., and C. P. Clarke. 2000. 'A Saxon intertidal fish weir at Collins Creek in the Blackwater Estuary'. *Essex Archaeology and History* 31: 125–46.

Hamerow, H. 1993. *Excavations at Mucking*, vol. 2, *The Anglo-Saxon Settlement*. London: English Heritage.

Hanson, K. 2013. 'Archaeological groundworks monitoring at Dengie Crops Ltd, Hall Road, Asheldham, Essex'. Unpublished report: Pre-Construct Archaeology Ltd. https://doi.org/10.5284/1038801 [accessed 8 March 2022].

Hart, C. 1957. *The Early Charters of Essex: the Norman period*. Leicester: Leicester University Press.

Hart, C. 1971. *The Early Charters of Essex*. Leicester: Department of English Local History, University of Leicester, Occasional Papers (1st ser.) 10 (rev. ed.).

Haslam, J. 1988. 'The Anglo-Saxon burh at *Wiginamere*'. *Landscape History* 10: 25–36.

Haslam, J. 2015. 'The two burhs of Maldon, Essex, and their antecedents'. *Transactions of the Essex Archaeological Society* (4th ser.) 6: 289–311.

Heppell, E. M. 2011. 'Saxon fishtraps in the Blackwater Estuary, Essex: monitoring survey at Collin's Creek, Pewet Island and The Nass 2003–2007'. *Transactions of the Essex Society for Archaeology and History* (4th ser.) 2: 76–97.

Hirst, S., and D. Clark. 2009. *Excavations at Mucking*, vol. 3, *The Anglo-Saxon Cemeteries*. London: English Heritage.

Hoggett, R. 2010. *The Archaeology of the East Anglian Conversion*. Woodbridge: The Boydell Press.

Howson, T. 2014. 'A pair of late medieval two-cell houses in an Essex village, and a regional context for the building type'. *Vernacular Architecture* 45: 67–80.

Hull, M. R. 1963. 'Roman gazetteer', in *Victoria County History of Essex III*. 35–203 London: University of London.

Ingle, C., and H. Saunders, H. 2011. *Aerial Archaeology in Essex: The role of the national mapping programme in interpreting landscape*. East Anglian Archaeology 136. Chelmsford: Essex County Council.

Jones, B., and D. Mattingly. 1990. *An Atlas of Roman Britain*. Oxford: Blackwell.

Kelly, S. E. 2004. *Charters of St Paul's, London*. London: British Academy.

Kemble, J. 2019. 'The early medieval place-name – Ingas'. *Essex Journal* 54 (2): 55–61.

Kowaleski, M. 1995. *Local Markets and Regional Trade in Medieval Exeter*. Cambridge: Cambridge University Press.

Lavender, N. J. 2000. 'Othona, Bradwell-on-Sea, Essex. Archaeological Survey: Synthesis of results'. Unpublished report: Essex County Council Field Archaeology Unit.

Laver, P. G. 1928. 'Sunecastre, or the camp at Asheldham'. *Transactions of the Essex Archaeological Society* 29: 180–85.

Letters, S. 2013. *Online Gazetteer of Markets and Fairs in England and Wales to 1516*. http://www.history.ac.uk/cmh/gaz/gazweb2.html [accessed 8 March 2022].

Lyte, H. C. M. 1906. *Calendar of Charter Rolls 1257–1300*. London: Public Record Office.

Medlycott, M. 1994. 'The Othona Community site, Bradwell-on-Sea, Essex: the extra-mural settlement'. *Essex Archaeology and History* 25: 60–71.

Mirrington, A. 2013. 'Transformations of Identity and Society in Essex, *c.* AD 400–1066'. Unpublished PhD thesis, University of Nottingham.

Mustchin, A. R. R., J. R. Summers, J. E. M. Cussans, A. Peachey and C. McClean. 2016. 'A Romano-British ladder system at Asheldham Quarry, Essex'. *Transactions of the Essex Archaeological Society* (4th ser.) 7: 129–41.

Myres, J. H. L., and B. Green. 1973. *The Anglo-Saxon Cemeteries of Caistor-by-Norwich and Markshall, Norfolk*. London: Reports of the Research Committee of the Society of Antiquaries of London 30.

Orzechowski, K. 2014. 'Land at Asheldham Quarry, Essex: Archaeological trench evaluation'. Unpublished report: Archaeological Solutions Report 4521.

Pestell, T. 2004. *Landscapes of Monastic Foundation*. Woodbridge: Boydell Press.

RCHME 1916. *An Inventory of the Historical Monuments in Essex*, vol. I. London: Royal Commission on the Historical Monuments of England, HMSO.

RCHME 1923. *An Inventory of the Historical Monuments in Essex*, vol. IV. London: Royal Commission on the Historical Monuments of England, HMSO.

Reaney, P. H. 1935. *The Place-Names of Essex*. Cambridge: English Place-Name Society.

Reynolds, A. 2013. 'Judicial culture and social complexity: a general model from Anglo-Saxon England'. *World Archaeology* 45(5): 699–713.

Rippon, S. 2018a. *Kingdom, Civitas, and County*. Oxford: Oxford University Press.

Rippon, S. 2018b. 'Changing landscapes? Land, people and environment in England AD 350–600'. In *Interpreting Transformations of Landscapes and People in Antiquity*, edited by N. Christie and P. D. Blasco. 95–112. Oxford: Oxbow.

Rippon, S. 2022. *Territoriality and the Early Medieval Landscape: The countryside of the East Saxon kingdom*. Woodbridge: Boydell & Brewer.

Rivet, A. L. F., and C. Smith. 1979. *The Place-Names of Roman Britain*. London: Batsford.

Roach Smith, C. 1865. 'Antiquarian researches at Bradwell juxta Mare'. *The Gentleman's Magazine*, October 1865: 403–8.

Rodwell, W. 1976. 'Some unrecorded archaeological discoveries in Essex, 1946–76'. *Essex Archaeology and History* 8: 234–48.

Rodwell, W., and K. Rodwell. 1977. *Historic Churches: A wasting asset*. London: Council for British Archaeology Research Report 19.

Round, J. H. 1903. 'Introduction to the Essex Domesday'. In *VCH Essex* I. 333–426. London: Archibald Constable.

Rumble, A. 1983. *Domesday Book: Essex*, Chichester: Phillimore.

Sawyer, P. H. 1968. *Anglo-Saxon Charters: An annotated list and bibliography*. London: Royal Historical Society. http://www.esawyer.org.uk/about/index.html [accessed 8 March 2022].

Secker, D. 2013. 'A re-used Anglo-Saxon cross shaft fragment from St Mary's Church, Newport'. *Transactions of the Essex Society for Archaeology and History* (4th ser.) 4: 222–3.

Smith, R. A. 1903, 'Anglo-Saxon remains'. In *VCH Essex* I. 35–203. London: Archibald Constable.

Sparrow, P. 2011, 'Othona: Roman extra-mural activity at the Othona Community site, Bradwell-on-Sea'. *Transactions of the Essex Society for Archaeology and History* (4th ser.) 2: 69–75.

Thornton, C. 2020a, 'Introduction'. In *VCH Essex* XII, part I, *St Osyth to the Naze: North-east Essex coastal parishes*. 1–58. Woodbridge: Boydell & Brewer.

Thornton, C. 2020b, 'St Osyth'. In *VCH Essex* XII, part I, *St Osyth to the Naze: North-east Essex coastal parishes*. 59–225. Woodbridge: Boydell & Brewer.

Tomlin, R. 1996. 'A five-acre wood in Roman Kent'. In *Interpreting Roman London: Papers in memory of Hugh Chapman*, edited by J. Bird, M. W. C. Hassall and H. Sheldon. 209–15. Oxford: Oxbow.

Tyler, S., and H. Major. 2005. *The Early Anglo-Saxon Cemetery and Later Saxon Settlement at Springfield Lyons, Essex*. East Anglian Archaeology 111.

Wade, K. 1980. 'A settlement site at Bonhunt Farm, Wicken Bonhunt, Essex'. In *Archaeology in Essex to AD 1500*, edited by D. Buckley. 96–102. London: Council of British Archaeology Research Report 34.

Watts, V. 2004. *The Cambridge Dictionary of English Place-Names*. Cambridge: Cambridge University Press.

Wilkinson, T. J., and P. L. Murphy. 1987. *The Hullbridge Basin Survey: Interim report no. 8*. 3–19. Chelmsford: Archaeology Section, Planning Department, Essex County Council [unpublished report in Essex Historic Environment Record].

Wilkinson, T. J., and P. L. Murphy. 1995. *The Archaeology of the Essex Coast*, vol. 1, *The Hullbridge Survey*. East Anglian Archaeology 71.

Wymer, J., and N. Brown. 1995. *Excavations at North Shoebury: Settlement and economy in South-east Essex 1500 BC–AD 1500*. East Anglian Archaeology 75.

Yorke, B. 1990. *Kings and Kingdoms of Early Anglo-Saxon England*. London: Seaby.

4
Cedd, Bradwell and the conversion of Anglo-Saxon England

Barbara Yorke

> Cedd established churches in various places and ordained priests and deacons to assist him in preaching the word of the faith and in the administration of baptism, especially in the *civitas* called *Ythancæstir* (Bradwell on Sea) in the Saxon tongue and also in the place called *Tilaburg* (Tilbury).[1]

In this brief passage Bede provides the essential information that links Cedd with the former Saxon Shore Fort at Bradwell on Sea as one of the two centres of his mission to the kingdom of the East Saxons. The few facts that we have for Cedd come from Bede's *Ecclesiastical History* (731), mostly provided by members of Cedd's foundation at Lastingham (North Yorkshire), and are summarised in Table 4.1. They gain more import when interpreted within a broader context of the history of the Anglo-Saxon conversion to Christianity and of the relationships between the different Anglo-Saxon kingdoms. The story of the Anglo-Saxon conversion often lingers on the foreign missionaries from Italy and Ireland who established the first mission stations, but equally important was the consolidation of their work by men like Cedd of the second generation, men whom they had trained and who knew how to promote Christianity among their own people. Cedd became bishop of the East Saxons but came from the kingdom of Northumbria and represented the influence both of the church of Lindisfarne, where he had trained, and of the powerful king of Northumbria, who was his patron.

Table 4.1 Timeline for the life of Cedd.

c. 620?	Birth of Cedd
635–51	Aidan bishop of Lindisfarne: educates Cedd at Lindisfarne
651–61	
653	Finán, bishop of Lindisfarne
	Cedd sent to Middle Angles by Bishop Finán, and then to East Saxons
	Baptism of Sigebert 'Sanctus', king of East Saxons
654	Cedd consecrated bishop of East Saxons
651x655	Foundation of Lastingham
664	Cedd *interpres* at Synod of Whitby
	Death of Cedd in plague at Lastingham (26 October)

Source: Compiled by the author.

Family and background

One of the few facts we know about Cedd is that he was the eldest of four brothers who, Bede says, 'were all famous priests of the Lord, a very rare thing to happen, and two of them reached the rank of bishop'.[2] Also notable about them was that all four – Cedd, Cynebill, Cælin and Chad – have names that are of British rather than Anglo-Saxon origin.[3] By 'British' in the context of this period one means those whose ancestors lived in the country during the Roman period. By the seventh century in the east of England people of British descent had intermingled with the Germanic incomers to produce a distinctive Anglo-Saxon culture in which Old English became the dominant language, but further west British culture continued with less outside influence, and a Brittonic language akin to Welsh was spoken. In some Anglo-Saxon kingdoms, notably those of Mercia and Wessex, some of the early kings had names that, like those in Cedd's family, were either Brittonic or incorporated Brittonic elements. These could have been the result of intermarriage with important British families when kingdoms were being established.[4] The parallel raises interesting questions about the status of Cedd's family, which may well have been significant, and either British or hybrid Anglo-British. As Bede says, for four brothers to have become priests was unusual, although there were other families in early medieval Europe who specialised in church appointments.[5] In Ireland this might happen when one ruler annexed the lands of another; it gave the defeated family status in the newly enlarged kingdom, and perhaps helped to reconcile areas over which they had held authority to new arrangements, but it also signalled that they were no longer rivals for secular power.[6] Could Cedd and his brothers have been entered into the church in comparable circumstances during the expansion of Northumbrian power in the early seventh century? Whatever the answer, it can be seen that Cedd and his brothers were influential individuals, closely linked with King Oswiu of Northumbria (642–70) and his nephew King Æthelwald of Deira (651–5).[7]

Cedd is first encountered in the *Ecclesiastical History* in 653, when he was one of the priests who went with Bishop Finán of Lindisfarne to assist in the conversion of the Middle Angles.[8] Subsequently Bede says that Cedd had been 'brought up' (*educatus*) at Lindisfarne,[9] and it is usually assumed that Cedd and his brothers entered Lindisfarne in the time of Finán's predecessor Aidan, who was the first bishop of Lindisfarne (635–51) and one of Bede's great ecclesiastical heroes (Figure 4.1). Aidan had been sent to Lindisfarne from the island of Iona, the influential monastic centre founded in 563 by St Columba, who was himself from the northern part of Ireland.[10] As Cedd was old enough to be appointed a bishop *c*. 654 (when one might expect him to have been aged at least 30), and all his younger brothers seem to have been priests by that date, a reasonable estimate for his birth would be around 620 – but that is no more than an educated guess.[11] He would then have been in his late teens when Aidan was appointed bishop of Lindisfarne in 635. Aidan is known to have recruited 12 English boys soon after his appointment to train up as missionaries,[12] and it is possible that Cedd and his brothers were part of this group.

Figure 4.1 The remains of the medieval church of Lindisfarne, on the site of the church founded by Aidan. Barbara Yorke.

Cedd and Northumbrian overlordship

King Oswiu of Northumbria was the most powerful king of the Anglo-Saxons from *c.* 650 until his death, and appears as the seventh such ruler in Bede's list of great overlords.[13] He had been a Christian from an early age when in exile among the Irish, but some of his contemporary kings had yet to be converted. Oswiu used conversion and the imposition of churchmen from Northumbria as a way of underpinning his overlordship, which otherwise rested largely upon his military superiority. That explains how Cedd came to be in the entourage of Bishop Finán among the Middle Angles in 653. Conversion was part of the alliance brokered between Oswiu and King Peada of the Middle Angles, which was also sealed by his marriage to Oswiu's daughter Alhflæd.[14] Next on Oswiu's list was the conversion of the East Saxon king Sigebert 'Sanctus', who 'about the same time' was persuaded by King Oswiu 'his friend' to be baptised as a Christian by Bishop Finán at one of Oswiu's royal estates near Hadrian's Wall known as *Ad Murum*.[15] The fact that Sigebert had to travel all the way from Essex to distant parts of Northumbria and his baptism by the Northumbrian bishop are indications of his political subservience to Oswiu. Another manifestation of this was that Oswiu summoned Cedd from the Middle Anglian province and sent him with another priest to preach to the East Saxons. When it was evident that a mission could be successful, Cedd returned to Northumbria and was consecrated bishop of the East Saxons by Bishop Finán.[16]

There are other indications of how Cedd was part of the Northumbrian royal establishment and worked to promote the position of King Oswiu and his family. Cedd subsequently baptised King Swithhelm of the East Saxons, successor of King Sigebert, but his baptism took place not in the East Saxon kingdom but in the neighbouring kingdom of the East Angles at the royal residence of Rendlesham with King Æthelwold of the East Angles as his sponsor.[17] The implication would seem to be that Æthelwold was also subject to Oswiu's overlordship, but was in turn Swithhelm's superior. Bede records something similar slightly later when the Mercian king Wulfhere (658–75) was the dominant overlord, and arranged the conversion of King Æthelwalh of the South Saxons. By accepting baptism in this way Æthelwalh recognised Wulfhere's superiority, and he was rewarded by being made overlord of the Jutish provinces of the Isle of Wight and the Meonware (Hampshire), which had recently submitted to Wulfhere.[18] In both cases there may have been a two-tier system of overlordship with Æthelwold of the East Angles and Æthelwalh of the South Saxons as median lords of Oswiu. But it was not

Æthelwold's bishop who carried out the conversion of King Swithhelm of the East Saxons but Cedd, because Cedd was Oswiu's major ecclesiastical agent in the area.

Cedd was also held in high regard by King Oswiu's nephew Æthelwald (son of his brother King Oswald (634–42)), who after 653 seems to have been subking under his uncle of the southern Northumbrian province of Deira (roughly corresponding to the later county of Yorkshire), which had once been an independent kingdom. Cedd's brother Cælin had at one time been a priest in the service of Æthelwald, and Bede says that it was through him that Æthelwald came to know Cedd as well. Æthelwald commissioned Cedd to found a religious house in his Deiran province where he (the king) could attend divine service and ultimately be buried.[19] Cedd's choice of location was Lastingham (Figure 4.2), which will be considered in greater detail later, but it is appropriate to mention here an incident when Cedd was cleansing the site through fasting and had to break off when a messenger suddenly appeared to summon him to the king. Cedd had to get his brother Cynebill, who was by then a priest, to complete the ritual for him rather than disobey a royal summons. The incident underscores Cedd's importance as an adviser to both Northumbrian kings. His position seems to have survived Æthelwald's fall from favour when he failed to support his uncle at the Battle of the River Winwæd in 655, which saw the death and defeat of Oswiu's major rival, King Penda of the Mercians.[20] Æthelwald is not heard of again, but Cedd's

Figure 4.2 The medieval church of Lastingham, probably on the site of the church founded by Cedd. Barbara Yorke.

position remained unchanged. Lastingham seems to have become fully his possession, which he was able to pass on to his brothers;[21] it is not recorded where Æthelwald was buried.

A final example of Cedd's high standing with King Oswiu was his role at the Synod of Whitby of 664. The king had called the council to decide whether Northumbria should continue to follow customs that had been introduced into Lindisfarne from its mother house of Iona that were at variance with those followed in other parts of England and Ireland, and even Rome itself.[22] Cedd acted as *interpres vigilantissimus*, 'a most diligent interpreter' for both sides. Bede's phrase is often taken to mean that Cedd acted as a translator, but the Latin *interpres* can have a broader meaning of 'negotiator' or 'expounder', suggesting a rather more active and key role.[23] Perhaps it was King Oswiu, who chaired the meeting, who particularly needed matters explained to him, as some of the disputed customs, particularly regarding methods used to calculate the date of Easter, were extremely complex.[24] When Oswiu decided against the customs of Lindisfarne, some of its clergy could not accept this rejection of the traditions of their mother house and left Northumbria. But Cedd abided by the king's ruling and continued as bishop of the East Saxons;[25] his brother Chad was appointed bishop of York.[26]

The establishment of Christianity among the East Saxons

Cedd's Northumbrian background is an important part of his biography that is needed to understand what preoccupations he brought to his role as bishop of the East Saxons, but it is now necessary to consider how his work fitted into the establishment of Christianity in the East Saxon kingdom. Christianity would have been introduced into Essex during the period of Roman rule, but it has proved difficult to find evidence of the continuation of Christian worship in eastern England after Britain ceased to be part of the Roman empire in the early fifth century.[27] The conditions do not seem to have existed for an organised church to continue to function, though there were parts of Britain where Christianity became more firmly embedded, and also contact with Christian areas overseas, especially Merovingian Francia.[28] The Prittlewell princely burial, which dates to around 600, contains Christian items and seems to demonstrate Christian influences.[29] Possibly they came via Kent, whose king, Æthelbert, in the late sixth century married Bertha, a Frankish princess and a Christian who came to England with a Frankish bishop called Liudhard.[30] Æthelbert's sister Ricule was married to King Sledd of the East Saxons,[31] and could have introduced some Christian practices into the province, but probably not any supporting infrastructure.

A more concerted effort to convert the East Saxon court and its subjects also came via Kent through the mission, led by Augustine, dispatched by Pope Gregory the Great in 596 to King Æthelbert's kingdom. In 604 the Italian Mellitus was consecrated bishop of London with the intention that he would act as bishop to the East Saxons, whose dominant king was Sæbert, the nephew of Æthelbert and his political subordinate.[32] To establish a bishop in London was a priority of Augustine's mission as Pope Gregory knew of its importance in the Roman period, and his vision of bringing the province of *Britannia* back into the church envisaged the establishment of two metropolitan sees at London and York.[33] London was an important trading centre in which a number of kingdoms seem to have had an interest, but in 604 King Æthelbert was the dominant power, and was claimed by Bede to have 'built the church of the apostle St. Paul in the city of London, in which Mellitus and his successors were to have their episcopal seat'.[34] Although King Sæbert was evidently baptised, Christianity was not adopted by all members of the royal house. After the deaths of Æthelbert and Sæbert (616x618), Sæbert's three sons, who had remined unbaptised, expelled Mellitus, and Æthelbert's son and successor Eadbald was not in a strong enough position to enable him to stay in London.[35] Mellitus returned to Kent, and eventually became the third (arch)bishop of Canterbury (619–24).

It would appear that Mellitus's mission to the East Saxons may not have been very productive, and Bede provides no positive details. But there is one possible intriguing link with the later mission of Cedd, though the evidence is inconclusive. In the twelfth century St Paul's, London, claimed to have a charter in which King Æthelbert granted land at Tillingham in Essex to Bishop Mellitus.[36] The charter is an evident forgery, and there is an alternative route by which the estate could have come to St Paul's as it was left to its community in the will of Bishop Theodred of London (died 951x953).[37] However, examination of the East Anglian estates in the will of Theodred (who also seems to have acted as bishop of part of East Anglia) suggests that these may in fact have been estates that he had 'borrowed' or leased for his personal use or that of his family and was now returning to their original ecclesiastical owners.[38] By analogy the implication could be that Tillingham belonged to St Paul's before the time of Theodred, and that the charter was subsequently forged to reinforce the claims. This is potentially interesting because it could indicate a possible link between the missions of Mellitus and Cedd. Tillingham is only a few miles south of Bradwell on the Dengie Peninsula and potentially was the centre (*ham*) of a large estate that could once have included Bradwell. Its first element is a rare male personal name 'Tilli' that is also the first element of Tilbury, the other site that Bede names as a foundation of Cedd in Essex.[39] It is possible that there was some long-standing link between Tillingham/Bradwell and Tilbury, that the two sites had been given to Mellitus as missionary bases and were passed on to Cedd, but the evidence is not strong enough for certainty.

There was a gap of over 30 years between the expulsion of Mellitus and the appointment of Cedd as bishop of the East Saxons *c*. 654 in which there does not seem to have been any formal episcopal provision for the province. It is therefore unlikely that Mellitus's episcopacy had much permanent legacy among the East Saxons, and Cedd was in effect restarting the mission from scratch. It must be stressed that, although Mellitus had been bishop of London and the see was revived when Wine was appointed by King Wulfhere of Mercia in 666, there is no evidence that Cedd had any connection with the city. He was bishop of the East Saxons but not bishop of London.[40] As Bede indicates in the passage quoted at the beginning of this chapter, he had two episcopal centres among the East Saxons at Bradwell and Tilbury from which he organised a church structure for the East Saxons by training up priests and deacons and establishing a network of local churches through which the population could be baptised.[41] There are indications that the East Saxon kingdom (which included areas outside the modern county of Essex) was frequently divided between two or more rulers.[42] Bradwell and Tilbury may well have been centres in two well-established divisions of Essex that were frequently under the control of different East Saxon kings. Bradwell was therefore not just a church site established by Cedd but actually the shared seat of his bishopric among the East Saxons from which his mission to the East Saxons was co-ordinated.

Bradwell and Lastingham

Bede provides relatively few details about Cedd's arrangements for Bradwell, but has more to say about Lastingham. The two foundations were made at about the same time. Bede says Cedd was already bishop of the East Saxons when Æthelwald invited him to found a monastery in his Deiran kingdom,[43] and as Cedd was only appointed bishop of the East Saxons *c*. 654 and Æthelwald disappears from view in late 655, work must have been proceeding in the two places at the same time. It therefore seems legitimate to suggest that some of what we know about the foundation of Lastingham could be relevant to Bradwell as well. Bede explains that the community of Lastingham were his main informants for the careers of Cedd and Chad, and more generally for some of the early history of the East Saxons and surrounding regions.[44] Bede indicates that Lastingham was Cedd's principal foundation, and although this may well be something his Lastingham informants wished to stress, it is nevertheless likely to have been the case. Although he was bishop of the East Saxons, Cedd remained part of the Northumbrian establishment and this was his base there. It was his own possession as abbot rather than one linked to his episcopal office and he was able to leave it to his brother Chad after his death. When Cedd died and was buried at Lastingham in 664, Bede records how 30 brothers from his monastery in the East Saxon province came to Lastingham 'wishing to live near the body of their father, or, if the Lord so willed, to die and be buried there'.[45] Bede refers only to one East Saxon *monasterium*, making it unclear whether Bradwell or Tilbury was meant, but perhaps we should not expect complete precision when Bede was writing almost 70 years later and the brothers may in fact have come from both foundations. Their loyalty was to their founder Cedd, not to the East Saxon province, though some of them presumably had been recruited locally. Bede's account refers somewhat scathingly to Cedd introducing a monastic rule to his East Saxon recruits 'so far as these rough people (*rudes*) were capable of receiving it'.[46] Was this the perspective at Lastingham of Cedd's East Saxon religious houses?

Cedd is said to have introduced to Lastingham 'religious observances according to the usage of Lindisfarne where he had been brought up',[47] which were themselves based on the monastic Rule instituted by Columba on Iona;[48] the same presumably applied to Bradwell and Tilbury as well. One rite Bede specifically refers to was purifying the site of Lastingham through prayer and fasting, which Cedd intended to do during the season of Lent, but was interrupted by a messenger from King Æthelwald so that the ritual had to be completed by his brother Cynebill.[49] Possibly such rituals were carried out in the Lindisfarne tradition to consecrate any new religious site, but Bede specifically says it was 'to cleanse the site … from the stain of former crimes', possibly a reference to a former Roman shrine or to prehistoric monuments in the vicinity.[50] Presumably similar rites of cleansing would have taken place at Bradwell for there are likely to have been Roman or Germanic shrines in the former Saxon Shore Fort.

Bede's account stresses the remoteness of Lastingham, on the edge of the North York Moors, 'amid some steep and remote hills which seemed better fitted for the haunts of robbers and the dens of wild beasts than for human habitation' (Figure 4.3).[51] Although topographically very

Figure 4.3 Aerial view of Lastingham (middle left), showing its position between Ryedale and the North York Moors. ©, and by kind permission of, Richard Morris.

different, Bradwell could also be seen as a physically challenging and remote site with some extreme weather that would fit the conventional idea of the asceticism of the Irish tradition of monasticism. However, in the case of neither Lastingham nor Bradwell would that represent the full picture, for both sites could also be seen as central to prosperous areas of strategic significance in the Roman period, in a Saxon Shore Fort on the eastern coast in the case of Bradwell,[52] and perched above the Ryedale valley in the case of Lastingham.[53] They were sites that offered both opportunities for monastic contemplation, and access to good routes of communication for a busy royal adviser and bishop like Cedd. Bede tells us that at Lichfield Cedd's brother Chad 'built himself a more retired dwelling-place not far from the church, in which he could read and pray privately with a few of his brothers',[54] and Cedd may have done something similar at both Lastingham and Bradwell.

One final point about Lastingham which may be relevant to understanding Bradwell in the time of Cedd was that the church built at Lastingham by Cedd would seem to have been of timber as there is reference to a stone church being built subsequently, perhaps in connection with Cedd's promotion as saint and evidently before Bede was writing in 731.[55] Many of the earliest churches to be built, especially in the north, were of timber.[56] The first church of York was a timber one, and so was that of Lindisfarne.[57] Timber building was what the Anglo-Saxons and Irish were familiar with, and so would be the tradition that Cedd would have expected to use.[58] Although at Bradwell there were stones readily available from the Saxon Shore Fort, and the church of St Peter's is built from these, even putting up a building from salvaged stone required workmen trained in specific skills, and where we have specific references, these seem to have been recruited from Francia (or possibly northern Italy).[59] Although the Italian missionaries had some early stone churches erected in Kent, in other parts of England stone churches seem to have been a secondary development after about 670, including at York and Lindisfarne. It is therefore possible that the existing church of St Peter's at Bradwell was not erected in the time of Cedd, but it was undoubtedly built because of Cedd and may have been closely associated with the promotion of his cult as a saint (as will be considered further below).

An Irish bishop among the East Saxons?

Certain aspects of Cedd's behaviour as bishop are distinctive and recall accounts of Aidan of Lindisfarne and of Columba of Iona, the founder of Lindisfarne's mother church (Figure 4.4). But here we must confront the issue of how far Bede records genuine instances of Cedd's behaviour and how far he was influenced by literary models of the expected behaviour of Irish-trained churchmen. It has been suggested that Bede may have had a history of Cedd and Chad independently written at Lastingham some time between 672 (the death of Chad) and 731,[60] which is certainly possible, but Bede does not specifically refer to a written source as he does, for example, to the *libellus* he had from the monastery of Barking.[61] Some of the information he received from the brothers of Lastingham may have come to him in written correspondence, but Bede can be presumed to have had opportunities to converse with fellow Northumbrian monks, especially as there seems to have been a fair amount of movement between the province's religious houses. Bede's own teacher, presumably at Wearmouth and Jarrow, was Trumbert, who had been brought up by Chad, probably at Lastingham but possibly at Lichfield (or even at both).[62] Established models existed in the Irish tradition of how a bishop might behave to have an impact on secular society, and these may have influenced how stories about Cedd were framed, but Cedd himself would have been brought up with these exempla and they are likely to have influenced his own behaviour. What is evident from the *Ecclesiastical History*

Figure 4.4 Statue on Lindisfarne of St Aidan, by Kathleen Parbury (1958). Barbara Yorke.

is that Bede had a very high regard for both Cedd and Chad, and for their mentor Bishop Aidan of Lindisfarne, and saw them as models of episcopal and monastic leadership.

Bishops in the Irish tradition could be quite fearsome in order to impress on recent converts appropriate standards of Christian behaviour. Bede recounts how Cedd had forbidden King Sigebert 'Sanctus' from associating with one of his own relatives whom Cedd had excommunicated because he regarded his marriage as unlawful. The king had ignored the prohibition and dined at his relative's house, but as he left Cedd confronted him. King Sigebert

> fell trembling at the bishop's feet, asking his pardon ... In his anger [Bishop Cedd] touched the prostrate king with his staff which he was holding in his hand, and exercising his episcopal authority, he uttered these words, 'I declare to you that because you were unwilling to avoid the house of this man who is lost and damned, you will meet your death in the very house'.[63]

Subsequently Sigebert was murdered by this relative and his brother as Cedd had prophesied.

The incident echoes another Bedan story in which Bishop Aidan publicly rebuked King Oswine of Deira (644–51) for complaining that he had given away a horse that was a gift from the king to a beggar in Christian charity: 'Surely the son of a mare is not dearer to you than the son of God?'[64] Aidan then prophesied that Oswine would die soon after, which did indeed occur, even though a swift apology to the bishop had saved him from a formal episcopal cursing. People did not normally speak to kings in this way, and it required conspicuous courage for the bishops to speak out, but doing so made a strong impression of their special character and of the power of the Christian God. The stories also make the point of how Christian principles might clash with traditional modes of behaviour. The two brothers who killed Sigebert claimed they had done it because 'they were angry with the king and hated him because he was too ready to pardon his enemies, calmly forgiving them for the wrongs they had done him, as soon as they asked his pardon'.[65] In practice both Sigebert 'Sanctus' and Oswine were probably killed by rivals for political power, but such actions could be represented as manifestations of divine vengeance.[66]

Bede also says that Chad as bishop of Lichfield modelled his behaviour on that of his brother Cedd as well as on their mentor bishop Aidan,[67] and so traits shared by Aidan and Chad may have been typical of Cedd as well. Bede particularly praised Aidan and Chad for their active pastoral care, which involved them travelling around to all parts of their dioceses, on foot, 'after the apostolic model', rather than on horseback. Though Cedd is described as dismounting when he confronted King Sigebert and can scarcely have made his journeys between Essex and Northumbria on foot, within his diocese he too is likely to have followed the practice of travelling and preaching on foot, which provided the opportunity to interact with people from all backgrounds.

Bede had the greatest respect for the episcopal standards of Cedd and Aidan, but he had major issues with some of their customs that differed from those approved in Rome, and these had come to a head at the Synod of Whitby.[68] Disputed areas included the form of tonsure and some aspects of how baptism was performed, but the one that caused the greatest problem was over the method used to calculate Easter. Lindisfarne used a calendar that had been introduced by Columba to Iona in the late sixth century which had become outmoded by the middle of the seventh century and, crucially, meant that in some years Easter was celebrated at a different time from other churches in the West, including in Rome. Many churches in Ireland had already adopted alternative calendars, but Iona and Lindisfarne felt obliged to follow the customs that had been established by Columba, and these were the traditions in which Cedd had been raised. When he became bishop of the East Saxons, Cedd would have found that some of Lindisfarne's practices were at variance with those Augustine had introduced from Rome, and had subsequently been updated,[69] or were followed by other missionaries who had been trained or had lived in Francia, such as Bishop Felix of the East Angles (630/31–647/8), who Bede says came from Burgundy.[70]

Such differences may also have caused problems for King Oswiu, whose major church in Northumbria was Lindisfarne but who exercised authority over other kingdoms that did not recognise its authority or practices. When his son Alhfrith took up with an ultra-Romanist party who were extremely hostile to Lindisfarne traditions, Oswiu called the Synod of Whitby in 664 to debate the issues, and decided that the Northumbrian church should from then on be in conformity with Roman practices. As we have seen, Cedd acted as 'interpreter' of the debates for King Oswiu, and readily accepted the Synod's ruling, which many of the Lindisfarne community felt unable to do. A possible interpretation is that Cedd had already decided that change was necessary and nudged Oswiu in the same direction. He would have been a representative, as was Oswiu himself after 664, of the so-called 'third party' who wanted to find a compromise between the extreme views of the two opposing 'Roman' and 'Celtic' parties.[71] Cedd may have come to this point of view because of his experiences in the south, but his brother Chad, who would seem to have been studying in Ireland at this time, may have been introduced to updated methods of calculating Easter there and influenced his brother. Chad was possibly at *Rath Melsigi* (Clonmelsh, County Carlow), and was certainly friendly with another Anglo-Saxon called Ecgbert who spent much time there and was responsible for persuading Iona to change its practices in 721.[72] Without that decision Bede might have had difficulty in writing about Lindisfarne alumni such as Cedd or Chad so favourably, as there was a very hostile reaction against anyone trained in the Lindisfarne tradition among many in the Northumbrian church establishment in the decades immediately after the Synod of Whitby.[73]

After Cedd

After the Synod Cedd seems to have visited his monastery at Lastingham, and while there caught the bubonic plague that was rampaging through the country; he died, presumably on 26 October, which became his major feast day. As recounted earlier, 30 brethren travelled from one or both of his East Saxon foundations to be with the body of their father Cedd. Sadly, they too caught the plague, and all but one small boy died.[74] This reads suspiciously like Bede's account of a subsequent plague visitation to Jarrow where all died except the abbot and one small boy.[75] It is perhaps not to be taken entirely literally. Bede adds the curious information that the boy subsequently realised that he had never been baptised, but this was speedily remedied. His survival in order to be baptised, and thus eligible for salvation, is presented as an instance of Cedd's intercession, and may have become a support for the claim that he was a saint.

The withdrawal of 30 individuals from Cedd's East Saxon foundations must have left the province somewhat bereft of functioning churchmen.[76] The East Saxons too were badly affected by the plague, which it has been suggested could have been of Black Death proportions.[77] The province was divided between two rulers, Sigehere and Sæbbi, and Sigehere and his portion of the East Saxon people revived public pagan worship while Sæbbi and his half continued to rely on the Christian God. Subsequently King Wulfhere of Mercia (659–74), when he was the dominant power in southern England, sent Bishop Jaruman of Lichfield (the main Mercian see) to sort out the defaulters, and Jaruman is said to have restored Christian order to the province.[78] In 666 Wine, who had been bishop of Winchester, purchased the see of London from Wulfhere, and the connection of London and the East Saxon bishopric was revived. At one point Wine seems to have been the only Anglo-Saxon bishop still standing, such had been the devastation of the plague, and after the Synod of Whitby he organised the consecration of Cedd's brother Chad as bishop of York with the aid of two British bishops.[79] When Theodore arrived from Rome to become archbishop of Canterbury in 669, he was very concerned about the legitimacy of any rituals involving British priests as many customs of the British church were not in conformity with those of Rome, and Chad was deposed,[80] but he was soon after appointed bishop of Lichfield instead.[81] Wine was succeeded as bishop of London by Eorcenwald in 675, an Anglo-Saxon probably connected to leading families in Kent and Francia. He founded the nunnery of Barking for his sister Æthelburh as well as the monastery of Chertsey (Surrey).[82] If the stone church of St Peter's Bradwell was not built by Cedd himself, it may well date from the time of Eorcenwald. From this point the East Saxons were firmly integrated into a unified English church under the authority of Archbishop Theodore.

Cedd, as we have seen, died and was buried at Lastingham. Bede says that he was first buried in the churchyard, but was subsequently moved into a stone church dedicated to St Mary and buried on the right side of the altar.[83] This translation of his body would have marked the point at which he was declared a saint, which at this date could be decided by a community itself after appropriate manifestations.[84] Richard Morris has suggested that two finely decorated pieces of stone sculpture from Lastingham could potentially be from the shrine of Cedd (Figure 4.5).[85] A vision of the soul of Cedd coming down from heaven with angels to collect the soul of Chad in heaven was described by Ecgbert in Ireland, who had known Chad in his youth.[86] Although Bradwell did not have the body of Cedd, it is quite likely that they had other relics associated with him which could act as a conduit to the saint, such as the staff with which he had prodded King Sigebert.[87]

Cedd's body did not remain at Lastingham. By the end of the Anglo-Saxon period it is recorded as being at Lichfield with the bodies of Chad and Ceatta, who is otherwise unknown but could have been another

Figure 4.5 (Left) Lastingham 07 and (right) Lastingham 08: two fragments from a possible shrine of Cedd at Lastingham. By courtesy of the Corpus of Anglo-Saxon Stone Sculpture, University of Durham.

relative.[88] It is not known when Cedd's remains were taken to Lichfield, but it was presumably after Bede completed the *Ecclesiastical History* in 731 and before 900, as it occurs in the first part of a list of saints' resting-places that is thought to have been compiled before that date.[89] One possibility could have been during the reign of King Offa of Mercia, when Lichfield was promoted to be an archbishopric in 787.[90] Cedd's second feast day of 7 January may relate to this translation.[91] In 1841 six bones were enshrined as relics in Birmingham Cathedral, and when these were examined and tested by radiocarbon dating they were found to represent three individuals, two of whom had lived in the seventh century and the third a century or so later.[92] These can be presumed to be what remains of Cedd, Chad and Ceatta.

Conclusion

Although, as with so many people of the seventh century, there are many gaps in what we know about Cedd, he was an individual who made his mark and ensured that Christian worship did not disappear again from Essex and the surrounding areas. Bede had heard only good things about him and was impressed by what he knew of him and of the high standards of his ministry. He brought the ethos of the Irish-founded churches of Iona and Lindisfarne to south-eastern England to join the eclectic mix of Christian culture from other parts of Europe and beyond to be found there. Bradwell is the main place in southern England where vestiges of Cedd can be found. The Saxon Shore Fort was one of his two episcopal centres, and even if he did not build the church of St Peter's himself, it is only there because of Cedd and is likely to have been erected in his honour and to support his cult. Cedd believed he had been put on earth for a purpose and to benefit others. St Peter's, Bradwell, is a fitting memorial for him today and deserves to remain a peaceful place where contemplation and prayer can still help those who come to seek it.

Notes

1 Colgrave and Mynors 1969, 282–5 (III, 22).
2 Colgrave and Mynors 1969, 288–9 (III, 23).
3 Insley 2003, 373–4.
4 Clark 1992, 463.
5 Fletcher 1997, 167–8, 193–227 passim.
6 Ó Corráin 2005, 585–90.
7 Pickles 2018, 93–113.

8   Colgrave and Mynors 1969, 278–81 (III, 21).
9   Colgrave and Mynors 1969, 288–9 (III, 23).
10 Charles-Edwards 2000, 308–26.
11 Farmer 2004; Sargent 2020, 48–9.
12 Colgrave and Mynors 1969, 308–9 (III, 26).
13 Colgrave and Mynors 1969, 148–51 (II, 5).
14 Colgrave and Mynors 1969, 278–81 (III, 21).
15 Colgrave and Mynors 1969, 280–5 (III, 22).
16 Higham 1999, 100–4.
17 Colgrave and Mynors 1969, 284–5 (III, 22).
18 Colgrave and Mynors 1969, 370–3 (IV, 13).
19 Colgrave and Mynors 1969, 286–9 (III, 23); Pickles 2018, 105–6.
20 Colgrave and Mynors 1969, 254–5 and 288–95 (III, 14 and 24).
21 Sargent 2020, 48–54.
22 Colgrave and Mynors 1969, 294–309 (III, 25); Charles-Edwards 2000, 391–415.
23 Farmer 2004.
24 Charles-Edwards 2000, 391–405; Dailey 2015.
25 Colgrave and Mynors 1969, 308–9 (III, 26).
26 The appointment was short-lived, and subsequently Chad was appointed bishop of Lichfield: Sargent 2020, 54–60. See further below.
27 Petts, 2003; Blair 2005, 10–34.
28 Charles-Edwards 2013, 192–241.
29 Blackmore et al. 2019.
30 Colgrave and Mynors 1969, 72–5 (I, 25).
31 Colgrave and Mynors 1969, 142–3 (II, 3); Yorke 1985, 31–2.
32 Colgrave and Mynors 1969, 142–3 (II, 3).
33 Colgrave and Mynors 1969, 104–7 (I, 29); Brooks 1984, 8–14; Flechner 2013.
34 Colgrave and Mynors 1969, 142–3 (II, 3); Naismith 2019, 40–66; Shaw 2018, 98–104.
35 Colgrave and Mynors 1969, 152–5 (II, 5).
36 Kelly 2004, no. 1, 135–7. See also Rippon, in this volume.
37 Kelly 2004, appendix 2, 225–8.
38 Pestell 2004, 81–6.
39 Kelly 2004, 84–5.
40 Whitelock 1975, 4–5; Shaw 2018, 99–103.
41 Colgrave and Mynors 1969, 282–5 (III, 22).
42 Yorke 1985, 25–31.
43 Colgrave and Mynors 1969, 286–9 (III, 23).
44 Colgrave and Mynors 1969, 4–7 (Preface); Sargent 2020, 48–54.
45 Colgrave and Mynors 1969, 288–9 (III, 23).
46 Colgrave and Mynors 1969, 284–5 (III, 22).
47 Colgrave and Mynors 1969, 288–9 (III, 23).
48 Herbert 1996, 9–46; Charles-Edwards 2000, 308–26 (no written Rule of Columban practice survives).
49 Colgrave and Mynors 1969, 286–9 (III, 23).
50 Wood 2009, 4–7; Morris 2015, 128–35.
51 Colgrave and Mynors 1969, 286–7 (III, 23).
52 Petts, in this volume.
53 Wood 2009; Morris 2015, 119–25; Pickles 2018, 135–41.
54 Colgrave and Mynors 1969, 336–9 (IV, 3).
55 Colgrave and Mynors 1969, 288–9 (III, 23).
56 Barnwell 2015, 212–14.
57 Colgrave and Mynors 1969, 186–7, 292–3 (II, 14; III, 25).
58 Ó Carragáin 2010, 19–26.
59 Cambridge 1999. For the fabric of the chapel see Andrews, in this volume.
60 Sargent 2020, 48–54.
61 Colgrave and Mynors 1969, 356–7 (IV, 7).
62 Colgrave and Mynors 1969, 342–3 (IV, 3); Sargent 2020, 51.
63 Colgrave and Mynors 1969, 284–5 (III, 22).
64 Colgrave and Mynors 1969, 258–9 (III, 14).

65 Colgrave and Mynors 1969, 284–5 (III, 22).
66 Higham 1999, 96–100.
67 Colgrave and Mynors 1969, 316–17, 336–7 (III, 28; IV, 3).
68 Charles-Edwards 2000, 391–415.
69 Dailey 2015.
70 Colgrave and Mynors 1969, 190–1 (II, 15).
71 Charles-Edwards, 2000, 320–1.
72 Colgrave and Mynors 1969, 224–5, 310–15 (III, 4; III, 28); Ó Cróinín 1984.
73 Stancliffe 2003.
74 Colgrave and Mynors 1969, 288–9 (III, 23).
75 Grocock and Wood 2013, 92–5 (*Life of Ceolfrith*, Chapter 14).
76 Cf. Rippon, in this volume.
77 Maddicott 1997.
78 Colgrave and Mynors 1969, 322–3 (III, 30); Yorke 1985, 18–19, 31–2.
79 Colgrave and Mynors 1969, 234–5, 316–7 (III, 7 and 28).
80 Colgrave and Mynors 1969, 332–7 (IV, 2).
81 Colgrave and Mynors 1969, 336–7 (IV, 3).
82 Colgrave and Mynors 1969, 354–7 (IV, 6); Whitelock 1975, 5–9; Kelly 2004, 110–12.
83 Colgrave and Mynors 1969, 288–9.
84 Rollason 1989, 23–59.
85 Morris 2015, 134–5; these are stones Lastingham 7 and 8 in Lang 1991, 170–1.
86 Colgrave and Mynors 1969, 344–5 (IV, 3).
87 Smith 2012.
88 Rollason 1978, 61–2.
89 Morris 2015, 128.
90 Sargent 2020, 35–40, 110–19.
91 Farmer 2004.
92 Greenslade 1996, 14–17; Sargent 2020, 120.

Bibliography

Barnwell, P. S. 2015. 'Conclusion: churches, sites, landscapes'. In *Places of Worship in Britain and Ireland, 300–950*, edited by P. S. Barnwell. 209–26. Donington: Shaun Tyas.
Blackmore, L., I. Blair, S. Hirst and C. Scull. 2019. *The Prittlewell Princely Burial: Excavations at Priory Crescent, Southend-on-Sea, Essex, 2003*. MOLA Monograph 23. London: Museum of London Archaeology.
Blair, J. 2005. *The Church in Anglo-Saxon Society*. Oxford: Oxford University Press.
Brooks, N. 1984. *The Early History of the Church of Canterbury*. Leicester: Leicester University Press.
Cambridge, E. 1999. 'The architecture of the Augustinian mission'. In *St Augustine and the Conversion of England*, edited by R. Gameson. 202–36. Stroud: Sutton Publishing.
Charles-Edwards, T. 2000. *Early Christian Ireland*. Cambridge: Cambridge University Press.
Charles-Edwards, T. 2013. *Wales and the Britons, 350–1064*. Oxford: Oxford University Press.
Clark, C. 1992. 'Onomastics'. In *The Cambridge History of the English Language*. vol. 1, *The Beginnings to 1066*, edited by R. M. Hogg. 452–89. Cambridge: Cambridge University Press.
Colgrave, B., and R. A. B. Mynors (ed. and trans.). 1969. *Bede's Ecclesiastical History of the English People*. Oxford: Clarendon Press.
Dailey, E. T. 2015. 'To choose one Easter from three: Oswiu's decision and the Northumbrian synod of A.D. 664'. *Peritia* 26: 47–64.
Farmer, D. H. 2004. 'Cedd'. *ODNB*. Online edition: https://doi.10.1093/ref.odnb/29986 [accessed 6 October 2020].
Flechner, R. 2013. 'St Boniface as historian: a continental perspective on the organization of the early Anglo-Saxon church'. *Anglo-Saxon England* 41: 41–63.
Fletcher, R. 1997. *The Conversion of Europe: From paganism to Christianity, 371–1386*. London: HarperCollins.
Greenslade, M. W. 1996. *Saint Chad of Lichfield and Birmingham*. Birmingham: Archdiocese of Birmingham Historical Commission.

Grocock, C., and I. Wood (ed. and trans.). 2013. *Abbots of Wearmouth and Jarrow*. Oxford Medieval Texts. Oxford: Clarendon Press.

Herbert, M. 1996. *Iona, Kells and Derry: The history and hagiography of the monastic familia of Columba*. Dublin: Four Courts Press.

Higham, N. 1999. 'Dynasty and cult: the utility of Christian mission to Northumbrian kings between 642 and 654'. In *Northumbria's Golden Age*, edited by J. Hawkes and S. Mills. 95–104. Stroud: Sutton Publishing.

Insley, J. 2003. 'Pre-conquest personal names'. In *Reallexikon der Germanischen Altertumskunde*, Band 23, edited by H. Beck, H. Steuer, R. Müller and D. Geuerich. 367–96. Berlin and New York: Walter de Gruyter.

Kelly, S. E. 2004. *Charters of St Paul's London*. Anglo-Saxon Charters 10. Oxford: Oxford University Press and the British Academy.

Lang, J. 1991. *Corpus of Anglo-Saxon Stone Sculpture*, vol. 3, *York and Eastern Yorkshire*. Oxford: Oxford University Press and the British Academy.

Maddicott, J. 1997. 'Plague in England in the seventh century'. *Past and Present* 156: 7–54.

Morris, R. 2015. 'Landscapes of conversion among the Deirans: Lastingham and its neighbours in the seventh and eighth centuries'. In *Places of Worship in Britain and Ireland, 300–950*, edited by P. S. Barnwell. 119–51. Donington: Shaun Tyas.

Naismith, R. 2019. *Citadel of the Saxons. The Rise of Early London*. London and New York: I.B. Tauris.

Ó Carragáin, T. 2010. *Churches in Early Medieval Ireland, Architecture, Ritual, and Memory*. New Haven, CT, and London: Yale University Press.

Ó Corráin, D. 2005. 'Ireland *c.* 800: aspects of society'. In *A New History of Ireland*, vol. 1, *Prehistoric and Early Ireland*, edited by D. Ó Cróinín. 549–608. Oxford: Oxford University Press.

Ó Cróinín, D. 1984. 'Rath Melsigi, Willibrord, and the earliest Echternach manuscripts'. *Peritia* 3: 17–49.

Pestell, T. 2004. *Landscapes of Monastic Foundation: The establishment of religious houses in East Anglia, c. 650–1200*. Anglo-Saxon Studies 5. Woodbridge: Boydell Press.

Petts, D. 2003. *Christianity in Roman Britain*. Stroud: Tempus.

Pickles, T. 2018. *Kingship, Society, and the Church in Anglo-Saxon Yorkshire*. Oxford: Oxford University Press.

Rollason, D. 1978. 'Lists of saints' resting-places in Anglo-Saxon England'. *Anglo-Saxon England* 7: 61–94.

Rollason, D. 1989. *Saints and Relics in Anglo-Saxon England*. Oxford: Blackwell.

Sargent, A. 2020. *Lichfield and the Lands of St Chad: Creating community in early medieval Mercia*. Studies in Regional and Local History 19. Hatfield: University of Hertfordshire Press.

Shaw, R. 2018. *The Gregorian Mission to Kent in Bede's Ecclesiastical History*. London and New York: Routledge.

Smith, J. 2012. 'Portable Christianity: relics in the medieval West'. *Proceedings of the British Academy* 181: 143–67.

Stancliffe, C. 2003. *Bede, Wilfrid, and the Irish*. Jarrow Lecture 2003. Newcastle upon Tyne: Jarrow Church.

Whitelock, D. 1975. *Some Anglo-Saxon Bishops of London*. Chambers Memorial Lecture 1974. London: University College.

Wood, I. 2009. *Lastingham in Its Sacred Landscapes*. Fifth Lastingham lecture 2008. Lastingham: Friends of Lastingham Church.

Yorke, B. 1985. 'The kingdom of the East Saxons'. *Anglo-Saxon England* 14: 1–36.

5
Put to good use: The religious afterlife of the Saxon Shore Forts

Richard Hoggett

Introduction

The chapel of St Peter-on-the-Wall is remarkable for a wide variety of reasons, many of which are explored in this volume. Dating from the latter part of the seventh century, it is one of the best preserved and most significant buildings from this period in southern England,[1] providing a rare and tangible link to the conversion period, during which the Anglo-Saxons embraced the Christian culture that was to shape English society for the next 1,500 years.[2] Foremost among the distinctive characteristics of St Peter's Chapel is its construction on the site of the former western gateway of the Roman fort of Othona, one of a network of forts that spanned the coast of south-east England, referred to collectively as the forts of the 'Saxon Shore'.[3] Historical, archaeological and architectural evidence indicates that, following a period of abandonment after the Roman withdrawal from Britain in the early fifth century, from the seventh century onwards many of these Shore Forts, and a large number of other Roman sites, were reoccupied and put to religious use as part of the Christianisation of the Anglo-Saxon kingdoms.

The deliberate construction of churches within the walls of former Roman forts was more than mere chance, and the strong correlation between the location of churches and former forts has often been observed and commented upon.[4] It is frequently suggested that such churches were situated in order to take advantage of the stonework that Roman ruins provided,[5] and (as David Andrews demonstrates in Chapter 1) this was certainly something that the architects of St Peter's

Chapel did, but a wider consideration of the evidence indicates that the selection of these specific locations was more than practical opportunism, being also a symbolic and meaningful act imbued with religious significance.

This chapter examines the evidence for the religious reoccupation of Othona and a selection of the other forts within the Saxon Shore network. While each site has a unique history and local context, such overarching comparisons enable the identification of cross-cutting themes within the wider conversion process, as part of which many former Roman structures, not just the Saxon Shore Forts, were repurposed as early ecclesiastical sites.

The Saxon Shore Forts

The Saxon Shore Forts have recently been defined by Historic England as 'a series of later Roman coastal defensive forts constructed to several different plans and portraying the development of Roman military architecture during the third and early fourth centuries, all apparently built in response to early Saxon raiders'.[6] The forts are located along the south-eastern coast of England and, from north to south, comprise the forts at Brancaster, Caister-on-Sea and Burgh Castle (all now in Norfolk, but the latter in Suffolk until 1974), Walton Castle (Suffolk), Bradwell on Sea (Essex), Reculver, Richborough, Dover and Lympne (Kent), Pevensey (East Sussex) and Portchester (Hampshire) (Figure 5.1). Although constructed at different times across a wide geographical area, and therefore not part of a deliberately planned scheme, these eleven forts are traditionally grouped together because nine of them were listed in a late fourth- or early fifth-century document called the *Notitia Dignitatum* ('Register of Dignitaries') as being under the control of the 'Count of the Saxon Shore' (*comes litoris Saxonici*) (Figure 5.2).[7] Neither Caister-on-Sea nor Walton Castle was specifically referred to in the *Notitia Dignitatum*, although the former is thought to have functioned as a pair with Burgh Castle and the omission of the latter is attributable to copyists' errors.[8]

The Shore Forts were all constructed in similar coastal locations, most often in sheltered tidal environments close to the open sea, from which most were protected by natural barriers.[9] During the intervening 1,500 years, many of these forts have been exposed to the dynamic forces of the sea and affected by coastal erosion. Walton Castle has been entirely destroyed, while the forts at Richborough, Reculver, Burgh Castle and Bradwell on Sea have all lost significant elements. Others now stand at

Figure 5.1 The locations of the Saxon Shore Forts, spanning the coast of Britain from The Wash to the Solent. Drawn by the author.

some remove from the sea and rivers which once they commanded, such as at Pevensey and Lympne.

Archaeological evidence indicates that many of the Shore Forts fell into disuse during the later fourth century, in some cases several decades before the 'official' withdrawal of the Roman presence from Britain following Honorius' 'rescript' of 410. Lympne was abandoned in the mid-fourth century, although whether this was due to the fort no longer being required by the military, or the onset of the landslides that were later to destroy the site is unclear. Likewise, the garrison was withdrawn from Reculver c. 360 and the pair of forts at Caister-on-Sea and Burgh Castle seems to have fallen out of use by c. 380. The fort at Richborough continued to be garrisoned until at least the late fourth century, when the site inexplicably witnessed the scattering of some 20,000 bronze coins issued between 395 and 402. A timber Christian church with hexagonal

Figure 5.2 A map identifying the Saxon Shore Forts, from a fifteenth-century Swiss copy of the *Notitia Dignitatum*. Othona is the first fort shown. Bodleian Library MS Canon. Misc. 378, fol. 153v. Bodleian Libraries, University of Oxford, CC BY-NC 4.0.

font was also constructed on the site during the late fourth or early fifth centuries. At other forts, Roman occupation continued into the fifth century, as was the case at Portchester, Pevensey, Brancaster, Bradwell and Dover.[10]

Very few studies of the Saxon Shore consider the post-Roman usage of the forts in anything more than a cursory fashion, yet individually and collectively they have a significant number of elements in common.[11] For example, the erosion that has affected many of the forts greatly enhances our understanding of environmental and coastal change since the Roman period.[12] Likewise, following the Norman Conquest, several forts were repurposed as the baileys of medieval castles, the ruins of which still stand at Pevensey and Portchester, while those at Burgh Castle have since been razed and Walton Castle has been destroyed completely by coastal erosion.[13] While the seventh-century St Peter's Chapel within the fort at Bradwell is a unique survival, it draws attention to the fact that many of the Shore Forts became the sites of Anglo-Saxon churches during the seventh and eighth centuries.[14]

Despite the continuing and widespread interest in the Shore Forts, the overview presented by Stuart Rigold in 1977 remains the most complete review of the Christian reoccupation of these forts published to date.[15] The repurposing of many of the Shore Forts was explored by Tyler Bell during his doctoral research, which focused on associations between Roman ruins and early Christian sites.[16] Likewise, the East Anglian forts have been assessed by the current author in the context of the conversion of East Anglia.[17] Unfortunately, a comprehensive review of the evidence from each of the Shore Forts lies beyond the scope of a chapter of this length, but the sections below present overviews of the archaeological and historical evidence from Bradwell on Sea and compare it to that from the neighbouring East Anglian sites of Walton Castle, Burgh Castle and Caister-on-Sea and the Kentish sites of Reculver and Richborough. While similar assessments could also be presented for the Shore Forts at Brancaster, Dover, Lympne, Portchester and Pevensey, the material evidence for the reoccupation of these sites is less certain and the historical sources are more ambiguous, although in almost every case an absence of evidence should not be considered to be evidence of absence.[18] It is hoped that future studies of this subject will be able to explore these sites more fully.

The Anglo-Saxon church at Bradwell on Sea

The Roman fort of Othona was constructed during the latter part of the third century, being one of the later forts that made up the Saxon Shore network.[19] Following its abandonment, the fort appears to have remained deserted until the mid-seventh century. In his *Historia ecclesiastica gentis anglorum*, Bede recorded how in 653, Cedd, a Northumbrian educated at Lindisfarne, began to evangelise the Middle Angles, following the conversion of their king, Peada, to Christianity.[20] Shortly afterwards, Cedd was elevated to the position of bishop of the East Saxons, and, having been consecrated at Lindisfarne in 654, he established churches, ordained priests and deacons, preached the faith and administered baptism, especially at *Ythancæstir*, the Anglo-Saxon name for Bradwell on Sea.

The achievements, influence and legacy of Cedd are explored in more detail by Barbara Yorke in Chapter 4, but notable among Cedd's later activities are his baptising Sigebert's successor, Swithhelm, son of Seaxbald, at the royal vill of Rendlesham in the neighbouring kingdom of East Anglia in 660. King Æthelwold of East Anglia, the brother of King Anna, was his sponsor.[21] The site at Rendlesham, in south-east Suffolk, enjoyed close links with the nearby royal burial ground at Sutton Hoo and is currently the subject of a research project investigating its Anglo-Saxon landscape.[22] As is discussed further below, by the time of this baptism, Æthelwold's precursors in the East Anglian royal family had already been instrumental in the religious reoccupation of several of the Shore Forts which lay within their kingdom.

St Peter's Chapel was constructed in the seventh century from the rubble of the Roman fort. Today, the chapel stands in splendid isolation, all surface traces of the fort having disappeared (see the cover image of this volume), although its walls survived, at least in part, until the seventeenth century, with small sections still remaining in the early twentieth century (see Figure 2.2). Archaeological and architectural investigations indicate that in its original form the church comprised a nave with flanking side chapels or *porticus*, a western porch and an apsidal chancel, linked to the nave by a double-arched opening (see Figure 1.4).[23] Nineteenth-century excavations revealed the presence of a cemetery surrounding the chapel, although its full extent was not exposed or recorded.[24]

St Peter's Chapel is undeniably a seventh-century Anglo-Saxon foundation, comprising a stone-built church with attendant cemetery, and it is generally assumed that the chapel is the church founded by Cedd, as indicated by Bede. However, several observers have commented on the resemblance between the chapel and other early churches built in Kent by Augustine and his successors, and its unusual location within the former gateway of the fort, rather than being located fully within the walls. They suggest that, rather than being Cedd's church, St Peter's Chapel may represent a second-generation church founded after 669, when Archbishop Theodore of Canterbury brought the kingdom of Essex under the influence of the Roman church emanating from Kent.[25] Irrespective of its true origins, St Peter's Chapel is a rare survival and contributes greatly to our understanding of the early church in south-eastern England. As is explored further below, its relationship with the site of the former Roman fort is significant, and is a characteristic it shares with other seventh-century churches founded on the former sites of Saxon Shore Forts.

East Anglia

Looking northwards from Bradwell and Essex, the adjacent Anglo-Saxon kingdom of East Anglia contained four Shore Forts: Walton Castle, Burgh Castle, Caister-on-Sea and Brancaster (Figure 5.1). Three of these sites – Walton Castle, Burgh Castle and Caister-on-Sea – are indicated by historical and archaeological evidence to have been the sites of seventh-century Christian foundations established as part of the conversion of the kingdom.[26] There is currently little evidence that the fort at Brancaster was subject to such reoccupation, although some tantalising discoveries support the possibility that such evidence may be discovered in the future.[27]

Walton Castle

Walton Castle was a Roman fort which stood on the coast near Felixstowe until it was destroyed by the sea in the eighteenth century (Figure 5.3). Antiquarian accounts describe a rectangular fort some 170m long, with round corner-bastions and bands of decorative red tile in its walls, making it broadly comparable with the forts at Bradwell and Burgh Castle, and suggesting a construction date in the later part of the third century.[28] Walton Castle was not listed in the *Notitia Dignitatum*, and we do not know its Roman name, but early descriptions indicate that it should be considered to be a Shore Fort. Although now completely lost, rubble traces of the fort can be seen on the foreshore during very low spring tides.

Like Bradwell, historical evidence suggests that Walton Castle became a significant early Christian site during the middle decades of the seventh century. Bede recorded that the first East Anglian king to come into contact with Christianity was Rædwald, who ruled the region in the first quarter of the seventh century and was baptised in Kent *c.* 604.[29] However, on returning to East Anglia he apparently lapsed; Christianity certainly did

Figure 5.3 Watercolour view of the ruins of Walton Castle, painted by Francis Grose in 1766. Te Papa (Museum of New Zealand) 1957-0009-121: Gifted by Archdeacon F. H. D. Smythe in 1957.

not become the dominant religion during his reign.[30] If Rædwald was indeed the individual buried in the famous ship burial at Sutton Hoo, then those who buried him clearly did not consider him to be a Christian.[31] Rædwald was succeeded by his son Eorpwald, who was converted to Christianity by Edwin of Northumbria in 627, although his conversion was literally short-lived, as he was assassinated not long afterwards.[32]

Eorpwald was in turn succeeded by his brother Sigebert c. 630. Described by Bede as 'a good and religious man'[33] and 'a devout Christian and a very learned man in all respects',[34] Sigebert had been in exile in Gaul during his brother's reign, where he had become a Christian, and Bede states that 'as soon as he began to reign he made it his business to see that the whole kingdom shared his faith'.[35] Unlike the reigns of his predecessors, that of Sigebert saw the true beginning of the East Anglian conversion for not only was the king a devout Christian himself but he also set a number of religious developments in motion, not least the creation of an East Anglian diocese.

Sigebert was aided in his efforts by Felix, a Burgundian bishop sent to East Anglia by Archbishop Honorius, perhaps in response to a request from Sigebert. In 630/1 Felix became the first bishop of the East Angles and Sigebert granted him the site of *Dommoc* to establish his bishopric.[36] Felix died 17 years later and *Dommoc* remained the sole East Anglian see until c. 673, when Archbishop Theodore divided the diocese and consecrated two bishops.[37] One bishopric continued at *Dommoc*, while a new see was established at Elmham.[38]

Dommoc is traditionally identified with the coastal town of Dunwich, although it has long been recognised that this association is largely without foundation.[39] Instead, several strong arguments can be made in favour of Walton Castle having been the site of *Dommoc*: Bede described the site as a *civitas*, an epithet also emphasised by the signatories of the Council of *Clovesho* of 803, indicating that *Dommoc* was a site with a significant Roman past, while several twelfth- and thirteenth-century documents clearly identify the site as lying at Felixstowe.[40] We do not know what Walton Castle's Roman name was, but Stuart Rigold suggested that *Dommoc* preserves an element of it, the full name having perhaps been *Dommucium*.[41] Walton Castle's location also makes its identification as *Dommoc* more favourable: after the Roman withdrawal it would have remained a significant landmark which stood at the maritime gateway to the royal heartland in south-east Suffolk – the Deben Valley contained both the burial ground at Sutton Hoo and the royal vill at Rendlesham – making Walton Castle a fitting site for the king's new bishopric and one that he was well within his rights to gift to Felix.

There is also evidence that a pre-Conquest church stood within the walls of Walton Castle. Shortly after the Norman Conquest, Roger Bigod built a castle within the Roman fort, and during the reign of William II (1087–1100) he is recorded as having granted Rochester priory the church of Walton St Felix, where it subsequently established a cell. This cell is also thought to have been sited within the fort in the first instance.[42] In 1154, Roger's son Hugh is recorded granting the priory land elsewhere in Walton in exchange for 'the land of their church where he built his castle'.[43] In the fourteenth century the priory moved again, to a site in the vicinity of St Mary's Church, Walton, where its remains were excavated in 1971.[44] From this evidence we know that the Bigod castle was constructed inside the walls of the Roman fort, and it would appear that the original church of St Felix was, too. While the dedication to St Felix must post-date his episcopate, it is suggestive that a church dedicated to the founding bishop of East Anglia should have stood within the walls of one of the probable candidates for his see.

The diocese of *Dommoc* prevailed until the ninth century, when the East Anglian dioceses were disrupted by Viking incursions. After the English reconquest of the region in the early tenth century only the see of Elmham was restored, and the new incumbents styled themselves bishop of the East Angles.[45] Like Bradwell, then, Walton Castle was a former Roman fort which became the focus of an early Christian foundation, in this case an early episcopal see rather than a monastic site, but it was not the only East Anglian Roman fort to witness occupation during this period.

Burgh Castle

Bede records that Sigebert also welcomed the Irish missionary Fursa to the kingdom and encouraged him to found a monastery at *Cnobheresburg*.[46] The location of *Cnobheresburg* is unknown but since the seventeenth century has almost universally been identified as the Roman fort at Burgh Castle. There is no strong evidence to suggest that this identification is correct, and Bede's description of *Cnobheresburg* as an *urbs* rather than a *civitas* suggests it was a non-Roman site,[47] but it is clear from archaeological evidence that Burgh Castle became a site of considerable religious significance during the seventh century, whether it was founded by Fursa or not.[48]

The late third-century fort of Burgh Castle – Roman *Gariannonum* – is strategically situated on the River Waveney and in the Roman period sat on the southern side of the Great Estuary, which provided maritime access to the regional capital at *Venta Icenorum* (Caistor St Edmund).[49] Today, its walls and external bastions survive on three sides; the west wall collapsed into the river shortly after the end of the Roman period.[50] The site was reoccupied from the seventh until at least the ninth centuries and, after the Norman Conquest, a motte was constructed for a timber castle in the south-western corner of the fort. The motte was only ploughed flat in 1837.[51] The site has been subject to several episodes of archaeological investigation – a series of trenches was dug along the western perimeter in 1850 and 1855 and excavation was conducted by Charles Green between 1958 and 1961 – but much of the fort's interior remains unexcavated.[52]

Green firmly believed Burgh Castle to be *Cnobheresburg* and confidently expected to discover the remains of Fursa's monastery. Indeed, so strong was his conviction that in the excavation records some layers were simply labelled 'Fursey'.[53] The flaws in Green's approach to interpretation are plain to see, but Burgh Castle *did* produce evidence for a significant phase of seventh- to ninth-century occupation. Excavation in the north-eastern corner of the fort produced a large quantity of Anglo-Saxon pottery, and in these same trenches Green recorded a number of oval structures, which he took to be the foundations of huts or monastic cells. However, Johnson questions whether these ovals survived to the extent that Green suggested or, indeed, whether they had actually existed at all.[54] Given the depth of the plough damage, it seems unlikely that any Anglo-Saxon built features, including any possible church, would have survived.

The only area of the fort in which Anglo-Saxon features were found in situ was in the south-western corner, where the motte had stood and the depth of overlying soil was consequently greater. Here the remains of an extensive cemetery were discovered, although the original ground surface from which the graves had been cut and several higher layers of burials had been destroyed.[55] This cemetery post-dated the Roman layers and was sealed beneath the eleventh-century motte, and radiocarbon dating suggests that the cemetery began in the early seventh century and continued into the late Anglo-Saxon period.[56] Whether identifiable as Fursey's monastery or not, it is clear that the former fort at Burgh Castle was a significant early Christian site.

Unlike some of the other examples discussed here, it is notable that the present parish church at Burgh Castle stands approximately 250m north-east of the fort (Figure 5.4). In 1993–4, a small excavation was

Figure 5.4 Aerial view of Burgh Castle from the south-west, showing the walls of the Roman fort (foreground) and the parish church (top left). © Norfolk County Council: Taken by Derek Edwards, 20 June 1990, TG4704/AJD/GBB1.

conducted to the south of the churchyard, revealing a number of Romano-British and late Anglo-Saxon agricultural ditches, suggestive of the church's having been relocated to its present site in the early Norman period, when the fort was converted into a motte and bailey castle.[57]

Caister-on-Sea

A similar sequence of reoccupation occurred at the nearby fort of Caister-on-Sea, situated on the opposite side of the Great Estuary to Burgh Castle. One of the earlier Shore Forts, built in the early third century, it was approximately 400m square and comprised an earthen rampart, stone wall and outer defensive ditch.[58] For a long time the site was considered to be a port or small township, but it has since been recognised that Caister-on-Sea was a fully fledged fort. The walls of the fort were standing in the seventeenth century, although they had been demolished by the eighteenth century, and the fort is now largely buried beneath modern housing.

There have been a number of small- and medium-scale excavations in and around the fort, many of them in response to development, but large areas of the fort's interior remain unexplored. Excavations undertaken by Charles Green between 1951 and 1955, prior to his work at Burgh Castle, revealed two ranges of Roman buildings, the southern gatehouse and a stretch of interior road, demonstrating that the fort fell out of use in the late fourth century. As at Burgh Castle, the overlying Anglo-Saxon archaeology had been greatly disturbed by later agriculture, although large quantities of Anglo-Saxon pottery and a number of *sceattas* were discovered. Very little Anglo-Saxon settlement evidence survived in situ, but excavations revealed evidence for two seventh- to ninth-century inhumation cemeteries – one inside the fort and one immediately to its south.[59]

In 1935, the remains of an inhumation cemetery were recognised in the north-east quadrant of the fort, although unfortunately no plans were made of the cemetery.[60] Green's excavation revealed isolated burials towards the centre of the fort, additional burials were discovered in the north-east corner in the 1960s and more recent housing development has revealed others, but beyond this the intramural cemetery remains elusive.[61] A number of inhumations were also revealed immediately to the south of the fort in 1932, more were discovered in 1946–7 and in 1954 a trench revealed at least 147 further burials. Estimates of the number of individual burials within this cemetery range from hundreds to thousands.[62]

It is clear that the intramural and extramural cemeteries at Caister-on-Sea are Anglo-Saxon and similar in character. It seems likely that the intramural cemetery had its origins in the seventh century, at the point when the ruined fort was presumably turned to ecclesiastical or monastic use in the manner described here for other forts. This cemetery seems to have continued into the late Anglo-Saxon period. We can be more certain about the extramural cemetery, attributed a start date of c. 720 on the strength of associated finds.[63] This cemetery also continued into the late Anglo-Saxon period. If the intramural cemetery was a part of the original Christian refoundation of the fort, it would seem that the extramural cemetery was founded later to accommodate the increasing numbers of burials that the site must have attracted as its influence grew.

As at Burgh Castle, rather than being situated within the walls of the fort, the medieval church at Caister-on-Sea stands some 300m to the east of the fort. The church was heavily restored in the late nineteenth century, but traces of thirteenth- and fourteenth-century masonry survive.[64] Unlike at Walton Castle and Burgh Castle, there is no evidence for a Norman reoccupation of Caister-on-Sea fort, which might have precipitated the relocation of an intramural church, yet the church's foundation in close proximity to the larger, extramural cemetery may indicate that this was a factor in its location.

Kent

Returning to Bradwell and travelling further south, the former Anglo-Saxon kingdom of Kent also contained four Shore Forts: at Reculver, Richborough, Dover and Lympne. This section examines in detail two of the four forts – Reculver and Richborough – which exhibit clear archaeological, architectural and historical evidence of Christian reoccupation during the Anglo-Saxon period. Of the other two forts, later historical sources suggest that a minster was founded at Dover in the 630s and that this was refounded and moved into the former Shore Fort in the 690s.[65] However, given the later development of the port of Dover, only limited excavations of the Shore Fort have taken place, revealing its south-west corner and traces of an earlier fort, with almost nothing being known about its interior.[66] Similarly, the ruins of the Roman fort at Lympne have witnessed limited exploration, primarily due to the later landslides which have significantly disrupted its remains.[67] Excavations have concentrated on reconstructing the lines of the walls and bastions, and the interior remains largely unexplored. In 1977, Stuart Rigold considered the possibility of the Christian reoccupation of the site to be an 'open question', and this remains the case today.[68]

Reculver

The Roman fort at Reculver – Roman *Regulbium* – was another foundation, dating from the early third century, and like Brancaster and Caister followed a simple square plan with rounded corners, surrounded by two V-shaped ditches. Situated at the northern end of the Wantsum Channel, which separated the mainland from the Isle of Thanet, the fort complemented Richborough, situated at the southern end of the channel creating a well-guarded harbour. The land to the north of Reculver has eroded to such a degree that the northern half of the site has been lost to the sea, but even within the southern half of the fort very little survives, with the exception of its southern and eastern gates.[69] Today the site is dominated by the pair of late twelfth-century towers that adorned the western front of the church founded at the centre of the fort in the seventh century, which was greatly enlarged during the medieval period, but which is now a precarious clifftop ruin.[70]

The Roman fort and its church have been a subject of interest for some 300 years. By the early nineteenth century, coastal erosion had encroached on the site to such a degree that the decision was taken to found a new church inland and take down the existing building. Demolition began in 1805, and the nave and chancel were removed quickly, but the pair of Norman towers at the western end were saved when the Trinity Board of Navigation bought the site and constructed sea defences around it.[71] Limited archaeological excavations of the fort's interior, including the church, were undertaken in 1877, 1923, 1927 and 1951.[72] Since the 1950s the site has been subject to a sporadic programme of rescue archaeology, which has revealed many of the fort's former Roman structures.[73]

The demolition of the church facilitated the excavation of its earlier phases and revealed that in its earliest incarnation the church comprised a simple nave and apsidal chancel with a curved interior and an angular exterior, from which doorways accessed rectangular northern and southern *porticus*. The nave featured northern, western and southern external doorways, and was connected to the chancel by a triple arch, similar to the double-arch at Bradwell (see Figure 1.6).[74] The two columns that supported the arches, clearly depicted in an engraving of the demolition of the church (Figure 5.5), were sold to a local landowner who re-erected them in an orchard near Canterbury.[75] They have since been

Figure 5.5 'Interior ruins of Reculver's church, Kent', drawn by I. Baynes, engraved by H. Adlard and published in Virtue's *Picturesque Beauties of Great Britain in a Series of Views: Kent* in 1838.

moved into the crypt of Canterbury Cathedral, where they have been reunited with a capital discovered on a nearby farm.[76]

Within the church, in front of the chancel arch, stood a carved stone cross which, like the columns of the chancel arch, was constructed from stone drums mounted one on top of the other and decorated with a variety of biblical scenes.[77] Leland described the cross in glowing terms when he visited the site between 1535 and 1543, although it appears to have been dismantled by the eighteenth century and the pieces scattered. Several fragments have since been rediscovered and brought back together, and are now on public display. The cross is unique, representing something of a syncretic fusion between Mediterranean and Anglo-Saxon art styles, and its position within the church suggests that the church was constructed around it in the later seventh century, although others date the cross to the ninth century.[78]

Although not mentioned by Bede, the Anglo-Saxon monastery at Reculver is the best-documented foundation within the walls of the Shore Forts, and the historical evidence complements the architectural and archaeological evidence discussed above. The *Anglo-Saxon Chronicle* records that in 669 Egbert, king of Kent, gave 'Raculf' to a priest named Bassa in order that he might found a minster.[79] The foundation's subsequent history is captured in a series of charters, the earliest of which dates from 679 and records a grant of land to the monastery's Abbot Berhtwald by King Hlothhere of Kent. As an indication of his status and prowess, Berhtwald was subsequently appointed archbishop of Canterbury in 692. A further royal grant was made *c.* 748x762 by King Eardwulf, who ruled west Kent, and *c.* 762x764 a further charter records the exemption of a ship belonging to the monastery from tolls and tribute at the port of Fordwich.[80] Another grant of land made by King Ealhmund is recorded in a charter dated 784, but by 811 it seems that the monastery was in the hands of the archiepiscopal see, as a charter records Archbishop Wulfred detaching land from Reculver church. Later charters indicate that by 817 Reculver had passed into the hands of the Mercian king, Coenwulf, but that it was regained by Wulfred in 821.[81]

Viking raiding affected the Kent coast throughout the ninth century, and it seems highly likely that the religious community at Reculver would have withdrawn inland, as was the case at other sites. The documentary evidence suggests that by the tenth century Reculver was no longer an important church and had passed to the control of the West Saxon kings: a charter of 949 records King Eadred granting Reculver to Archbishop Oda and the Canterbury community.[82]

Ultimately, the former monastic church at Reculver remained a parish church until the events of the early nineteenth century described above, but it seems that at least two additional buildings with possible Anglo-Saxon origins formerly stood in the northern half of the fort. To the north-east of the church was a building known as the 'Chapel House', which incorporated Roman stonework and had an arch formed of Roman tile in the Anglo-Saxon fashion but was lost to the sea in 1802.[83] Similarly, a cottage to the west of the church, which engravings show incorporating an Anglo-Saxon doorway, was demolished in 1781.[84] It is possible that either or both buildings were contemporary, or even earlier, monastic buildings and may have functioned as additional churches, a trait that would be perfectly in keeping with the known topography of Anglo-Saxon minsters.[85]

Richborough

The Shore Fort at Richborough – Roman *Rutupiae* – is one of the best-preserved and most extensively excavated examples from the group. Located on a small island at the southern end of the Wantsum Channel, it is also the site that has the longest history, as Richborough was the landing point of the invading Claudian army in 43. The fort and its wider environs have been subject to considerable antiquarian and archaeological interest since the eighteenth century,[86] and were extensively excavated by Bushe-Fox and the Society of Antiquaries between 1922 and 1938.[87] More recently, the fort and its environs have been subject to an extensive campaign of geophysical survey and excavation which has shed new light upon the conclusions of the earlier work.[88] Excavations have revealed the defensive ditches of a first-century temporary camp, which was subsequently replaced by a military supply base. Around 85–90, space was cleared within the base for a large rectangular monument, which probably comprised a four-way triumphal arch celebrating the Roman conquest of Britain. During the second and third centuries, the supply base developed into an extensive town and port, complete with an amphitheatre to its south. In the later third century, the central part of the town was levelled, and the triumphal arch converted into a signal station. Around 270 this, too, was destroyed to make way for the construction of the Saxon Shore Fort.

The fort itself was rectangular, encompassing an area of around 4.5ha, and featured rounded corner bastions with projecting rectangular bastions spaced along the intervening lengths of wall. The walls of the fort survive on three sides, in places over 8m high, while the eastern wall and the eastern ends of the northern and southern walls have been lost to erosion.[89] The defences were more substantial and architecturally advanced than the other forts in the scheme, with the masonry from the former triumphal arch used to construct parts of the walls and decorate their facings. Despite extensive excavation, the interior layout of the fort is not well established, although the *principia* was located centrally on the site of the former great monument. A stone bath block and two other stone buildings were identified, and it is presumed that many of the other structures within the fort were of timber construction.[90]

The fort's administrative functions apparently broke down in the later fourth century, with the withdrawal of the Roman garrison, but the site continued to be occupied into the fifth century. During this period, a Roman rectangular timber Christian church with an apsidal chancel was founded within the north-western corner of the fort. This structure was overlooked during the original excavation but subsequently identified from site records, and was served by an external hexagonal baptismal font located to its north-east.[91] This church was relatively short-lived, and both it and the wider fort fell into disuse during the later fifth or early sixth centuries.

Having witnessed a brief Christian presence during the later Roman period, the abandoned fort became the focus of Christian activity during the seventh century. During the course of Bushe-Fox's excavation, the foundations of a small stone chapel were discovered in the eastern part of the fort, which later records indicate was dedicated to St Augustine, the missionary who had led the Gregorian mission to convert the Anglo-Saxons and who had reputedly landed in Thanet (some sources indicate at Richborough) in 597.[92] Although the earliest documentary references to this chapel are from later in the medieval period, and no architectural elements of the chapel survive, it is accepted that the foundation of the chapel was much earlier. Historical sources indicate that the chapel continued to be used until at least 1601 and also that it held a relic – a tile bearing the impression of a footprint – said to have been formed when Augustine first set foot on Kentish soil.

From its archaeological remains, in its final form the chapel of St Augustine comprised an apsidal-ended chancel, with nave and two western annexes, the inner interpreted as a porch and the outer perhaps housing a flight of steps. The apsidal chancel was a later addition, built around an earlier chancel, while the western wall of the nave also belonged to this earlier phase of construction, with the north and south walls of the nave having been rebuilt. In its original form, the chapel consisted of a rectangular chancel measuring 14ft × 10ft (4.2m × 3m), a nave measuring 36ft × 16ft (11m × 4.9m) and the two western annexes.[93]

The chapel was surrounded by a graveyard, with only one burial, that of a child, recorded within the building. Burials beneath the extensions to the building indicate that this cemetery belonged to the earlier phase of occupation. Stuart Rigold noted that a large number of seventh- to ninth-century coins were discovered in the vicinity of this cemetery, which he interpreted as coins placed in the graves or offerings from the chapel, in either case indicating that the chapel was an Anglo-Saxon foundation and very likely to share the same seventh-century origins as the other sites discussed here.[94] As the excavator, Barry Cunliffe, noted, 'it may well be that the first masonry chapel replaced an earlier timber structure dating back to the seventh century'.[95]

The religious reuse of roman structures

In Britain, associations between early ecclesiastical sites and extant Roman ruins have long been recognised, although it was not until the 1970s that they began to be studied in a systematic fashion.[96] Such associations are also commonplace in continental Europe, particularly Gaul and Italy, although it must be remembered that most of these European sites were continuously occupied from the Roman period onwards.[97] By contrast, within most of lowland England there was a distinct hiatus between the end of Roman occupation and this ecclesiastical reoccupation.[98] The evidence discussed above clearly indicates that the former Shore Forts were deliberately targeted by the early church, but why should early ecclesiastics have considered ruinous Roman sites to be such suitable locations for their foundations?

One traditionally cited explanation is the ready source of quarried stone that Roman buildings provided for the new churches.[99] While logistics were clearly a factor, in the neighbouring kingdom of East Anglia the building of stone churches did not begin in earnest until the late eleventh century, meaning that for 400 years church-builders had no need of quarried stone. It is true that once churches began to be built of stone in these areas Roman sites *were* quarried for their raw materials, but this is arguably a secondary process which has somewhat muddied the water. A more compelling explanation is to be found not in pragmatic considerations but in the symbolic connotations carried in the seventh century by all things Roman.

It is clear from wider historical sources that by the seventh century the Roman church had come to regard itself as the natural successor to the Imperial Roman state, in both actual and metaphorical senses, and from the evidence of his own writings Pope Gregory approached the conversion of the English not only as the evangelisation of a new people but also as the spiritual reclamation of a lost Roman province.[100] This sentiment was expressed very clearly in Gregory's letter to Augustine of 601, in which he set out a vision of a Christianised England that was based on the administrative structure of late Roman Britain: archbishoprics were to be established in London and York, the capitals of *Britannia Superior* and *Inferior* respectively, while additional bishoprics were to be founded in accordance with the network of regional *civitas* capitals.[101] Indeed Mellitus, a member of the mission, was appointed bishop of the East Saxons in 604 with his see in London, and presumably established the first missionary bases in the province.[102] Driven by this ideological approach – the pursuit of *Romanitas* – it is no surprise that on their arrival in Britain the missionaries of the Roman church should not only have recognised the extant remains of Roman buildings for what they were, but would have considered them to be extremely appropriate sites within which to found new Roman churches and literally attempt to rebuild Rome.[103]

Doubtless as a result of specific requests from the missionaries, many ruinous Roman forts became the subject of royal gifts so that they might be reoccupied and put to ecclesiastical use. As has been seen, many of the Saxon Shore Forts were reused in this manner, as were a considerable number of forts along Hadrian's Wall and elsewhere.[104] Nationwide, more than 46 early ecclesiastical sites, many of them directly attributable to missionaries of the Roman church, are associated with Roman forts or enclosures, while more than 200 other churches are associated with broader classes of Roman buildings.[105] In every case of a reappropriated fort it is the walled enclosure itself that seems to have been of greatest importance to the occupiers, rather than the presence of any particular building within it. Tellingly, these enclosures were not used for defensive purposes – indeed, many would not have been defensible by the seventh century – but the walls served to mark the boundary between the secular exterior world and the religious precinct within, while simultaneously providing a strong symbolic link with the Roman past.[106]

As well as an overarching ideology, within these wider statistics it is clear that we are not witnessing a single homogenised approach to the reuse of Roman sites, just as we do not see a single conversion to Christianity. As several regional studies of religious conversion have demonstrated, the ways in which Christianity took root were many and various, as new ideologies and practices were mapped onto those of the existing population.[107] Such regional variation is also evident in the sites discussed here, with the historical development, architectural and archaeological remains of St Peter's Chapel being much more akin to those at Reculver and Canterbury than they are to those at the East Anglian sites at Walton Castle, Burgh Castle and Caister-on-Sea.

In the cases of Bradwell and Reculver, we are arguably seeing the direct Romanising influence of the Augustinian mission on the early church in Kent and Essex. Bede tells us that at the time of Augustine's arrival in 597, King Ethelbert of Kent's wife was a practising Christian, with her own church of St Martin on the outskirts of Canterbury, which she shared with the missionaries on their arrival.[108] Augustine was subsequently granted a church, said to be of Roman origin, which was still standing in Canterbury and this was appropriated as the new cathedral.[109] After this, he was granted land on which he founded his own monastery dedicated to SS Peter and Paul.[110] Around 620, still in Canterbury, the church of St Mary was constructed to the east of the abbey church,[111] and shortly afterwards, further to the east, the church of St Pancras was built.[112] The striking architectural similarities between many of these churches, including those at Bradwell and Reculver, have often led to them being discussed as a group, variously referred to as 'St Pancras Type', 'Augustinian Type' or simply 'Kentish' churches.[113]

While such discussions can be rightly criticised for focusing on similarities rather than differences, they are indicative of a unifying ideological approach taken to the foundation of new churches which was established in the decades following the Augustinian mission.[114] Indeed, it is notable that the churches that exhibit the closest similarities are second- and third-generation churches, dating from the middle decades of the seventh century, rather than from the immediate aftermath of Augustine's arrival. Architecturally, these phases are also distinguished by the use of Gallic-influenced architectural features in the earliest missionary churches, giving way to distinctly Italianate architectural styling in the mid-seventh century. Eric Cambridge has argued convincingly that this reflects a shift away from an initial phase of royal patronage into a more consolidated phase of church-building led by subsequent waves of Continental missionaries, and the strong preference for the reoccupation of Roman sites noted here was also an intrinsic part of this cultural appropriation.[115]

We see a different picture in the kingdom of East Anglia, where a timber architectural tradition at odds with that of Kent and Essex prevailed, and consequently no traces of any similar Anglo-Saxon churches have been found inside the East Anglian Shore Forts. Their equivalent must surely have existed, and their absence may be explained by the organic nature of the original structures and the subsequent disturbance that occurred at each site. In this regard, it is notable that in all three of the East Anglian examples discussed here the later medieval church was founded outside the walls of the associated Roman fort, indicating that, unlike their stone equivalents, timber churches were much more impermanent and consequently more easily abandoned or relocated. At Walton Castle there is historical evidence for the survival of the church until the Norman Conquest, but the disruption of the dioceses caused by the tenth-century Viking incursions and the fact that only the later diocese of Elmham was refounded indicate that whatever remained at *Dommoc* had diminished greatly since its seventh-century heyday. Following the Conquest, a land swap saw the fort at Walton converted into a castle and the medieval church was established outside the walls. Similarly, the sites at Burgh Castle and Caister-on-Sea both appear to have floundered during the late Anglo-Saxon period and it is possible that they, too, fell victim to the Viking raids, either directly or via precautionary measures taken against attack from the sea. In the case of Burgh Castle, there is further evidence for a similar land swap occurring when the fort was converted to a castle following the Norman Conquest and the church relocated (see Figure 5.4). One wonders how different these sites would appear today had stone churches been constructed within them during the seventh century.

Taken together, it is clear that the former Saxon Shore Forts played an instrumental part in the evangelisation of their respective territories, as did other forts elsewhere, and once early ecclesiastics had occupied these Roman enclosures, they became stations from which missionaries could begin their work within the local population. A good indication of the degree of success enjoyed by these early missionaries is provided by the extent of the Christian cemeteries associated with some of the Roman sites described above. For example, excavations at Burgh Castle revealed a cemetery containing several hundred burials, and the intramural cemetery at Caister-on-Sea was of a similar size, while the extramural cemetery was much larger, comprising hundreds or even thousands of burials. From the quantity of burials discovered it would seem that each of these sites had a zone of influence that extended far beyond its walls, with individuals from the surrounding area being buried within or close to the fort. However, the later histories of all of the sites discussed here suggest that, after the initial phase of the conversion effort in the seventh century, the significance placed on the reoccupation of former Roman forts waned as the Church became more widely established and Christianity became engrained in Anglo-Saxon society. As has been seen, in some cases the churches founded as part of the conversion effort continued to thrive, as was the case at Reculver until the nineteenth century, while in other cases, such as at Bradwell and Richborough, the churches fell out of use and were repurposed or demolished, so that only architectural ruins or archaeological remains survive.

Finally, while reoccupied Roman sites such as those discussed here were important, they represent only part of the wider picture of conversion and the establishment of the Anglo-Saxon Church. Although Roman sites were clearly attractive to the early waves of Christian missionaries for a variety of reasons, that is not to say they were occupied to the exclusion of other sites, and there are many sites that were either converted to a Christian purpose or founded anew during the conversion period. In many cases, reoccupied Roman sites are only the most archaeologically obvious form of site employed in this manner and, because of their visibility, happen to be the sites that have attracted the most archaeological attention. As is apparent from the preceding discussions, in many instances the evidence for the Christian reuse of Short Forts has been an incidental discovery made while investigating the Roman phases, and there is a genuine concern that much ephemeral material pertaining to these later phases has been stripped away, unrecorded.

Conclusion

The Roman withdrawal from Britain in the early fifth century did not result in the erasure of the existing Roman infrastructure, and the Anglo-Saxon landscape contained the remains of Roman towns, villas, settlements and roads. Many of these were old even at the end of the Roman period and by the seventh century would have been in poor condition, if not entirely ruinous. Dilapidated Roman masonry buildings, sometimes of immense size, would have been particularly awe-inspiring in a period characterised by modest timber architecture; small wonder, then, that later Anglo-Saxon poets referred to such ruins as *enta geweorc* – 'the work of giants'.[116]

When Roman Christianity was reintroduced to these shores by the arrival of Augustine in Kent in 597, these Roman ruins were identified and reappropriated by early missionaries, who at Pope Gregory's behest were driven by an ideological desire to evangelise the Anglo-Saxons while at the same time reclaiming the lost Roman province of *Britannia*. During the first half of the seventh century the conversion effort expanded rapidly from its south-eastern bridgehead, and this is the context within which the former Saxon Shore Forts discussed here, together with numerous other Roman sites, were reoccupied and put to Christian use.

Whether it represents the monastery founded by Cedd in 653 or a second-generation building dating from later in the seventh century, Bradwell's chapel of St Peter-on-the-Wall is one of the best-preserved and most significant buildings from this period in southern England. Irrespective of its true origins, the chapel is a very rare survival and contributes greatly to our understanding of the early church in south-eastern England, both in terms of what we can learn about the site itself and also in terms of what it can tell us about the other sites discussed here with which it has many elements in common. Although each site has a unique history and local context, such comparisons enable the identification of overarching themes within the conversion effort, in which Roman forts clearly played an important part in cementing the ideology of the Roman church among the Anglo-Saxon people. Despite over 150 years of archaeological interest, there is still a lot more for us to learn about the religious landscape of the seventh century, and, like its dedicatee, St Peter's Chapel holds one of the keys.

Notes

1 Taylor and Taylor 1965, 91–3; Andrews, in this volume.
2 Mayr-Harting 1991; Fletcher 1997; Gameson 1999; Yorke 2006; Dunn 2009; Hoggett 2010a.
3 White 1961; Johnson 1976; Johnson 1977; Maxfield 1989; Pearson 2002, 2003; Fields 2006; Historic England 2018; Pearson, in this volume.
4 Rigold 1977; Rodwell and Rodwell 1977; Morris and Roxan 1980; Morris 1983, 40–5; Rodwell 1984; Blair 1992, 235–46, 2005, 188–90; Bell 1998, 2005; Hoggett 2010a, 2010b; Semple 2013, 131–8; Fafinski 2021.
5 For example, Morris 1983, 43–5; Eaton 2000.
6 Historic England 2018. On possible non-defensive functions see Pearson, in this volume.
7 White 1961, 33–55; Johnson 1976, 34–63; Pearson 2002, 11–38.
8 Darling with Gurney 1993; Pearson 2002, 15–16; Hassall 1977, 8.
9 Green 1961; Burnham 1989; Pearson 2002, 99–124.
10 Johnson 1976, 134–56; Pearson 2002, 167–70.
11 Johnson 1976, 153–6; Pearson 2002, 170.
12 Green 1961; Burnham 1989; Fulford et al. 1997; Pearson 2002, 99–124; Murphy 2014.
13 Goodall 2018; Porter 2020; Johnson 1983; Fairclough and Plunkett 2000.
14 Rigold 1977.
15 Rigold 1977.
16 Bell 1998, 2005.
17 Hoggett 2010a, 2010b.
18 Rigold 1977; Bell 1998, 2005; Hoggett 2010a.
19 National Heritage List for England entry no. 1013834. On the fort and its wider landscape setting see Pearson and Rippon, in this volume.
20 Colgrave and Mynors 1969, 278–81 (III, 21).
21 Colgrave and Mynors 1969, 281–5, quote at 285 (III, 22).
22 Scull et al. 2016.
23 Lewin 1867, 447–8; Chancellor 1877; Laver 1909; Taylor and Taylor 1965, 91–3; Andrews, in this volume.
24 Lewin 1867, 448–9.
25 For example, Peers 1901; Baldwin Brown 1925, 101–2; Rigold 1977, 72–3; Cambridge 1999; Bell 2005, 196.
26 Gallyon 1973; Hoggett 2010a, 2010b.
27 Hoggett 2010a, 2010b.
28 Fox 1911, 287–91; Johnson 1976, 41–3; Fairclough and Plunkett 2000, 419–26; Pearson 2002, 19–21.
29 Stenton 1959; Dumville 1976.
30 Colgrave and Mynors 1969, 189–91 (II, 15).
31 Williams 2001; Carver and Fern 2005.
32 Colgrave and Mynors 1969, 189–91 (II, 15).
33 Colgrave and Mynors 1969, 267–9 (III, 18).
34 Colgrave and Mynors 1969, 189–91 (II, 15).
35 Colgrave and Mynors 1969, 189–91 (II, 15).
36 Colgrave and Mynors 1969, 189–91 (II, 15).
37 Colgrave and Mynors 1969, 349–55 (IV, 5).
38 Rigold 1962; Wade-Martins 1980.
39 Rigold 1961, 1974; Haslam 1992; Hoggett 2010a, 35–44.
40 Haddan and Stubbs 1871, 546–7; Campbell 1979, 40; Rigold 1961, 57–8, 1974, 9.
41 Rigold 1961, 59.
42 Rigold 1974, 98–100; Davison 1974, 142–3; Pestell 1999, 303–4; Fairclough and Plunkett 2000, 451–2.
43 Davison 1974, 143.
44 West 1974.
45 Wade-Martins 1980, 3–11.
46 Colgrave and Mynors 1969, 269–76 (III, 19).
47 Campbell 1979, 35–7; Hoggett 2010a, 44–6.
48 Johnson 1983, 60–5. Hoggett 2010a, 56–60.

49 Johnson 1976, 37–41; Pearson 2002, 17–19.
50 Johnson 1983, 43–5.
51 Johnson 1983, 118–20.
52 Harrod 1859; Johnson 1983.
53 Johnson 1983, 7–8.
54 Johnson 1983, 37–9.
55 Johnson 1983, 55–60.
56 Johnson 1983, 111–12; Jordan et al. 1994, 27–8.
57 Wallis 1998.
58 Pearson 2002, 15–16; Darling with Gurney 1993, 8–15.
59 Darling with Gurney 1993, 37–45.
60 Rumbelow 1938, 180–2.
61 Rumbelow 1938, 180–2; Darling with Gurney 1993, 45.
62 Darling with Gurney 1993, 45–61.
63 Darling with Gurney 1993, 252.
64 Pevsner and Wilson 1997, 424–6.
65 Rigold 1977, 73; Bell 2005, 210.
66 Amos and Wheeler 1929; Johnson 1976, 51–3; Pearson 2002, 29–31.
67 Roach Smith 1850; Johnson 1976, 53–6; Cunliffe 1980; Hutchinson et al. 1985; Pearson 2002, 31–4.
68 Rigold 1977, 73.
69 Johnson 1976, 45–8; Pearson 2002, 24–5; Philip 1981, 2005.
70 Dowker 1878b; Taylor and Taylor 1965, 503–9.
71 Dowker 1878b; Taylor and Taylor 1965, 503–9; Kelly 2008, 67.
72 Roach Smith 1850; Dowker 1878a, 1878b; Peers 1928; Jessup 1936; Thompson 1953; Philip 2005, 11–13.
73 Philip 2005.
74 Dowker 1878b; Peers 1928; Taylor and Taylor 1965.
75 Roach Smith 1850, 197; Taylor and Taylor 1965, fig. 248.
76 Kent Archaeological Society 1860; Taylor and Taylor 1965; Kozodoy 1986, 69.
77 Peers 1928; Clapham 1951; Taylor 1968; Kozodoy 1986.
78 Kozodoy 1986; Taylor 1968; Kelly 2008, 80–1.
79 Swanton 2000, 34–5; Kelly 2008, 71–2.
80 Kelly 2008, 74–80.
81 Kelly 2008, 80–1.
82 Kelly 2008, 81–2.
83 Kelly 2008, 70.
84 Kelly 2008, 70.
85 Blair 1992.
86 Pearce 1968.
87 Bushe-Fox 1926, 1928, 1932, 1949; Cunliffe 1968.
88 Wilmott and Smither 2020.
89 Wilmott and Smither 2020.
90 Johnson 1976, 48–51; Johnson 1981; Philip 1981; Pearson 2002, 26–8.
91 Brown 1971.
92 Bushe-Fox 1928, 34–40.
93 Bushe-Fox 1928, 34–40.
94 Rigold 1968, 1977; Bell 2005, 233.
95 Cunliffe 1968, 251.
96 Rigold 1977; Rodwell and Rodwell 1977; Morris and Roxan 1980; Morris 1983, 40–5; Rodwell 1984; Blair 1992, 235–46; Bell 1998, 2005; Fafinski 2021.
97 For example, James 1981; Percival 1997.
98 Bell 2005, 38–68; Dunn 2009, 43–56.
99 Morris 1983, 43–5; Eaton 2000, 10–35.
100 Bell 2005, 26–7.
101 Martyn 2004, 11–39.
102 Colgrave and Mynors 1969, 142–3 (II, 3).
103 Blair 1988, 44, 1992, 235–46, 2005, 188–90; Bell 1998, 5–8, 2005, 16–22; Semple 2013, 132–6; Fafinski 2021.

104 Rigold 1977; Bell 1998, 14–15.
105 Bell 2005.
106 Blair 1988, 46, 1992, 235–41, 2005, 188–90; Bell 1998, 15–16; Semple 2013, 132–8; Fafinski 2021.
107 For example, Yorke 2006; Dunn 2009; Hoggett 2010a.
108 Taylor and Taylor 1965, 143–5.
109 St John Hope 1918; Taylor and Taylor 1965, 148.
110 Taylor and Taylor 1965, 134–43.
111 Taylor and Taylor 1965, 145.
112 Taylor and Taylor 1965, 146–8.
113 Micklethwaite 1896; Peers 1901, 1929; Fernie 1983, 34–9; Cambridge 1999.
114 Cambridge 1999.
115 Cambridge 1999.
116 Grocock 2015.

Bibliography

Amos, E. G. J., and R. E. M. Wheeler. 1929. 'The Saxon-Shore fortress at Dover'. *Archaeological Journal* 86: 47–58.
Baldwin Brown, G. 1925. *The Arts in Early England: Anglo-Saxon architecture*. 2nd ed. London: John Murray.
Bell, T. 1998. 'Churches on Roman buildings: Christian associations and Roman masonry in Anglo-Saxon England'. *Medieval Archaeology* 42: 1–18.
Bell, T. 2005. *The Religious Reuse of Roman Structures in Early Medieval England*. Oxford: British Archaeological Reports.
Blair, J. 1988. 'Minster churches in the landscape'. In *Anglo-Saxon Settlements*, edited by D. Hooke. 35–58. Oxford: Blackwell.
Blair, J. 1992. 'Anglo-Saxon minsters: a topographical review'. In *Pastoral Care before the Parish*, edited by J. Blair and R. Sharpe. 226–66. Leicester: Leicester University Press.
Blair, J. 2005. *The Church in Anglo-Saxon Society*. Oxford: Oxford University Press.
Brown, P. 1971. 'The church at Richborough'. *Britannia* 2: 225–31.
Burnham, C. P. 1989. 'The coast of south-east England in Roman times'. In *The Saxon Shore: A handbook*, edited by V. A. Maxfield. 12–17. Exeter: University of Exeter Press.
Bushe-Fox, J. P. 1926. *First Report on the Excavation of the Roman Fort at Richborough, Kent*. Oxford: Society of Antiquaries.
Bushe-Fox, J. P. 1928. *Second Report on the Excavation of the Roman Fort at Richborough, Kent*. Oxford: Society of Antiquaries.
Bushe-Fox, J. P. 1932. *Third Report on the Excavation of the Roman Fort at Richborough, Kent*. Oxford: Society of Antiquaries.
Bushe-Fox, J. P. 1949. *Fourth Report on the Excavation of the Roman Fort at Richborough, Kent*. Oxford: Society of Antiquaries.
Cambridge, E. 1999. 'The architecture of the Augustinian mission'. In *St Augustine and the Conversion of England*, edited by R. Gameson. 202–36. Stroud: Sutton Publishing.
Campbell, J. 1979. 'Bede's words for places'. In *Names, Words and Graves*, edited by P. Sawyer. 34–54. Leeds: University of Leeds.
Carver, M. and C. Fern. 2005. 'The seventh-century burial rites and their sequence'. In *Sutton Hoo: A seventh-century princely burial ground and its context*, edited by M. Carver. 283–313. London: British Museum Press.
Chancellor, F. 1877. 'St Peter's on the Wall, Bradwell Juxta Mare'. *Archaeological Journal* 34(1): 212–18.
Clapham, A. 1951. 'Some disputed examples of pre-Conquest sculpture'. *Antiquity* 25(100): 191–5.
Colgrave, B., and R. A. B. Mynors (ed. and trans.). 1969. *Bede's Ecclesiastical History of the English People*. Oxford: Clarendon Press.
Cunliffe, B. (ed.) 1968. *Fifth Report on the Excavation of the Roman Fort at Richborough, Kent*. Oxford: Society of Antiquaries.
Cunliffe, B. 1980. 'Excavations at the Roman fort at Lympne, Kent 1976–8'. *Britannia* 11: 227–88.

Darling, M., with D. Gurney. 1993. *Caister-on-Sea Excavations by Charles Green, 1951–55*. Gressenhall: East Anglian Archaeology.

Davison, K. 1974. 'History of Walton Priory'. *Proceedings of the Suffolk Institute of Archaeology* 33(2): 141–9.

Dowker, G. 1878a. 'The Roman castrum at Reculver'. *Archaeologia Cantiana* 12: 1–13.

Dowker, G. 1878b. 'Reculver church'. *Archaeologia Cantiana* 12: 248–68.

Dumville, D. 1976. 'The Anglian collection of royal genealogies and regnal lists'. *Anglo-Saxon England* 5: 23–50.

Dunn, M. 2009. *The Christianization of the Anglo Saxons c. 597–c. 700*. London: Continuum.

Eaton, T. 2000. *Plundering the Past: Roman stonework in medieval Britain*. Stroud: Tempus.

Fafinski, M. *Roman Infrastructure in Early Medieval Britain*. Amsterdam: Amsterdam University Press, 2021.

Fairclough, J., and S. Plunkett. 2000. 'Drawings of Walton Castle and other monuments in Walton and Felixstowe'. *Proceedings of the Suffolk Institute of Archaeology and History* 39(4): 419–59.

Farmer, D. H. 2004. 'Cedd'. *ODNB*. Online edition: https://doi.10.1093/ref.odnb/29986 [accessed 10 March 2022].

Fernie, E. 1983. *The Architecture of the Anglo-Saxons*. London: Batsford.

Fields, N. 2006. *Rome's Saxon Shore: Coastal defences of Roman Britain, AD 250–500*. Oxford: Osprey Publishing.

Fletcher, R. 1997. *The Conversion of Europe: From paganism to Christianity, 371–1386*. London: Harper Collins.

Fox, G. 1911. 'Romano-British Suffolk'. In *VCH Suffolk* I, edited by W. Page. 279–320. London: Constable.

Fulford, M., T. Champion and A. Long (eds). 1997. *England's Coastal Heritage*. London: English Heritage.

Gallyon, M. 1973. *The Early Church in Eastern England*. Lavenham: Terence Dalton.

Gameson, R. (ed.) 1999. *St Augustine and the Conversion of England*. Stroud: Sutton Publishing.

Goodall, J. 2018. *Portchester Castle*. London: English Heritage.

Green, C. 1961. 'East Anglian coast-line levels since Roman times'. *Antiquity* 35: 21–8.

Grocock, C. 2015. '*Enta geweorc*: the ruin and its contexts reconsidered'. In *The Material Culture of the Built Environment in the Anglo-Saxon World*, edited by M. Clegg Hyer and G. R. Owen-Crocker. 13–36. Liverpool: Liverpool University Press.

Haddan, A., and W. Stubbs (eds). 1871. *Councils and Ecclesiastical Documents Relating to Great Britain and Ireland*, vol. III. Oxford: Clarendon Press.

Harrod, H. 1859. 'Excavations made at Burgh Castle, Suffolk, in the years 1850 and 1855'. *Norfolk Archaeology* 5: 146–60.

Haslam, J. 1992. '*Dommoc* and Dunwich: a reappraisal'. *Anglo-Saxon Studies in Archaeology and History* 5: 41–5.

Hassall, M. 1977. 'The historical background and military units of the Saxon Shore'. In *The Saxon Shore*, edited by D. E. Johnson. 7–10. London: Council for British Archaeology.

Historic England. 2018. *Saxon Short Forts: Introductions to heritage assets*. Swindon: Historic England.

Hoggett, R. 2010a. *The Archaeology of the East Anglian Conversion*. Woodbridge: Boydell.

Hoggett, R. 2010b. 'The early Christian landscape of East Anglia'. In *The Landscape Archaeology of Anglo-Saxon England*, edited by N. J. Higham and M. J. Ryan. 193–210. Woodbridge: Boydell & Brewer.

Hutchinson, J. N., C. Poole, N. Lambert and E. N. Bromhead. 1985. 'Combined archaeological and geotechnical investigations of the Roman fort at Lympne, Kent'. *Britannia* 16: 209–36.

James, E. 1981. 'Archaeology and the Merovingian monastery'. In *Columbanus and Merovingian Monasticism*, edited by H. Clarke and M. Brennan. 33–55. Oxford: BAR International Series 113.

Jessup, R. F. 1936. 'Reculver'. *Antiquity* 10(38): 179–94.

Johnson, D. E. (ed.) 1977. *The Saxon Shore*. Research Report 18. London: Council for British Archaeology.

Johnson, S. 1976. *The Roman Forts of the Saxon Shore*. London: Paul Elek.

Johnson, S. 1979. *The Roman Forts of the Saxon Shore*. 2nd ed. London: Paul Elek.

Johnson, S. 1981. 'The construction of the Saxon Shore Fort at Richborough'. In *Collectanea Historica: Essays in memory of Stuart Rigold*, edited by A. Detsicas. 23–31. Maidstone: Kent Archaeological Society.

Johnson, S. 1983. *Burgh Castle: Excavations by Charles Green 1958–61*. Gressenhall: East Anglian Archaeology.
Jordan, D., D. Haddon-Reece and A. Bayliss. 1994. *Radiocarbon Dates*. London: English Heritage.
Kelly, S. 2008. 'Reculver Minster and its early charters'. In *Myth, Rulership, Church and Charters: Essays in honour of Nicholas Brooks*, edited by J. Barrow and A. Wareham. 67–82. Aldershot: Ashgate Publishing.
Kent Archaeological Society. 1860. 'The columns of Reculver church'. *Archaeologia Cantiana* 3: 135–6.
Kozodoy, R. 1986. 'The Reculver cross'. *Archaeologia* 108: 67–94.
Laver, H. 1909. 'St Peter's Chapel, Bradwell-on-Sea'. *Transactions of the Essex Archaeological Society* 11(2): 85–9.
Lewin, T. 1867. 'On the castra of the *Littus Saxonicum*, and particularly the castrum of *Othona*'. *Archaeologia* 41(2): 421–52.
Martyn, J. (ed. and trans.) 2004. *The Letters of Gregory the Great*. 3 vols. Toronto: Pontifical Institute of Mediaeval Studies.
Maxfield, V. A. (ed.) 1989. *The Saxon Shore: A handbook*. Exeter: University of Exeter Press.
Mayr-Harting, H. 1991. *The Coming of Christianity to Anglo-Saxon England*. 3rd ed. Philadelphia: Pennsylvania State University Press.
Micklethwaite, J. T. 1896. 'Something about Saxon church building'. *Archaeological Journal* 53: 293–351.
Morris, R. 1983. *The Church in British Archaeology*. York: Council for British Archaeology.
Morris, R., and J. Roxan. 1980. 'Churches on Roman sites'. In *Temples, Churches and Religion*, edited by W. Rodwell. 175–209. Oxford: British Archaeological Reports.
Murphy, P. 2014. *England's Coastal Heritage: A review of progress since 1997*. London: English Heritage.
Pearce, B. W. 1968. 'The history of excavation at Richborough'. In *Fifth Report on the Excavation of the Roman Fort at Richborough, Kent*, edited by B. Cunliffe. 251–3. Oxford: Society of Antiquaries.
Pearson, A. 2002. *The Roman Shore Forts: Coastal defences of southern Britain*. Stroud: Tempus Publishing.
Pearson, A. 2003. *The Construction of the Saxon Shore Forts*. BAR British Series 349. Oxford: British Archaeological Reports.
Peers, C. R. 1901. 'On Saxon churches of the St Pancras Type'. *Archaeological Journal* 58: 402–34.
Peers, C. R. 1928. 'Reculver: Its Saxon church and cross'. *Archaeologia* 77: 241–56.
Peers, C. R. 1929. 'The earliest Christian churches in England'. *Antiquity* 3(9): 65–74.
Percival, J. 1997. 'Villas and monasteries in late Roman Gaul'. *Journal of Ecclesiastical History* 48: 1–21.
Pestell, T. 1999. 'An Analysis of Monastic Foundation in East Anglia c. 650–1200'. Unpublished PhD thesis, University of East Anglia.
Pevsner, N., and B. Wilson. 1997. *Norfolk I: Norwich and North-East*. London: Penguin.
Philip, B. 1981. 'Richborough, Reculver and Lympne: a reconsideration of three of Kent's late Roman shore-forts'. In *Collectanea Historica: Essays in memory of Stuart Rigold*, edited by A. Detsicas. 41–9. Maidstone: Kent Archaeological Society.
Philip, B. 2005. *The Excavation of the Roman Fort at Reculver*. Dover: Kent Archaeological Rescue Unit.
Porter, R. 2020. *Pevensey Castle*. London: English Heritage.
Rigold, S. 1961. 'The supposed see of Dunwich'. *Journal of the British Archaeological Association* 24: 55–9.
Rigold, S. 1962. 'The Anglian cathedral of North Elmham, Norfolk'. *Medieval Archaeology* 6: 67–108.
Rigold, S. 1968. 'The post-Roman coins'. In *Fifth Report on the Excavation of the Roman Fort at Richborough, Kent*, edited by B. Cunliffe. 217–23. Oxford: Society of Antiquaries.
Rigold, S. 1974. 'Further evidence about the site of "*Dommoc*"'. *Journal of the British Archaeological Association* 37: 97–102.
Rigold, S. 1977. '*Litus Romanum* – the Shore Forts as mission stations'. In *The Saxon Shore*, edited by D. E. Johnson. 70–5. London: Council for British Archaeology.
Roach Smith, C. 1850. *The Antiquities of Richborough, Reculver, and Lymne*. London: John Russell Smith.

Rodwell, W. 1984. 'Churches in the landscape: aspects of topography and planning'. In *Studies in Late Anglo-Saxon Settlement*, edited by M. Faull. 1–23. Oxford: Oxford University Department of External Studies.

Rodwell, W., and K. Rodwell. 1977. *Historic Churches: A wasting asset*. London: Council for British Archaeology.

Rose, E. 1985. 'A note on the demolition of the walls of the Roman fort'. In *Excavations at Brancaster 1974 and 1977*, edited by J. Hinchcliffe with C. Green. 188–9. Gressenhall: East Anglian Archaeology.

Rumbelow, P. 1938. 'Finds on a Roman site at Caister-on-Sea, Norfolk'. *Norfolk Archaeology* 26: 178–82.

St John Hope, W. 1918. 'The plan and arrangement of the first cathedral church of Canterbury'. *Proceedings of the Society of Antiquaries* 30: 136–58.

Scull, C., F. Minter and J. Plouviez. 2016. 'Social and economic complexity in early medieval England: a central place complex of the East Anglian kingdom at Rendlesham, Suffolk'. *Antiquity* 90: 1594–1612.

Semple, S. 2013. *Perceptions of the Prehistoric in Anglo-Saxon England*. Oxford: Oxford University Press.

Stenton, F. 1959. 'The East Anglian kings of the seventh century'. In *The Anglo-Saxons*, edited by P. Clemoes. 43–52. London: Bowes and Bowes.

Swanton, M. (trans. and ed.) 2000. *The Anglo-Saxon Chronicles*. London: Phoenix Press.

Taylor, H. M. 1968. 'Reculver reconsidered'. *Archaeological Journal* 125: 291–6.

Taylor, H. M., and J. Taylor. 1965. *Anglo-Saxon Architecture*, vol. I. Cambridge: Cambridge University Press.

Thompson, F. H. 1953. 'Excavations at Reculver, Kent, 1951'. *Archaeologia Cantiana* 66: 52–60.

Wade-Martins, P. 1980. *Excavations in North Elmham Park, 1967–1972*. Gressenhall: East Anglian Archaeology.

Wallis, H. 1998. 'Excavations at Church Loke, Burgh Castle, 1993–4'. *Norfolk Archaeology* 43: 62–78.

West, S. 1974. 'The excavation of Walton Priory'. *Proceedings of the Suffolk Institute of Archaeology* 33(2): 131–52.

White, D. A. 1961. *Litus Saxonicum: The British Saxon Shore in scholarship and history*. Madison, WI: The State Historical Society of Wisconsin.

Williams, H. 2001. 'Death, memory and time: a consideration of mortuary practices at Sutton Hoo'. In *Time in the Middle Ages*, edited by C. Humphrey and W. M. Ormrod. 35–71. Woodbridge: Boydell.

Wilmott, T., and Smither, P. 2020. 'The plan of the Saxon Shore Fort at Richborough'. *Britannia* 51: 147–74.

Yorke, B. 2006. *The Conversion of Britain, 600–800*. Harlow: Pearson Education.

6
Early medieval monasteries on the North Sea coast of Anglo-Saxon England
David Petts

Today, the journey to Bradwell involves leaving the A roads and heading off down country lanes, and out into the flat landscapes of the Tillingham and Bradwell Marshes, seated between the slow estuarine flows of the Blackwater and the Crouch. This is 'deep Essex'. As the tarmac gives way to gravel and the sight, sound and smell of the North Sea envelops the senses, it is hard to resist the feeling of coming to the edge of things. Marsh and coast are liminal locations par excellence – constantly in a state of flux, neither truly land nor truly sea. Indeed, for those in search of the spiritual, Bradwell is a classic 'thin place', where the divide between this world and a world beyond is at its most attenuated. For the modern viewer, Bradwell is indeed a liminal place, both physically and spiritually.

However, this physical sense of the Dengie Peninsula being remote, distant, isolated, is not inherent in the topography of the site. In this chapter, I want to reorientate our perception of Bradwell – rather than framing it as somewhere on the edge, I want to place it, and other early medieval monastic coastal sites, as places at the centre of things. To do this, we need to move away from perceptions of space underpinned by terrestrial points of view, and instead to navigate our ways through the land- and seascapes of an early medieval world, where the sea was central. In particular, I want to argue that the middle Anglian period (600–800) was one where the coast of southern and eastern England from the Humber to the Solent saw the emergence of a new relationship between human societies and the coast, not just spiritually but also socially and economically. This new turn to the coast in the seventh century was one that transcended monastic sites, to encompass other forms of exchange and the exploitation of economic resources.

Monasteries and seascapes

Although Christianity initially emerged in the arid landscapes of Palestine, its wider expansion soon meant that early ecclesiastical sites had to engage with the sea- and island-scapes of the East Mediterranean. Eremitic ascetic practice spread across the islands both sides of Italy.[1] By the early fifth century, island monasticism had reached the western Mediterranean, most notably at les Îles Lérins, off Cannes, founded by Honoratus by 410, with monasteries on Île Saint-Honorat and Île Sainte-Marguerite, and it was soon joined by other insular ecclesiastical sites further west along the coast on the Îles d'Hyères.[2] Given Lérins' connections with late antique British churchmen, it is no surprise that island monasteries should be such a feature of early Christianity in Ireland and western Britain.[3] Here, many of the most important early monastic sites were located on islands – most spectacularly Columba's late sixth-century foundation on Iona, off the western tip of Mull (Argyll, Scotland), but also sites such as Inishmurray, High Island, Illaunloughan and the striking Sceilig St Michael.[4] It has been persuasively argued that we see not just the transplantation of a Mediterranean insular monastic tradition to the colder waters of the North Atlantic, but also a dialogue with existing indigenous practices that had long imbued islands – both natural and artificial (crannogs) – with a seam of ritual significance and symbolic importance.[5] This grafting of exogenous and endogenous attitudes to sanctifying island and maritime space became embedded in the ritual geography and cosmogony of the Irish church. It is thus not surprising that, when Oswald brought the Irish tradition of Christianity to Northumbria in the 630s, with the assistance of monks from Iona, his first establishments should both have been on small, offshore, tidal islands: Lindisfarne and Hartlepool (the latter now no longer an island, but clearly surrounded by the sea in the seventh century).[6]

Over the seventh and eighth centuries, an enthusiasm for planting monastic sites on coastal or estuarine sites along the North Sea coast became embedded in Northumbrian ecclesiastical tradition.[7] The pre-Viking monastic sites at Abercorn, Aberlady, Tyninghame, Auldhame, Coldingham, Lindisfarne, Alnmouth, Tynemouth, Jarrow, Monkwearmouth, Hartlepool, Whitby and possibly Filey were all situated in immediate proximity to the sea.[8] Offshore islands were also extensively co-opted for religious use – both for communal and eremitical purposes. An early medieval religious presence has been adduced for a number of islands in and around the Firth of Forth, including the Isle of May, Inchcolm and Bass Rock, as well as, further south, the Inner Farne and Coquet Island off the coast of Northumberland.[9] In some cases, such as at Lindisfarne, the coalescing of multiple littoral and insular ecclesiastical sites, including Lindisfarne itself, St Cuthbert's Island, Inner Farne and probable early medieval church sites at Tweedmouth and Beadnell, resulted in the development of distinct maritime seascapes of sanctity held together by visual intervisibility, regular communication between sites and economic interdependence.[10] It is quite possible that a similar land-/seascape of ecclesiastical activity continued further down the east coast of southern Northumbria, but here the encroachment of the sea has led to considerable coastal erosion, destroying any potential survival of archaeological evidence. Documentary sources certainly attest to the presence of a hermitage inhabited by Wilgils (father of St Willibrord) 'on the headlands that are bounded by the North Sea and the river Humber'.[11]

Given the Irish and Northumbrian predisposition to coastal locations, it is no surprise that, as mission from the north and west extended into East Anglia and southern England, key ecclesiastical establishments should be established on coastal and tidal riverine locations. The earliest coastal foundation was probably Saint Felix's *Dommoc* (probably Walton, near Felixstowe, or possibly Dunwich – both Suffolk) established *c.* 629–31.[12] While Felix had come from landlocked Burgundy, he was probably influenced by Columbanus, who had himself once been resident at the coastal monastery of Bangor (County Down). More direct Irish influence came in the form of Fursa, who, like Felix, received royal patronage from Sigebert, king of East Anglia. It was Sigebert, *c.* 630, who gave him the site of *Cnobheresburg* – probably Burgh Castle, near Great Yarmouth – also on the coast.[13] Thus, when the Northumbrian mission started its engagement with southern and eastern England, they entered a milieu that already featured coastal monasticism. When Sigebert *Sanctus* (king of the East Saxons) gave Cedd the site of *Ythancæstir* (Othona) in 653, he seems to have been mimicking his East Anglian namesake in planting monastic sites within old Roman coastal forts.[14] Meanwhile, Cedd's foundation at Tilbury was on the lower reaches of the Thames, also in a low-lying, watery, tidal landscape.[15] Even before Wilfrid converted ostensibly pagan Sussex, there was already a monastery at Bosham (West Sussex) under Dicul, an Irish monk. Its location was described as surrounded by woods and the sea ('silvis et mari circumdatum').[16] When Wilfrid founded his first monastery in the kingdom, it too was in a coastal location. Bede described the peninsular position of this new foundation at Selsey ('Island of the Sea Cows') in detail.[17]

Between the interstices of these known, datable coastal ecclesiastical sites with Irish or Northumbrian connections, we can also see the emergence of other early ecclesiastical establishments. Starting at the Solent, there are hints of a monastery, erstwhile home of Wynfrith (Boniface) at Nursling around the head of the tide of the River Test (Hampshire).[18] Along the south side of the Thames Estuary and the north Kent coast, we see a series of coastal foundations of seventh-century date – Reculver, founded in 669 by Egbert of Kent, Minster-in-Thanet, Minster-in-Sheppey and, of course, the episcopal seat at Rochester itself.[19] We can add to this hints of an ecclesiastical site at Sandwich/Richborough based on the presence of two unusual early burial markers, and a reference to Wilfrid making a landing at a port of safety at Sandwich.[20] There is also pre-Viking sculpture at Preston-by-Faversham.[21] On the north side of the Thames there are further recorded monastic sites at Barking and Wakering, with arguments for a minster at Mersea, bringing us back round to the Blackwater and Bradwell itself.[22] Moving further north into Suffolk and Norfolk, we can also find the emergence of further coastal and estuarine monastic sites. We have already noted *Dommoc* and *Cnobheresburg* – and whatever their precise locations, there is solid or circumstantial evidence for some kind of early ecclesiastical presence at Burgh Castle, Caister-on-Sea, Dunwich and Walton Castle. To these we can add early sites at Stutton, Iken and Blythburgh in Suffolk.[23]

Figure 6.1 View across the Alde Estuary towards Iken. David Petts.

While it is tempting to characterise the adoption of coastal, island and estuarine sites for ecclesiastical purposes as particularly typical of the Irish and Northumbrian churches, it is clear that such locations were co-opted for religious purposes across most of the North Sea and Channel coasts of England. Whilst the practice may have been introduced initially via mission from the north and west, it was adapted with alacrity. It is important also to appreciate that it is likely that we are under-recognising the presence of early coastal church sites in southern and eastern England. While stone sculpture of eighth-/ninth-century date is widespread in northern England, Scotland and Ireland, it is far less extensive in southern and eastern England, primarily due to a lack of decent sources of stone.[24] This means it is less easy to identify possible early ecclesiastical sites that have not been picked up in textual sources. We also have areas of the coastline that have suffered coastal erosion on various scales – for example, parts of the north Norfolk coast, Lincolnshire and Suffolk have all seen ongoing coastal erosion over a considerable time. We know that both Dunwich and Walton Castle have almost entirely been lost to the sea, and it is quite possible that other sites of potential relevance may also have gone (see Figure 5.3).

The dynamic nature of the shoreline also raises another issue, which affects how we frame the contexts within which such sites sit. The rocky land- and seascapes of northern England and the Atlantic coast are characterised by projecting headlands, cliffs and islands. In many areas, such as Argyll, the west coast of Ireland and, to a lesser extent, the Firth of Forth, shorelines are archipelagic, defined by the widespread distribution of islands. These northern seascapes feel very different from the more subdued and low-lying coastal margins of England south of the Humber. Given this, it is tempting to see the coastal scapes of the south and east as being less complex and impressive than those further north. However, we need to factor in the extent to which the east coast of England has changed since the early Middle Ages.[25] There are two related factors that have had an impact on the shape of the current coastline. The first is the widespread reclamation of marshland.[26] Coastal salt marshes were once far more widely spread along the southern and eastern coasts from the great Fens around The Wash to the large swathes of marshland around the mouths of the Thames, the Blackwater and the Crouch in Essex, as well as the Pevensey Levels (East Sussex) and Walland and Romney Marshes and the Wantsum Channel (Kent).[27] As well as these large open stretches of marshland, there were many smaller-scale areas of marsh and saltflats around smaller river mouths sometimes extending well inland – for example, the creeks of East Anglian rivers such as the

Stour, the Orwell, the Alde, the Blyth, the Waveney, the Yare and the Bure were also fringed by marshland. There were also other areas of coastal marshland not specifically associated with rivers – such as along much of the north Norfolk coast. Even allowing for the impact of sea-level rise, and human intervention (such as large-scale peat cutting in what is now the Norfolk Broads), the extent of marsh, fen and swamp was far greater than it is today. However, these areas have been drained and reclaimed, shedding their intertidal characteristics and making access through them to more solid ground less complex. Settlements that had previously been more clearly on the edge of coastal, tidal regimes, with direct access to the open sea by boat, found themselves stranded inland as the character of the coast changed. The low-lying levels of the coastline have also resulted in the need to protect land from coastal flooding and storm surges, particularly as what had previously been marshland and fen was being reclaimed. This again resulted in the construction of dykes, banks and drainage ditches with the intention of preventing, or at least controlling, the flow of water in both directions between land and sea.

The end result of these campaigns of civil engineering has been a progressive 'tidying' and 'hardening up' – the very shape of much of the coastline has been fundamentally altered. In the early medieval period, the reach of the sea would have been much further inland than it is today – tidal regimes would have been more physically apparent, and micro-topographical variation would have been much more significant, when it meant the difference between wet or dry feet. The sense of a permeable coast would have been far more apparent, problematising the relationship between sea and dryland, the fresh and the salt; one particular consequence would have been a marshscape that would have been more archipelagic – islands (tidal and complete) and isolated headlands and peninsulas would have been far more present than they are today: not just the shallow, shifting islands that characterise the muddy Essex coast but more substantial, free-standing islands embedded within complex landscapes of coastal and inland marsh, mudflat and shingle spits.[28] The most obvious example of this would have been the great monastery at Ely – now 30 miles inland, but at its foundation surrounded by open marsh which reached northwards to The Wash.[29] Given the extent of the Great Fens, reaching far inland from The Wash, the fen edge settlements of Norfolk, Suffolk and Cambridgeshire were not a world away in landscape and topographical terms from more obviously coastal sites such as Bradwell.[30] With much of the East Anglian coast pierced by creeks and inlets, fringed with marsh and salt-flat and tidal regimes extending far inland, the distinction between the worlds of blue, green and brown water would have been blurred. The watery word of the Southumbrian coast would have had a fractal complexity that rivalled that of the Inner Hebrides.

Glorious isolation?

We are left with what appears to be a low-lying waterscape – often difficult to move through dry-shod, particularly in winter, and open to biting easterly winds. It is tempting to see this as confirmation of the remoteness and isolation of this landscape and coastal landscapes in general. The motif of fen and marsh as being a difficult, untamed and spiritually chaotic ecological niche is one that comes through strongly in some textual sources. Beowulf, of course, framed meres and fens as the natural habitat of Grendel and his mother.[31] The eighth-century *Life of Saint Guthlac* describes the 'most dismal' Fens as 'a very long tract, now consisting of marshes, now of bogs, sometimes of black waters overhung by fog, sometimes studded with wooded islands, and traversed by the windings of tortuous streams', and proceeds to characterise it explicitly as 'a vast desert' in which Guthlac could St Anthony-like confront his demons as a hermit.[32] At a large scale, Christian cosmology particularly associated the (Atlantic) ocean as being situated on the periphery of the known world, with Jerusalem at the centre. This perspective saw it as the home of malign demonic forces.[33] Yet, while the notion of isolation and remoteness is a seductive explanation for the distribution of ecclesiastical sites, in reality the situation is more complex. It has long been recognised that the trope of retreating to the desert to confront demons used commonly in narratives of the establishment of monastic sites is often belied by reality. Whether we look at Lastingham (like Bradwell, associated with Cedd), described as 'more suitable for the haunts of robbers and the dens of wild beasts than for human habitation',[34] despite its proximity to the densely settled landscape of Ryedale (see Figure 4.3), or think of Lindisfarne only a few miles from the major Northumbrian palace site at Bamburgh as the puffin flies, it is clear that tropes of isolation/ desert do not always chime comfortably with the more mundane reality. Even hermitages, where one would expect isolation to be essential, are often far more centrally located than usually appreciated. Peter Brown has emphasised the role of the holy man as a mediator in social tensions and an impresario of sanctity across the early Christian world.[35] The fact that Cuthbert was forced to build his cell higher to block out the constant stream of callers to his hermitage on the Farnes, and that Guthlac's island fastness on Crowland seems to have been a regular destination for a range of visitors, is a reminder that whatever the best intentions of island hermits, they could rarely escape the outside world.[36] Indeed, the regular presence of visitors provided the grist for the production of the miracles that were required for construction and maintenance of sanctity.

If the trope of coastal and island monasticism can be seen to be as extensive in Southumbria as it is in the north, however, there are still some differences between these two regions. Even in the later sixth century, before the advent of Christianity into southern and eastern England, there is growing evidence for an increasing symbolic engagement directly with the interface between land and sea, whether on exposed coastlines or in more estuarine contexts. The most obvious examples of this are the two boat burial sites from Suffolk – Snape and Sutton Hoo. Snape, the slightly earlier of the two, dates to the mid-sixth century, and included several log boats as burial containers as well as the larger boat burial.[37] The barrows here would have been visible both from the broad tidal expanse of the Alde Estuary, and probably the open sea. The presence of boat burials, as well as high-status grave goods, indicates the importance of the cemetery, although it probably evolved out of a more typical cremation cemetery in the later fifth century. Sutton Hoo meanwhile was also situated on a bluff overlooking the tidal reaches of the Deben – its elaborate early seventh-century burial assemblage needs no rehearsal here – and it was almost certainly connected to the key royal site at nearby Rendlesham.[38] Local and regional elites were clearly deliberately situating burial sites with reference to estuarine landscapes, with this maritime connection underlined by the use of boats as part of the mortuary rituals at both sites.

Other important early burial sites in locations close to estuaries are known from Ipswich and Southampton. Slightly later in date, perhaps mid- to late seventh-century, at Ipswich, a group of at least seven barrows were located on the south bank of the Orwell at Stoke Quay.[39] Standing on a break of slope, these would have been clearly visible from the river. A very similar group of burials was found at Southampton on the St Mary's Stadium site, which appears to have its origins in the later sixth century but flowered in the seventh century.[40] Here, yet again, the cemetery was located close to the tidal waters of the lower stretch of the Itchen heading out into Southampton Water. The St Mary's Stadium burials pre-date the emergence of Hamwic as an *emporium* in the eighth century. However, it has been argued that they may have been part of an earlier royal estate situated at the mouth of the Itchen that managed trade in agricultural produce from the surrounding area.[41] Although not as impressive as Snape or Sutton Hoo, burials such as St Mary's Stadium and Stoke Quay indicate a clear interest in the seventh century in utilising important locations in estuarine contexts for burial and the associated ritual activity that came with it.

The utilisation of coastal landscapes could be subtle. This can be seen at Prittlewell, Southend (Essex), the site of a late sixth-century princely burial.[42] Although 1½ miles from the Thames Estuary (nearly 5 miles wide at this point), the elaborate chambered mound grave and its associated cemetery were not positioned to exploit this major topographic feature and would not have been visible from navigation on the Thames. Instead, the cemetery was oriented towards the north, particularly the northward-flowing Prittle Brook, which is a tributary of the River Roach, which itself debouches into the Crouch as it flows along the southern edge of the Dengie Peninsula. This places the Prittlewell cemetery firmly within the braided tidal landscape of the Roach–Crouch–Blackwater estuary complex. While the Prittlewell cemetery precedes the establishment of the monastery at Bradwell by a little over 50 years, there is evidence for early medieval fabric within the church of St Mary, Prittlewell, a short distance to the south of the cemetery.[43] It has been argued that this surviving fabric, a blocked round-headed doorway arched with reused Roman tile, may be as late as tenth- or early eleventh-century in date.[44] However, there are persuasive arguments for there being two axially aligned churches at this site.[45] While the latest versions of these churches appear to date architecturally to the tenth/eleventh centuries, and there is certainly a revival of the practice of such 'paired' churches in the tenth century, it was also a phenomenon found earlier, in the seventh to early ninth century, with the obvious (and nearest) parallel being at Canterbury. Therefore, the presence of an important ecclesiastical focus emerging out of the ritual landscape that originated with the cemetery cannot be entirely dismissed.[46]

The later seventh century and early eighth century saw yet further engagements with coastal landscapes on the North Sea and Channel coasts, with the emergence and consolidation of a North Sea trading zone connecting England from the Humber to the south coast with mainland Europe, particularly north-east France, the Low Countries, northern Germany and beyond into Scandinavia and the Baltic. This involved the movement of both archaeologically visible material, such as the import of ceramics, quernstones and honestones into England, as well as the probable trade of a range of organic goods, including textiles, leather, slaves and foodstuffs.[47]

In England, this trading system has traditionally been framed as primarily hung on four key nodal sites – Ipswich (Suffolk), York (*Eoforwic*), Southampton (*Hamwic*) and London (*Lundenwic*).[48] These sites all seem to have emerged as important focal sites around the same time – *Hamwic, Eoforwic* and *Lundenwic* seem to have coalesced as trading sites around the turn of the eighth century, with Ipswich emerging as centre a little earlier (probably in the mid- to late seventh century). Not surprisingly, given the maritime nature of this trade, these sites were all located on major rivers or tidal estuaries with easy access to the sea – and, as such, they provide an important counterpoint to the ecclesiastical coastline presence.

Whether such *emporia* are seen as top-down, royal interventions aimed at directly stimulating long-distance trade links or as sites that developed more organically, and which were simply exploited by burgeoning royal families for tax purposes, it is clear that other social actors were engaged with the same coastal and riverine contexts along the North Sea and Channel coasts as the early church. Significantly, the presence of the Stoke Quay and Buttermarket cemeteries at Ipswich and the St Mary's Stadium cemetery at Southampton imply that these were already important locations within the social and perhaps economic landscapes of East Anglia and the south coast.

However, while the emergence of the trans-North Sea exchange network in the later seventh and early eighth century is traditionally framed in terms of international exchange between the large *emporia*, it is increasingly clear that there was both direct continental exchange to smaller sites, as well as secondary redistribution from the *emporia*.[49] Many of these second-tier sites were situated in coastal or fen edge locations. *Sandtun,* West Hythe (Kent), which appears at some points to have had connections with the nearby monastic site at Lyminge, emerges around 700.[50] Its ceramic assemblage is probably indicative of direct cross-Channel contacts, but the presence of Ipswich ware and shell-tempered wares (probably from elsewhere on the south coast or the Thames Estuary area) is testament to lateral coastal movement as well. Further north, fen edge settlements such as Burnham, adjacent to the mouth of the River Burn on the north coast of Norfolk, and Wormegay, on a former island on the fen edge, both have finds assemblages including coinage and pottery (both Ipswich Ware and foreign imports).[51]

One of the real challenges, however, when trying to identify these small coastal and waterside settlements, is the basic issue of distinguishing between secular and ecclesiastical establishments. Particularly without full excavation, the artefactual fingerprints of imported pottery recovered via fieldwalking and middle Anglo-Saxon metalwork picked up through metal-detecting surveys are very similar for both secular estates and monasteries. Unpicking the nature of activity at Bradwell itself is challenging due to the lack of large-scale modern excavation, although it is clear that the site has its origins as a monastery. Crude excavation in the nineteenth century that focused on Roman remains at the site, did, nonetheless, retrieve some objects of early medieval date, including a metal mount, possible fragments of millefiori, two styli and some iron objects.[52] There are a small number of early medieval coins recorded from the vicinity of Bradwell – a Series N sceatta and a Series S sceatta, as well as a Frisian Series E sceatta; all indicate coin use at the site in the early to mid-eighth century.[53] Furthermore, the presence of a mid-ninth-century styca of Aethelred II of Northumbria and ninth-century coinage from Mercia and Wessex extends the use of coinage at the site.[54] The presence of Frisian and Northumbrian coinage testifies to links both northwards and eastwards. There is also tentative ceramic evidence for wider exchange at Bradwell – a small number of Ipswich Wares are recorded from the site, and fieldwalking to the north of the fort enclosure has also collected ceramics that may date to as late as the tenth century.[55] However, while Bradwell was clearly involved in local, regional and international exchange from the late seventh century onwards, it is not easy to integrate this archaeological perspective with our historical understanding of monastic activity at the site, for which documentary evidence is relatively sparse. Does the material from Bradwell testify to a monastic site engaging in trade and exchange over a period of several centuries, or was the monastic dimension of the site limited to the mid-seventh century, with a subsequent transformation into a secular exchange focus?[56]

Even when more substantially excavated sites such as Flixborough (Lincolnshire) and Brandon (Suffolk) are assessed, without clear textual attestation it is not easy to define the nature of their occupation. A particular challenge is that sites may go through multiple phases of activity – potentially coming into and falling out of monastic control.[57] We have already seen the site at *Sandtun*, which is not first attested as being donated to Lyminge until around 30 years after the site was established; and it has been argued by the excavators that Flixborough passed through various stages of secular and ecclesiastical control.[58] The wider challenge of distinguishing between monastic and lay management of sites has been recognised in other areas of Britain: for example, it has been argued that both Whithorn and Portmahomack originated as secular settlements before transferring into monastic hands.[59] We also need to be aware that within the basic binaries of ecclesiastical and secular are likely to be subdivisions. For example, Bede in his letter to Egbert tried to distinguish between rigorously managed *monasteria* and those which were essentially intended as a 'tax dodge' by a secular elite.[60] Equally we might also distinguish between larger, more substantial ecclesiastical foci and the estates which were dependent on them, and those which may have been largely managed and populated by secular tenants. In parts of early medieval England where stone is more common, the presence of carved stone monuments is often taken as a 'diagnostic' tool that distinguishes between secular and ecclesiastical sites, but on the coast south of the Humber where good quality stone is rare, pre-Viking ecclesiastical sculpture is incredibly uncommon, while arguments about the other potentially diagnostic features of ecclesiastical character, such as the presence or absence of evidence of literacy, including styli and inkwells, runs the risk of being circular in nature.

The fact remains that we have a range of sites from along the fen edge and North Sea coast – such as Brandon, Bawsey, Butley, Wormegay and Babingley – for which good arguments can be made for both secular and religious dimensions:[61] a situation complicated by the potential of sites to shift in character over time. While in some ways this presents an interpretative challenge to the archaeologist, the very fact that it *is* so hard to distinguish between monasteries and a middle-level secular sites is itself an important point. We need to acknowledge the significance of their archaeological similarity; the basic fact remains that we see an emergence and consolidation in the seventh and eighth centuries of a new component of the settlement hierarchy along the North Sea coast. These settlements are foci for exchange (archaeologically visible in the presence of coinage and imported pottery), increasingly specialist production of a range of goods, including textiles (perhaps also destined for exchange) and, through the multiplicity of styli, evidence for a pragmatic literacy being used as a tool for bureaucracy and administration in addition to scholarship. In some ways, discussions about whether an abbot or a thegn was the senior manager of a particular site misses the wider point. Both monasteries and secular estate centres were fulfilling very similar roles and functions, as centres for production and exchange. Rather than focusing on disaggregating the two forms of management, we should concentrate on understanding the underlying drive and processes that result in them appearing archaeologically so similar – in terms of on-site activity, artefactual signature and landscape location – in the first place. Whether monastic or lay, such sites occupied very similar social and physical niches in the wider landscape – with the importance of coastal and fen edge positions being clear.

To return to our point of departure, the key argument of this chapter is that we need to resist the urge to characterise the occupation of coastal locations by ecclesiastical sites as an urge towards isolation and remoteness: quite the opposite. The complex mosaics of sea, sand, estuary and marsh that comprised the North Sea littoral were already being embraced for their symbolic valency before the spread of Christianity. The presence of sites such as the boat burials at Snape and Sutton Hoo in Suffolk, both in proximity to major estuaries, indicates the importance of the sea in the internal mythology of local rulers well before the establishment of a network of coastal monastic sites. The continued situating of cemeteries in locations with clear views to and from major waterways, such as Ipswich and Southampton, is testament to a continued fascination with the interface between land and sea that seems to run parallel to the increasing church presence on the coast. It is salutary to realise that in the mid-seventh century in Suffolk, while Botolph was founding his monastery at Iken on the tidal reaches of the River Alde, just 20 miles south-west, the *emporium* at Ipswich was emerging on the tidal reaches of the River Orwell. In between the two, on a marsh island at the mouth of the River Ore, stood Butley, which within decades was home of a site producing a range of imported ceramics, glassware and coins, as well as being the focus of a substantial cemetery, which remains poorly understood by scholars.[62] Butley has been variously interpreted both as a secular trading site and an unattested monastic establishment – and it is

Figure 6.2 Reconstruction of the Saxon settlement at Barber's Point by David Gillingwater, published in *Life and Death at Barber's Point* as part of the Touching the Tide project for the Coast & Heaths Area of Outstanding Natural Beauty, funded by the National Lottery Heritage Fund.

a classic example of a site caught in the intersection in function and purpose between *emporia* such as Ipswich and monasteries such as Iken.

The appearance of coastal monastic sites along the North Sea coast thus needs to be seen not simply as a purely Christian occupation of a land–sea interface that was mapped onto religious cosmology as a 'desert'. Instead, this was a place where symbolic associations were already being constructed in the pre-Christian period, and also one where other social actors were engaged in developing complex, interlinked landscapes of long-distance and local exchange. To characterise the coasts and fen edge settlements of eastern and southern England as entirely liminal zones, freighted with symbolism and ideology, or entirely as a zone with clear pragmatic advantages for the articulation and facilitation of newly emerging networks of exchange, is to miss the bigger picture. The church occupation of sites such as Bradwell was part of a wider process of the establishment of a new Middle Anglo-Saxon settlement hierarchy that encompassed both secular and ecclesiastical elites and has roots in a pre-Christian as well as Christian symbolic constructions of space.

Notes

1. Belcari 2013; Istria and Pergola 2013.
2. Arnaud 2003; Tréglia 2003; Codou and Lauwers 2009.
3. Codou and Lauwers 2009; Ó Carragáin 2013.
4. Horn et al. 1990; White Marshall 2005; O'Sullivan and Ó Carragáin 2008; Scally 2014; Campbell and Maldonado 2020.
5. O'Sullivan 2009; Ó Carragáin 2013.
6. Petts 2017a, 2009.
7. Daniels 2007; Petts 2009.
8. For example, Cramp 2005; Stronach 2005; Daniels 2007; Crone and Hindmarch 2016; Petts 2017a.
9. Fawcett 1989; James and Yeoman 2008.
10. Petts 2009.
11. Reischmann 1989.
12. Colgrave and Mynors 1969, 109–11 (II, 15); Pestell 2004, 20. See Hoggett, in this volume.
13. Colgrave and Mynors 1969, 270–1 (III, 19); Pestell 2004, 56.
14. See Hoggett, in this volume.
15. Colgrave and Mynors 1969, 284–5 (III, 22).
16. Colgrave and Mynors 1969, 372–3 (IV, 13).
17. Colgrave and Mynors 1969, 374–5 (IV, 13)
18. Collier 1990.
19. Blair 2005; Kelly 2008.
20. Colgrave 1985b, 13; Tweddle et al. 1995.
21. Tweddle et al. 1995.
22. Colgrave and Mynors 1969, 354–7 (IV, 6); Blair 2005, 215; Secker 2019.
23. Pestell 2004.
24. Schofield 1996; Petts 2017b.
25. Compare Rippon, in this volume.
26. For reclamation of marsh around Bradwell see Bruce and Thornton, in this volume.
27. For example, Rippon 2000; Long et al. 2007; Barber and Priestley-Bell 2008.

28   For the landscape around Bradwell in the early medieval period see Rippon, in this volume.
29   Barrowclough 2010; Woolhouse et al. 2019.
30   Oosthuizen 2017.
31   Estes 2017.
32   Colgrave 1985a.
33   O'Loughlin 1997; Petts 2019; Ó Carragáin 2013.
34   Colgrave and Mynors 1969, 286–7 (III, 23); Cf. Rippon and Yorke, in this volume.
35   Brown 1971.
36   For example, Colgrave 1985c; Bede's prose *Vita Sancti Cuthberti*, Chapter 18.
37   Filmer-Sankey and Pestell 2001.
38   Carver 2005; Scull et al. 2016.
39   Brown et al. 2020.
40   Stoodley 2010.
41   Yorke 1982; Stoodley 2002.
42   Blackmore et al. 2019.
43   Blackmore et al. 2019, 13–14.
44   Secker 2016.
45   Secker 2016, 131–4.
46   Gittos 2013, 55–102.
47   Hodges 1982, 2006; Blinkhorn 1999; Loveluck and Tys 2006; for the role of trade and exchange in the burgeoning of northern French coastal monastic sites see Bavuso 2022.
48   For example, Hodges 1982; Crabtree 2018.
49   Davies 2010; Loveluck and Tys 2006; Tys 2020.
50   Gardiner et al. 2001.
51   Pestell 2003, 2014; Rogerson 2003; Davies 2010.
52   Borough of Colchester 1947/48.
53   Portable Antiquities Scheme: ESS-B5EB76; EMC 1977.0003, 1986.0418. On the coins see Rippon, in this volume.
54   Portable Antiquities Scheme: ESS-B5A2F7; Bonser 1998; Challis 1992, 2, no.3.
55   Rodwell 1976; Medlycott 1994.
56   Mirrington 2013.
57   Loveluck 2001.
58   Loveluck 2001.
59   Maldonado 2011, 180–207; Carver et al. 2016.
60   Blair 2005, 101.
61   Davies 2010; Tester et al. 2014.
62   Fenwick 1984.

Bibliography

Arnaud, A. 2003. 'Les îles de Lérins, Sainte-Marguerite et Saint-Honorat (Cannes, Alpes Maritimes)'. In *Des îles côte à côte. Histoire du peuplement des îles de l'antiquité au Moyen Âge*, edited by Michel Pasqualini, Pascal Arnaud and Carlo Varaldo. *Bulletin archéologique de Provence*, supplément 1: 175–90.
Barber, G., and G. Priestley-Bell. 2008. *Medieval Adaptation, Settlement and Economy of a Coastal Wetland: The evidence from around Lydd, Romney Marsh, Kent*. Oxford: Oxbow.
Barrowclough, D. 2010. 'Expanding the horizons of island archaeology: islandscapes imaginary and real, Ely: the case of the dry island'. *Shima: The International Journal of Research into Island Cultures* 4(1): 27–46.
Bavuso, I. 2022. 'Monastic foundations and coastal interactions in the Normandy Peninsula'. In *Transitions and Relationships over Land and Sea in the Early Middle Ages of Northern Europe*, edited by A. Richardson, M. Bintley, J. Hines and A. Seaman. Neue Studien zur Sachsenforschung. 89–101. Brunswick: Braunschweigisches Landesmuseum.
Belcari, R. 2013. 'Monachesimo insulare tirrenico: fonti documentarie e attestazioni materiali a Montecristo e nelle altre isole dell'arcipelago toscano'. *Hortus Artium Medievalium* 19: 79–97.

Blackmore, L., I. Blair, S. Hirst and C. Scull. 2019. *The Prittlewell Princely Burial: Excavations at Priory Crescent, Southend-on-Sea, Essex, 2003*. London: Museum of London.

Blair, J. 2005. *The Church in Anglo-Saxon Society*. Oxford: Oxford University Press.

Blinkhorn, P. 1999. 'Of cabbages and kings: production, trade, and consumption in middle-Saxon England'. In *Anglo-Saxon Trading Centres: Beyond the emporia*, edited by M. Anderton. 4–23. Glasgow: Cruithne Press.

Bonser, M. J. 1998. 'Single finds of ninth-century coins from Southern England: a listing'. In *Kings, Currency and Alliances: History and coinage of southern England in the ninth century*, edited by M. A. S. Blackburn and D. N. Dumville. 199–240. Woodbridge: The Boydell Press.

Borough of Colchester. 1947/48. *Report of the Museum and Muniment Committee for the Period April 1st 1947 to March 31st 1948*. 20–31. Colchester: Colchester Borough Council.

Brown, P. 1971. 'The rise and function of the holy man in late antiquity'. *Journal of Roman Studies* 61: 80–101.

Brown, R., S. Teague, L. Loe, B. Sudds and E. Popescu. 2020. *Excavations at Stoke Quay, Ipswich: Southern Gipeswic and the parish of St Augustine*. East Anglian Archaeology 172. Norwich: East Anglian Archaeology.

Campbell, E., and A. Maldonado. 2020. '"A New Jerusalem at the ends of the earth": interpreting Charles Thomas's excavations at Iona Abbey, 1956–63'. *Antiquaries Journal* 100: 374–407.

Carver, M. 2005. *Sutton Hoo: A seventh-century princely burial ground and its context*. London: British Museum.

Carver, M. 2009. 'Early Scottish monasteries and prehistory: a preliminary dialogue'. *Scottish Historical Review* 88: 332–51.

Carver, M., J. Garner-Lahire and C. Spall. 2016. *Portmahomack on Tarbat Ness: Changing ideologies in north-east Scotland, sixth to sixteenth century AD*. Edinburgh: Society of Antiquaries of Scotland.

Challis, K. D. 1992. 'Early and Middle Saxon Essex'. Unpublished MPhil thesis, University of Nottingham.

Codou, Y., and M. Lauwers (eds). 2009. *Lérins. Une île sainte de l'antiquité au Moyen Âge*. Turnhout: Brepols.

Colgrave, B. (ed. and trans.) 1985a. *Felix's Life of Saint Guthlac*. Cambridge: Cambridge University Press.

Colgrave, B. (ed. and trans.) 1985b. *The Life of Bishop Wilfrid by Eddius Stephanus*. Cambridge: Cambridge University Press.

Colgrave, B. ed. 1985c. *Two Lives of St. Cuthbert*. Cambridge: Cambridge University Press.

Collier, C. 1990. 'Romsey Minster in Saxon Times'. *Proceedings of the Hampshire Field Club and Archaeology Society* 46: 41–52.

Colgrave, B., and R. A. B. Mynors (eds and trans.) 1969. *Bede's Ecclesiastical History of the English People*. Oxford Medieval Texts. Oxford: Clarendon Press.

Crabtree, P. 2018. *Early Medieval Britain: The rebirth of towns in the post-Roman west*. Cambridge: Cambridge University Press.

Cramp, R. 2005. *Wearmouth and Jarrow Monastic Sites*, vol. I. London: English Heritage.

Crone, A., and E. Hindmarch. 2016. *Living and Dying at Auldhame, East Lothian: The excavation of an Anglian monastic settlement and medieval parish church*. Edinburgh: Society of Antiquaries of Scotland.

Daniels, R. 2007. *Anglo-Saxon Hartlepool and the Foundations of English Christianity: An archaeology of the Anglo-Saxon monastery*. Hartlepool: Tees Archaeology.

Davies, G. 2010. 'Early medieval "rural centres" and West Norfolk: a growing picture of diversity, complexity and changing lifestyles'. *Medieval Archaeology* 54(1): 89–122.

Estes, H. 2017. *Anglo-Saxon Literary Landscapes: Ecotheory and the Anglo-Saxon environmental imagination*. Amsterdam: University of Amsterdam Press.

Fawcett, R. 1989. *Inchcolm Abbey and Island*. Edinburgh: HMSO.

Fenwick, V. 1984. '*Insula de Burgh*: Excavations at Burrow Hill, Butley Suffolk 1979–1981'. *Anglo-Saxon Studies in Archaeology and History* 3: 35–54.

Filmer-Sankey, W., and T. Pestell. 2001. *Snape Anglo-Saxon Cemetery: Excavations and surveys, 1824–1992*. Ipswich: Suffolk County Council.

Gardiner, M., R. Cross, N. Macpherson-Grant and I. Riddler. 2001. 'Sandtun, continental trade and non-urban ports in mid-Anglo-Saxon England: excavations at Sandtun, West Hythe, Kent'. *Archaeological Journal* 158: 161–290.

Gittos, H. 2013. *Liturgy, Architecture and Sacred Places in Anglo-Saxon England*. Oxford: Oxford University Press.

Hodges, R. 1982. *Dark Age Economics*. Bristol: Duckworth.

Hodges, R. 2006. 'Dark Age Economics revisited'. In *Goodbye to the Vikings? Re-reading early medieval archaeology*. 63–71. London: Duckworth

Horn, W., J. White Marshall and G. Rourke. 1990. *The Forgotten Hermitage of Skellig Michael*. Berkeley: University of California Press.

Istria, D., and P. Pergola. 2013. 'Moines et monastères dans les îles des mers Ligure et Thyrrénienne (Corse, Sardaigne, archipel toscan et archipel ligure)'. *Hortus Artium Medievalium* 19: 73–8.

James, H., and P. Yeoman. 2008. *Excavations at St Ethernan's Monastery, Isle of May, Fife, 1992–7*. Perth: Tayside & Fife Archaeological Committee.

Kelly, S. 2008. 'Reculver Minster and its early charter'. In *Myth, Rulership, Church and Charters: Essays in honour of Nicholas Brooks*, edited by J. Barrow and A. Wareham. 67–82. Farnham: Ashgate.

Long, A., M. Waller and A. Plater. 2007. *Dungeness and Romney Marsh: Barrier dynamics and marshland evolution*. Oxford: Oxbow.

Loveluck, C. P. 2001. 'Wealth, waste and conspicuous consumption. Flixborough and its importance for middle and late Saxon rural settlement studies'. In *Image and Power in the Archaeology of Early Medieval Britain*, edited by H. F. Hamerow and A. McGregor. 79–130. Oxford: Oxbow.

Loveluck, C. P., and D. Tys. 2006. 'Coastal societies, exchange and identity along the Channel and southern North Sea shores of Europe, AD 600–1000'. *Journal of Maritime Archaeology* 2: 140–69.

Maldonado, A. 2011. 'Christianity and Burial in late Iron Age Scotland, AD 400–650'. Unpublished PhD thesis: University of Glasgow.

Medlycott, M. 1994 'The Othona Community site, Bradwell-on-Sea, Essex: the extra-mural settlement'. *Essex Archaeology and History* 25: 60–71.

Mirrington, A. 2013. 'Transformations of Identity and Society in Essex, c. AD 400–1066'. Unpublished PhD thesis: University of Nottingham.

Oosthuizen, S. 2017. *The Anglo-Saxon Fenland*. Bollington: Windgather Press.

Ó Carragáin, T. 2013. 'The view from the shore: perceiving island monasteries in early medieval Ireland'. *Hortus Artium Medievalium* 19: 209–20.

O'Loughlin, T. 1997. 'Living in the ocean: the significance of the patristic understanding of oceanus for writings from Iona'. In *Studies in the Cult of Saint Columba*, edited by C. Bourke. 11–23. Dublin: Four Courts Press.

O'Sullivan, A. 2009. 'Early medieval crannogs and imagined islands'. In *Relics of Old Decency: Archaeological studies in later prehistory; Festschrift for Barry Raftery*, edited by G. Cooney, K. Becker, J. Coles, M. Ryan and S. Sievers. 79–87. Dublin: Wordwell.

O'Sullivan, J,. and T. Ó Carragáin. 2008. *Inishmurray: Monks and pilgrims in an Atlantic landscape*. Cork: Collins.

Pestell, T. 2003. 'The afterlife of "productive" sites in East Anglia'. In *Markets in Early Medieval Europe: Trading and 'productive sites', 650–850*, edited by T. Pestell and K. Ulmschneider. 122–37. Macclesfield: Windgather Press.

Pestell, T. 2004. *Landscapes of Monastic Foundation: The establishment of religious houses in East Anglia, c. 650–1200*. Woodbridge: Boydell & Brewer.

Pestell, T. 2014. 'Bawsey – a "productive site" in West Norfolk'. In *Landscape and Artefacts: Studies in East Anglian Archaeology presented to Andrew Rogerson*, edited by S. Ashley and A. Marsden. 139–66. Oxford: Archaeopress.

Petts, D. 2009. 'Coastal landscapes and early Christianity in Anglo-Saxon Northumbria'. *Estonian Journal of Archaeology* 13(2): 79–95.

Petts, D. 2017a. '"A place more venerable than all in Britain": the archaeology of Anglo-Saxon Lindisfarne'. In *The Lindisfarne Gospels: New perspectives*, edited by R. Gameson. 1–18. Leiden and Boston, MA: Brill.

Petts, D. 2017b. 'Places and spaces: some reflections on reconstructing the spatial organisation of Northumbrian monasteries'. In *Early Medieval Monasticism in the North Sea Zone: Proceedings of a conference held to celebrate the conclusion of the Lyminge excavations 2008–15*, edited by G. Thomas and A. Knox. 43–54. Oxford: Oxford University School of Archaeology.

Petts, D. 2019. 'Ecclesiastical tidescapes: exploring the early medieval tidal world'. *Norwegian Archaeological Review* 52(1): 41–64.

Reischmann, H.-J. (ed. and trans.). 1989. *Willibrord – Apostel der Friesen: seine Vita nach Alkuin und Thiofrid*. Darmstadt: Wissenschaftliche Buchgesellschaft.

Rippon, S. 2000. *The Transformation of Coastal Wetlands: Exploitation and management of marshland landscapes in north west Europe during the Roman and medieval periods* Oxford: Oxford University Press.

Rodwell, W. J. 1976. 'Some unrecorded archaeological discoveries in Essex, 1946–75'. *Essex Archaeology and History* 8: 234–8.

Rogerson, A. 2003. '"Productive" sites in West Norfolk'. In *Markets in Early Medieval Europe: Trading and 'productive sites', 650–850*, edited by T. Pestell and K. Ulmschneider. 110–21. Macclesfield: Windgather Press.

Scally, G. 2014. *High Island (Ardoileán), Co. Galway: Excavation of an early medieval monastery*. Dublin: The Stationery Office.

Schofield, 1996. R. 'Regional Geology'. In *Corpus of Anglo-Saxon Stone Sculpture*, vol. 4, *South-East England*, edited by D. Tweddle, M. Biddle and B. Kjølbye-Biddle. 10–20. Oxford: Oxford University Press.

Scull C., F. Minter and J. Plouviez. 2016. 'Social and economic complexity in early medieval England: a central place complex of the East Anglian kingdom at Rendlesham, Suffolk'. *Antiquity* 90(354): 1594–1612.

Secker, D. 2016. 'The late Saxon and early Romanesque churches at St Mary, Prittlewell, Essex'. *Medieval Archaeology* 60: 115–37.

Secker, D. 2019. 'The church of SS Peter and Paul, West Mersea, Essex: an Anglo-Saxon minster on a major Roman villa site'. *Journal of the British Archaeological Association* 172(1): 1–23.

Stoodley, N. 2002. 'The origins of Hamwic and its central role in the 7th century as revealed by recent archaeological discoveries'. In *Central Places in the Migration and Merovingian Periods*, edited by B. Hårdh and L. Larsson. 317–31. Acta Archaeologica Lundensia 8(39). Lund: Lunds Universitets Historiska Museum.

Stoodley, N. 2010. 'Burial practice in seventh-century Hampshire: St Mary's Stadium in context'. In *Burial in Later Anglo-Saxon England, c. 650–1100 AD*, edited by S. Ashley and A. Marsden. 38–53. Oxford: Oxbow.

Stronach, S. 2005. 'The Anglian monastery and medieval priory of Coldingham: Urbs Coludi revisited'. *Proceedings of the Society of Antiquaries of Scotland* 135: 395–422.

Tester, A., S. Anderson, I. Riddler and R. Carr. 2014. *Staunch Meadow, Brandon, Suffolk: A high-status Middle Saxon settlement on the fen edge*. East Anglian Archaeology 151. Bury St Edmunds: Suffolk County Council Archaeological Service.

Tréglia, J.-C. 2003. 'L'occupation des îles d'Hyères durant l'antiquité tardive'. In *Des îles côte à côte. Histoire du peuplement des îles de l'antiquité au Moyen Âge*, edited by Michel Pasqualini, Pascal Arnaud and Carlo Varaldo. *Bulletin archéologique de Provence*, supplément 1:127–32.

Tweddle, D., M. Biddle and B. Kjølbye-Biddle. 1995. *Corpus of Anglo-Saxon Stone Sculpture,* vol. 4, *South-East England*. Oxford: Oxford University Press.

Tys, D. 2020. 'Maritime and river traders, landing places, and emporia ports in the Merovingian period in and around the Low Countries'. In *The Oxford Handbook of the Merovingian World*, edited by B. Effros and J. Lund. 765–96. Oxford: Oxford University Press.

White Marshall, J. 2005. *Illaunloughan Island: An early medieval monastery in County Kerry*. Dublin: Wordwell.

Woolhouse, T., M. Hinman and B. Sudds. 2019. 'Recent discoveries at Ely Cathedral, Cambridgeshire: Aetheldreda's Gate, the church of Holy Cross and the possible boundary of the Anglo-Saxon monastery'. *Archaeological Journal* 176(1): 159–95.

Yorke, B. A. E. 1982. 'The foundation of the Old Minster and the status of Winchester in the seventh and eighth centuries'. *Proceedings of the Hampshire Field Club and Archaeological Society* 38: 75–84.

7
Land, marsh and sea: Transformations in landscape and farming at Bradwell on Sea, c. 1086–c. 1650

Kevin Bruce and Christopher Thornton, assisted by Neil Wiffen

This chapter places the site of the chapel of St Peter-on-the-Wall within the evolving economy and landscape of Bradwell on Sea between the late eleventh and the early seventeenth centuries, tracing the role of both human and natural influences on the chapel's wider setting. As Bradwell is a large parish, some 5,236 acres in 1901,[1] the focus is on evidence pertaining to its north-eastern parts, closest to the chapel and most likely to be affected by the proposed power station developments. Two key strands to the economic development of Bradwell in the Middle Ages and into the sixteenth century were the considerations of its lords and residents and the impact of their activities on the environment. The chapter therefore begins with a reconstruction of landownership in that area before investigating changing population and wealth, the pattern of farming, the changing nature of the marshlands and associated reclamations and sea defences and, finally, the significance of ancillary occupations such as fishing and coastal trade.

Landownership

Bradwell on Sea had a complex landowning structure, with probably 11 separate landholdings recorded in Domesday Book (1086). The descent of Bradwell's manors was described by Morant in 1768, but he omitted or misidentified certain estates existing in 1086. Round improved on some of Morant's identifications, but a later account of landholding by Brown again appears quite muddled.[2] Our research has enabled us to trace most estates forward from 1086 and to plot their boundaries provisionally (Figure 7.1).[3] The three medieval manors of most significance for understanding landscape change around St Peter's Chapel are East Hall, Battels and Down Hall (including Tanyes and Tomlyns Wick), while in the Tudor period new farms or expanded estates called New Wick and Wymarks partly reshaped landholding (Figure 7.2).

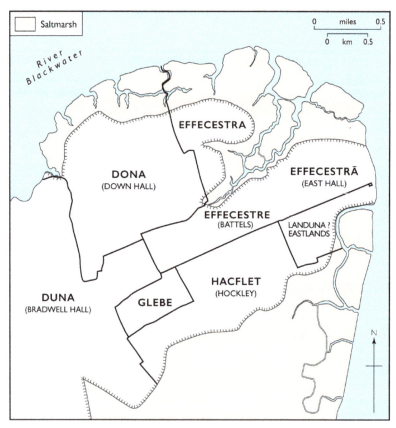

Figure 7.1 Reconstruction of probable boundaries of Domesday Estates (1086) in north-east Bradwell on Sea. K. Bruce; redrawn by Mrs Cath D'Alton.

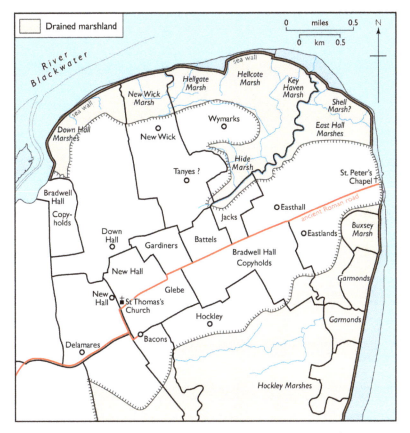

Figure 7.2 Reconstruction of boundaries and location of medieval and Tudor estates (to c. 1650) in north-east Bradwell on Sea. K. Bruce; redrawn by Mrs Cath D'Alton.

East Hall

In 1086 two manors in Bradwell called Effecestrā/e shared the same philological origin as the name of the earlier settlement of *Ythancæstir* (Othona), where, according to Bede, Cedd built his church.[4] It seems probable, therefore, that those two manors, plus land in the same vill held by three freemen, represent portions of an earlier estate associated with the site of the Saxon Shore Fort and St Peter's Chapel. The total assessment of their lands amounted to 4½ hides plus 20 acres (560 acres; Table 7.1).[5] It is possible that the monastic endowment had been more substantial, perhaps comprising the whole of Bradwell which at a little over 30 hides

Table 7.1 Domesday manors in Bradwell, tenants-in-chief and sub-tenants, 1066 and (1086).

Place/Estate in 1086 (see note 1)	Hides (h.) and acres (a.)	Tenant in 1066	Tenant-in-chief 1086	Sub-tenant 1086	Notes (and later manorial identity)
Effecestrā (1)	1½ h. + 20 a.	Thorkill, a free man	Monastery of St Valery	–	Manor of East Hall
Effecestrā	1½ h.		Monastery of St Valery	3 free men	Held of the manor of East Hall and probably later forming part of it
Effecestre (2)	1½ h.	Ingulf, a free man	Hugh de Montfort	Wulfmaer	Manor of Battels
Duna (3)	14 h.	Siward	Ranulf de Peverel		Manor of Bradwell Hall (held in demesne)
(of) Duna	[1½ h.]	[Siward]	Ranulf de Peverel	Ascelin	Held of the manor of Bradwell Hall; hides probably part of above hidation
(in) Duna	5 h. – 6 a.	[Siward]	Ranulf de Peverel	8 free men	Probably held of the manor of Bradwell Hall
Dona (4)	2 h. + 20 a.	Moding	Eudo Dapifer	Richard	Identified as the manor of Down Hall (note 2)
Landuna	½ h. + 20 a.	4 free men	Eudo Dapifer	Richard	Tentatively identified as Eastlands farm

Acleta	1½ h. + 10 a.	Moding	Eudo Dapifer	Richard	Uncertain.
Hacflet (5)	2 h. + 30 a.	Alweard, a free man	Bishop of Bayeux	One of the bishop's knights. The church holds 40 a.	Tentatively identified as the manor of Hockley (note 3)
Hacflet	[30 a.]	A free man (outlawed)	Bishop of Bayeux	Land taken by Swein of Essex	Part of above; acreage probably part of above entry
ESTIMATED HIDATION	29½ hides + 94 a.				

Notes:

(1) Estates are arranged under the five tenants-in-chief, their primary estate in Bradwell being labelled (1) to (5).

(2) See chapter text, pp. 184–5.

(3) Previously identified as 'Bradwell Quay': J. H. Round, 'Bradwell iuxta Mare', *Transactions of the Essex Archaeological Society*, New Series 16 (1923), 52–4. Topographical reconstruction and the location of the church (glebe) estate suggests Hockley is more plausible: K. Bruce, 'The Manor of Hacflet in Bradwell – a reappraisal', *Essex Society for Archaeology and History Newsletter* 187 (Autumn/Winter 2018), 9.

Source:

A. Williams and G. H. Martin (eds), *Little Domesday Book, Essex* (London, 2000), ff. 21, 24, 53v, 74v, 149v.

was similar in scale to other early church holdings in Essex,[6] but the correspondence of the estate and place name seems compelling.

The first of these two estates (Effecestrā), covering land in the north-west corner of Bradwell including St Peter's Chapel, was held by the Benedictine abbey of St Valery-sur-Somme from 1086 until 1391 (Table 7.1; Figures 7.1 and 7.2). It had apparently been granted to the monastery as a reward for the successful intervention of their prayers to assist the weatherbound ships of William the Conqueror's fleet.[7] All of St Valery's English properties lay in Essex, administered from their principal house at Takeley Priory.[8] Confirmations to the priory by Henry I (c. 1130) and Henry II (1163 and c. 1180) indicate that Effecestrā was renamed La Waule/Walle, a name possibly deriving from the extant walls of the Roman Saxon Shore Fort astride which St Peter's Chapel sits.[9] La Waule continued to be used into the fourteenth century, but by 1371 the name East Hall had been adopted.[10] Earlier, in 1324–5, Takeley Priory and its lands had been taken into the king's hands as an alien priory, and although it was restored 'at farm', the monastic house apparently struggled financially thereafter.[11] In 1391 the abbot and convent sold the priory and its estate to William of Wykeham for his foundation of New College (Oxford), the college retaining East Hall manor until 1865.[12]

New College leased out the East Hall estate from 1395, and from 1451 a continuous series of leases survives in the Bodleian Library.[13] One important lessee was John Causton (Cawston), who was granted a 20-year lease in 1504 at £20 per annum.[14] Two years later Causton was described as the lord's bailiff, and he owned the adjacent Jacks Farm, part of Battels manor, to which he added 'Blyres', a copyhold of East Hall, by purchase in 1515.[15] The surviving building at East Hall was probably built in the time of Causton, as it comprises a timber-framed three-bay high-end cross-wing of c. 1500, all that remains of a once larger house that would have continued to the north.[16]

In 1522 a Writtle yeoman, William Pincheon (Pynchon), obtained the lease on the same terms, which he renewed in 1538.[17] William, and his father Henry before him, had long been tenants of New College lands in Writtle, so would have been favourably positioned to secure the East Hall lease when it became available.[18] The Pincheon family continued to hold the lease through five generations – William, John, William (and afterwards his widow, Rose), Edward and John, until the last of these died in debt in 1654.[19] With their ownership of other nearby estates, such as Battels and Wymarks (see below), the Pincheons became the most important farmers in the area of St Peter's Chapel in the sixteenth and earlier seventeenth centuries.

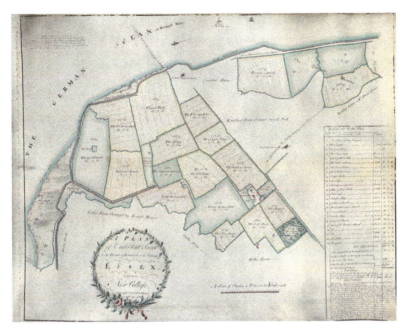

Figure 7.3 Map of East Hall Farm in 1768, an estate belonging to New College, Oxford, from 1391 to 1865. St Peter's Chapel is at the top of the map (New College Archives, Oxford, NCA 14758/3 © Courtesy of the Warden and Scholars of New College, Oxford).

Battels

The second portion of the vill (Effecestre), located immediately to the west towards Down Hall, was held by Hugh de Montfort in 1086 and tenanted by Wulfmaer (Table 7.1; Figures 7.1 and 7.2). The demesne tenancy later passed to the Bataille or Batayl family, from whom it was later renamed the manor of Battels (Battles; Batailles).[20] The Bataille family were present in Bradwell by 1207, when the abbot of St Valery granted Emery (Almeric) Bataille one carucate (in other words, one hide) in La Waule as well as other freehold lands and Garmonds (Gurmonds/Garmunds) Marsh.[21] The Bataille family continued to hold their manor until the mid-fourteenth century, through Emery (d. 1252), Saer (d. 1292) and Edmund (d. 1333).[22] Edmund died without issue, leaving his sister Margaret, aged 40, as his heir.[23]

The full descent of the manor for the remainder of the fourteenth century and most of the fifteenth has not been traced, but in the first

LAND, MARSH AND SEA: TRANSFORMATIONS

quarter of the fifteenth century the manor was apparently divided into three parts held by different families.[24] By 1485 the manor had passed to the Higham family, for an abutment recorded the lands of Thomas Higham called 'Batayles hyde'.[25] The manor was later held by Anthony Higham (d. 1540), followed by his son Robert.[26] A lease shows Robert in possession c. 1544–51, but he had apparently disposed of the estate before making his will in 1558.[27] The Higham family also leased Battels out, for on his death in 1543 John Brooke the elder (I) held a lease of 'Hyghehams Lands', and the Brooke family eventually bought the manor, probably in the time of John Broke the younger, of Great Baddow. The latter's son Stephen held it at his death in 1581.[28] Stephen's heirs sold the manor to Rose Pincheon, the widow of William Pincheon.[29] The estate was then effectively incorporated into the Pincheons' Wymarks estate and held by the family until Rose and William's grandson John Pincheon became indebted and mortgaged the manor of Battels along with all his Wymarks properties (see below) to Henry Carter. When he died in 1629, Carter willed that, should the mortgage not be redeemed, the estate's ownership should descend to his son, another Henry. Additionally, at the time of his death, Carter had possessed Hellgate Marsh, Smiths Marsh, Skinner's Marsh and Dunnyngs Marsh, all former Pincheon properties, and held of the Warden and Fellows of New College as lords of East Hall manor.[30] However, it seems likely that Pincheon's mortgage was redeemed with the help of his brother-in-law Sir William Luckin of Little Waltham, as by 1641 Battels was in Luckin's possession (see below, Wymarks).

Down Hall

The major portion of the vill called Duna was held by Ranulf de Peverel by 1086, in three portions totalling 20½ hides (Table 7.1).[31] The largest portion (14 hides), which Ranulf held in his own demesne, can safely be identified with the manor of Bradwell Hall.[32] It thus covered much of the centre and west of the parish, bordering the Blackwater Estuary on the north but well away from the open coast (Figure 7.1). Round set out a case that a later division of Ranulf's estate led to the creation of a separate manor (Down Hall).[33] Yet another estate called Dona, assessed at two hides and 20 acres lay in the ownership of Eudo Dapifer and his sub-tenant Richard. They also held two separate landholdings called Landuna (½ hide and 20 acres) and Acleta (1½ hides and 10 acres), making a total estate of c. 530 acres. Eudo's estate had much 'pasture for sheep', indicating a coastal location (Table 7.1),[34] and this landholding is regarded here as a more probable candidate for the origin of Down Hall (Figures 7.1 and 7.2). However, another suggestion by Round, that Landuna equated to the later Eastlands Farm, seems more plausible.[35]

Although the above reconstruction remains provisional, for the purposes of this article it is sufficient to note that between the thirteenth and early sixteenth centuries the demesne tenancy of the small manor of Down Hall descended in the Doune/Downe family, who took their name from the vill or manor. A John de la Doune held the manor in 1254 and was succeeded by a Thomas de la Doune, probably his son, recorded in 1284.[36] Thomas, or a descendant of the same name, died in 1306 and was succeeded by his daughter Margaret, a minor aged eight.[37] Margaret must have married, as at the time of her death in 1343 she was succeeded by her daughter Joan, wife of John le Cok.[38] The estate later returned to the male line of the Doune family, being held by Edward de la Doune (d. 1400).[39] In the early fifteenth century it was held by Edwards's son John, who died in 1426 and it then passed to his son Robert de la Doune, a minor aged four.[40] At Robert's death in 1502 he held Down Hall manor together with two further estates called Tanyes and Tomlyns Wick and their marshlands, measuring at least 894 acres.[41]

In 1504 Robert de la Doune's indebted son and heir William sold Down Hall to John Christmas of Colchester, and this was followed in 1512 by a further sale of Tanyes, Tomlyns Wick, Hellcote Marsh and Keyhaven marshes to Thomas Christmas.[42] The purchasers were members of a wealthy clothier dynasty of Colchester who built up a large landed estate in Essex in this period.[43] In 1562, their descendant George Christmas, his wife Bridget and their tenant John Brooke the younger apparently mortgaged Down Hall to Robert Christmas and John Turner for £800. George Christmas still held the manor at his death in 1565, with four messuages or bercaries (sheep wicks) and tenements, called West Wick, Tawneys (probably meaning Tanyes), Tomlyns Wick and Shortes, in Bradwell, Tillingham and St Lawrence.[44]

The Christmas family were also absentee landlords, buying the estate as investors but leaving the farming to tenants. John Brooke the elder (I) of New Hall held the lease on his death in 1543. John also leased 'Hyghehams lands' (that is, Battels manor) and owned other lands in Bradwell, Asheldham and Pagelsham. He bequeathed the leases of Down Hall and Battels jointly to three of his sons, Robert, John 'the elder' (II) and John 'the middle'. To a fourth son, John 'the younger', he instead left his marsh called Pilverins (Pylferyns), but wished it to remain with his lease of Down Hall; later evidence implies that the whole estate eventually passed to the youngest son.[45]

In 1576 John Christmas began the process of disposing of his Bradwell estate, selling two messuages, two cottages, two gardens and 580 acres to John Brooke for £400.[46] The latter was apparently John Brooke 'the younger', who had advanced further in the world and at his death in 1581 was described as 'gentleman' of Brook Hall in Great Baddow. Very probably he had earlier inherited the lease of Down Hall, placing him in a good position to buy half the estate. His will indicates that his purchase probably included Tanyes and Tomlyns Wick (Figure 7.2; see below), and he settled this estate jointly on his four grandsons, sons of his son Robert, who was made responsible for their maintenance. In addition, he also held other lands including 'Keyhaven Marsh, Pilverins, C[h]ristmas Crofts, Jakes and one little parcel of Hidehill, being a way from Jakes unto Keyhaven Marsh' (for locations see Figures 7.2 and 7.5).[47] In 1601 the four Brooke grandsons, some of whom had sold their portions, took their father to court, claiming that he had withheld monies from them.[48] One grandson's quarter was apparently acquired by Robert Wade, son-in-law of their grandfather and therefore their uncle, who in 1597 sold it to Matthew Rudd, a Chelmsford lawyer.[49] Another quarter may have passed after the death of one grandson to his own father, Robert Brooke, who in 1601 sold it to John Coleman.[50]

In 1580 John Christmas sold the second half of the manor, probably representing the main demesne farm, to Walter Mildmay for £360.[51] Four years later it was sold by Walter and his wife, Mary, to Thomas Mildmay.[52] Then, in 1590, Thomas Mildmay and his wife, Alice, sold a quarter of these lands in Bradwell to Robert Wade for £200.[53] In 1611 it was recorded that the Down Hall estate was leased by Thomas Mildmay to John Coleman of New Wick.[54] Thomas continued in possession of the remainder of the manor, which he held at his death in 1612, being succeeded by his grandson William Mildmay.[55] What brought the Christmas and Mildmay families to purchase Down Hall remains uncertain, although as clothiers the former may have desired to secure supplies of wool from the marshland flocks, even though it would not have been of the highest quality. Both families probably also appreciated the leisure opportunities provided by the landscape, reserving certain rights to themselves. In a Down Hall lease of 1576, John Christmas reserved the fishing, fowling, hawking and hunting on the premises for himself, his heirs and his servants whenever they visited.[56] Similarly, when Thomas Mildmay leased the estate in 1593, he reserved the right to visit with a party of up to 20 persons for up to two nights and two days when they could occupy the hall, great parlour and chamber over it, and little parlour. The tenant also had to provide meals and sustenance for their horses.[57]

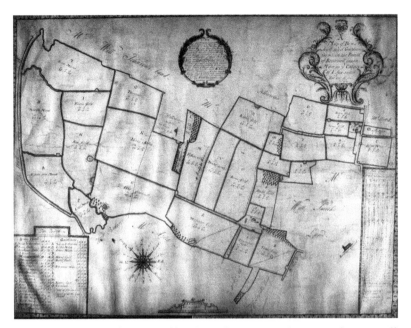

Figure 7.4 Map of Down Hall and Gardiners Farm in 1753. The sea wall on the Blackwater Estuary is on the left of the map. The core of the estate remained as it was in the Middle Ages, but the names of many fields had changed. Reproduced by kind permission of the Essex Record Office; ERO, D/DCm P13.

Tanyes and Tomlyns Wick

During the Middle Ages the Doune family of Down Hall owned a subsidiary estate called Tanyes. It was apparently named after its subtenancy by the le Tany family, for in 1320 a Robert de la Doune had granted 120 acres of marsh in Bradwell to John le Tany.[58] In 1502 it comprised a messuage, 100 acres of land, five acres of meadow, five acres of wood and 60 acres of 'internal' marsh, 200 acres of 'foreign' marsh (that is, saltmarsh), a marsh called Hellcote Marsh on the west of Keyhaven and 80 acres of 'foreign' marsh on the west of Keyhaven called Shellmarsh.[59] These details and field names in other sources indicate that Tanyes was located to the east of Down Hall and north of Battels (Figure 7.2).[60] Its medieval house may be associated with the site of a 'reasonably high-status medieval building' uncovered during archaeological investigations in May 2020 beside the perimeter track of the Second World War Bradwell Bay airfield.[61]

A second subsidiary estate of Down Hall lay at Tomlyns Wick, first recorded in 1428.[62] By 1502 it was described as a 'barkery' (sheep wick) measuring 240 acres and worth £5 yearly.[63] The 'wick' element of its name indicates that the estate was the site of a coastal dairy farm, several similarly named wicks being located on the East Hall estate and, indeed, on other parts of the Essex coast, such as St Osyth and Clacton.[64] The name Tomlyns Wick has now been lost, but our topographical reconstruction places it on the western side of Down Hall near the coast, probably equating to the later Down West Wick (that is, the wick to the west of Down Hall). Both Tomlyns Wick and Tanyes were held and leased with New Wick by the early seventeenth century (see below).

New Wick

The earliest mention of an estate called New Wick (Newwick, Nuwick) occurred in 1575, when John Christmas granted a lease of Down Hall and Down West Wick to Robert Wade of Bradwell, yeoman, for £40. Excepted from the lease were New Wick in the occupation of John Brooke of Great Baddow, and 40 acres at Keyhaven already in the occupation of Robert Wade.[65] The house at New Wick, now demolished, was possibly a replacement for that at Tanyes on a new site; perhaps it was built for or by the Brooke family and later passed to John Coleman, who purchased lands from Robert Brooke in 1601 (see above). After Coleman died in 1611, disputes over the estate arose between his (remarried) widow and his executor Matthew Rudd, and afterwards between Rudd's (remarried) widow and Coleman's children, with a chancery suit of 1624 naming Coleman's Bradwell holdings as New Wick, Tomlyns and Tanyes.[66] As Coleman had also leased Down Hall from Mildmay, it is apparent that the whole block of land continued to be farmed by a single person over the later sixteenth and earlier seventeenth centuries.

Wymarks

As described above, during the Middle Ages both East Hall and Down Hall manors, covering the area later to be occupied by the existing and the proposed power stations, were owned or leased as a number of demesne farms and additional marshland dairy farms. The area between East Hall and Down Hall/Tanyes/New Wick comprised a mixture of copyhold and freehold properties, both large and small, including many marshes. The c. 1500 rental of East Hall shows six different tenants holding both freehold and copyhold properties of varying sizes.[67]

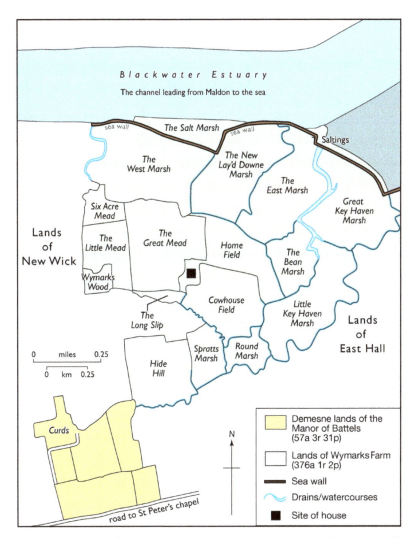

Figure 7.5 Map of Wymarks Farm in 1714, lying between the Down Hall and East Hall estates, representing the culmination of the Pincheon family's land acquisitions which they held until the mid-seventeenth century. Drawing by the authors from ERO, T/M 301/1; redrawn by Mrs Cath D'Alton.

That rental also identifies properties that were *not* part of the manor, namely, Wymarks, Jakes, Hide Hill, Northlands and Tanyes (as considered above), and some of the marshes on the northern shore, and provides the names of their owners or tenants. This whole area was eventually to be consolidated as a single estate in the ownership of the Pincheon

Table 7.2 Domesday economic statistics: population, ploughs and value, 1066 and (1086).

Place	Villani 1066 (1086)	Bordarii 1066 (1086)	Servi 1066 (1086)	Men's ploughs	Lord's ploughs	Value 1066 (1086)
Effecestrā (1)	–	2 (3)	2 (1)	(1)	1 (1)	£2 (£3 10s.)
Effecestrā	–	–	–	(1)	–	(£1)
Effecestre (2)	–	2 (2)	1 (0)	(½)	(1)	(£1 10s.)
Duna (3)	2 (4)	3 (15)	12 (6)	2 (3)	5 (5)	£10 (£13)
Duna	–	–	–	–	–	£1 of above valuation
Duna	–	6 (6)	–	2½ (2½)	–	£3 (£4 10s.)
Dona (4)	–	2 (2)	2 (2)	–	1 (1)	(£3)
Landuna	–	–	–	½ (1)	0 (½)	(10s.)
Acleta	–	1 (1)	–	–	1 (1)	£2 (£2 10s.)
Hacflet (5)	–	4 (10)	–	1 (1)	–	£3 (£4 11s.)
TOTAL 1066	2	20	17	6	8	£20
TOTAL 1086	(4)	(39)	(9)	(10)	9½	£34 1s.
% change	+100%	+95%	–47%	+66%	+25%	+70%

Notes
(1) Estates are arranged under the five tenants-in-chief, their primary estate in Bradwell being labelled (1) to (5).

Source:
A. Williams and G. H. Martin (eds), *Little Domesday Book, Essex* (London, 2000). ff. 21, 24, 53v, 74v, 149v.

family, lessees of East Hall, and was named after their farm at Wymarks (Figures 7.2 and 7.5).

The process apparently began in 1530, when William Pincheon acquired 20 acres of arable and 2 acres of meadow, possibly representing the core holding at Wymarks.[68] It was his son John who considerably increased the family's holdings in Bradwell, for c. 1559 he acquired three portions of East Hall's copyhold and freehold land and Eastlands Farm, to the south of East Hall, from Robert Higham.[69] His son and heir, William, was only 19, so the properties were managed by his widow, Jane. In 1584 she purchased a further 140 acres of marshland from Robert and Margaret Wade.[70] This was possibly part of Tanyes (to the west), as Margaret was the sister of Robert Brooke, both being offspring of John Brooke of Great Baddow, who also owned land in the Wymarks area (see above). In 1588 William Pincheon purchased 97 acres of marsh from Robert Brooke and his wife, Joan, and John Brooke his nephew,[71] possibly representing Keyhaven Marsh. William died c. 1590, but the accumulation of land continued as in 1595 his widow, Rose, then added the manor of Battles (see above).[72]

The remainder of East Hall's freehold and copyhold lands were later in the hands of William and Rose's son Edward (d. 1627), followed by his son John. In 1634 the latter's sister Elizabeth became the second wife of Sir William Luckin of Little Waltham, who also owned Delamares Farm in Bradwell. It appears that John Pincheon approached his brother-in-law for a loan, possibly to recover Battels manor, but using Wymarks as security on which he defaulted; by 1641 Sir William and Elizabeth Luckin were in possession as they then leased Battels, Hide Hill, Wymarks and Curds to the occupant and farmer William Malden of Mundon.[73] All these lands continued to be held together as Wymarks Farm, which by 1714 comprised c. 434 acres, including the demesne lands of Battels manor (c. 58 acres) (Figure 7.5).

Wealth and population

Interpreting the value given for Domesday estates is fraught with difficulties,[74] but two aspects of Bradwell's survey entries are worthy of comment (Table 7.2). First, its overall assessment had risen by 70 per cent between 1066 and 1086. Although that calculation clearly overestimates growth because some estates had no value recorded for the earlier date, it is clear from individual entries that values had risen: for example at East Hall, Bradwell Hall (two parts), 'Acleta' and Hockley. Rising local prosperity on the eastern coast of Dengie hundred contrasted with many instances of falling manorial values across the coastal hundreds of the county.[75] Second, the 1086 valuations per hide of coastal manors such as East Hall (4.2*d*. per acre) were much higher than that of inland manors such as Bradwell Hall (1.86*d*. per acre),[76] suggesting that additional wealth was generated by coastal resources such as marshland dairying, fishing and trade (see below).

Bradwell's enumerated population grew between 1066 and 1086 from 39 to 52, while the number of 'villagers' (*villani*) had doubled from two to four, that of 'smallholders' (*bordarii*) had virtually doubled from 20 to 39, while that of slaves (*servi*) had nearly halved from 17 to 9. If all, including the slaves, were heads of household, applying an omission figure of 5 per cent and using a multiplier of 4.0 or 5.0 per household, the local population may be estimated as lying between *c*. 218 and *c*. 273 in 1086.[77] Over half the enumerated people (31) were listed under Bradwell Hall (Duna) and its sub-estates. The three manorial estates under consideration in this article had much smaller populations and, as in later centuries, they probably comprised single manorial farmsteads with attached dependent workers, with perhaps a few subsidiary tenant farms scattered nearby.

In the high Middle Ages the large rural parish appears to have been relatively wealthy. For the subsidy of 1237–8 Bradwell paid the highest amount (£5 0*s*. 1*d*.) out of the 15 vills recorded for Dengie hundred, although the return did not include Great Maldon, Tillingham and Southminster.[78] The latter three vills paid the highest amounts in the 1327 and 1334 subsidies, but Bradwell still lay in sixth or seventh position out of 19 places in the hundred, similar to the assessments for the neighbouring coastal parish of Dengie and the large parish of Purleigh.[79] A typical pyramid of wealth was demonstrated by the 29 Bradwell taxpayers in 1327, with 16 paying under 1*s*., eight between 1*s*. and 4*s*., and three between 6*s*. and 10*s*. None of them had occupational surnames suggestive of trade or manufacture, with the exception of one 'le Smyth'. Edmund Bataille, lord of the manor of Battels, was among the highest taxpayers.[80] With little sign of industry, the parish's wealth must have been based on its large acreage and fertile coastal farms, well placed for the export of produce by water.

There are no adequate sources available for measuring the growth of Bradwell's population during the Middle Ages, but it probably reached a peak in the early fourteenth century.[81] Nevertheless, the impact of the Black Death of 1348–9 and subsequent outbreaks of plague may be seen in the total of 217 people over the age of 14 who paid poll tax in 1377, probably equating to a total population of *c*. 300.[82] By the later fourteenth century, therefore, the population had fallen back to a level only slightly higher than three centuries previously. Recovery seems improbable during the fifteenth century, given the trends demonstrated by tithing-penny evidence from central and northern Essex.[83] Changes in land use and production at Bradwell in the later Middle Ages should be seen in the context of this severe demographic trough.

Bradwell's population is unlikely to have benefited from the late medieval industrial growth that buoyed many parts of north and north-east Essex, especially Colchester, Braintree/Bocking and Coggeshall. By 1524/5 the parish's relative wealth even seems to have declined within Dengie hundred, for its tax assessment placed the parish in only 11th position out of 20 communities (excluding Maldon). In that year Bradwell had 44 named taxpayers, of whom 26 were assessed on goods, 17 on wages and one on land. Within the parish there was a concentration of wealth in the hands of John Brooke the elder (I), lessee of Down Hall, assessed at £92 13s. 4d. Brooke's own wealth was far in excess of the next six highest assessments lying between £15 and £21, and contrasted sharply with the nominal £1 assessments of the 17 men assessed on their labour. Indeed, his assessment comprised one quarter of that of the whole parish and he was also the 16th highest taxpayer in Dengie hundred.[84]

The parish's population levels probably declined further through the fifteenth century along the lines exhibited by many rural communities in central and western Essex.[85] While Bradwell's 44 taxpayers in 1524 were only exceeded in number within Dengie hundred by Purleigh (49), Southminster (68), Burnham (89) and the larger town of Maldon (193), the absolute population probably remained low.[86] If households averaged five people, and an allowance is made for a proportion of exempt (perhaps one third to one half), Bradwell's total population seems unlikely to have much exceeded that existing a century and a half earlier (c. 300). Renewed growth thereafter was probably also slow, for as late as 1670 the parish had only 77 properties paying hearth tax (including 18 exempt), almost half of which (35) having just one hearth and probably being cottages for labourers and fishermen.[87] Unsurprisingly, the medieval farming and settlement pattern remained largely unchanged in later centuries, as exemplified by a county map of 1777.[88]

Agriculture

All of the manors studied in this chapter included two main land types influencing forms of agricultural production. The spur of higher land forming the north-eastern peninsula of Bradwell, based on river terrace sands and gravels overlying London Clay, produced fertile loamy soils, easily worked and free-draining, that were suitable for arable farming. Around the coastline to the north, against the Blackwater Estuary, and to the east, facing the Outer Thames Estuary, lay large areas of low-lying saltmarsh formed of alluvium.[89] In its undeveloped state the saltmarsh was valuable as sheep pasture, but after inning and draining it could be used for both cattle and sheep and could also be cropped. The balance of land use between arable and pasture, and on the marshlands between saltmarsh and drained marsh, changed over time in response to economic trends influenced by population, market demand and economic specialisation.

Low hidations and small populations on the estates later known as East Hall, Battels and Down Hall suggest that arable production was relatively limited in the late eleventh century (Tables 7.1 and 7.2). Upland pasture and meadow were perhaps also in short supply as few horses, cattle and pigs were enumerated. The only recorded woodland (for 50 pigs) existed on the Bradwell Hall estate. A more notable feature of Bradwell's economy, and one that has been highlighted by previous studies, is the importance of marshland grazing identified by the term 'pasture for sheep' (Table 7.3). The entries relate to the large belt of intertidal saltmarsh along the Essex coast, especially prominent in Dengie hundred, where the sheep were grazed on wick (dairy) farms to produce large quantities of cheese and butter.[90] As only a limited amount of marsh had been 'inned' and converted to fresh marsh by banking and draining before 1200,[91] it seems probable that the sheep were mostly grazed on the saltmarsh, being moved to higher ground during bad weather and in winter.

Bradwell's pastures were assessed at 1,010 sheep, but unevenly distributed. Bradwell Hall, located inland, had pasture for only 50 sheep, indicating limited access to marshland. In contrast, manors directly nearer the coast were endowed with more significant shares: Effecestrā (East Hall; 300 sheep), Effecestre (Battels; 200 sheep), Dona (Down Hall; 100 sheep), Acleta (Tanyes(?); 100 sheep) and Hacflet (Hockley(?); 260 sheep). Three also had substantial sheep flocks: Effecestrā (216 sheep), Dona (159 sheep) and Acleta (80 sheep). It is also relevant that the abbey of St Valery owned 2½ hides and 'pasture for 200 sheep' in the adjacent parish of Dengie, known as the manor of Bacons, for a portion of Bacons called Buxsey Marsh adjoined East Hall's Garmonds Marsh (Figure 7.2).[92]

An informative snapshot of economic conditions at East Hall before the Black Death is provided by a survey from 1324. The manor house and the easements of the houses were worth 2s., the pleas and perquisites of

Table 7.3 Domesday economic statistics: pasture, woodland, animals and fisheries, 1066 and (1086).

Place	Pasture for	Woodland for	Horses	Cattle	Sheep	Pigs	Other
Effecestrā (1)	(300 sheep)	–	–	(3)	(216)	(20)	1 fishery
Effecestrā	–	–	–	–	–	–	–
Effecestre (2)	(200 sheep)	–	–	–	–	–	–
Duna (3)	(50 sheep)	(50 pigs)	–	–	–	–	–
Duna	–	–	–	–	–	–	–
Duna	–	–	–	–	–	–	–
Dona (4)	(100 sheep)	–	1 (3)	(3)	120 (159)	–	–
Landuna	–	–	–	–	–	–	–
Acleta	(100 sheep)	–	–	2 (2)	80 (80)	9 (9)	–
Hacflet (5)	(260)	–	–	–	–	–	1 fishery
TOTAL 1086	(1,010 sheep)	(50 pigs)	(3)	(8)	(455)	(29)	2 fisheries

Notes

(1) Estates are arranged under the five tenants-in-chief, their primary estate in Bradwell being labelled (1) to (5).

Source:

A. Williams and G. H. Martin (eds), *Little Domesday Book, Essex* (London, 2000), ff. 21, 24, 53v, 74v, 149v.

the court 1*s*. 6*d*. and the rents of assize £2 6*s*. 9½*d*. There were 138 acres of arable land worth £2 19*s*., two acres of mowing meadow worth 4*s*., Garmonds Marsh for a plough team and 100 sheep worth £1 5*s*., and another marsh for 80 sheep worth 13*s*. 4*d*. per year. Customary tenants provided 248 days of labour service (*opera*) worth 10*s*. 4*d*.[93] Account rolls from the same year show that 100½ acres were sown on the demesne, comprising 38 acres of wheat, 5 acres of mixed grain (*mixtillum*) and 8½ acres of rye in the winter, and 40½ acres of oats, 2 acres of barley, 1½ acres of beans and 5 acres of peas in the spring. The similarity between the winter-sown and spring-sown acreages (51½: 49) suggests a balanced rotation, but apparently with only 37½ acres left fallow. Expenses indicate a well-maintained farm, with 400 perches of furrows or watercourses ploughed before the spring sowing for drainage, and the smith paid for iron work on agricultural equipment and shoeing horses.[94]

As in the eleventh century, a key economic feature was the sheep flock grazed on the coastal marshes. In 1324 the demesne farm was stocked with seven rams, 124 ewes and 108 lambs, but optimum stocking was probably higher as the skins of two rams, 36 ewes and 12 lambs that had died were sold in the same year. Among the manorial servants were two shepherds and an indoor servant (*inhewe/inhughe*; possibly a dairyman).[95] The economic importance of the flock was also reflected in various maintenance expenditures. In 1324 6 gallons of tar and butter were purchased for treating sheep, foot rot being one threat to their health. The sheepfold in Garmonds Marsh required the work of a thatcher and his mate, while the walls were plastered anew at a total cost of 1*s*. 6*d*., details indicating an enclosed roofed structure for the protection and milking of the ewes (a 'bercaria').[96] Following damage caused by 'an inundation of the sea', possibly the same storm which overwhelmed sea defences at Stepney on New Year's Eve 1323, work in repairing three watercourses in the same marsh and making good with earth cost 6*s*. 8*d*.[97]

Rights of access to Garmonds Marsh was a significant local issue as the marsh did not lie contiguously with the East Hall demesne, being separated from it by Eastlands Farm and Buxsey Marsh (Figure 7.2). In 1308 an important local landowner called John de la Mare had granted to the monks of St Valery a way for their cattle to reach Garmonds through his farm of Eastlands 'when the height of the tide hindered their passage'.[98] Reference to the tide is explained by the separation of Garmonds Marsh from the rest of East Hall manor by a substantial tidal creek running from the coast westwards to Hockley Farm, which remained open until *c*. 1500 (Figure 7.1). The right of way to Garmonds Marsh past Eastlands Farm was still shown on an estate map of 1768 (Figure 7.3). Much earlier still, in 1207, as has already been noted, Emery Bataille had been granted a share of the same marsh by the abbot of St Valery. As his manor of Battels lay inland from the coast, the grant also included 'the ways appertaining to the said marsh' and Emery also received 80 sheep from the abbot (probably the stock allocation for that part of the marsh).[99]

Another account roll for East Hall from 1371–2 reflects changes wrought by the Black Death, although this was perhaps an unusual year in which the demesne farm was being restocked.[100] Arable cultivation had about halved since half a century earlier, with just 15 acres of rye being sown by the road leading to the chapel, 4 acres of peas, 1 acre of vetches and 32 acres of oats (total 52 acres). Significantly, no sowing of wheat was recorded, and much of the produce seems to have been expended on the farm. From the rye available after seeding various food liveries were dispensed: the ploughmen were paid just 1 quarter and 4½ bushels, while the shepherd at Blakesdonewick received 6 quarters and 4 bushels and another shepherd at Garmondswick 4 quarters and 7 bushels. The stock account reveals a large-scale restocking by purchase: seven cows before calving, two rams and another received as a gift, and 203 ewes, although 13 died. A final entry records the ewes apparently received in customary rents as totalling 66 in Blakesdonewick and 94 in Garmondswick, plus at Easter another 20 in Blakesdonewick and 50 in Garmondswick when milking (total 230, of which 70 milking). These entries imply the manor's tenants also kept large numbers of sheep.

Comparisons can be drawn with the more modest manor of Battels, where at his death in 1252 Emery Bataille held just a messuage, 68 acres of arable, pasture for 50 sheep, and £1 3s. 3½d. rent, plus another estate in Bradwell, where there was pasture for 120 sheep and 8s. 4d. rent. If the latter represents his portion of East Hall's Garmonds Marsh (see above), its stocking had apparently increased by 50 per cent since 1207.[101] In the late thirteenth century his son Saer Batayl still held the marsh's lease.[102] In 1274–5 it was also recorded that Saer owed a debt of £1 10s. to the king and that the bailiff of the hundred had distrained upon his marsh and fishery, probably indicating that these were among his most valuable assets.[103] After Saer's death in 1292 his estate comprised a messuage worth 2s., 20 acres of arable land worth 6s. 8d., marshland pasture worth £1 6s. 8d., a fishery worth 4s., rents of assize worth 18s. 10d., labour services worth a total of 6s. 9½d., the view of frankpledge and court perquisites worth 3s. and minor rents in wax, cumin and eggs worth 7d.[104] The estate probably included more land, as in 1317 Edmund Bataille granted a freehold subtenancy to John and Constance le Keu

(Coo or Cook), comprising a messuage, 40 acres of land, 2 acres of meadow and £2 rent.[105] On Edmund's death in 1333, the core of Battels remained a capital messuage, 20 acres of arable, 40 acres of saltmarsh and 10s. from rents of assize.[106]

The medieval farming landscape at Down Hall was similar. In 1306 Thomas de la Doune's estate comprised 126½ acres of arable, 2 acres of meadow, two parts of a marsh and a windmill, 8s. rent from freemen and the rent and work of a single customary tenant worth 2s. 3d. Further lands in Bradwell held of other lords, principally John de la Mare, amounted to 73½ acres and two parts of a marsh.[107] Upon her death in 1343 Margaret at Doune held a messuage and 102 acres of arable land, of which 81½ acres were sown with wheat, rye and oats. She also had an 'external' marsh (that is, saltmarsh) worth 5s. and an old and debilitated windmill worth 7s. per annum. In addition, 40 acres of arable, another 'external' marsh and 2s. rent were held of the heirs of John de la Mare, plus another 30 acres from Thomas Baynard. Margaret had also held in dower, after the death of her former husband, Edmund Bataille (of Battels manor), a third part of a messuage and 43 acres of land and 10 acres of marsh, of the inheritance of Robert Baron (Baround), kinsman and heir of Edmund.[108]

When Edmund de la Doune died in 1400, the family's Bradwell estate again comprised several distinct portions: (a) a messuage (Down Hall), a ruined windmill, 100 acres of arable, 4 acres of meadow, 2 acres of pasture, 40 acres of 'external' marsh, a broken weir, 10s. 4d. rent and the view of frankpledge valued at 1s.; (b) another messuage (Tanyes) with 100 acres of arable, 5 acres of meadow, 10 acres of 'external' marsh, 1 acre of wood, five old broken weirs and 12s. rent; (c) a third messuage with 60 acres of arable, 1 acre of pasture, 30 acres 'external' marsh and 5s. rent; and (d) another estate of 30 acres.[109] On the death of John de la Doune in 1426 the estate core of Down Hall was essentially identical, but showed signs of decay as the messuage (called 'le Ferehous') and a grange (barn) were worth nothing and the site of the windmill was now 'vacant'.[110] In 1428 an assignment of dower to John's widow, Katherine, gave her one third of the above estate, including the lower part of the house called 'Fer[e]hous' and one third of the grange on the northern side.[111]

In summary, by the high point of expansion in the early fourteenth century all three manors had arable farms on the higher land. A wide variety of crops, as evidenced for East Hall in 1324, were grown. It is also probable that well before the Black Death the main estates had 'inned' and drained some of their saltmarsh and built or extended sea walls, but the archaeological and historical work necessary to uncover the chronology on the Dengie Peninsula has yet to be conducted.[112] Certainly, however, the process was not complete by the mid-/late fourteenth century, as substantial 'external' marshes were recorded on Down Hall manor in both 1343 and 1400. Investment probably halted after the Black Death, while increasingly stormy conditions made existing sea defences vulnerable.[113] The impact of plague on the estates in the vicinity of St Peter's Chapel can also be detected. On Down Hall manor the reduction of the cultivated area and a windmill in ruins by 1400 (it was still abandoned in 1427),[114] reflects falling market demand for bread grain and flour milling. Correspondingly, rising living standards led to greater demand for meat, wool and dairy products, so it seems likely that Bradwell's sheep became more valuable and even more numerous in the later Middle Ages.

Descriptions of the manors and other estates near St Peter's Chapel in the Tudor period suggest that the pastoral sector was dominant and probably expanding. When the Pincheons were adding to the Wymarks estate in the 1580s, much of the land had already been inned and drained, with Jane Pincheon purchasing 100 acres of fresh marsh to 40 acres of saltmarsh in 1584 and William Puncheon 100 acres of fresh marsh to just 7 acres of saltmarsh in 1588.[115] In 1593 the manor of Battels was said to comprise just 10 acres of arable alongside 10 acres of meadow and 60 acres of pasture.[116] Most evidence relates to Down Hall, where in 1502 there had been 100 acres of land (arable), compared with 4 acres of meadow, 80 acres of pasture, 100 acres of 'foreign' marsh, plus 200 acres of 'foreign' marsh called Hellcote Marsh and another 80 acres of 'foreign' marsh called Shellmarsh (for locations, see Figure 7.2). The 'foreign' marshes were saltmarsh, indicating a substantial area yet to be 'inned' (see below),[117] but in the following century it seems that much of the saltmarsh was drained. At this date it seems likely that the newly drained marsh was used for an expansion of cattle dairying rather than for arable production. When Down Hall was mortgaged in 1562, it was described as having 400 acres of arable, 20 acres of meadow, 300 acres of pasture, 40 acres of wood, 400 acres of marsh and £2 rent, clearly rounded figures but ones that probably reflect the balance of land use.[118] This is confirmed by later sales of 1576 and 1580, when one part of the manor, probably comprising Tanyes and Tomlyns Wick, had 200 acres of arable, to 10 acres of meadow, 150 acres pasture, 20 acres of wood, 140 acres of fresh marsh and 60 acres of saltmarsh,[119] and the other part, probably the Down Hall demesne, had 200 acres of arable, 12 acres of meadow, 100 acres of pasture, 20 of acres of wood, 300 acres of marsh and 30s. rent.[120]

Contemporary sea wall construction was recorded in the sale of Tanyes and Tomlyns Wick in 1590, when the transaction excluded 8 rods (c. 40m) of marsh or sea wall newly erected by Thomas Mildmay on part of a marsh called 'Fernewell', a parcel of Down Hall manor, extending to the head of an old wall at New Wick.[121] In 1593 the Down Hall tenant had to repair and maintain sea defences which included the 'new wall' and new gutters in the wall in Far Newell marsh.[122] Later maps indicate that 'inning' was virtually complete by the eighteenth century: in 1714 Wymarks had about 220 acres of enclosed marsh to just 11 acres of saltings, in 1753 Down Hall had no appreciable saltmarsh and in 1768 East hall had about 100 acres of enclosed marsh to 32 acres of saltings and its sea walls were noted as 'old' (Figures 7.3, 7.4 and 7.5). The map of Wymarks gives a good indication of the nature of the northern marshes before reclamation; a wide fleet was preserved behind the sea wall when Keyhaven Creek was sealed off and the formerly tidal creeks and rills were preserved as field boundaries as far inland as Battels (Figure 7.5).

As will be demonstrated below, increased farming profits from supplying London with dairy products lay behind the draining of the marshlands. Evidence of high stocking levels is found in a legal suit in 1624, when the heirs of John Coleman attempted to recover their inheritance. They stated that their father, landowner at New Wick and lessee at Down Hall, had a 'great estate' at the time of his death with '60 kine, 300 sheep, 30 horses, mares, geldings and colts and divers[e] oxen and … carts, ploughs'. They also indicated that Coleman had a sideline in growing hops, perhaps on the same site as the 'Hop Field' shown on the Down Hall estate close to Bradwell Waterside in 1753 (Figure 7.4). They further claimed that 'at the several places … [he] kept there also several great dairies and had at the time of his decease great quantities of wool, butter and cheeses at the several farms and places before of the said stock and goods worth at least a 1,000 marks', probably referring to his operations at Tomlyns Wick and New Wick.[123]

How far this pattern extended throughout Bradwell can be investigated by analysing the occupational designations of 63 testators whose wills survive between 1565 and 1604 (Table 7.4). The data only represent the social level, status and gender of people who routinely made formal wills, thereby including the wealthy, such as those who held leases of the main estates, and the middling sort, but excluding most women and the poorer elements of society.[124] Five of the only six women recorded were widows, no labourers or servants were identified by status designation and only one tradesman (a shoemaker). Forty per cent of testators did not describe their status or occupation, but examination of the contents of their wills indicates that at least one third of them, and probably many more, were also landowners or farmers like the large group (33 per cent) clearly designated as farmers. Many others drew at least part of their living from agriculture, including the two clergymen, two people classified as unmarried and some of the mariners.

No early probate inventories survive for Bradwell, but the wills contain some details elucidating the nature of local farming concerns. A yeoman testator, Henry Saffold (d. 1590), who possessed land in both Bradwell and Tillingham, left bequests to his wife including 18 dairy cows and 50 ewes, a bay gelding and a bay colt, all his poultry and eight seams of wheat.[125] Another testator with a large dairying concern was William Hodge (d. 1588), who bequeathed his lease of 'Dillimers' (that is, Delamares in Bradwell) stocked with 28 cows and 100 ewes.[126] Jakes Born, evidently a wealthy farmer, left to his son five cattle and 20 of the best ewes 'that goeth at East Hall' (he was probably renting pasture there).[127] Members of the husbandman class often had similar stock: Richard Payne (d. 1587) bequeathed to his daughter 10 of his best sheep and three cows.[128] The 'single woman' Dorothy Parker (d. 1566) had a joint share of stock with her sister and from the will of their husbandman father, John Porter, that comprised seven cows, a heifer, 60 sheep, five crones (old ewes), five lambs, as well as horses, colts, hogs and pigs.[129]

Fisheries

A number of early medieval fish weirs, large permanent structures constructed with heavy posts driven into the mud or sand that supported wattle-type fencing in a funnel or V-shape to trap fish on the ebbing tide, have been discovered in the Blackwater Estuary. One lies on the north side of Pewet Island (off Bradwell Waterside) and the other off Sales Point (about 1,200m from St Peter's Chapel).[130] The latter is of especially complex form and has been radiocarbon dated to *c*. 670; in both date and scale it seems likely to have been linked to ecclesiastical ownership and an early monastic community at St Peter's Chapel.[131] It may be represented by the fishery recorded at East Hall in 1086, while a second fishery was listed on Hacflet (Hockley) manor at the same date (Table 7.3).[132]

Whether or not the largest weirs were maintained into the later Middle Ages is uncertain, for smaller traps (often called kiddles) seem to have become favoured perhaps due to structural changes in the industry or target species.[133] By 1292 there was a 'fishery on the sea sands' on Battels manor worth 4*s*.[134] In 1324 East Hall manor received an income of

5s. 1½d. from its fish traps on the coast.[135] Many weirs and kiddles were held by East Hall tenantry around 1400, sometimes subdivided into half shares.[136] In 1397, for example, William and Johanna Sampwell applied for a licence to place half of two weirs 'at farm' to Robert and Amys Bubbe for five years at 15s. per annum, the lessees to repair and maintain their carpentry. In the following year Robert and Amys took on yet more weirs in two separate transactions, three of them named as La Rose, Maltere and Lotham.[137] These transactions reveal the high value of the weirs and their probable use for commercial fishing. Their catch may have been destined for local urban markets such as Maldon, but as Galloway has shown, there was a large-scale market for fish in medieval London which partly drew upon the weirs along the Essex and Kent coasts in the outer Thames Estuary.[138]

The fishing industry may have encountered some problems by the fifteenth century, for there were 'broken' weirs on Down Hall lands c. 1400. In the period 1436–8 another fishing weir was reported as damaged by the sea and repairs were being undertaken on the sea walls on Hockley manor.[139] Erosion certainly proved a problem at Clacton in Tendring hundred, only a few miles away by sea, where fish weirs were being swept away somewhat later, c. 1500.[140] Nonetheless, on East Hall manor new kiddles were being constructed and rented to tenants in 1497, developments perhaps in response to changes on the coastal marshes and sands. One was located on the lord's sand opposite a certain 'waste' marsh called North Germannes, another to the south of the first lay opposite Garmonds Marsh and another three were on the lord's sand opposite 'East Hall Marsh'.[141] Shortly afterwards, c. 1500, a rental of East Hall recorded £1 11s. rent from 14 kiddles and two fish weirs. In 1508 Thomas Tele took a weir called 'Petyrwere' situated in the stream between Rosewere on the east and Clamfletewere on the west, again with a condition that he had to repair it.[142] The possible site of some of these weirs or kiddles has been located by aerial photography and foot survey lying in the mud north-east of St Peter's Chapel but closer to the shoreline than the Sales Point weir. Perhaps 'Petyrwere' was named in relation to the chapel, although St Peter was a fisherman and thus fishermen were sometimes termed 'petermen'.[143]

Tudor wills reveal continuing local fishing activity, although only one testator, 'Elles' Garrowolde (d. 1598), was identified as a 'kiddleman'.[144] Other testators who designated themselves as mariners (or a similar term) but also bequeathed nets, together with their boats, must have drawn at least part of their income from fishing. Examples include John Bennett (d. c. 1597), who bequeathed to his son John half his hoy and half his nets at the age of 23,[145] and the sailor Gregory Jacob (d. 1600), who left half his boat and half his nets to Richard Tye (possibly Gregory's business partner). Although not stated, the other half of the boat probably descended to Gregory's wife and son.[146] Some of Bradwell's inhabitants clearly belonging to the class of 'fisher-farmers', often found in coastal communities, who were able to combine farming with seasonable activities in fishing and probably also seaborne trade.[147] Clement Bond (d. 1574), a mariner and probably another fisherman, left cattle to his wife as well as his boats and nets 'and all other my craft which I have towards the sea'.[148] In 1602 the reasonably well-to-do mariner Abraham Bennett, who owned a house with a hall and chamber, also grew peas and barley.[149] Robert Lovedaie (d. 1600), who owned two boats and another substantial house with parlours and solars, was also another farmer, as he had corn and cheese in his parlours, grew wheat, barley and peas, and had at least three cows and seven sheep.[150]

Shipping and trade

As population and commerce grew in scale between the twelfth and fourteenth centuries, so a major part of the harvest, especially of wheat, may have been destined for market sale. In 1283 John de la Mare obtained grants to hold both a Monday market and a fair at Bradwell, part of a pattern of commercial development in thirteenth-century Essex involving 'a comparatively rapid growth of coastal trade through minor market centres'.[151] It was apparently successful, as only two years after its foundation an agreement was struck between John and the bishop of London, who owned a long-standing market at nearby Southminster. The agreement allowed John's Bradwell market to continue, with right of way to it for traders and their carts and wagons via the bishop's bridge in Southminster called 'Ledebridge', while in return traders coming by sea who wished to attend the bishop's market were allowed to land their goods at John's quay at Bradwell called Hokflete without paying toll or wharfage.[152] The landing was probably on the waterway named Hokflete that passed through the marshes belonging to Hockley and from which it took its name (Figure 7.1).

It remains uncertain whether Bradwell had developed a sizeable maritime community at this time for records of naval service for the fourteenth century do not record any ships, masters or mariners from the parish; local shipping seems to have been dominated by Maldon and Burnham.[153] But the new Bradwell market must have benefited the locality, for agricultural products such as wheat and cheese could be transported easily by sea to important towns and markets such as Maldon, St Osyth and Colchester, as well as to London, which was the nearest metropolitan market for ports on the Essex coast south of Colchester that faced the Thames Estuary.[154] One documented example of the transport of grain from East Hall by ship occurred in 1324, when 3 quarters and 1 bushel of wheat and 5 quarters of oats were shipped by boat to Maldon and delivered to Richard Perers, sheriff of Essex, for the king's use.[155] The case reflects not only the method by which Bradwell's produce must largely have been exported but also how Essex coastal manors could suffer the demands of the crown for provisions in support of military operations.[156]

Bradwell lay under the jurisdiction of the port of Maldon for customs purposes, the latter place itself being a member of the head port of Ipswich.[157] Maldon's customs officials oversaw many small landing places and wharves in coastal parishes along the Blackwater Estuary, where farmers could load grain directly into ships more conveniently than using the narrow channel to Maldon.[158] In 1565 a survey revealed three such landing places at Bradwell,[159] the first being described as 'a Creek in Bradwell water leading from out of the main sea plain west towards Maldon'. That location is likely to be Bradwell Wharf, depicted on the 1777 county map opposite Pewet Island, now known as Bradwell Waterside.[160] The second and third were described as 'two common lading places' in 'Bradwell stream' called, respectively, Stansgate and Bradwell. The former was actually outside of the parish, lying along the Blackwater Estuary to the west of Bradwell, while a later survey from 1579 indicates the latter to be Keyhaven, a landing place on the marshes between East Hall and Down Hall to the north-west of Wymarks.[161] The absence of Hokflete from the survey suggests that the wharf there was no longer accessible, probably blocked by a new sea wall. Keyhaven may have only dealt with the trade of neighbouring farms, so most trade to and from the parish of Bradwell probably passed through Bradwell Waterside. It was probably the single landing place or haven at Bradwell recorded in yet another survey from 1566, described as having 10 ships, nine masters and owners, and seven mariners, and sharing a customs deputy with Tillingham.[162]

Out of Bradwell's 63 Tudor testators, only six (9.5 per cent) bequeathed boats, but not all of these were identified by their wills as mariners thus indicating wider community involvement with seafaring (Table 7.4). Their relatively small vessels were described by a variety of terms, including hoy (a small coastal trading vessel) and ketch (a small

Table 7.4 Bradwell occupations as indicated by 63 wills, 1565–1604.

Designation of occupation or status	Number	Percentage
Yeoman	6	9.5
Husbandman	15	23.8
Clergymen	2	3.2
Mariner, sailor or sea-faring man	6	9.5
'Kiddle-man', i.e. fisherman	1	1.6
Shoemaker	1	1.6
Widow	5	7.9
Single man (i.e. bachelor)	1	1.6
Single woman (i.e. spinster)	1	1.6
Unstated	25	39.7
Total	63	100.00

Source: Emmison, *Essex Wills*, vols 1–9; TNA, PROB 11/44/159; PROB 11/27/146; PROB 11/96/404; PROB 11/93/187; PROB 11/99/232.

fishing craft, but one adaptable for other uses including coastal trade). As in other Essex coastal communities like St Osyth, the vessels were subdivided into shares between family members (as a result of inheritance) or between investors.[163] When Timothy Tredsall, a member of a significant family of local maritime traders, died at an unknown date between 1583 and 1592, he bequeathed half his ketch called the *George* to his daughter Elizabeth (the other half probably descending to his widow, Helen).[164] The same ketch was then recorded in the will of Gregory Payne (d. 1594), a seafaring man who owned land in Bradwell, and who bequeathed cattle and leased land but also left half of the ketch called the *George* and the cock (a small boat) called the *Duck* to his wife's daughter, called Elizabeth Tredsall. It seems probable that Payne had married Timothy's widow, thus acquiring her share of the ketch, but after his death the whole vessel was reunited in the hands of Timothy and Helen's daughter.[165]

The port of Maldon's sixteenth- and seventeenth-century shipping and associated mercantile activity were explored in great depth by Bronwen Cook using port books (customs accounts).[166] This source contains a wealth of information on ships, masters, merchants, merchandise and voyages, although unfortunately their incomplete survival means full statistical analysis is not possible. Cook's study shows that Bradwell was one of the more important shipping points, alongside Maldon, Burnham and Althorne, benefiting from its location at the tip of the Blackwater Estuary and the deeper water available at Bradwell Waterside. In the late sixteenth century, the parish had a small but thriving community of ship masters who earned their living shipping local agricultural produce to London and other destinations. Seven masters were recorded with more than 10 voyages, the most active being Thomas London (1588–1611; 59 voyages). The Tredsall family, mentioned above, were important, including both John Tredsall (1566–81; 26 voyages) and Timothy Tredsall (1574–89; 28 voyages).[167] Cargoes of wheat, oats and barley were all exported from Bradwell, usually to the major and growing market of London.[168] Large amounts of dairy produce, in the form of cheese measured in weys (336lb) and butter in barrels, were shipped to London (about two-thirds) and Kent (about one third), revealing the main markets for Bradwell's coastal dairies.[169] An example of a typical trading voyage occurred on 7 October 1568, when the *Mary* of Bradwell, weighing 9 tons, mastered by John Elliott, travelled from Maldon to Gravesend (Kent) with 12 weys (4,032lb) of cheese and two barrels of butter for the yeoman John Baker of Tillingham.[170]

Between 1565 and 1602 vessels from many landing places were involved in the trade in dairy produce, but the largest number were from Bradwell and Burnham on either flank of the marshlands. Voyages were made under contract for merchants, and sometimes farmers, from across Dengie hundred. Some Bradwell shipments were made for merchants chiefly operating out of other havens such as Maldon or Burnham, but one of the more important was John Wakeman of neighbouring Tillingham, for whom 35 shipments were recorded.[171] Many other voyages were on behalf of specialist London merchants from the city livery companies, such as salters, fishmongers and cheesemongers. Among the most important was Sir John Leman (a fishmonger), who together with Francis Bridges was responsible for shipping over 600 weys (201,600lb) of cheese and butter in Bradwell vessels between 1574 and 1577. By the time of his death in 1632, the wealthy and successful Leman, who became mayor of London in 1616, had also accumulated much landed property across 12 parishes of Dengie hundred, including Bradwell, Dengie and Southminster.[172]

The early seventeenth century was the highpoint of the dairying industry and export trade in Bradwell and neighbouring parishes (Figure 7.5). Cheese and butter production continued, but subsequently their relative importance waned as arable production, particularly of oats and wheat, began a resurgence. These adjustments reflected changes and increases in market demand and consequent regional adjustments to

Table 7.5 Major exports of produce from Bradwell, 1565–1703.

Produce Type	1565–1602	1603–1653	1668–1703
Dairy produce (weys)	1,965	446	238
Wheat (quarters)	204–333	238–331	12,007
Oats (quarters)	433–757	1,260–1,950	26,865–30,046
Barley (quarters)	20–60	140	318–540

Source: Cook 2005, 108–131, 164–7.

production. By the period 1668–1703 Bradwell ships took about 16 per cent of wheat freights from the port district of Maldon, chiefly to London.[173] Production of wheat displaced rye as demand for finer bread grain increased once more, while oats were principally for feeding the capital's horses. Smaller quantities of other produce were also exported, including seed crops, hops, wool and firewood.[174] Individual shipments in the 1640s demonstrate the scale of grain shipments and also give some flavour of the variety of goods. In 1642 John Dewbank sent seven horsepacks of wool to Colchester for its clothmakers, while Daniel Goodwyn of Bradwell despatched 30 weys of cheese and butter (10,080lb) in the *Sarah* and 60 quarters of oats and 10 quarters of wheat in the *Peter and Mary* (a Bradwell barge) to London.[175] In 1643 Goodwyn and Nicholas Blackwell of New Wick farm, with other local farmers, used the *Peter and Mary* to send 360 quarters of oats and 40 quarters of wheat to London.[176]

Summary

This chapter has considered the development of the north-east part of Bradwell on Sea close to St Peter's Chapel over the six centuries following the Norman Conquest. Landholding in the area was already complex in 1086, and although further research is needed, the area was clearly structured around three small estates (East Hall, Down Hall and Battels) possessing small arable farms as well as adjacent wicks associated with dairying on the marshes. Down Hall and Battels manors had few freemen or customary tenants, and even though East Hall manor's assized rents and labour services, plus its manorial servants, imply a slightly larger population, it was never more than a hamlet.

The importance of the coastal fisheries and marshland to the economy of the estates was a constant theme. Two fisheries were recorded in 1086, the one at East Hall perhaps being associated with the major early medieval fish trap discovered lying off Sales Point. Many fish weirs and kiddles used by the manors' tenantry in the later Middle Ages were recorded because of their value in rents and fines. In contrast, little information could be uncovered about medieval coastal fishing using nets or trawls, although those techniques must certainly have been employed.[177] By the Tudor period the catching of fish using nets appears to have been a by-employment for Bradwell's fisher-farmers. In both periods fishing would have been not only for subsistence but also on a commercial basis to supply urban markets accessible by sea.

In 1086, and presumably long before, there were substantial sheep flocks on the coastal saltmarshes; these were organised as coastal dairy farms called wicks. Before 1348 there was also substantial arable production on the higher ground, and market development would have seen both dairy produce and grain, especially wheat, traded at Bradwell's market and exported by sea to London and other destinations. The late fourteenth and the fifteenth centuries were probably a time of retrenchment, certainly for the arable economy, although sustained demand for meat and dairy products may have further emphasised the pastoral sector. By the sixteenth century there are signs that rising demand, perhaps especially from London, further enhanced Bradwell's pastoral economy, seen most clearly in the large-scale late Tudor dairying industry.

The chronology of 'inning' and sea defence matches the development of the farming economy. While some expansion of sea walls and drainage probably occurred up to the fourteenth century, there was then a temporary halt, with much saltmarsh remaining. A new phase evidently began in the sixteenth century, perhaps accelerating in the second half, with the drainage of most remaining saltmarsh around the headland stretching from Down Hall on the west to East Hall and St Peter's Chapel on the east. It seems probable, on the evidence of maritime trade, that the money to invest in drainage and new sea walls was generated by successful commercial farming at Bradwell. At first greater profits were generated by the Tudor dairying industry, including involvement by important London merchants, but by the mid-seventeenth century larger-scale cereal growing was provisioning the same market. More 'capitalistic' farming was accompanied by significant changes in landholding, with external investment by the Mildmay and Christmas families and the formation of new estates by rising yeoman farming families such as the Brooke and Pincheon families.

Notes

1. Minchin 1907, 346.
2. Morant 1768, vol. 1, 374–8; Round 1903, 391–2; Brown 1929, 103–55.
3. A full modern analysis of Bradwell's manors awaits the progress of the *VCH*.
4. Reaney 1935, 211. See also Breeze 2020, 11–15.
5. The hide in Essex representing a nominal 120 acres.
6. For example, Barking (30 hides), Southminster (30 hides), the Naze (30 hides), Clacton (20 hides): Round 1903, 334; Thornton 2020a, 9.
7. Williams and Martin 2000, fol. 21; Fowler 1907, 199.
8. Fowler, 1907, 199.
9. Salter 1929, charter nos 29, 30, 32; Round 1903, 392 and note 3; Reaney 1935, 210. Reaney's discussion does not clearly differentiate between application of the 'Walle' name to the estate/vill and as a descriptive suffix to the name of the chapel.
10. NCA, 9166.
11. TNA, E 106/7/3.
12. Fowler 1907, 199–200; Brown 1929, 143; NCA, 1353; NCA, 7774.
13. Steer 1974, 243 (NCA, 2343); transcripts of Bodleian MS ch. Essex in ERO, T/A 316/175–226.
14. ERO, T/A 316/176.
15. NCA, 20 (7 July 1506); NCA, 18.
16. NHLE 1110940 (accessed 2 August 2021); unpublished survey by Tim Howson, Maldon District Council Conservation Officer (2015).
17. ERO, T/A 316/177–8.
18. Newton 1970, 73; Steer 1974, 282.
19. ERO, T/A 316/177–202; TNA, PROB 11/241/209.
20. Round 1903, 392 and note 1.
21. *Feet of Fines, Essex*, vol. 1, 42 (no. 233).
22. TNA, C 132/13/5; C 133/21/1; C 135/35/31.
23. TNA, C 135/35/31.
24. *Feet of Fines, Essex*, vol. 3, 243 (no. 103); *Cal. Inq. p.m.*, vol. 22, 652–3 (no. 751).
25. Brown 1929, 139 (John, possibly in error?), 157 (Thomas); BL Add. Ch. 9262.
26. Morant 1768, vol. 1, 376; TNA, C 142/62/65; C 142/69/81.
27. TNA, C 1/1219/37–9.
28. TNA, C 142/199/73.
29. *Feet of Fines, Essex*, vol. 6, 134 (no. 12).
30. Morant 1768, vol. 1, 376; TNA, PROB 11/155/427.
31. Williams and Martin 2000, fol. 74v. For Ranulf de Peverel: Round 1903, 346; Taylor 2000, 20.
32. Round 1903, 392.
33. Round 1903, 392 and notes 4–7.
34. Williams and Martin 2000, fol. 49v; Round 1903, 493. For Eudo: Round 1903, 347–8; Taylor 2000, 20, 23.
35. Round 1903, 493 note 5.
36. Morant 1768, vol. 1, 376.
37. *Cal. Inq. p.m.*, vol. 4, 235.
38. *Cal. Inq. p.m.*, vol. 8, 296.
39. *Cal. Inq. p.m.*, vol. 18, 35.
40. *Cal. Inq. p.m.*, vol. 22, 612–13.
41. TNA, C 142/15/87; Morant 1768, vol. 1, 377; Brown 1929, 130.
42. TNA, C 131/86/33; TNA C 131/251/11; Brown 1929, 132; ERO, D/DB T129 (24 November 1512).
43. Britnell 1986, 210.
44. *Feet of Fines, Essex*, vol. 5, 96 (no. 16); Morant 1768, vol. 1, 377.
45. TNA, E179/108/160 (the 1st assessment); ERO, D/ABW 3/93.
46. *Feet of Fines, Essex*, vol. 5, 204 (no. 8).
47. TNA, PROB 11/63/587; ERO, T/M 301/1.
48. TNA, C 2/Eliz/B16/59.

49 *Feet of Fines, Essex*, vol. 6, 139 (no. 24).
50 *Feet of Fines, Essex*, vol. 6, 177 (no. 3).
51 *Feet of Fines, Essex*, vol. 5, 240 (no. 8).
52 *Feet of Fines, Essex*, vol. 6, 30 (no. 55). The description was the same less 10 acres of wood, and the marshland was described as 7 acres of fresh marsh and 100 acres of salt marsh.
53 *Feet of Fines, Essex*, vol. 6, 75 (no. 18).
54 ERO, D/AER 19/80.
55 Morant 1768, vol. 1, 377.
56 ERO, D/DB T129 (deed 1 December 1575).
57 ERO, D/DB T129 (deed 9 September 1593).
58 *Feet of Fines, Essex*, vol. 2, 199 (no. 849).
59 TNA, C 142/15/87.
60 Field names from an inquisition of 1427 (TNA, C 139/36/84), a charter of 1485 (Brown 1929, 157) and a rental of East Hall manor from *c.* 1500 (NCA, 18).
61 Information from Maria Medlycott, Senior Historic Environment Consultant, ECC Place Services.
62 *Cal. Inq. p.m.*, vol. 23, 85.
63 Morant 1768, vol. 1, 377; TNA, C 142/15/87.
64 Thornton 2020a, 38–9.
65 ERO, D/DB T129 (1 December 1575).
66 ERO, D/AER 19/80; TNA, C 2/JasI/C14/24 (1611); TNA, C 3/338/2 (1624).
67 NCA, 18; NCA, 19.
68 *Feet of Fines, Essex*, vol. 4, 177 (no. 8).
69 *Feet of Fines, Essex*, vol. 5, 139 (no. 6); TNA, C 3/144/84. For his ownership of Eastlands Farm at his death: TNA, C 142/173/41.
70 *Feet of Fines, Essex*, vol. 6, 26 (no. 6), under her (second) married name, Jane Willson.
71 *Feet of Fines, Essex*, vol. 6, 63 (no. 17).
72 *Feet of Fines, Essex*, vol. 6, 134 (no. 12).
73 Morant 1768, vol. 1, 377; ERO, D/DH VID7, VID10, VID74; TNA C 7/214/83; TNA, PROB 11/356/314.
74 Darby 1977, 208–31, esp. 220–31; Macdonald and Snooks 1986, 77–96.
75 Finn 1971, 249–59; Thornton 2020a, 13, 53.
76 Calculation based on a hide = 120 acres.
77 Darby 1977, 87–91.
78 Fowler 1930, 30.
79 Glasscock 1975, 84; Ward 1983, 89–94.
80 Ward 1983, 92.
81 Smith 1991, 37–49.
82 Using a multiplier of 1.4. Data from Fenwick 1998, 175.
83 Poos 1991, 91–110.
84 TNA, E179/108/160.
85 Britnell 1986, 86–97; Poos 1991, 91–110.
86 TNA, E179/108/160 (the first assessment). Cf. Sheail 1998, 89.
87 Ferguson et al. 2012, 440–1.
88 Chapman and André 1777, plate XIV.
89 British Geological Survey 2000/2010; Soil Survey of England and Wales 1983.
90 For an explanation of the formula and its link to Essex marshlands: Round 1903, 369–74; Darby 1977, 149–50, 157–9; Hart 1993, 185–7.
91 Galloway 2013, 7–8.
92 Williams and Martin 2000, fol. 21; Morant 1768, vol. 1, 369–70.
93 TNA, E 106/7/3.
94 TNA, SC 6/1125/11.
95 TNA, SC 6/1125/10; SC 6/1125/11. For the Middle English word *Inhewe* see Fisher 1997, 24.
96 TNA, SC 6/1125/10; SC 6/1125/11. Cf. Dyer 1995.
97 TNA, SC 6/1125/11; Galloway 2007, 372.
98 Morant 1768, vol. 1, 377. Morant did not give his source, but it was probably New College 9790/632.
99 *Feet of Fines for Essex*, vol. 1, 42 (no. 433).

100 Following paragraph based on NCA, 9166.
101 *Cal. Inq. p.m.*, vol. 1, 62–3; TNA, C 132/13/5; Morant 1768, vol. 1, 376.
102 NCA, 9790/633.
103 *Rot. Hund.*, vol. 1, 159.
104 *Cal. Inq. p.m.*, vol. 3, 15–16; TNA, C 133/62/1.
105 *Feet of Fines for Essex*, vol. 2, 175 (no. 595).
106 *Cal. Inq. p.m.*, vol. 7, 363; TNA, C 135/35/31 [the extent is damaged].
107 *Cal. Inq. p.m.*, vol. 4, 235; TNA, C 133/121/19; Morant 1768, vol. 1, 376.
108 *Cal. Inq. p.m.*, vol. 8, 296; TNA, C 135/69/14.
109 *Cal. Inq. p.m.*, vol. 18, 35; TNA, C 137/7/43; Morant 1768, vol. 1, 376.
110 *Cal. Inq. p.m.*, vol. 22, 612–13.
111 *Cal. Inq. p.m.*, vol. 23, 85.
112 Galloway 2013, 9; Gardiner 2005, 73–83.
113 Galloway 2007, 373–4, 2013, 12–13.
114 *Cal. Inq. p.m.*, vol. 22, 612–13.
115 *Feet of Fines, Essex*, vol. 6, 26 (no. 6), under her (second) married name, Jane Willson; *Feet of Fines, Essex*, vol. 6, 63 (no. 17).
116 *Feet of Fines, Essex*, vol. 6, 134 (no. 12).
117 TNA, C 142/15/87; Morant 1768, vol. 1, 377; Brown 1929, 130.
118 *Feet of Fines, Essex*, vol. 5, 96 (no. 16).
119 *Feet of Fines, Essex*, vol. 5, 204 (no. 8).
120 *Feet of Fines, Essex*, vol. 5, 240 (no. 8).
121 ERO, D/DB T129 (1 Jan. 1591).
122 ERO, D/DB T129 (deed 9 Sept. 1593).
123 TNA, C 3/338/2.
124 Goose and Evans 2000, 44–7.
125 *Essex Wills*, vol. 5, 163 (no. 613).
126 *Essex Wills*, vol. 5, 91 (no. 331).
127 *Essex Wills*, vol. 8, 52 (no. 230).
128 *Essex Wills*, vol. 5, 81 (no. 284).
129 *Essex Wills*, vol. 8, 124 (no. 529).
130 NHLE 1019105, 1019103 (accessed 2 August 2021).
131 Strachan 1998, 274–82, esp. 276, 278–80; Murphy and Brown 1999, 17; see also Rippon, in this volume.
132 Strachan 1998, 281.
133 Thornton, 2020a, 40–1.
134 *Cal. Inq. p.m.*, vol. 3, 15–16.
135 TNA, SC 6/1125/11.
136 NCA, 20.
137 NCA, 20 (3 May 1397; 15 April 1398).
138 Galloway 2021, esp. 265–70.
139 TNA, SC 837/3, 4.
140 Cooper and Chapman 2020, 257.
141 NCA, 20 (30 Sept. 1497).
142 NCA, 18.
143 Aerial photographs and fieldwork by K. Bruce. For 'petermen': Galloway 2021, 252.
144 *Essex Wills*, vol. 7, 8 (no. 33).
145 *Essex Wills*, vol. 6, 102 (no. 514).
146 *Essex Wills*, vol. 7, 37 (no. 184).
147 For an Essex example: Galloway 2021, 254.
148 *Essex Wills*, vol. 9, 20 (no. 103).
149 *Essex Wills*, vol. 7, 57 (no. 275).
150 *Essex Wills*, vol. 7, 69 (no. 354).
151 *Cal. Charter Rolls*, vol. 2, 265–6; Letters, 2003, 126. Quotation from Britnell 1981, 19.
152 *Feet of Fines for Essex*, vol. 2, 53 (no. 336); Letters 2003, 126, 136. The details of the agreement suggest it resulted from an earlier stand-off over access rights between John and the bishop.
153 Ships from Althorne and Creeksea were also recorded. Ayton and Lambert 2017, 98–142.
154 Campbell et al. 1993, 48, 182.
155 TNA, SC 6/1125/10; SC 6/1125/11 (which has 4 quarters and 6 bushels of oats).

156 In this instance perhaps associated with provisioning for the war of Saint-Sardos in Gascony: Phillips 2010, 461–8. See also: Wiffen 2019, 11–20.
157 Cook 2005, 19–20.
158 Cook 2005, 88–90.
159 TNA, E 178/2124. See also Dickin 1924, 158.
160 Chapman and André 1777, plate XIV.
161 TNA, SP 12/135.
162 TNA, SP 12/39 (22), fol. 66.
163 Thornton 2020b, 155.
164 *Essex Wills*, vol. 5, 150 (no. 558).
165 *Essex Wills*, vol. 6, 67 (no. 338).
166 We are grateful to Bronwen Cook for allowing us to cite from her thesis: Cook 2005.
167 Cook 2005, 289–91.
168 Cook 2005, 101–2, 109–11, 124–5.
169 Cook 2005, 161–2.
170 Cook 2005, 409.
171 Cook 2005, 345.
172 Cook 2005, 161–5, 349, 351 (and note 41); R. Ashton, 'Leman, Sir John (1544–1632)', *ODNB*: https://doi.org/10.1093/ref:odnb/16420 [accessed 2 August 2021].
173 Cook 2005, 114.
174 Cook 2005.
175 TNA, E 190/605/9.
176 TNA, E 190/605/11.
177 Galloway 2021, 255–8.

Bibliography

Ayton, A., and C. Lambert. 2017. 'Shipping the troops and fighting at sea: Essex ports and mariners in England's wars, 1337–89'. In *The Fighting Essex Soldier. Recruitment, war and society in the fourteenth century*, edited by C. C. Thornton, J. Ward and N. Wiffen. 98–142. Hatfield: University of Hertfordshire Press.
Breeze, A. 2020. 'A Celtic-Roman mystery: the name Othona'. *Essex Journal* (spring): 11–15.
British Geological Survey. 2000/2010. 1:50000 Scale Geology series, England and Wales Sheet 224/242, Colchester and Brightlingsea. Bedrock and Superficial Deposits.
Britnell, R. H. 1981. 'Essex markets before 1350'. *Essex Archaeology and History* 13: 15–21.
Britnell, R. H. 1986. *Growth and Decline in Colchester, 1300–1525*. Cambridge: Cambridge University Press.
Brown, H. 1929. *History of Bradwell-on-the-Sea*. Chelmsford: J. H. Clarke & Co.
Campbell, B. M. S., J. A. Galloway, D. Keene and M. Murphy. 1993. *A Medieval Capital and Its Grain Supply*. Historical Geography Research Papers ser., no. 30.
Chapman, J., and P. André, 1777. *Map of Essex from an Actual Survey Taken in 1772, 1773, and 1774*. London.
Cook, B. 2005. 'The coastal trade of Maldon, c. 1565–c. 1702'. Unpublished PhD thesis, University of Essex.
Cooper, J., and A. Chapman. 2020. 'Great and Little Clacton'. In *VCH Essex* XII (part 1), edited by C. C. Thornton and H. Eiden. 226–93. Woodbridge: Boydell & Brewer.
Darby, H. C. 1977. *Domesday England*. Cambridge: Cambridge University Press.
Dickin, E. P. 1924. 'Notes on the coast, shipping, and sea-borne trade of Essex, from 1565 to 1577'. *Transactions of the Essex Archaeological Society*, new series 17: 153–64.
Dyer, C. 1995. 'Sheepcotes: evidence for medieval sheepfarming', *Medieval Archaeology* 39: 136–64.
Emmison, F. G. (ed.) 1989–1994. *Essex Wills*, vols 5–9. Chelmsford: Essex Record Office.
Fenwick, C. C. (ed.). 1998. *The Poll Taxes of 1377, 1379 and 1381*, part 1, *Bedfordshire–Leicestershire*. Oxford: Oxford University Press.
Ferguson, C., C. Thornton and A. Wareham (eds). 2012. *Essex Hearth Tax Return Michaelmas 1670*. London: British Record Society.
Finn, R. W. 1971. *The Norman Conquest and Its Effect on the Economy*. London: Longman.
Fisher, J. L., revised A. Powell and W. R. Powell. 1997. *A Medieval Farming Glossary of Latin and English Words*. Chelmsford: Essex County Council.

Fowler, R. C. 1907. 'Religious houses'. In *VCH Essex* II, edited by W. R. Page and J. H. Round. 84–201. London: Archibald Constable & Co.

Fowler, R. C. 1930. 'An early Essex subsidy'. *Transactions of the Essex Archaeological Society*, new series 19: 27–37.

Galloway, J. A. 2007. 'Marine flooding in the Thames Estuary and tidal river c. 1250–1450: impact and response'. *Area* 39(3): 370–9.

Galloway, J. A. 2013. 'Coastal flooding and socio-economic change in eastern England in the Later Middle Ages'. *Environment and History* 19(2): 173–207.

Galloway, J. A. 2021. 'Fishing the Thames Estuary in the later Middle Ages: environment, technology and the metropolitan market for fish c. 1250–1550'. *Imago Temporis. Medium Aevum* 15: 243–71.

Gardiner, M. 2005. 'Archaeological evidence for the exploitation, reclamation and flooding of salt marshes'. In *Water Management in Medieval Rural Economy (Ruralia* V), edited by J. Klápste. 73–83. Turnhout: Brepols.

Glasscock, R. E. (ed.) 1975. *The Lay Subsidy of 1334*. London: Records of Social and Economic History, new series ii.

Goose, N., and N. Evans. 2000. 'Wills as an historical source'. In *When Death Do Us Part: Understanding and interpreting the probate records of early modern England*, edited by T. Arkell, N. Evans and N. Goose. 38–71. Oxford: Leopard's Head Press.

Hart, C. 1993. 'Essex in the late tenth century'. In *The Battle of Maldon. Fiction and Fact*, edited by J. Cooper. 171–204. London: Hambledon Press.

Letters, S. (ed.) 2003. *Gazetteer of Markets and Fairs in England and Wales to 1516*. London: List and Index Society, Special Series, vol. 32, part 1.

Macdonald, J., and G. D. Snooks. 1986. *Domesday Economy. A new approach to Anglo-Norman history*. Oxford: Clarendon Press.

Minchin, G. S. 1907. 'Table of population, 1801–1901'. In *VCH Essex* II, edited by W. R. Page and J. H. Round. 342–54. London: Archibald Constable & Co.

Morant, P. 1768. *The History and Antiquities of the County of Essex*, vol. 1. London.

Murphy, P., and N. Brown. 1999. 'The archaeology of the coastal landscape'. In *The Essex Landscape in Search of Its History*, edited by L. S. Green. 11–19. Chelmsford: Essex County Council.

Newton, K. C. 1970. *The Manor of Writtle. The development of a royal manor in Essex c. 1086–c. 1500*. London and Chichester: Phillimore.

Phillips, S. 2010. *Edward II*. London and New Haven, CT: Yale University Press.

Poos, L. R. 1991. *A Rural Society after the Black Death: Essex, 1350–1525*. Cambridge: Cambridge University Press.

Reaney, P. H. 1935. *The Place-Names of Essex*. Cambridge: English Place-Name Society.

Round, J. H. 1903. 'The Domesday Survey'. In *VCH Essex* I, edited by W. R. Page and J. H. Round. 333–598. London: Archibald Constable & Co.

Salter, H. 1929. *Facsimiles of Early Charters in Oxford Muniment Rooms*. Oxford: Oxford University Press.

Sheail, J. 1998. *The Regional Distribution of Wealth in England as Indicated in the 1524/5 Lay Subsidy Returns*, edited by R. W. Hoyle. London: List & Index Society, special series, 29, part II.

Smith, R. M. 1991. 'Demographic developments in rural England, 1300–1348: a survey'. In *Before the Black Death: Studies in the 'crisis' of the early fourteenth century*, edited by B. M. S. Campbell. 25–78. Manchester: Manchester University Press.

Soil Survey of England and Wales 1983. Soils of England and Wales, Sheet 4, Eastern England, Scale 1:250000, Map and Legend. Cranfield.

Steer, F. W. 1974. *The Archives of New College Oxford*. London and Chichester: Phillimore.

Strachan, D. 1998. 'Inter-tidal stationary fishing structures in Essex: some fourteenth-century dates'. *Essex Archaeology and History* 29: 274–82.

Taylor, P. 2000. 'Introduction'. In *Little Domesday Book, Essex*, edited by A. Williams and G. H. Martin. 9–35. London: Alecto Historical Editions.

Thornton, C. C. 2020a. 'Introduction: St Osyth to the Naze'. In *VCH Essex* XII (part 1), edited by C. C. Thornton and H. Eiden. 1–58. Woodbridge: Boydell & Brewer.

Thornton, C. C. 2020b. 'St Osyth'. In *VCH Essex* XII (part 1), edited by C. C. Thornton and H. Eiden. 59–225. Woodbridge: Boydell & Brewer.

Ward, J. 1983. *The Medieval Essex Community: The lay subsidy of 1327*. Chelmsford: Essex County Council.

Wiffen, N. 2019. 'Supplying the army: the contribution of Essex to provisioning the forces of Edward III, c. 1337'. *Essex Journal* (spring): 11–20.

Williams, A., and G. H. Martin (eds). 2000. *Little Domesday Book, Essex*. London: Alecto Historical Editions.

Part II
St Peter's Chapel and its modern contexts

8
'A building of altogether exceptional interest': The rediscovery of St Peter's Chapel in the nineteenth century, and its restoration in the twentieth

James Bettley

On 26 October 1864 the Essex Archaeological Society (EAS) gathered at Bradwell on Sea for 'one of the most interesting meetings of this society that has been held in this county', to consider 'one of the most interesting discoveries of the day' which had recently been made there.[1] The South Essex Estuary and Reclamation Company, incorporated in 1852 for the purpose of reclaiming mud banks and marshland for agricultural use by means of sea walls, was in the process of enclosing some 800 acres of 'redeemable land' at the mouth of the River Blackwater.[2] To make the sea wall it was necessary to construct a tramway for bringing extra earth, and as they were digging at the side of a field they uncovered a section of Roman wall. This came to the attention of the landowner, John Oxley Parker of Woodham Mortimer Place, who recognised its significance and organised further excavation in addition to the company's (see Figure 2.1). It was known that Bradwell was the location of the Saxon Shore Fort of Othona, but it was thought to have lain further out to sea. Parker was convinced that this was what had been found, and experts in the field such as Charles Roach Smith and Thomas Lewin agreed.[3]

This discovery drew attention to the only structure that stood above ground, St Peter's Chapel, to which little serious thought appears to have been given hitherto. Morant had recorded it in 1768 as a former chapel of ease to St Thomas's, Bradwell, but 'when it was founded, and by whom', he did not know.[4] He said it was in ruins, but although it was no longer in

Figure 8.1 Interior of St Peter's Chapel, looking west, 1907. Photograph by Alfred Wire. Vestry House Museum, London Borough of Waltham Forest.

use as a chapel it had been put to good use as a barn by the late seventeenth century and remained as such in 1864.[5]

As the chapel came under scrutiny, the first to pronounce on it, in a paper read to the assembled members of the EAS in October 1864, was the Rev. Frederick Spurrell, rector of Faulkbourne and author of a number of papers on archaeological matters.[6] Only with some difficulty did he accept that it had been built as a chapel; in particular, the lack of windows suggested otherwise, and theories included that it was built as a sea mark, or as a pharos or watch tower, or even that it had, after all, been built as a barn, and was the last surviving structure of a town lost to the sea. But the east–west orientation suggested to Spurrell that it had been built as a chapel, and the evidence of the stonework supported the previous existence of an apse or chancel, recorded by Morant as having existed in 1442. As to the date, Spurrell dismissed the suggestion that it was a Roman building: the walls contained Roman tiles, but so did a great many Essex churches – in a county with no building stone to speak of, any material that came to hand was liable to be reused. The quoins suggested to him a Saxon building, but other details made him think that it was in fact Norman, built soon after the Conquest.

Frederic Chancellor, Essex's leading architect and expert on the county's churches, many of which he had restored, disagreed to the extent that he thought the building was later than Norman.[7] However, the Rev. Guy Bryan, rector of Woodham Walter, drew attention to Bede's identification of this place with St Cedd, and the rector of Bradwell, John Warner, hoped that it would be possible to prove that it was Saxon, a hope supported by the landowner, J. O. Parker.[8] After a further paper by Spurrell on the Roman remains the members adjourned to the King's Head for a 'good dinner'.[9]

Chancellor, who worked with Parker on the excavations, published his thoughts on the chapel in the *Archaeological Journal* in 1877, and concluded that it was built 'for ecclesiastical purposes' at the latter end of the twelfth century. He based his argument on the presence or remains of buttresses, seven in all, which in his experience were never to be found on Saxon or, indeed, Norman buildings. Bede said that Cedd had built his church in *Ythancæstir*; Chancellor took the view that this was separate from Othona, and that Cedd's church had therefore disappeared along with the city.[10]

Chancellor's views on dating were known to, and supported by, H. W. King, who visited the chapel in 1874 as part of his survey of Essex churches. He differed from Chancellor, however, in thinking that the chapel was built on the site of St Cedd's church 'to supply the wants of a scattered population remote from the parish church of this extensive parish'. The printing, verbatim, of King's unpublished account as part of a report of the Essex Archaeological Society's visit to Bradwell in 1897 in the *Transactions of the Essex Archaeological Society* in 1898 suggests that this version of events continued to be accepted.[11]

Perhaps there was a degree of local loyalty towards Chancellor, whose 1877 paper was written in response to one by Thomas Lewin in which he had 'no hesitation in pronouncing that in this tattered and dilapidated edifice we have the veritable handiwork of the old Saxon missionary Bishop Cedd'. Moreover, he compared the chapel, in a passing reference, to St Augustine's church (St Pancras) at Canterbury.[12] In this respect Lewin was anticipating the most authoritative account of the chapel, a paper of 1901 by Charles Peers, 'On Saxon churches of the St Pancras type', in which he developed a hypothesis put forward by J. T. Micklethwaite in 1896 regarding a group of churches belonging to the years following the reintroduction of Christianity to the south of England at the end of the sixth century: St Martin and St Pancras in Canterbury, St Mary and St Ethelburga, Lyminge, and St Andrew, Rochester (all in Kent); St Peter-on-the-Wall; and possibly the Old Minster at South Elmham (Suffolk). Peers, like Micklethwaite, dismissed Chancellor's dating and concluded that St Peter's 'may with considerable reason be identified as the church built by Cedd for his Essex converts from the ruins of the Roman Othonae [sic]'.[13]

We have seen how, in 1864, churchmen such as the rectors of Bradwell and Woodham Walter were anxious that St Peter's should be identified as St Cedd's church. This seemed to have been confirmed by Peers and others, but the matter assumed a greater, symbolic importance in 1914 with the creation of what would become known as the diocese of Chelmsford. As early as 1906 a writer in the *Church Times* hoped that 'the present generation of Essex Churchmen, now that they are taking steps to have a Bishop of their own, may be moved ... to rescue this once long sanctified site from desecration, so the offering of the Holy Sacrifice may be renewed within its walls'.[14] Chelmsford was chosen as the site of the cathedral in 1908, but the name of the new diocese was not immediately settled. The Rev. J. Charles Cox, antiquary and prolific writer on ecclesiological topics, was quick to publish *The Cathedral Church and See of Essex*, in which he proposed 'Essex' as a form of tribute to St Cedd, termed 'Bishop of the East Saxons' by Bede. He included in his book a description of St Peter's as 'assuredly one of the most interesting of hallowed buildings throughout the whole of England', and ended by saying, 'surely the days cannot be far distant when this, the most ancient shrine of the Christian faith in the kingdom of the East Saxons and the present Diocese of Essex, will be once more rescued for the worship of the Most High.'[15]

Such thoughts seem to have been shared by the authorities in the new diocese, because at the cathedral's first annual meeting in 1915 it was resolved to approach J. O. Parker's son, Christopher William Parker, about the chapel, with a view to its being restored to sacred use.

The upshot was that on 15 June 1916 the chapel was conveyed by Parker to a body of trustees comprising the bishop of Chelmsford (Rt Rev. J. E. Watts Ditchfield), the bishop of Barking (Rt Rev. Thomas Stevens) in his capacity as archdeacon of Essex, the rector of Chelmsford (Canon H. A. Lake), the rector of Bradwell (Rev. J. R. B. Owen), C. W. Parker and his son John Oxley Parker. The long-term plan was for the chapel to be conveyed to the chapter, but although the assembly of honorary canons was referred to as such it was not as yet legally constituted; that did not come about until 1935. Meanwhile the trustees had full power of ownership over the chapel, with 18ft of land on all four sides and a 4ft-wide right of way from the end of the farm track.[16]

Something had to be done to turn the building back from a barn into a place of worship. The obvious person to give advice was Charles Peers, who had visited the chapel with J. T. Micklethwaite in 1900. Peers (who would be knighted in 1931) was an architect by training, with experience as an archaeologist; he was editor of the *Archaeological Journal*, 1900–3, and then architectural editor of the *Victoria County History*. In 1910 he was appointed Inspector of Ancient Monuments in the Office of Works, and in this capacity had been involved in repairs to St Botolph's Priory, Colchester, after 1912. Early in his tenure came the Ancient Monuments Consolidation and Amendment Act of 1913, which established the Ancient Monuments Board, the forerunner of English Heritage, with the

Figure 8.2 Visit by the Essex Field Club, 6 August 1910. Photograph probably by Alfred Wire. Kevin Bruce Collection.

power to take scheduled ancient monuments into public ownership and require their owners to apply for permission before altering or demolishing them.[17]

Peers returned to Bradwell in October 1915 at the request of C. W. Parker and Canon Lake, and made proposals for the chapel's repair. His guiding principle was that 'the church should remain without the slightest suspicion of "restoration", far more impressive in its venerable simplicity than any furnishings could make it'. He even considered that paving or boarding the earth floor would be out of place. He had no doubt that it was proper for the Office of Works to take an interest in the chapel, which he considered 'a building of altogether exceptional interest on account of its early date', but it was felt that nothing should be done until after the end of the war. The work would then be carried out by the Office of Works at the cost of the trustees.[18]

Things got under way in May 1919 with a further report by Arthur Heasman, the Office of Works' architect in charge of the project. He was cautious in pointing out some of the practical difficulties. The remoteness of the location would add to the cost with regard to transport of labour and materials. There was no debris on the site that could be reused for repairs, and although sand and shingle could be taken from the seashore, moving it would be difficult. There were no suitable local builders or

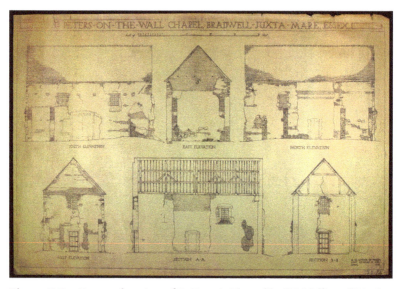

Figure 8.3 Survey drawing of St Peter's Chapel by HM Office of Works. Essex Record Office.

Figure 8.4 St Peter's Chapel under restoration, c. 1919–20, showing the north and west walls. © Historic England Archive.

contractors who could undertake the work or who could supply plant. The nearest railway station, Southminster, was 9 miles away, but material could be brought by barge to Bradwell Waterside, a distance of about 3½ miles. A foreman experienced in dealing with historic buildings was essential, and W. T. Knapp was seconded to Bradwell from Framlingham Castle in Suffolk. The plant also came from Framlingham.[19]

In accordance with Peers's principles, the minimum necessary was done to make the building usable as a chapel. The large cart entrance in the south wall was filled with stonework similar to that of the rest of the wall, but set back a little so that the infill would never be mistaken for original work. This was done mainly with new Clipsham and Kentish Ragstone, as well as such old face stones and Roman bricks as were turned up during excavation. The doorway in the west wall was reopened, as were original windows in the north, south and west walls; the new oak door and window frames were made at Caernarfon Castle. The roof was made weathertight, its timbers repaired following the same method used at Westminster Hall and Eltham Palace Hall. A carpenter came up from the Tower of London. Wykeham Chancellor, son of Frederic and himself an architect (and Chelmsford diocesan surveyor), was responsible for the brick platform at the east end and designed the simple altar that stood on it, made of oak from the roof of Chelmsford Cathedral.[20]

The restoration came at just the right time for publication in 1923 of the relevant volume of the Royal Commission on Historical Monuments'

Figure 8.5 St Peter's Chapel from the south, 1925. Photographed by John Harry Pledge. © Historic England Archive.

survey of Essex, which included a photograph of the restored chapel and one of the Office of Works' detailed measured drawings of the walls. The conclusion was that 'the chapel is almost certainly that built by Bishop Cedd in c. 654 at Ithancester [*Ythancæstir*]'.[21]

Peers had thought in 1915 that the work could be done for £250, but the estimate in 1919 was £550; of this, the trustees guaranteed £300 and hoped to raise the balance by public subscription. In the end, after some negotiation over the payment of out-of-pocket expenses of Office of Works staff, the cost to the trustees was £443 11s.[22] What really mattered, however, was that the chapel was ready to be re-dedicated by the bishop of Chelmsford on 22 June 1920. For the first service, Holy Communion at 8.15 a.m., Canon Henry Sanders presented a silver-gilt chalice and paten. Otherwise, the furnishings were minimal: as well as Chancellor's altar (which he donated), there were chairs provided by Alderman Clement W. Parker.[23]

From 1922 the cathedral chapter held an annual service on or near to the anniversary of the re-dedication, with an address by speakers who included Charles Peers in 1922 and Wykeham Chancellor in 1923. By 1926 this was sufficiently established to be referred to as the annual pilgrimage; in that year a bishop's chair was dedicated, the gift of Oxley Durant Parker, and in 1934 a credence table was presented by Miss Dorcas Parker.[24] About 120 people had attended in 1926; by 1936 that number had risen to 300. The latter year also saw the formation of the Society of Friends of St Peter and St Cedd.[25] The following year, 1937, was notable because, as well as the regular pilgrimage on 16 June, on Sunday 4 July there was a Roman Catholic pilgrimage to 'a spot which might be called the cradle of English Catholicism'. It was organised by Father George Steadman of Burnham-on-Crouch, with nearly 500 pilgrims coming by coach from as far as Southend and Tiptree. The clergy robed at Eastlands Farm and the procession to the chapel was headed by a fife and drum band from Wapping. The Rev. F. W. Galpin, an honorary canon of Chelmsford since 1917 and closely associated with the chapel, wrote to the *Essex Chronicle* welcoming this new development. Roman Catholic pilgrimages were repeated in 1938 and 1939.[26]

A further development was a separate pilgrimage, Anglican but High Church in character, organised by the Brentwood station of the Seven Years Association.[27] The first was held in 1936, and by 1938 it seemed well established. The day began with a service at St Thomas's, Brentwood, before the pilgrims travelled to Bradwell, where there was a procession led by thurifer, crucifer, acolytes and servers from Brentwood and Southend, and priests from various other Essex churches. The pilgrims returned to Brentwood for a solemn thanksgiving in St Thomas's. The 1938 pilgrimage was notable for the attendance of the Archimandrite Nicholas of the Russian Orthodox Church, formerly tutor to the children of Tsar Nicholas II. There was one further pilgrimage in 1939, when over 120 people took part.[28]

The Brentwood pilgrimages were of lasting significance for St Peter's because one of the pilgrims, a member of the Seven Years Association and worshipper at St Thomas's, was a young architect named Laurence King. A lifelong resident of Brentwood, where he set up practice in 1932, he made his name with the design of St George's, Brentwood, consecrated in 1934, and by the following year he had opened an office in London.[29] He was on friendly terms with Canon Owen, the rector of Bradwell, and his wife, and it is therefore not surprising that in July 1939 he was asked to inspect the chapel, following which he recommended reroofing.[30] The matter was discussed by the cathedral chapter the following April, and King's report was referred to Sir Charles Nicholson (the cathedral's architect), who approved of King's proposals in March 1941; following this, an estimate was prepared by a local builder, H. W. Dowsett. Nicholson agreed with King that no attempt should be made to go back to thatch or shingles with which the building might originally have been roofed, remarking presciently that '"restoration" of the entire building would be pure guesswork for the most part & therefore undesirable even if financially possible'.[31]

In the meantime, C. W. Parker's original intentions had been realised and the chapel had been conveyed to the chapter, this body having been formally created in 1935.[32] The trustees appointed in 1916, although they held particular positions or were members of the Parker family, had been appointed as individuals and remained trustees when they left their respective positions; but by 1938 all save J. O. Parker had died. Actual management was in the hands of a committee, on which a member of the donor's family should be represented, and in practice this involved holders of many of the same positions. Thus it was that in April 1938 the managers (the bishop of Chelmsford, the bishop of Barking – now archdeacon of West Ham rather than Essex), the provost of Chelmsford Cathedral and the rector of Bradwell) asked Parker to convey the chapel to the chapter; this was executed on 20 June 1939. This time the chapel came with a little more land: 25ft to the north, 22ft to the west, 50ft to

Figure 8.6 St Peter's Chapel from the south, 1942, showing damage to the roof, and barbed wire and other military debris. © Historic England Archive.

the east, and 23ft to the south, with an additional portion at the southwest corner for the apparent purpose of taking in the old shed that stood there. The following May access was improved by the granting of a 9ft-wide right of way for repairs only.[33]

It seems that advantage was not immediately taken of this right of way as far as the roof was concerned, but, in any case, money spent on it would have been wasted: in November 1941 it was damaged by an explosion of landmines. The rector, P. N. Maitland, immediately informed Canon Curling, the clerk to the chapter, but Chancellor, the diocesan surveyor, did not find out about it until the following January, and by the time he came to report to the Ministry of Works (as it now was) in March 1942 he found, as well as obvious damage to the tiles, that the roof timbers were spreading to a worrying degree. There was, however, no significant damage to the walls. Emergency repairs were carried out in June under Chancellor's direction.[34] The site was occupied by the army (as it had been in the First World War), and the surrounding ground was heavily mined. There was further damage in 1943 caused by engineers detonating unrequired explosives, and the Ministry of Works obtained an undertaking that there would be no further detonation in the vicinity of the chapel; but the colonel responsible did not accept liability and pointed out that an aircraft had crashed near by and that the damage might have been the result of this incident.[35]

The more extensive repairs envisaged by Chancellor had to wait until after the war. Following his death in 1945 the task fell to Laurence King, himself now diocesan surveyor. In October 1947 Maitland issued an appeal for funds; the war damage to the south side of the roof had been patched up, but subsequently gales had stripped the tiles off the north side so that the whole roof now needed to be replaced.[36] King had already been appointed as architect: his specification of work is dated May 1947. Dowsett & Sons submitted an estimate for the work in June 1947 (£961 19s. 1d.) and a building licence was issued on 1 September. Delays were caused by the difficulty of obtaining timber, then by the bad condition of the track, which prevented lorries reaching the chapel, and when the timber was finally delivered it was found to be of the wrong dimensions; but work was in hand by the time King reported in April 1948, and it was completed in June. As part of the re-roofing the roof was plastered between the rafters for the first time, which not only helped keep the chapel clean but also showed off the timbers to greater advantage. Repairs were also carried out to the windows and doors, and the internal face of the stonework was cleaned down. The total cost of the work was £984 19s. 9d.[37]

Figure 8.7 Interior of St Peter's Chapel, looking east, 1947. Photograph by Anthony F. Kersting. Distributed under a Creative Commons CC BY-NC 4.0 licence by the Courtauld Institute of Art.

King had ambitions for the building that went far beyond re-roofing, however: 'the building in its present form is too reminiscent of the period of the desecration when it came to be used as a farmer's barn.' He wanted to pave the floor: 'it would then be possible to kneel in this church which few worshippers are prepared to do today on the earth.' He wanted to plaster and limewash the walls internally; he had found traces of plaster at high level and argued that the rough stonework would not originally have been left exposed (see Figure 1.7). This work would 'do much to remind the pilgrim that this is in fact a House of Prayer rather than a restored farmer's barn', and in taking this attitude he clearly demonstrated the different approach to the building which he took as a church-going architect, as opposed to that of the conservative archaeologist Peers. King disliked the furnishings too; for the time being he did not seek to replace the altar, but he did not approve of the altar cross ('ungainly' in itself, and 'unknown in Saxon times') and recommended instead a large hanging cross on the east wall:

> a Saxon rood showing the figure of the living Christ would be in perfect character with the building. I am of the opinion that all the recommendations made in this report would greatly improve the building and would assist in recreating the atmosphere that existed when it was the first Cathedral of Essex.[38]

King did not get his way as far as plastering the walls was concerned, but the paving was carried out, albeit with slight difficulty. The Ministry of Works approved the idea, but on condition that an archaeological excavation be carried out before the laying of a permanent floor. This would have meant an unacceptable delay, and a compromise was reached in the form of cement paving slabs laid on sand, which could easily be taken up for any future excavation. In April 1949 King repeated his thoughts on the hanging cross, illustrating his report with a proposal for the east end of the chapel; the form of the cross was inspired by the carved stone Saxon rood at Romsey Abbey, Hampshire, although King also referred to the carved crucifixion at St Matthew's Church, Langford, Oxfordshire. This proposal too was accepted, and the crucifix was painted on wood by Francis Stephens, the first work in a long association between King and this important artist and designer of ecclesiastical furnishings and stained glass.[39]

The re-roofing, paving and installation of the crucifix were completed in time for the pilgrimage on 28 June 1949, attended by over 250 pilgrims led by the bishops of Chelmsford, Colchester and St Albans. King delivered a lecture on the history of the chapel with, by way of epilogue, a glimpse into the future, when the chapel might be reconstructed as it was in the time of St Cedd. About £1,000 had been spent on the restoration; now £4,000 was called for.[40] King's proposals, initially made in his reports to the cathedral chapter in 1948 and 1949, were published in a booklet with a foreword by the bishop of Chelmsford (Henry Wilson), which proclaimed 'our happy duty to restore St Cedd's Cathedral eventually to its original state'; Francis Stephens provided the attractive illustrations.[41]

Figure 8.8 Laurence King's proposals for restoring St Peter's Chapel to its presumed Saxon appearance, 1948. © Shenstone and Partners. Source: Essex Record Office.

The chapel in its present form was the nave of the original church. The excavations in 1864–5 had revealed the former existence of an apse at the east end, and at the west end was a porch, its walls then still standing to a height of about 2ft, that presumably formed the base of the 'small Tower with two Bells' recorded by Morant in 1768 (see Figure 1.2). In the south wall were the remains of a doorway and on the north side evidence of a rectangular structure interpreted by Lewin as a sacristy or vestry.[42] Comparison with the other churches studied by Peers led to the conclusion that there had been a *porticus* or chamber on either side of the chapel, overlapping the nave and apse. It was King's hope that these features – porch-tower, *porticus*, apse – might be reconstructed, and the east wall of the chapel replaced with a triple-arched screen between the nave and the apse. He considered it to be not only an aesthetic improvement, but a practical and ideological one too:

> Though there may be some who, out of either conservatism or sentiment, would prefer to see the building as a restored barn, which though of unique archaeological interest, has little aesthetic

appeal, there are many others who would prefer to see it carefully and reverently restored with all the ancient features preserved. The building would then take on the form it had in St Cedd's time, and would be transformed from its secular appearance into a church where the worship of the Faithful can in decency and all seemliness be offered once more in what is not unlikely to be the oldest Christian building in England.[43]

It is not surprising that these proposals generated controversy. Some, indeed, did not like what King had already done. Colonel E. A. Loftus of West Tilbury, self-styled 'pedagogue', wrote 'with considerable emotion' to the Ministry of Works, deploring the 'hideously ornate crucifix of large design painted in the most lurid colours, now in situ over the altar. I was so depressed with the incongruity of the concrete slabs and this rood, that I walked away… lest I should express my feelings inappropriately' to the rector, who was showing off the chapel to a party of visitors.[44]

The Chief Inspector of Ancient Monuments at the Ministry of Works, Bryan O'Neil, supported King's proposals, following the advice of the Inspector for England, Paul Baillie Reynolds, who met King and the rector on site in January 1950. Baillie Reynolds felt that the chapel, if restored, would be more often used for worship, observing that 'the motive of the restoration appears to be the same as that which prompted the original construction of the church, namely the Glory of God'; and he felt that there was enough evidence of missing features, supplemented by comparison with what survived at Reculver and St Pancras, Canterbury, to allow for reconstruction. He concluded:

> This scheme of restoration will undoubtedly tend to the better preservation of the monument, which is what the [Ancient Monuments Department] strives to secure. If it were in our charge we should not restore it, neither should we use it for worship. But since it belongs to the Church which wishes to use it for its ecclesiastical purpose, restoration to its ecclesiastical plan is the logical result. It will do no harm to the existing Saxon remains; it will on the other hand materially aid their proper preservation.[45]

The principal opposition came from the Council for British Archaeology, whose president, D. B. Harden, particularly objected to the breaching of the east wall and to the additions, which, in the opinion of the Council, falsified the history of the building.[46] Similar representations were made to the Minister of Works, Richard Stokes, by Eric Fletcher, MP for East

Islington and member of council (later president) of the British Archaeological Association: '*Any* restoration must be highly conjectural and speculative and will clutter a building of almost unique importance with modern paraphernalia which cannot fail to falsify it ... I cannot believe that the Chief Inspector of Ancient Monuments can be enthusiastic about the proposal.' But Stokes replied that the Chief Inspector 'believes that the work, so far from being highly conjectural, is almost certainly a sound reconstruction', and moreover 'the Church will be restored to its original purpose, as a place of worship, and in addition will give the casual visitor a much better idea of what a Saxon Church really looked like ... I must make it clear that the scheme has my full support.'[47]

Fletcher also wrote that he had been told that the Royal Fine Art Commission 'regard the whole scheme as distasteful and unsuitable'. The matter had indeed been referred to the Commission by the Council for British Archaeology, and the Commission's chairman, Lord Crawford, took the trouble to write personally to the bishop of Chelmsford explaining why they could not support the scheme. The chapel was 'an almost unique document in the early history of the Church and of Ecclesiastical architecture in this country: as indeed it is in Europe'. The reconstruction must be largely conjectural, and character and atmosphere would be lost: 'it would be very sad, we feel, if the authenticity of this almost unique record were sophisticated by any such reconstruction.' Lord Crawford had decided to write to the bishop (in addition to the secretary of the Commission writing to the architect) because the architect 'naturally defends his proposals ... and also because it appears to us that the scheme involves principles which are only in part related to the architectural problem'.[48]

In terms of the ground plan, King's scheme was, as the Ministry of Works acknowledged, better than conjectural, and could have been supported by further excavation (the outline of the *porticus* and apse are now marked out on the ground). Although Baldwin Brown, in 1925, had conjectured that the building was unlikely to be Cedd's, and 'may conceivably represent a rebuilding under Kentish direction of a simpler oratory perhaps of wood that had been reared by Cedd', this argument was dismissed by the Taylors in their authoritative *Anglo-Saxon Architecture* (1965). They also disagreed with Brown's theory (put forward more emphatically by H. Malcolm Carter in 1966) that there had been only two arches rather than three between the nave and the apse.[49] Above ground, however, there was little certainty, and the west tower in particular owed much to King's imagination. Lord Crawford questioned the columns in the proposed arcade, 'based on those which used to be in a church in Kent', namely, St Mary, Reculver, discovered by Peers in 1926 and preserved at Canterbury Cathedral. The conjectural reconstruction published by Carter in 1966 shows a building of a very different and much simpler character (compare Figure 1.9).[50]

It was apparent that King's scheme would continue to be controversial, and it would have cost a lot of money; it is not clear what finished it off, but it seems the idea was quietly dropped. There was other work to do. The old shed that stood to the south-west of the chapel, and served as a vestry, collapsed and was replaced with a new vestry, designed by King, in 1953.[51] This incurred the displeasure of the Ministry of Works, because of the possible damage done to archaeological remains by the foundations, but they did not find out about it until 1955, by which time it was too late to do anything other than issue a reprimand.[52] The annual pilgrimages continued, with special celebrations in 1954, 'St Cedd's Year', including a broadcast service from the chapel on 2 May and a rally at West Ham United football ground on 19 June. At the pilgrimage itself on 3 July, 6,000 people attended an open-air service at Bradwell, on the spot where St Cedd had landed 1,300 years before. Another notable landmark was the first joint Anglican and Roman Catholic pilgrimage in 1971.[53]

Still King hankered after improving the internal appearance of the chapel, and in March 1964, at the request of the provost, Eric Gordon, he submitted proposals. He repeated the dislike of the wooden altar that he had expressed in 1948, and proposed one of stone with a central support as being more dignified: 'it would recapture some of the atmosphere of the early Church'. There was no need for an altar cross, given the rood on the east wall (which needed some touching up), but he proposed a pair of wrought-iron candlesticks, and a plain carpet in front of the altar. The credence table 'is a typical product of an ecclesiastical emporium. I would like to see this got rid of and a plain simple credence table substituted.' A prayer desk was similarly dismissed. A 'rather horrid wrought-iron candle stand' should be removed and replaced with wrought-iron candle brackets fixed to the walls. In the north wall there was a recess in which he would like to see a statue of St Cedd. Display boards and a table at the back of the chapel should be specially designed for the building. The metal stacking chairs were 'very unfortunate'; benches that could be moved back against the walls, or specially designed stacking chairs in wood, would be preferable. Externally, he still felt that the chapel looked too much like a barn, and he suggested a Christian emblem fixed to the wall above the entrance door.[54]

The provost took the sensible precaution of sending King's ideas to an ad hoc 'committee of taste' consisting of Dr G. H. S. Bushnell of

Cambridge University, H. Malcolm Carter of Layer Breton, L. C. Evetts of the University of Newcastle's Department of Fine Art and Professor Francis Wormald of the Institute of Historical Research, University of London. There was a distinct lack of enthusiasm. Nobody liked the statue. Opinion was divided as to what would be the most suitable form of altar. Some sort of external emblem was generally felt appropriate, but not the one designed by King. Carter felt that a free-standing cross some distance from the west door 'would be more suited to the weatherbeaten situation'. He didn't like King's rood on the east wall but agreed that it would look better in its original position rather than the higher position to which it had been moved by the previous incumbent. He also pointed out that the altar cross and candlesticks had been given as a memorial and could not simply be discarded.[55]

Most of what King disliked about the interior remains, although the chairs were replaced with simple oak benches in 1966. However, in 1985 the bishops of Chelmsford and Bradwell consecrated a new stone altar, a plain slab on a cruciform supporting pillar designed by Gerald Shenstone. Set into the pillar are stones from the three other communities connected with St Cedd's ministry: Holy Island, Lindisfarne, where he was trained by St Aidan; the island of Iona, where St Aidan

Figure 8.9 Interior of St Peter's Chapel, 2020, showing the hanging crucifix by Francis Stephens, 1949, and altar by Gerald Shenstone, 1985. N. Hallett.

was trained; and Lastingham, Yorkshire, where St Cedd built a monastery and died. As King would have wished, it has no frontal, and has no need of one.[56]

Although King regarded his work as incomplete in 1964, the transformation of St Peter's from a 'tattered and dilapidated edifice' in a remote corner of the county to a shrine at the spiritual heart of the diocese was a remarkable one.[57] In the century since 1864 it had been identified with near certainty as the church built by Cedd when he came to Essex from Lindisfarne in the seventh century, and after initial doubts most were satisfied that it was the very building and not a later replacement. It took its place in the select group of the earliest English churches. A conservative restoration by Charles Peers had preserved its primitive character but enabled the chapel to be rededicated as a place of worship and to serve not just as a powerful symbol for the newly created diocese of Chelmsford but also as a place of pilgrimage, initially for Anglicans and then for Roman Catholics as well. It had survived being in an exposed position for centuries, so a few more gales it could take in its stride, but being in the front line of two world wars was a new experience and one that brought it close to destruction. In Laurence King it found a champion who was a devout Christian with decided views on what was seemly and a very particular High Church aesthetic that was not to everybody's taste. But however appropriate it may have been for City churches and others that he successfully restored, at Bradwell what the *Church Times* called 'the Laurence King treatment' was simply not what was called for.[58] In seeking to recreate the church as he believed it would have looked in Cedd's day, and which he believed to be a more suitable setting for worship than a building which to him still looked like a barn, he failed to understand the appeal that the building had (and still has) for those who revere it. Peers wrote of 'its venerable simplicity', Carter of its 'great but holy solemnity'.[59] These are the qualities that most people admire in the building and which King, with the best and most sincere of intentions, would have destroyed.

Notes

1 *Chelmsford Chronicle*, 28 October 1864, 3; Roach Smith 1865, 403.
2 South Essex Estuary and Reclamation Act, 1852 (ERO, D/DMb O3 and T/M 264/1).
3 Roach Smith 1865. Roach Smith was probably also responsible for the article in the previous volume of *The Gentleman's Magazine* (218 (1865): 67–71), which summarises the account published in the *Chelmsford Chronicle*; Lewin 1868.
4 Morant 1768, vol. 1, 377.

5 Lease of 'All that Barne commonly called or knowne by the name of St Peters Chappell', 28 October 1686 (ERO, D/DC 21/5–6; Steer 1950).
6 *Chelmsford Chronicle*, 28 October 1864, 3.
7 *Chelmsford Chronicle*, 28 October 1864, 3.
8 *Chelmsford Chronicle*, 28 October 1864, 3.
9 *Chelmsford Chronicle*, 28 October 1864, 3.
10 Chancellor 1877.
11 ERO, T/P 196/6, 205–9; subsequently published in the *Transactions of the Essex Archaeological Society* 6 (1898). 352–4.
12 Lewin 1868 (offprint in ERO, T/P 124/1).
13 Micklethwaite 1896; Peers 1901.
14 *Church Times*, 21 September 1906, 350: 'An Essex Pilgrimage. By a Peripatetic Parson'. The writer also suggested that the site 'is healthy and probably well suited for a clerical retreat, or possibly for some small religious foundation'.
15 Cox 1908, 3–7. He had written at greater length about St Peter's in *The Builder* (Cox 1906). *The Reliquary and Illustrated Archaeologist*, which he edited, published articles on St Peter's by J. Charles Wall (Wall 1908) and Henry Laver (Laver 1909).
16 ERO, D/DGe T142; D/P 94 addl (A14562, box 1, part 4).
17 Thurley 2013, 66–83; Cooper 1994, 306. The Bradwell site was scheduled as a monument in 1924; the chapel itself was listed Grade I in 1959 (Historic England, list entry numbers 1013834 & 1110942).
18 TNA, WORK 14/451, 22 October 1915.
19 TNA, WORK 14/451, 12 May 1919.
20 TNA, WORK 14/451, 2 December 1919, 29 April 1920.
21 Royal Commission on Historical Monuments (England) 1923, 15–16. Peers was appointed as one of the commissioners in 1921.
22 TNA, WORK 14/451, 31 May 1921.
23 *Essex Chronicle*, 25 April 1919, 6, and 25 June 1920, 6; Benton et al. 1926, 110; Brown n.d. [1929], 20–2.
24 *Essex Newsman*, 26 June 1926, 1, and 3 July 1926, 1; *Essex Chronicle*, 13 July 1934, 10.
25 *Essex Chronicle*, 26 June 1936, 7.
26 *Essex Chronicle*, 18 June 1937, 7, 9 July 1937, 2, 16 July 1937, 7, 10 June 1938, 7, and 28 July 1939, 2.
27 The Association, formed in 1933, was open to Anglo-Catholic laity (men and women) who would still be under the age of 40 in 1940 (*Church Times*, 13 October 1933, 408).
28 *Church Times*, 10 July 1936, 54, 18 June 1937, 782, 8 July 1938, 38, and 7 July 1939, 5; *Essex Chronicle*, 8 July 1938, 7.
29 Bettley 2015, 39–58.
30 ERO, D/P 94 addl (A14562, box 1, part 4), 13 July 1939. King wrote to Mrs Owen on 22 July 1938 following the pilgrimage that year, a letter chiefly of interest for discussion of Tom Driberg as a suitable purchaser of the rectory (now Bradwell Lodge) (ERO, T/P 124/1). Canon J. G. Owen was to retire in January 1939 (*Essex Chronicle*, 6 January 1939, 9); he was the son of J. R. B. Owen, the rector, who was one of the 1916 trustees, and grandson of Edward Owen, rector from 1870, who owned the advowson and passed it down the generations.
31 *Essex Chronicle*, 26 April 1940, 5; ERO, D/P 94 addl (A14562, box 1, part 4), 17 March 1941.
32 Tuckwell 2013, 160–3.
33 ERO, D/P 94 addl (A14562, box 1, part 4). In 1955 it was decided that the chapel should be administered by the cathedral council, rather than the chapter, with a subcommittee controlling the finances (ERO, D/C 1/4/4). Any alterations to the building would still have to be approved by the chapter, and use of the chapel other than for diocesan purposes was at the discretion of the rector of Bradwell.
34 ERO, D/P 94 addl (A14562, box 1, part 4), 6 November 1941; TNA, WORK 14/1719, January–August 1942. Chancellor refers to damage 'by enemy agency', but from Maitland's letter it seems to have been a Home Forces landmine.
35 TNA, WORK 14/1719, July–September 1943. *The Spectator*, 14 August 1920, 201–2, noted the background of 'sandbagged trenches and many coils of rusty wire' at the re-dedication service. Even after the Second World War there was concern about RAF use of the Dengie Flat as a range (TNA, WORK 14/1719, 22–4 November 1948).

36 *Essex Chronicle*, 10 October 1947, 6; *The Sphere*, 13 December 1947, 340–1; undated appeal leaflet, ERO, D/P 94 addl (A14562, box 1, part 4).
37 King's reports, April 1948 and April 1949, ERO, D/F 102/2/1 (1948 only), D/P 94 addl (A14562, box 1, part 4).
38 King's report, April 1948 (ERO, D/F 102/2/1).
39 Bettley 2015, 45; *The Times*, 8 May 2002, 33 (obituary of Stephens); leaflet by Canon Hugh Beavan, 2003.
40 *Essex Chronicle*, 1 July 1949, 6; unidentified cutting, 'Pilgrims at ancient shrine: past history and future plans', 2 July 1949 (private collection); King 1949–50; Steer 1950.
41 Anonymous 1949 (ERO, LIB/E/BRADS6).
42 Lewin 1868, 448; Morant 1768, vol. 1, 377.
43 Anon. 1949 (ERO, LIB/E/BRADS6).
44 TNA, WORK 14/719. For Loftus see *Who Was Who* 2007.
45 TNA, WORK 14/719, 11 August 1950.
46 TNA, WORK 14/719, 3 January 1951.
47 TNA, WORK 14/719, 19 and 28 September 1950. Fletcher was co-author of various papers on Saxon churches, such as Fletcher and Jackson 1944.
48 ERO, D/P 94 addl (A14562, box 1, part 4), 18 July 1950.
49 Brown 1925, 101–4; Taylor and Taylor 1965, 1: 91–3; Carter 1966, 18–19.
50 Carter 1966, 11; Newman 2013, 508.
51 ERO, D/P 94 addl (A14562, box 1, part 4).
52 TNA, WORK 14/1719, September 1955–January 1956.
53 *Church Times*, 8 January 1954, 24, 12 March 1954, 195, 30 April 1954, 333, and 9 July 1954, 521; *The Sphere*, 24 April 1954, 152; ERO, D/P 94 addl (A14562, box 1, part 4).
54 ERO, D/P 94 addl (A14562, box 1, part 4), March–August 1964.
55 ERO, D/P 94 addl (A14562, box 1, part 4), March–August 1964.
56 Burling *c*. 1985; Carter 1987, 18.
57 Lewin 1868, 447.
58 *Church Times*, 11 September 1959, 10.
59 Peers quoted in Brown n.d. [1929], 21; Carter 1966, 20.

Bibliography

Anon. 1949. *The Ancient Chapel of St Peter-ad-Murum Bradwell-juxta-Mare Essex Built by St Cedd Apostle of Essex circa* A.D. *654*. Chelmsford: Diocese of Chelmsford.
Benton, G. M., F. W. Galpin and W. J. Pressey. 1926. *The Church Plate of the County of Essex*. Colchester: Benham & Co.
Bettley, J. 2015. 'Laurence King and Faith Craft'. In *All Manner of Workmanship: Papers from a symposium on faith craft*, edited by R. Gage. 39–58. Downton: Spire Books.
Brown, G. B. 1925. *The Arts in Early England: Anglo-Saxon architecture*. London: John Murray.
Brown, H. n.d. [1929]. *St Peter's-on-the-Wall, Bradwell-on-Sea*. Chelmsford: J. H. Clarke & Co.
Burling, S. *c*. 1985. 'Memories of St Peter's Chapel, Bradwell-on-Sea, 1963–1976'. Unpublished typescript.
Carter, H. M. 1966. *The Fort of Othona and the Chapel of St Peter-on-the-Wall, Bradwell-on-Sea, Essex*. Chelmsford: The Provost and Chapter of Chelmsford.
Carter, H. M. 1987. *The Fort of Othona and the Chapel of St Peter-on-the-Wall, Bradwell-on-Sea, Essex*. Chelmsford: St Peter's Chapel Committee.
Chancellor, F. 1877. 'St Peters on the Wall, Bradwell juxta Mare'. *Archaeological Journal* 34: 212–18.
Cooper, J. (ed.). 1994. *A History of the County of Essex*, vol. IX. *The Borough of Colchester*. Oxford: Oxford University Press.
Cox, J. C. 1906. 'St Peter-on-the-Wall, Bradwell-on-Sea'. *The Builder* 91: 314–16.
Cox, J. C. 1908. *The Cathedral Church and See of Essex*. London: Bemrose & Sons.
Fletcher, E., and E. D. C. Jackson. 1944. '"Long and short" quoins and pilaster strips in Saxon churches'. *Journal of the British Archaeological Association* 9: 12–29.

King, L. 1949 and 1950. 'Saint Peter-ad-Murum, Bradwell-juxta-Mare. Lecture given at Bradwell on the occasion of the Diocesan Pilgrimage on Wednesday the 29th June, 1949'. *Chelmsford Diocesan Chronicle* 35: 75–6, 83–4, 91–2, 98–9, and 36: 7–8, 14–15.

Laver, H. 1909. 'St Peter ad Murum'. *The Reliquary and Illustrated Archaeologist* 15: 39–50.

Lewin, T. 1868. 'On the Castra of the Littus Saxonicum, and particularly the Castrum of Othona'. *Archaeologia* 41: 421–52.

Micklethwaite, J. T. 1896. 'Something about Saxon church building'. *Archaeological Journal* 53: 293–351.

Morant, P. 1768. *The History and Antiquities of the County of Essex*. London: T. Osborne.

Newman, J. 2013. *Kent: North-East and East*. The Buildings of England. New Haven, CT, and London: Yale University Press.

Peers, C. R. 1901. 'On Saxon churches of the St Pancras type'. *Archaeological Journal* 58: 402–34.

Roach Smith, C. 1865. 'Antiquarian researches at Bradwell-Juxta-Mare'. *The Gentleman's Magazine and Historical Review* 219: 403–8.

Royal Commission on Historical Monuments (England). 1923. *An Inventory of the Historical Monuments in Essex*, vol. IV. London: HMSO.

Steer, F. W. 1950. 'Saint Peter-ad-Murum, Bradwell-juxta-Mare: a footnote'. *Chelmsford Diocesan Chronicle* 36: 31.

Taylor, H. M., and J. Taylor. 1965. *Anglo-Saxon Architecture*. Cambridge: Cambridge University Press.

Thurley, S. 2013. *Men from the Ministry: How Britain saved its heritage*. New Haven, CT, and London: Yale University Press.

Tuckwell, T. 2013. *Coming of Age: The life and times of Chelmsford Cathedral, 1914–2014*. Bloomington, IN: Xlibris.

Wall, J. C. 1908. 'St Peter ad Murum'. *The Reliquary and Illustrated Archaeologist* 14: 257–63.

Who Was Who. 2007. 'Loftus, Col Ernest Achey'. https://doi.org/10.1093/ww/9780199540884.013.U16648.

9
'And withal a great silence':
The spiritual landscape of the Othona Community and St Peter-on-the-Wall

Ken Worpole

This chapter explores the establishment of the Othona Community adjacent to the St Peter's Chapel at Bradwell in 1946. Its founders, drawn by the isolated setting at the mouth of the Blackwater Estuary where it meets the North Sea, along with a perceived spiritual quality emanating from the presence of the ancient Christian chapel, set about re-purposing a collection of military Nissen huts to create a community dedicated to peace and mutual understanding. Once established as an intentional community, over time the Othona project has gone on to adopt a strong ethos of environmental sustainability, through becoming self-sufficient in energy supply, combined with the recycling of all waste products, and the encouragement of low-consumption lifestyles.

The choice of location raises interesting questions with regard to the often-cited concept of 'spirit of place' now gaining increasing attention, as travellers, geographers and landscape historians attempt to define the concept in a globalised world that seems to be depleting in topographical and cultural distinctiveness. The German sociologist Max Weber was early in suggesting that industrialisation and secularisation had led to a 'disenchanted world', devoid of authenticity or affect, one of the central themes of Alexandra Walsham's seminal book *The Reformation of the Landscape*.[1] In the UK, programmes to reconstitute 'local distinctiveness', such as that promoted by the environmental organisation Common Ground, have been supplemented in urban and suburban environments by the popularity of 'place-making' schemes, similarly committed to reinstating 'a sense of place' if not 'spirit of place'. The discussion is necessarily freighted with religious implications, and David Petts's chapter on early coastal monasticism and Johanna Dale's history of the pilgrimage tradition, both published in this book, provide locally specific evidence to complement Alexandra Walsham's examination of the long history of Christian anxieties about the pagan origins of 'spirit of place'.[2]

In the final part of the chapter, the unusually extensive Essex coastline, with its isolated marshlands, islands and estuaries, is shown to have provided a location for a number of religious and political communitarian projects, as well as therapeutic retreats, leading to the idea of it being a 'sanctuary' or 'spiritual' landscape. This recuperative quality applies not only to small groups or intentional communities but to individuals as well, and is clearly illustrated in Stuart Oliver's study of how two significant figures in twentieth-century British politics – Nobel Prize-winning author and politician Norman Angell and Labour MP Tom Driberg – both found escape on the Blackwater shoreline, which in the former's case Oliver described, as 'a retreat from a threatening world'.[3] Regarded this way, the qualities of withdrawal, silence and of being at the edge of the world, rather than at its centre, have become much valued. For this and other reasons there is a strong case for conserving these qualities wherever possible as an endowment for future generations.

The origins of the Othona Community

The Othona Community was established in 1946 by RAF padre Norman Motley as a religious retreat, a place where British and German Christians could meet in a spirit of reconciliation following the catastrophe of the Second World War. Early members occupied a handful of redundant wartime Nissen huts tucked behind the sea wall (Figure 9.1), just 200 yards from the isolated chapel of St Peter-on-the-Wall, a solitary four-square building exercising a profound presence in an empty landscape, and one of only a handful of seventh-century church buildings still extant in England. A simple chapel with a steep pitched roof, St Peter's stands tall on the horizon when viewed from across the Blackwater Estuary, equal to the nearby monolith of the former Bradwell Power Station. One modern-day pilgrim, Polly Clarke, wrote in 2006 that her small party walked there on the last day of 2005 to see 'two power stations, their profiles sharp against the wide sky; set barely a mile apart, they remain respectful strangers, mutually incomprehensible, divided by fourteen centuries'.[4] Both, they realised, exercised a strong presence in the landscape, their impact deriving from very different kinds of energy. The geographical

Figure 9.1   Medlar Cottage, the Othona Community. Ken Worpole.

position of the chapel is integral to its presences and energy: 'To come to the chapel at Bradwell, we know that we have come to the end of all buildings, to the end of the road, to the end of the track, to the end of the land ... this chapel always seems to symbolise standing on the edge.'[5]

Close to the chapel, badgers, profuse in the area and noisily evident at night as I have heard myself, still work ceaselessly on the remaining ruins of the old Roman fort of Othona, from which the community takes its name. Much of the stonework of the fort was reclaimed for St Peter's construction, and as a result dozens of holes, tunnels and mounds of excavated sand and rubble render the woodland copse, where the fort once stood, uneven and disturbed territory. The only other building in the vicinity is a small weatherboard bungalow, Linnets Cottage, originally erected to house signal station personnel, once belonging to wildfowler Walter Linnet, and until recently used for birdwatching, re-badged as the Bradwell Bird Observatory. Close by, a decaying wooden observation tower keeps watch over Bradwell Cockle Spit and St Peter's Bay. In summer months the shingle and shell beach here is home to the beautiful but rare yellow horned poppy, a protected species, now a defining species of the East Anglian coast, while nearby gulls and waders patrol the mudflats and saltmarsh at low tide: prominent among them is the redshank, 'sentinel of the marshes'.

It feels like the end of the world in more ways than one. If sanctuary has a geography, and I think it does, then the extensive saltmarshes, estuaries and islands of Essex (there are more than 30 of the latter) have long provided places of retreat for humans and wildlife, the Dengie Peninsula foremost among them. A long-standing member of the Othona Community (and theologian), Andrea-Renée Misler, has described how Othona is 'a place where people come who are on the brink of something new, on a threshold'.[6] It was for precisely such reasons that Motley chose to establish his community at Bradwell, as well as knowing of the existence of St Peter's, the closest thing he knew to the religious landscape of Iona, where his friend George McLeod had established a community in 1938. In her chapter, Dale points to the many historic connections between Bradwell, Iona and Lindisfarne, most recently re-established through new forms of pilgrimage.[7] It was McLeod who famously described Iona as what in Celtic culture was described as a 'thin place' where, in his words, 'the membrane between the world and the other world, between the material and the spiritual, was very permeable'.[8] Motley felt the same about this small corner of the world on the Essex coast.

In his history of the Othona Community, Much Ado about Something, Motley recalled the day in March 1946 when he and his wife and two others drove to Bradwell to see the site that was to become the location of their great experiment:

> On that vivid afternoon we came under the spell of that ancient building and of the whole area of the Blackwater Estuary. St Peter's is situated a few hundred yards from the south shores of the river at the point where it enters the North Sea. There, one can breathe. The land on which we stood is almost a peninsula, with the mile-wide estuary to the north and Bradwell Bay behind – and all round, and curving to the south, the North Sea. The cry of the curlew was heard, and a variety of maritime flora and many sea birds were evident on the saltings; and withal, a great silence.[9]

Motley's background was in line with the formative experiences of a number of other religious and political activists who shaped the Essex communitarian tradition, including William Booth of the Salvation Army, George Lansbury and many lesser-known priests and nonconformist ministers. Born into a large working-class family in east London, he was a member of the choir at St John of Jerusalem church in Hackney, an avid student of religion and music, and by the age of 16 was teaching a Workers' Educational Association evening class on the music of

Beethoven. As a military chaplain during the war, Motley organised a series of discussion groups that grew to become the 'Answer-Back' movement, encouraging men and women of all ranks to 'debate such matters as the evils of war and the existence of a living God'. This movement, whose origins Motley describes in his history of the Othona Community, eventually became known as the 'Nails' movement, the name deriving from a miniature crucifix welded from four simple nails and distributed in their hundreds during the war.[10] In later life he described himself as 'one who has been left-wing all his life in the Keynes, Temple, Attlee, Lansbury tradition'.[11]

In time the community at Bradwell was joined by a sister community at Burton Bradstock in Dorset, which opened in 1964. The site was chosen as Motley had seen another ancient chapel, St Catherine's, on the coast near Chesil Beach during one of his flying operations during the war, and had been equally committed to creating a community there. This came about some years later, though its general identity was subsumed under the name of the older centre at Bradwell. In a mission statement updated and published in 2007, the two centres are described as being part of one larger initiative:

> The Othona Community is an open Christian Community, whose purpose is to provide, mainly through its two centres in Essex and Dorset, a welcoming, accepting place with a pattern of work, worship, study and play where people of different beliefs, cultures, classes, abilities and ages can discover how to live together, learn from each other, explore together the relationship between faith and life with a view to a more positive action in the world, and encourage one another in caring for the world and its people.[12]

The Nissen huts at Bradwell – which are still there almost 80 years later – stood the community in good stead in its early years, but eventually new buildings were added, piecemeal (Figure 9.2). Motley and his small group of full-time residents began to take an interest in the possibility of growing some, if not all, of their own food, and for a while made arrangements to lease land from a nearby farmer. In time ideas of self-sufficiency also gained ground, as being at one with the religious principles that governed the community, which, like so many other communal attempts in living, owed much to the monastic tradition. For Andrea-Renée Misler it represents 'a *vita mixta* of action and contemplation in the Franciscan tradition'.[13] In a newsletter issued by the community in summer 2016, Motley's son-in-law Richard Marshall recalled that 'he

Figure 9.2 One of the original wartime Nissen huts, first home of the Othona Community. Ken Worpole.

always seemed a very human and well-read person, who grew out of East End socialism'.[14] Motley himself wrote in one of his published letters that 'we can begin to *incarnate* our concern for intelligent conservation by using more land to produce food – fruit and vegetables and flowers'.[15] He further added that 'self-sufficiency is encouraged, bringing out latent qualities and helping achieve unity'.[16]

Starting from small beginnings, the Bradwell community has grown in size to become a settlement in its own right, attracting up to 1,500 visitors a year, who come for as little as a single night or can stay for up to three weeks, but no more. These visitors need to be accommodated and fed. While the hospitality, food and sociability are generous and welcoming to all, the accommodation is comfortable but basic. Given that as soon as Motley had seen St Peter's Chapel he decided in his own words 'to pitch his tent there', it was clear that it was the unique landscape and history of the site that enraptured him, not the site's potential for a fully blown architectural endeavour. Since then, the community has constantly favoured low-energy, low-maintenance buildings, preferably re-purposed from older stock as indeed St Peter's Chapel itself was. But nothing ever goes to waste in such remote settings, as is evident in the bricolage of old and new, rough and ready elements that make up many of the farm compounds and outbuildings elsewhere on the Dengie Peninsula.

Today's campus – some now prefer to call it an eco-village – consists of the original Nissen huts now used for storage only, a shed/workshop and a caravan, a demountable former NatWest Bank used for administrative purposes, five permanent yurts, a modern timber and brick pavilion block, the Motley Building, where meetings are held and food served, and a weatherboard bungalow, Medlar Cottage, for resident staff (Figure 9.3). Opened in 1994, the Motley Building is now the heart of the settlement, with a south-facing long, covered terrace called The Stoep, where people can sit at tables outside overlooking the Quad, meet and talk, and work things out. The most recent addition to the building stock is the Solar Building, a residential dormitory (Figure 9.4), constructed from rammed earth excavated on site, straw bales and timber. Its interior floor tiling was salvaged from the refurbishment of one of London's Underground stations. The dormitory block is raised high off the ground to provide additional flood protection, a growing anxiety along the east coast, with good reason.

What at first sight is an extremely improvised and eccentric collection of buildings is interconnected – one might even say incarnated – by an intricate energy and waste disposal system, now tried and tested

Figure 9.3 The permanent sleeping yurts at Othona. Ken Worpole.

Figure 9.4 The Solar Building at Othona, made out of compacted clay dug from the ground below and elevated above flood level. Ken Worpole.

over years of extensive modification and use. One medium-size wind turbine, together with a series of photo-voltaic panels, provides all the electricity needed for a residential campus that can accommodate up to 70 people at any one time – lighting, heating, cooking, hot water, along with servicing a variety of other needs. All 'grey water' and sewage is collected, broken down and pumped into a series of reed-beds where it is filtered naturally in stages, before returning to the soil and water table. Thus it stands in quiet rebuke to the former nuclear power station close by, and in greater harmony with the neighbouring Bradwell Wind Farm on land and the Gunfleet Sands Wind Farm offshore.

Utility services and energy distribution networks are hidden in plain sight. In the washrooms all the plumbing is on show, supported by pressurised tanks and pumps whirring on and off, while sensors switch lights and heating on and off as required by human activity, all of the switch gear, fuse-boxes, openly accessible to view and mounted on plywood casings for immediate access. The buildings and plant rooms quietly hum with the noise of pumps, electrical resets and feedback systems, adding to the sense of human and environmental integration. Adaptability, reuse, multi-purpose functioning come with the territory.

After all, in its 1,300 years nearby St Peter's Chapel has variously been 'a monastery, a chapel-of-ease, a beacon, a lighthouse, a smugglers' hideaway for contraband, a barn and a billet'.[17]

Though the community no longer owns farmland, it has its own orchards, polytunnels, vegetable beds and herb gardens. This improvised approach to establishing the wherewithal of life is embedded in the history and geography of Essex, with the county's long tradition of plotland settlements, self-built bungalows and chalet dwellings, seaside shacks, caravan sites and smallholdings.[18] The fact that, in the early days of the hut and tent community, water was collected daily from a standpipe at a neighbouring farm, in a dustbin mounted on wheels, continues the pioneering history of the early twentieth-century plotlanders, who often had to do the same, as they too established self-built communities in more peripheral parts of Essex.

Othona and 'spirit of place'

Alexander Pope's much-cited aphorism 'Consult the genius of the place in all' is too often employed, in the absence of evidence, to serve as an accepted truth of landscape aesthetics and its philosophical underpinnings, an idea I have discussed and challenged elsewhere.[19] Yet the *genius loci*, like the pathetic fallacy, of which more shortly, often obscures more than it enlightens in explaining the emotional impact that place exerts on the human imagination. That this is much disputed territory is evident from one seminal encounter in the world of modern philosophy, at which twentieth-century English and French philosophers realised that they occupied two wholly different worlds with regard to the relationship between human perception and the material world – and the creation of meaning.

On the evening of 11 January 1951 the English logical positivist A. J. Ayer gave a lecture in Paris on 'The Idea of Truth and Contemporary Logic'. Afterwards Ayer was taken to a bar by his hosts, Georges Bataille, Georges Ambrosino and Maurice Merleau-Ponty, where the discussion continued until the early hours of the morning. At one point Ayer made the simple assertion that there was a sun before man existed, which caused astonishment. All three French philosophers thought the proposition meaningless, as without a subject there to witness or experience the phenomenon, it couldn't be said to possess any human meaning or descriptive reality. Without a subject, they contended, there is no object. In short, no world could be said to exist before humans came along and created it through language and shared understanding.

On these grounds 'spirit of place' cannot be considered a quality inherent in a particular configuration of earth, rocks, trees and rivers, but is a symbolic construct, embodying a unique mix of geological, historical, religious and aesthetic narratives attached to a place over time. Nevertheless, there are few, if any, landscapes in the world that have not been altered by human activity, some designed to impose function and meaning in quite conscious ways, through agriculture, industry and, in the case of the East Anglian coast, through sea defences and, most recently, programmes of coastal 'managed retreat'.[20] There are other views of course. 'Landscape may have no plot but it has much by way of revelation', the novelist Anne Enright has written of her own work.[21] Yet revelation itself depends on already extant categories of understanding or experience, according to philosopher William James, who claimed that, 'There are no specifically religious emotions any more than there are specifically religious acts. Religion draws on common emotions and common acts.'[22] James was writing about personal, not organisational, forms of belief but nevertheless implying that even quasi-transcendental experiences are made up of a mixture of inner psychological dispositions compounded by environmental factors – such as weather conditions, quality of light, architectural or topographical grandeur – which combine to produce the overwhelming emotional experiences commonly referred to as moments of revelation or epiphany.

The 'end of the world' setting of the Othona Community, with its vast skies and limitless horizons beyond the sea wall, along with the flat and windswept fields to the rear, clearly does exert a powerful sense of being in a liminal place; nevertheless, this can be explained rationally, and is not harmed by so doing. Revelation is part of the Othona tradition. On the pilgrim track which leads to St Peter's from Bradwell village there has always been a sign which claims that 'In this place the word is revealed to you.' The 'pathetic fallacy' shares some of the same ambivalences as the concept of revelation. The term was first elaborated by John Ruskin in volume 3 of *Modern Painters*, in which he discussed the process by which human feelings and understandings shape, and are shaped by, topography.[23] For Ruskin himself, though, it was a process by which mind and place could become trapped in an inescapable web of feeling, often leading to baseless sentimentality.

Perhaps it is only artistic representation that allows us to step back and dispassionately to interrogate what it is we feel about certain landscape conditions and why we do so. This is why writers and artists, especially perhaps photographers, become adept at employing particular weather conditions, time of day, selective framing of place and incident, to construct an atmosphere and representation that appears authentically true to inherent qualities of a landscape, as it means and feels to them. The essentialism is theirs, not that of the place itself.

In her recent study *Spirit of Place: Artists, Writers & the British Landscape*, Susan Owens provides an erudite and comprehensive history of landscape representation imagined in prose or poetry or through the visual arts.[24] One difficulty with her approach is its underlying chronological determinism: century by century, decade by decade, one innovation in landscape practice and appreciation leads to the next, so that in the book's section on grand landscape design, we encounter Lancelot 'Capability' Brown, then William Kent, then Humphrey Repton, in what is by now an overfamiliar exercise in baton-passing.

Such chronological problems are compounded by the way tastes change in relation to different regional topographies and boundaries, as landscapes fall in or out of favour according to the spirit of the age (another elusive spirit or *Geist*). In the eighteenth century, according to Owens, reference to 'the eastern counties' principally concerned Lincolnshire, Cambridgeshire and Norfolk as far as tourists of the picturesque were concerned. Suffolk and Essex were only enlisted into the eastern territories in the late nineteenth century (except for the case of John Constable's *oeuvre*), while the right of Essex to belong to East Anglia continues to remain contested. Yet the two latter counties have provided some of the most important territory for understanding and representing landscape, especially in the twentieth century, whether in the work of Paul Nash, Edward Bawden, Eric Ravilious, Prunella Clough, Maggi Hambling, Benjamin Britten, Sylvia Townsend Warner, John Cowper Powys (notably in his overlooked East Anglian novel *Rodmoor*) and, more recently, in the writings of W. G. Sebald, Richard Mabey, Mark Cocker, Roger Deakin, Robert Macfarlane, Jules Pretty, Sarah Perry, Melissa Harrison and others.

In the work of these artists and writers, spirit of place is not inherent or essentialist but is often contested territory, disrupted by war, flooding or migration. As a result, the region's saltmarshes, fens, vast skies and winter seas seem more fitting to the mood of a world no longer grounded in traditional narratives of national history or geography. These writers and artists suggest that, when it comes to spirit of place, cycles of both dwelling *and* displacement are necessarily involved in a struggle that can never be finally resolved. Mutability is all.

Essex, with its 350 miles of shoreline, is especially susceptible to such conditions and interpretations, and therefore predisposed to artistic fascination and representation. In itself it is a liminal space, a borderline between the fixed (or apparently fixed) land surface and the ever restless and changing sea. The wide coastal skies and changing cloud formations play their part too. On this matter much recent understanding on the post-Romantic and post-Darwinian perception of the shoreline – as a place for self-consciousness, a place of foreboding but also of promise and escape too – comes from historian Alain Corbin's magisterial study *The Lure of the Sea*. For the Greeks, Romans and early Christians, he suggests, the formlessness of the sea and its uncontrollability posed serious problems of placing within a formal taxonomy of substance and origins. Flood narratives are found in many creation myths, whether as a new beginning or a punishment for human cupidity.

Because the shoreline is characteristically a site where much of the early fossil record was first uncovered, its identity and aura is that of a place where the long past of geological time seems confirmed. On nearby Mersea Island, just a mile from Othona, the bones of monkeys, bears, elephants and hippopotamuses have been found in the river gravels beneath the beaches at Cudmore Grove, and similar finds are still being recorded. A few miles in the other direction from Mersea Island, buried in the estuary mud of the River Roach – a tributary of the River Crouch which marks the southern limit of the Dengie Peninsula – are the remains of Darwin's ship *The Beagle*, which ended its life plying trade as a local goods carrier. For the Romantics the seashore was a place for self-knowledge, as well as hope for travel and a fresh start, the spirit quickening as the mind imagined escaping to other more exotic worlds and cultures.

In an essay, 'Sea and the Contemporary Gaze', written to accompany a catalogue of British marine art, Janette Kerr writes:

> When we stand and gaze with our twenty-first-century eyes on the sea, what do we see? Stories of sea have long captured us with notions of longing and passion, of discovery and loss, of determination, hardship and survival, and the lure of foreign lands has sent us on countless journeys of exploration and conquest. As a metaphor for the unconscious, the pull and push of the sea upon our imagination is no less powerful now than it has ever been.[25]

One work not featured in the exuberant collection of essays and illustrations edited by Kerr and Payne, from which the above essay comes – and particularly germane to the Othona story – is a film by Dutch artist Bettina Furnée: *Lines of Defence*. This eloquent recording of coastal erosion on the Suffolk coast at Bawdsey, just 30 miles to the north of Othona as the crow flies, and documented over a single year using time-lapse photography, is an astonishing work. I remember seeing the film at one of the now legendary 'Place' weekend cultural forums at Snape Maltings about 10 years ago: it left the audience silent in admiration and melancholy awe. Before our eyes, the cliffs, fields, hedges and buildings of a tiny section of East Anglia disappeared in rapid succession as the sea reclaimed the land.

An essentialist version of 'spirit of place' provides theological challenges, sidestepped by Motley when he rhapsodised on the numinous qualities of the remote site of Othona. Yet, as Alexandra Walsham discusses at length in her study cited earlier, the idea that particular places embody aspects of the sacred is essentially a pagan concept, and one that Protestantism has historically been keen to extirpate. 'The central place that the veneration of nature occupied in the pagan religions of the British Isles,' Walsham writes, 'though poorly documented, can hardly be contested. The ritual practices of its earliest residents appear to have focused upon sites in the environment that were perceived to be the dwelling places of the gods or apertures through which human beings could gain access to them.'[26]

Yet the absorption of earlier cultures and understandings is characteristic of all syncretic belief systems, though less expected perhaps in a part of England with a strong nonconformist tradition, especially among the agricultural and labouring poor, the last vestiges of which are still evident on the Dengie Peninsula. Close to Othona, in the villages of Steeple and Tillingham, chapels belonging to the Peculiar People, an evangelical sect unique to Essex, can still be found. Established by a Rochford labourer, James Banyard, in the 1840s, at its height the sect attracted significant congregations in rural areas, where it built more than 50 village chapels.[27] I became fascinated by the 'Peculiars' from an early age, as, for a while in the late 1950s, our family lived next door to the chapel at Daws Heath and we could hear the singing and chanting during Sunday services. The sect's beliefs had set them apart from most other Christian denominations through their refusal to call on medical help, believing that only faith could provide healing for sick bodies. On the rare occasions when families failed to call a doctor for a child whose illness resulted in death, the sect was shunned by the wider community, as it was during the First World War when young men belonging to the Peculiar People were imprisoned for refusing to take part in the war.

Land, life and a new settlement

The 'Peculiars' were not alone in making a connection between rural life, religious belief and a refusal to bear arms against their fellow men and women. Following the carnage of the First World War, a fast-growing pacifist movement – whose adherents included men who had won military honours in the trenches themselves – began to occupy an influential space in the public and political domain. The result was the creation of the Peace Pledge Union (PPU) in 1934, initially for men only but expanded to include women in 1936, and by the outbreak of the Second World War it claimed some 140,000 members. One of its founders was Vera Brittain, whose 1933 memoir *Testament of Youth* recounted the heartbreaking impact on families back home of the deaths of so many hundreds of thousands of young men in that war. The book made her immediately a figure of conscience across the world. At the PPU she was supported by her close ally the Rev. Dick Sheppard, possibly one of the most charismatic Anglican priests ever to claim the national stage.

To their credit, some of the movement's chief exponents, including Vera Brittain and the influential writer and critic John Middleton Murry, realised that to maintain some moral credibility they would have to offer an alternative form of national endeavour in times of conflict, and this they did: productive work on the land. In an essay on the history of *The Adelphi* magazine – a largely Christian socialist and pacifist journal edited for much of its life by Middleton Murry – historian Michael H. Whitworth observed that 'By the 1940s, the journal was calling for a national renaissance based on an agricultural renaissance, a position derived from Murry's pacifism.'[28] The growing overlap between pacifism and agrarianism, was not only promulgated by the PPU. In addition to Murry's enthusiasm for agricultural communes, Methodist minister and PPU member Henry Carter had started to organise the Christian Pacifist Forestry and Land Units. Likewise, the Quakers had also had a hand in setting up a number of farming initiatives, as work on the land was classified as a 'reserved occupation', which meant it was regarded in many cases, but not all, as a legitimate alternative to joining the armed forces.

Pacifism and new forms of communal agrarianism were now seen to be part of the same new world view, and East Anglia was a favourite place for these experiments. Two of them, the Adelphi Centre at Langham, near Colchester (1934–42), and Frating Hall Farm (1942–54), close to Clacton, were projects that attracted a number of theological and political intellectuals in support, developing some of the most important reflections on the relationship between Christian ethics, communitarianism and the land question (not just of who owned it but how it was to be farmed sustainably). The period of the Frating Hall Farm community overlaps with the early years of the Othona Community, not many miles away, though whether they knew of each other's endeavours is unrecorded. Even so, they not only shared a Christian ethos but, in addition to their farming activities, saw themselves, as Frating did, as providing a sanctuary for refugees and even German prisoners-of-war. Once again, the spirit of East Anglian nonconformism shone a light on the ethical nature of the land question that still glimmers in the region.

In 1947 George Woodcock – poet, anarchist, friend and later biographer of George Orwell, and a pacifist who would spend much of the Second World War himself working on a farm in Suffolk – published a short book, *The Basis of Communal Living*, reporting on these new communities:

> In the years before and during the war, there has been a strong movement to found communities in Britain, arising largely out of the peculiar circumstances of the British pacifist movement at the beginning of the war. The communities which arose during this period were numerous, running into several hundreds. Some lasted only a few months – others are still alive and thriving after seven or eight years. Their sizes range from two or three up to a hundred members; their theoretical approaches were equally varied, ranging from Christian mysticism to materialist anarchism, while they presented a variety of economic structures, and their functions ranged from farming units to living communities in towns, from free schools to travelling theatre groups. The majority, however, were connected in some way with agriculture.[29]

The Society of Friends – more commonly known today as the Quakers – also took an interest in supporting smallholding schemes after the First World War, noted earlier. Known as 'Group Holdings', and aimed at unemployed miners, the first scheme was launched at Potton in Bedfordshire, but the idea soon came to north-east Essex at Ardleigh, again near Colchester. This led subsequently to the formation of the Land Settlement Association (LSA) in 1932, able to attract government funding. According to Marina O'Connell, a chronicler of the LSA and until recently a smallholder herself at Ardleigh, said that the organisation

> bought up farms across the country and divided them into groups of 50–80 holdings of 4–10 acres each. Each holding had a modern

home and was equipped with piggeries, chicken sheds, machinery sheds, glasshouses and more. Approximately 1,000 holdings were created over 21 sites.[30]

In a short time Ardleigh became a regional stronghold for market gardening, remnants of it still evident today in a scattering of glasshouses, vegetable and flower beds, orchards and outbuildings, a few of which still remain in commercial use. The pre-war initiatives at Ardleigh blossomed again after the Second World War, when in 1951 a Conservative government revived the scheme, and Lawford and Ardleigh in Essex again became a focus for the creation of new smallholdings, orchards and market gardens. At their high point, the LSA gardens 'provided about 78% of salad in the UK wholesale market', according to O'Connell. Eventually cheap imports of food started to arrive in the UK, and the growing power of the supermarkets led inevitably to the 'economies of scale' resulting from more industrialised forms of farming, and the LSA declined, finally coming to an end in the 1980s.

For O'Connell it was much more than small-scale food production that was lost in the process. So too were many skills, friendships and places of convivial and playful endeavour:

> When the holdings were in full flow in the 60s and 70s people use the words idyllic, utopia, paradise over and over. Hard work yes, but also a time of friendships, community and making a good living. People who were children at that time told stories of how they 'free ranged' across the holdings with other children, how their parents were there on site, but very busy. The generation that were the growers in the 1960s and 1970s told me stories of collaboration on the holdings. How they shared knowledge and information freely as they were not competing with each other. One retired grower told me very proudly about how they experimented with their crops from very high skill base and not from an intellectual or college base.[31]

It was a significant episode in modern agricultural history, today being revived by the proliferation of organic and niche fruit and vegetable smallholdings and orchards in the county and beyond.

Riparian, estuarian and coastal Essex, too often characterised as remote, un-picturesque and of marginal economic interest or landscape value, is in fact of immense significance in environmental and religious terms. It has always been a sanctuary landscape, and one in possession of other-worldly qualities that have been eroded elsewhere to our human detriment. Norman Motley was not the first to appreciate this. Two generations before him the Rev. Sabine Baring-Gould had been dispatched to the same territory to preach the word of God, though in his case he came to loathe the Blackwater marshlands and their inhabitants, though his well-publicised abhorrence says more about him than it does about the people he found there. A generation later, by contrast, Norman Angell found respite here after the horrors of the First World War. Nevertheless, it was Motley's fierce attachment that found the key to matching theology with topography, and the success of the Othona Community has more than redeemed his vision.

We remember that St Peter's was largely constructed out of Roman stones, and that the new buildings at Othona are made out of clay excavated from the ground beneath. The world remakes itself from finite resources, and the remote estuarine landscape at Bradwell is where, in Burkean terms, we should respect the past, conserve the present and endow future generations with something of inestimable human value. The 'great silence' of St Peter's and Othona does not imply consent to disruptive change in these perilous times.

Notes

1   Walsham 2011, 336.
2   Walsham 2011, 82.
3   Oliver 2014, 189–206.
4   Clarke 2006, 25.
5   Martin Wallace cited in Misler 2017, 168.
6   Misler 2017, 162.
7   Dale, in this volume. These links are also commemorated in the altar, consecrated in 1985: see Bettley, in this volume.
8   Cited in Misler 2017, 234.
9   Motley 2007, 12.
10 Motley 2007, 3–5. See also Marshall 2016, 13–19.
11 Motley 1986, 29.
12 Misler 2017, 134.
13 Misler 2017, 15.
14 Marshall 2016, 12.
15 Motley 1986, 31.
16 Motley 1986, 31.
17 Misler 2017, 67.
18 See for example, Hardy and Ward 2004; Darley 2018.
19 Worpole and Orton 2013, especially the bibliography.
20 'Managed retreat' is the name given to programmes of managing tidal waters not through obstruction but through allowing the sea to interpenetrate with the land in some areas by realigning sea walls, or dispensing with them altogether.
21 Enright 2015.
22 James 2012, 30.
23 Ruskin 1856, 166–83.

24 Owens 2020.
25 Kerr 2014, 26.
26 Walsham 2011, 19.
27 Sorrell 1979.
28 Worpole 2021, 39.
29 Hardy 2000, 46.
30 O'Connell 2014, 5.
31 O'Connell 2014, 5.

Bibliography

Brittain, V. 1933 *Testament of Youth*. London: Victor Gollancz.
Clarke, P. 2006. 'The day Saint Cedd discovered the Dengie Peninsula'. *The Essex Protector*. Essex: CPRE Essex.
Corbin, A. 1995. *The Lure of the Sea*. London: Penguin Books.
Darley, G. 2018. 'From plotlands to new towns'. In *Radical ESSEX*, edited by H. Dixon and J. Hill. 101–21. Southend: Focal Point Gallery.
Enright, A. 2015. 'A return to the western shore: Anne Enright on yielding to the Irish tradition', *The Guardian*, 9 May. https://www.theguardian.com/books/2015/may/09/return-western-shore-anne-enright-yielding-irish-tradition [accessed 28 November 2022].
Hardy, D. 2000. *Utopian England: Community experiments, 1900–1945*. London: E & FN Spon.
Hardy, D., and C. Ward. 2004. *Arcadia for All: The legacy of a makeshift landscape*. Nottingham: Five Leaves.
James, W. 2012. *The Varieties of Religious Experience*. Oxford: Oxford University Press.
Kerr, J. 2014. 'Sea and the contemporary gaze'. In *The Power of the Sea: Making waves in British art, 1790–2014*, edited by J. Kerr and C. Payne. 26–35. Bristol: Sansom & Co.
Marshall, J. 2016. *Norman Motley: Portrait of a man of vision*. Market Harborough: Matador.
Misler, A.-R. 2017. 'The Othona Community: "A Strange Phenomenon"'. Unpublished PhD thesis, University of Birmingham.
Motley, N. 1986. *Letters to a Community, 1970–1980*. Bradwell: The Othona Community.
Motley, N. 2007. *Much Ado about Something: A history of the Othona Community*. Bradwell: The Othona Community.
O'Connell, M. 2014. 'Land settlement schemes in East Anglia'. *Managed Retreat*. Freesheet, Essex.
Oliver, Stuart. 2014. 'Life in an in-between landscape: Norman Angell, Tom Driberg and the Blackwater marshlands'. *Cultural Geographies* 21(2): 189–206.
Owens, S. 2020. *Spirit of Place: Artists, writers & the British landscape*. London: Thames & Hudson.
Ruskin, J. 1856. *Modern Painters*, vol. 3. London: George Routledge & Sons.
Sorrell, M. 1979. *The Peculiar People*. Exeter: The Paternoster Press.
Walsham, A. 2011. *The Reformation of the Landscape: Religion, identity and memory in early modern Britain and Ireland*. Oxford: Oxford University Press.
Woodcock, G. 1947. *The Basis of Communal Living*. London: Freedom Press.
Worpole, K. 2018. 'The road to Othona'. In *Radical ESSEX*, edited by H. Dixon and J. Hill. 43–67. Southend: Focal Point Gallery.
Worpole, K. 2021. *No Matter How Many Skies Have Fallen: Back to the land in post-war Britain*. Dorset: Little Toller Books.
Worpole, K., and J. Orton. 2013. *The New English Landscape*. London: Field Station London.

10
A case study in vulnerability: Bradwell A, a trial environment for nuclear power
Gillian Darley

The post-war landscape

To modern eyes, the story of how Bradwell on Sea was identified as the location for a first-generation nuclear power station in 1955 is both alarming and scarcely credible. The public inquiry in 1956, the first of many such, made apparent the threadbare state of national protection for either the natural or the historic environment, let alone appreciation of vulnerable landscape settings, particularly ones as reticent and obscure as this stretch of the Essex coast. Those mounting an opposition had little firepower, while the government appeared surprisingly cavalier, arguing the case for a new electrical supply rather than on wider planning grounds. All this made the site around St Peter-on-the-Wall extremely vulnerable to the emerging development, both the ancient structure itself and the wider ecology of the tip of the Dengie Peninsula. The only existing statutory protection was Ancient Monument status for Othona fort, which lay largely underground.[1] The impact of the proposed Bradwell A had to be considered without a planning framework against which recognised objections could be offered and the likely outcome measured and scrutinised. This chapter covers the period up to and during the 1956 public inquiry, in which local people and concerned individuals attempted to make their case at a time when procedures and adequate knowledge were equally wanting. Given that the presence of Bradwell A is used to justify further development, with the boundary of the proposed main development site coming to within 150m of the chapel, the original decision to site a nuclear power station at the mouth of the Blackwater deserves close scrutiny.

After the last war Bradwell Bay was a desolate, seemingly redundant, RAF air base on the eastern extremity of south-east Essex. A concrete landing strip and structural remnants were all that remained to signal its strategic importance when it had housed one of the ingenious Fog Investigation and Dispersal Operation (FIDO) systems, a corridor of flaming pipelines to assist planes landing in fog or bad weather.[2] In January 1953 the USAF assumed management of the Dengie Flats Gunnery Range, a missile firing range well out to sea, and so Bradwell Bay became a small part of NATO's Cold War defence. Nearby sat a tiny church, commemorating one of the earliest Christian sites in the country, perched on the nose of the Dengie Peninsula, where the Blackwater Estuary meets the North Sea. In the late 1940s it was looking very vulnerable and for a time sprang a sizeable hole in the roof, collateral damage from the firing range, as the authorities all but admitted.[3] Those few pilgrims, religious or antiquarian, who steadfastly wended their way out to St Peter-on-the-Wall were shocked yet irresistibly moved by what they found.

It still takes patience and a long perspective to catch, and then celebrate, the understated quality of this easterly landscape. Modern environmental thinking defines marshland and coastal or estuarial saltings as ecologically important 'intangible heritage', in theory at least offering protection for vulnerable yet significant landscapes. But in the immediate post-war years there was negligible concern for such a fragile ecology and scarcely any recognition of what is now seen as cultural significance, that subtle personal response loosely defined as 'sense of place'.[4] More comprehensively than elsewhere on the Dengie, many acres of the northern peninsula, those around Bradwell on Sea and running down towards the Crouch, were converted from grazing marsh veined with meandering saltwater creeks into permanently cultivated arable land with geometric drainage ditches. Radical transformation through insensitive reclamation had begun much earlier but was given momentum, and funding, by post-war agricultural policy.[5] Only intervention by bodies such as the Essex Wildlife Trust (set up in 1959) and the RSPB (founded in 1889 but newly energised) secured substantial swathes of vulnerable habitat from the relentless march of agribusiness.

J. A. Baker's *The Peregrine*, originally published in 1967, was a powerful cry against the repercussions of such officially sanctioned vandalism. Purporting to be a journal of a single year, the book concertinaed its author's observations made over the previous decade as he explored what Mark Cocker calls his 'bicycle-bounded territory', an arc east of Chelmsford and out to the coast. Baker's despair colours and dominates his account, with the elusive raptor centre-stage. His diaries, discovered well after the book was republished almost 40 years later by the *New York Review of Books*, add valuable, precise detail. [6] Then, in 1971, prompted by the scheme to develop Foulness Island into an airport called Maplin Sands, Baker wrote an article for the RSPB magazine, 'On the Essex coast'. Vast areas of bird habitat would be, he suggested, lost to the incursions of jets, motorways and 'electricity-generating "temples"'.[7] Of these, only Bradwell A already existed.

In the mid-1950s, the historian W. G. Hoskins had unleashed a jeremiad against the detritus of the post-war landscape. The final paragraphs of *The Making of the English Landscape* inveighed against the 'obscene shape of the atom-bomber' in the skies, the arterial bypass, bombing ranges, battle training and tanks.[8] The poet and pundit John Betjeman sounded off about 'poles and wires' in the *Architectural Review*, and there too the architectural polemicist Ian Nairn fulminated against the 'morbid' scene that he termed 'universal Subtopia', his special issue on the topic quickly reissued as a book, titled *Outrage* (1955).[9] In the teeth of these justified storms of environmental indignation, the thankless but essential task of accommodating the infrastructure of daily life to meet the needs of the population was left to a handful of professionals, who adopted, where possible, that essentially multidisciplinary approach described by Sylvia Crowe as 'landscape planning'.[10] Crowe would become the landscape architect at Bradwell.

Due to its geography, the Dengie Peninsula, once coastal trade died away and roads and railways came to dominate, has come to feel remote from the rest of Essex, even retaining elements of long-lost Essex dialect into modern times, as if to match the patchy survival of its remaining coastal landscape. But the relative remoteness of the area and its scant population nudged the Dengie ahead in the stakes to house a Magnox nuclear power station. The siting of this first generation of reactors was based on the calculations made by T. M. Fry in 1955 at Harwell Research Station, whose initial criteria were 'all expressed in terms of limits on the population distribution around reactor sites'.[11] As models changed, the importance of an economically viable location overcame matters such as optimal evacuation times in case of disaster. But the first of the seven public inquiries, that into Bradwell in 1956, was viewed as a 'Test Case'.[12]

If the arguments about siting relating to population were carefully made, the protection for the natural ecology and landscape was negligible. This stretch of coastal countryside hardly suggested a National Park – then or now – but nor were any more fine-grain measures yet available, ranging from Areas of Outstanding Natural Beauty (AONB) and Sites of Special Scientific Interest (SSSI) to listed building measures.[13] The crucial countywide land-use plan offered no help since the document that would determine the future location of industry, new housing and infrastructure in Essex was still far from ready, under preparation by the county council in distant Chelmsford. The first National Parks reflected a view of landscape rooted in eighteenth- and early nineteenth-century romanticism, both of the pen and of the paintbrush.[14] The Dengie Peninsula did not and does not conform to established canons of natural beauty. Unsurprisingly, dramatic mountains and lakes, moors, valleys and picturesque downland were the raw material of the new National Parks, with the Derbyshire Peak District the first to be designated in 1951. In the eastern counties, it was not until 1976 that the Norfolk Broads were grudgingly accorded 'equivalent status' to a National Park.

The Dengie Peninsula was not inaccessible even if it felt remote, just 50 miles from London and from 1899 served by a train line running to Southminster. This particular stretch of the Essex coast has always been insidious in its charms and had a way of catching its advocates in the rear-view mirror. John Betjeman revelled in the near-Gothic folk melodrama of *Mehalah*,[15] set out on the mudflats around Mersea Island just across the mouth of the Blackwater from St Peter's, but for Michael Morpurgo the impact of his childhood years in Bradwell was direct and visceral. His vivid memories weave through his writing, including several children's stories, notably *Homecoming* (2016),[16] and take on extra resonance in the face of a decommissioned Bradwell A and a proposed Bradwell B.

Arriving in Bradwell, seven-year-old Michael and his older brother explored the territory on bicycles, heading out, heads down into the wind, towards the sea wall, past the remnants of the air base and on to the minute church, set slightly above the foreshore of saltmarsh and shell-strewn beach. Locals, such as Mr Dowsett the village builder-cum-handyman, knew that St Peter's was not just any old chapel-turned-barn but the very first church in this country, Saxon and, as such, of resounding significance.[17] The ramshackle little fragment was an eloquent mosaic of stone and brick, much of it gleaned and recycled from the Roman-era fort beneath it. Once there, the boys could huddle against the seventh-century walls, a sheltered ringside seat for sightings of hares, larks, foxes, kestrels, deer and more – these were, Morpurgo writes, days of 'sheer exhilaration'.[18]

An announcement in the local paper that Bradwell on Sea was being considered as the site for a Magnox atomic power station had a dramatic effect. The village fell into warring camps, in which the Morpurgo boys' mother became an active opponent of the scheme. As if reflecting the wider schisms, her second marriage fell apart and they left. In 2018, on what would have been her 100th birthday, the family returned. Sitting just as they did as children, their backs against the ancient sun-warmed walls, the vacant hulk of the now moribund nuclear power station loomed behind, out of sight.

The programme

A Programme for Nuclear Power was published as a government white paper in February 1955 even as Calder Hall, the first Magnox nuclear reactor, was already under construction close to Windscale, one of several plants where military-grade plutonium was produced. Until then electricity had been considered as no more than a by-product of the nuclear defence programme.[19] As Ian Welsh notes, shifting the emphasis onto ambitious civil power development away from the military one 'revealed the intensity of the euphoria and the tendency to indulge in transcendent symbolism'.[20] The white paper, largely written by the Chairman of the UK Atomic Energy Authority (UKAEA), Edwin Plowden, was a 24-page manifesto, pointing to a heady future of cheap power, seductively 'clean' (involving no coal dust) jobs and prosperity, and aiming to situate the UK at the cutting edge of a novel technology. The Central Electricity Authority (CEA), to become the Central Electricity Generating Board (CEGB) in 1958, was responsible for the national supply of electricity from all existing sources and would soon add nuclear to the mix. Rapid 'series ordering' would facilitate the construction of 12 atomic power stations.[21] They would be operational within ten years and provide 25 per cent of national electricity needs. In fact, that level of nuclear energy was not achieved until the 1990s.

The UKAEA had been set up the previous year with the passing of the Atomic Energy Authority Act. It was a 'quasi autonomous government organisation receiving its funding from Parliament in the form of an annual vote', and this little-scrutinised sum was, incredibly, more than that accorded to the entire Department of Energy.[22] With that, the UKAEA 'in effect became the sole repository of nuclear expertise within the country and the positive disposition towards risk-taking became a prominent part of the organisation's culture'.[23] The programme stood, emblematically and practically, for rapid modernisation at home and potentially offered immense economic benefits through the sale of reactor design across the world. A month before the publication of the white paper, Christopher Hinton, the head of the engineering division of UKAEA, addressed a public meeting in Thurso regarding the proposed experimental fast-breeder research station at Dounreay, saying, somewhat ambiguously, 'clearly only the fact that we consider there is a remote risk would cause us to build a factory in a remote area like this'.[24] In this case the exploratory nature of the scheme, announced (before the location was chosen) in a 1953 white paper, involved both highly innovative and little-tested technology as well as social issues, involving what Linda Ross terms 'a unique form of employment-based migration to the Highlands' but also offering employment prospects for local people in a remote area which had suffered continuous depopulation.[25]

On the wider stage, as nuclear tests continued around the world, a very different setting for civil nuclear development was needed, and it was crucially important to bring the carrot of economic revival into the picture. A more reassuring public information campaign, together with Hinton's alluring honesty, helped to present what Jonathan Hogg refers to as 'a façade of certainty'.[26] An atomic energy exhibition was staged in Thurso Town Hall in April 1955, promoted as 'a beginning to help you to understand nuclear energy'. Caithness would soon have what Ross calls a population of 'nuclear citizens'.[27] Meanwhile, the search for suitable reactor sites commenced. The terms under which the National Park Commission (set up in 1949) operated meant that it could not effectively challenge preferred sites but merely argue about the design and scale of the buildings and the vulnerability of the surrounding landscapes of exceptional natural beauty. Once the hard-fought 'amenity clause', Section 37 of the 1957 Electricity Act, became law, the applicants, thanks to a government amendment at the report stage in the House of Lords, had to 'take into account any effect which the proposals would have on the natural beauty of the countryside or on any such flora, fauna, features, buildings or objects'.[28] As Francesca Church has shown, the Council for the Preservation of Rural England (CPRE) in the 1930s valuably considered the understanding of amenity to be 'both education and educator', hoping that its effects might usefully 'delineate the 'proper' relations between people, environment, and practices'.[29] When challenged, the boundaries between these and government policy were subject to great tension. At a three-day public inquiry into Trawsfynydd power station held in February 1958, the commission expressed its strong reservations about the intended site on a reservoir in the Snowdonia

National Park, suggesting acidly that 'anyone reading the National Parks Act would not expect to find an Atomic Station within its boundary'.[30]

But the UKAEA was now in the driving seat, and the overall ambition, even insouciance, of the programme was signalled by statements such as 'although we are still only at the edge of knowledge of its peaceful uses, we know enough to assess some of its possibilities'.[31] In his summing up, counsel to the objectors at Bradwell would consider the authority to be both 'self-accountable and inscrutable' – largely due to its unwillingness to divulge, let alone answer, still unresolved technical questions.[32] In October 1956 the young Queen Elizabeth opened Calder Hall power station. While the nation might have risked losing 'our sense of wonder', given the rapid pace of modern technical revolutions, she happily proclaimed 'that sense has been dramatically restored by the advent of the atomic age'.[33]

In *Questions of Power* Bill Luckin characterised two camps in the pre-war ascendancy of electricity, the 'triumphalists' and the 'traditionalists'.[34] The former were unquestionably the post-war winners. Only seven of the 12 chosen sites were to be subject to public inquiry between 1956 and 1961. These procedures, lasting just a few days, were for the benefit of the Minister of Fuel and Power (until 1954 the Minister of Supply and after 1957 the Minister of Power) and stood for the consolidation of ministerial policy over the civil nuclear programme. The minister had already dictated the terms of reference and was the ultimate 'judge' in the case, taking the final decision based on what he deemed to be in 'the national interest'.[35]

But what section of the public were the government and its scientific advisers seeking to persuade? As Sophie Forgan points out, the 'informed layman', rather than a broader popular audience, was the target.[36] Despite that, early public inquiries were conducted in a determinedly parochial fashion, with meetings kept local and only those on the electoral register qualified to express their opinion. As we shall see, informed opposition was met with a measure of hostility. Up to then, the public received a facile, reassuring message on atomic science: for example, at the 1951 Festival of Britain, in Glasgow's Hall of the Future, where 'suspended as it were between yesterday and tomorrow, is a display on present-day atomic research'. That will determine, trilled the guidebook writer, 'whether we are entering an age of undreamed-of plenty and comfort, or whether we are working out our complete extinction'.[37]

Smart government-sponsored publications (as Forgan suggests, helpful for high-quality recruitment) spread the message, and the UKAEA engaged in a rapid public relations strategy. When Dounreay, in Caithness, was chosen for the fast-breeder reactor location in 1954, there was no public consultation, the local MP was staunchly supportive and the planning authority was 'consulted' on the basis of very limited information (citing confidentiality). Without a public forum dissent remained unrecorded and allowed 'a dominant narrative of positivity based upon opportunity'.[38] And yet, as Ross argues, in time Caithness became home to a population that was gradually familiarised to nuclear reality.[39] The strategy has been described as the 'decide-announce-defend' principle.[40] The use of brief public inquiries in the fast-moving early civil nuclear programme, even if suggesting a measure of openness, did little to offer effective scrutiny or deal with complex policy issues. But there were to be setbacks with the disaster at Calder Hall's pile 1 in October 1957 suddenly illustrating the immense dangers, and the scale of the unknown, that were hidden within the civil nuclear programme. As if to intensify the situation, the Campaign for Nuclear Disarmament was founded in 1958. Not all 'informed laymen' were acquiescent.

Preparing for a civil nuclear future

With Hiroshima a recent memory, the scale, speed and manner of development of the post-war civil nuclear programme were driven by a heightened, and continuing, public sensitivity about safety. Official secrecy and sophisticated government public relations worked in tandem. When concerned individuals and public bodies were confronted with the reality, as opposed to carefully prepared advance publicity, they found themselves underprepared for the complexities ahead. Public inquiries were 'frequently the only formal opportunity open to the public to question the siting of a nuclear facility; they were a rare point of contact between the public, national groups, such as the Council for the Protection of Rural England, policy-makers and industry'.[41] By the time a proposal came before an inquiry, it would be at a relatively advanced stage, and yet the stated terms of reference hardly touched on safety and siting. Until the 1957 Electricity Act, the constraints were those relevant to hydro-electric power and the valuable landscapes of mountain and lake where these power stations were sited. With the 'amenity clause' now embedded in legislation, the 1958 Dungeness public inquiry saw Nature Conservancy (established 1949) fielding its inspiring Director-General, Max Nicholson. He gave compelling evidence of the dangers the power station would present to the vulnerable and rare shingle ecology, although his words did nothing to alter the outcome.[42] But 'amenity' gave added weight to landscape design as an important mitigator of the scale and impregnability of the new generation of power stations.

The man with the unenviable task of identifying and then justifying suitable sites was Douglas Clark, the Station Development Officer of the CEA. His search began immediately, using maps and aerial surveys. John Cockcroft of the UKAEA had directed that sites should be wherever coal was unavailable and to be within easy reach of major users.[43] Enormous dependable supplies of water would be needed for cooling. Clark homed in on the Essex coast around the Blackwater and on the Severn Estuary in Gloucestershire. Once Clark identified the 'sufficiently remote' site at Bradwell, it had fallen to Essex County Council to assess the development – albeit with their collective hands tied behind their backs. At the public inquiry the county authority's ready acquiescence in a massive infrastructure project involving multiple unknowns raised pertinent and probing questions especially from Tom Driberg, until very recently the Labour MP for Maldon. He doubted the breadth of consultation and, therefore, just how democratic the process in County Hall, Chelmsford, had been, remarking, 'I would just like to say this, that there was no debate in the Essex County Council on this matter in the full Council.' It had only been discussed by the 'appropriate' committee, and he believed they 'did not take fully into account all the various non-material and non-economic considerations'.[44] Essentially the county council did not have the expertise to consider a proposal of such complexity. No wonder that when Sizewell A, a pair of Magnox reactors, was proposed on the Suffolk coast at Leiston two years later, there was no pretence of a public inquiry, nor had East Suffolk County Council even granted planning permission when the construction tenders went out. As Christine Wall describes, by then, much of the local opposition was strongly political (in part, avowedly Communist), and there were fears that this could easily get out of hand. Interestingly, Wall recounts the experiences of local people and those employed on the construction site. The 'nuclear citizens' of Caithness would not prove to be any kind of model here, and the assault on local democracy that Sizewell A presaged and maintained was strongly resisted.[45]

Of the first two sites, Berkeley and Bradwell, respectively in the west and the east of England, only Bradwell had aroused sufficient concern to justify a public inquiry. Much of that opposition was due to Driberg's efforts. John Betjeman, his friend since Oxford in the 1930s, joined the fray. In his 'City and Suburban' column in the *Spectator* of 9 December 1955 he wrote that the minister, Mr Geoffrey Lloyd, whom he described as a 'weak sort of man' had failed to consult any relevant preservation interests, 'or any other body which is concerned with what is left that is beautiful'. He feared that matters on the Blackwater Estuary (as at Berkeley) would be settled 'with town clerks and borough surveyors and little private huddles in the local councils.'[46]

In the New Year, the CEA started their consultation, determinedly local. In late January and early February 1956, a loftily titled 'nuclear engineering exhibition' featuring a large model of Calder Hall was held in Bradwell Village Hall, followed by a public meeting (Figure 10.1).[17] It was explained that the proposed Magnox station would not require the forest of cooling towers, but it quickly became clear that the authorities had little further idea of either the scale or the appearance of the proposed plant in Essex. It would be revealed at the public inquiry that almost all aspects of the design, including the essential technology, remained work in progress. Tom Driberg remarked at the inquiry that the exhibition and meeting had left many questions unanswered.[48] Calder Hall was the only atomic reactor yet built in England, begun in 1953 and becoming operational in 1956. It was the first atomic reactor in the world to supply

Figure 10.1 The model of Calder Hall displayed at Bradwell Village Hall, photograph originally published in the *Maldon and Burnham Standard*, 2 February 1956. Kevin Bruce Collection.

domestic electricity. Alongside it, Windscale, later renamed Sellafield, was a nuclear research station and plutonium production facility. In 1957 it suffered a catastrophic fire in one of its two reactors, about which the public would hear surprisingly little. The fire, which started during routine maintenance, was ascribed by a committee of inquiry held a month later to 'a combination of human error, poor management and faulty instruments'. That damning judgement, not to mention contaminated milk, did not offer reassurance.[49]

At Bradwell the key opposition body, the Blackwater and Dengie Peninsula Protection Association, had been formed at impressively high speed. They collected over 500 signatories to a letter of objection and claimed some 400 supporters, making up a wide coalition of local businesses and residents. Community action drove an organic, highly effective campaign and over 100 objectors were present throughout the days of the hearing.[50] The opposition was faced with 'the unassailable position of the nuclear enterprise', as Ian Welsh puts it, pointing out that it was unable to call expert witnesses to challenge the cast-iron 'certainties' put forward by the UKAEA (which, he suggests, were quite tentative).[51] From the beginning, the national press took little serious interest in the proposals for Bradwell, even though The *Times* had suggested that the success of the entire prospective nuclear power programme depended on it. Fears of irradiated oysters and burrowing worms on yacht hulls made for better copy, and press coverage 'bordered on the inane at times'.[52]

Locally, concerned residents were already discovering that essential information was hard to glean. It was only from a scrappy notice pinned up in the village post office that they learned that fuel and hazardous radioactive material would arrive and depart from the power station by the narrow lanes of the Dengie Peninsula, the radioactive material 'in suitable containers'.[53] It set a worrying tone, and an atmosphere that ran from controlled news management to deeply inadequate public information. Bradwell Parish Council called a meeting in mid-March, promising a formal vote for all those on the electoral roll. The CEA fielded their top men. Clark was described in the Maldon paper as an Orwellian figure, a technocrat who answered questions with care. Identifying the site had been a process of elimination, as the Thames Estuary both above and below Tilbury was ruled out and the government forbade access to Shoeburyness, a Ministry of Defence site.[54] The vote went the CEA's way – 115 in favour, 32 against, and an unrecorded number of abstentions (Figure 10.2). One supporter introduced a rather ingenious angle, hoping that the new power station would save the community from an existing intrusion, the 'hideous bombing range practice and low-level flying'.[55]

Figure 10.2 Voting at the Bradwell Parish Council meeting, photograph originally published in the *Maldon and Burnham Standard*, 22 March 1956. Kevin Bruce Collection.

The public inquiry

The local now ceded to the, at least nominally, national. Bradwell was the first in a series of seven public inquiries. The inspector, H. W. Grimmitt, would preside at Trawsfynydd and over two more, although after the 1957 Electricity Act he was joined by a planner colleague representing the Ministry of Housing and Local Government. The inquiry process itself was little tried and hugely pressured. The procedure was confused and confusing, from loose timetabling to last-minute insertion of extra witnesses, from the introduction of matters of relevance to those entirely beyond the issue.[56] The stumbling conduct of the short and absurdly limited hearing is only the first of many shocks for a modern observer, used to the complexity and sophistication, let alone long duration, of such events.

The first day of the Bradwell public inquiry took place on 26 April 1956 in the underwhelming, if homely, surroundings of Bradwell's own village hall. The lead counsel for the CEA, Harold Willis QC, set the scene by reading out substantial sections of the white paper,[57] rather as Lewis Silkin had quoted from Thomas More's *Utopia* when he introduced the New Towns programme to the House of Commons in 1946.[58] Driberg had organised a deputation to meet the Minister of Fuel and Power in London on 24 February, and the concerns that the February deputation to the minister had listed, now referred to by Willis as the 'stereotyped' objections, were also described.[59]

Over a total of five non-consecutive days in late April and early May, with the rest of the proceedings held in the Congregational Chapel, Maldon, Willis revealed just how unprepared the authorities were, presumably due to the extraordinary speed with which the programme was being rolled out and the pressure being exerted by government to fulfil the challenging new policy.[60] Many conditions 'in regard to matters of detail' still had to be met. These included 'plans showing the siting, design and external elevations of the proposed buildings and means of access to the site'.[61] Over the days more gaps were to emerge. Information on road access was muddled and, in part, incorrect, and the large questions of danger, contamination and other hazards were, at best, answered with educated guesses. The CEA was even vague on 'precise engineering details' which included fuel design and the precise nature of graphite. Without peer group review or exposure in the public realm, the UKAEA could retain its authority on safety, so 'central to the legitimation of the fledgling industry', while assuming that the uncertainties would be dealt with by scientific advances in the future.[62]

In fact, safety was far from the most pressing worry for the objectors, coming fourth in the list of concerns they had presented to the minister at their February meeting. Of these, Harold Willis QC listed industrialisation of a rural area, visual intrusion and road conditions as taking precedence over 'the possible danger'.[63] Yet early calculations, starting with those by T. M. Fry at Harwell in 1955, emphasised the importance of siting nuclear reactors at maximum distance from existing centres of population, in view of what Willis termed 'the experimental nature of the project'.[64] But as the perceptive landscape architect Nan Fairbrother neatly put it in *New Lives, New Landscapes*, if safety was of no concern, how was it that locations for nuclear power stations required 'sufficiently remote situations for a nervous safeguard against dangers declared non-existent'?[65] In an internal report on proceedings at Bradwell, the director of public relations for UKAEA, Eric H. Underwood, even expressed concern that 'there would appear to be a danger of public opinion underrating the risk and pressing for a siting policy less cautious than the one we have adopted'.[66] His department appeared to have done its job too well.

Far more difficult to characterise and so entirely missing from Willis's list was the essential nature of the vulnerable site. From the start witnesses struggled to articulate that intangible 'sense of place' that the CEA's choice of site threatened. The continued viability (or not) of the important oyster business on the Blackwater, the concerns of the inshore fishermen and worries about water (both its quality and temperature), equally from the rivers board and the yachting community, were clear and could be treated seriously. These interests had their representatives and marshalled their arguments to good effect. Yet on land use planning the inquiry was bound to struggle since, as Driberg knew, the County Development Plan under which major schemes fell was very far from ready, as Enoch Powell told his questioners in the House of Commons that autumn.[67]

Driberg's recently elected Conservative successor, Brian Harrison MP, was staunchly supportive of the choice of Bradwell, despite a questionable grasp of its historic significance. The remote peninsula already had pioneer status, since it had been visited by early Christian missionaries. By comparing St Peter's, a Saxon church, to a Magnox atomic power station, the new MP, the first Australian to sit in the House, did little to burnish his own standing. Why should a tiny stone cell dating to the seventh century stand in the way of a brave future, flagging up all kinds of British ambitions? The nuclear power option here, as elsewhere, came dressed in gauzy promises of new jobs, housing and improved amenities. During the inquiry it emerged that the majority of jobs would be construction-related, with workers housed in local towns, but once it was in operation, only relatively few, highly skilled employees would be required.[68]

Viewed from Whitehall, Westminster or even Chelmsford, the civil nuclear programme could hardly have been more exciting – or the waters more uncharted. At the public inquiry into Oldbury in April 1960 a representative of the National Farmers' Union, frequent objectors on these occasions (particularly regarding fears of irradiated milk from dairy herds), conveyed their growing levels of anxiety, 'a natural lay concern at the ever-rapid stepping up in the production of a potential Frankenstein monster, full control of which did not appear to be guaranteed'.[69] Opinions did not fall neatly on political lines. The right-wing editor and commentator James Wentworth Day protested angrily that the start date for Bradwell, requiring a labour force of 2,000, had been given out as March 1957.[70] It smacked suspiciously of the inquiry being a foregone conclusion and, as Wentworth Day put it, showed the 'sheer despotism' of the ministry.

The barrister representing the objectors' association, J. B. Herbert, had questioned Donald Clark closely about the nature of the area. He ranged over employment, still almost entirely agricultural, the seasonal and local holidaymakers on the estuary, the various spots favoured by birds and, above all, the likely physical impact of the power station. He lingered over the effect that the great blocky structure would have upon the diminutive church. 'From St Peter's Chapel this power station will be perfectly obvious, will it not?' Clark admitted 'if you stand with your back to the sea, and if there are no trees nearby, I expect you will see it; but if you stand at St Peter's Chapel looking out to sea, of course, you will not see it.' Herbert's response came, rapier quick: 'If you do not look in the direction of the power station, of course, I do not suppose you will see it.'[71]

The most startling aspect of the inquiry to modern eyes is the way in which the opposition was painted as exemplifying wilful interference rather than expressing their valid concerns. For all their efforts to confront the juggernaut of the civil nuclear programme, putting up strong arguments against this 'Test Case' on which 'the further advance of the nuclear programme was dependent',[72] the CEA and its counsel, Harold Willis QC, chose to dismiss them as individuals or organisations duped and orchestrated by wily outsiders – above all, Driberg. But the arguments of the association, alongside those of the voluntary sector – a tiny contingent compared with those NGOs and action groups that would confront a comparable case today – could not be dismissed for all their lack of firepower.

Enter the CPRE

The most influential and effective dissenting witness then available was the CPRE.[73] Founded in 1926, the body had assumed the role of guardian of the countryside in the face of uncontrolled suburban development. Its eminent founder, Sir Patrick Abercrombie, had seen the Town and Country Planning Act (1947) into law and with that Green Belt protection and early moves towards historic building legislation. He was the pre-eminent shaper of the post-war environment, which still bore the influence of what David Matless has termed the 'planner-preservationists' of the inter-war years.[74] The CPRE was represented at the public inquiry by its assistant secretary, Mervyn Osmond.[75] Much of the CPRE's active work was carried out by a web of regional committees, largely in areas of acknowledged landscape beauty. No such committee existed in Essex. Osmond had been briefly at the Bar before the war but afterwards moved to the CPRE. One early strand of his work was a commission (shared with the Commons Preservation Society) from the Ministry of Town and Country Planning to look at the 'general amenity implications' of the Services Land Requirements review, which considered the release or retention of the wartime defence estate. At one point he was handling a case a day, so perhaps RAF Bradwell Bay had already crossed his desk.

Osmond told the inquiry that his organisation was a federation of some 45 bodies 'interested in various ways in the preservation and welfare of the English countryside'.[76] Although this inquiry was under the aegis of the Ministry of Fuel and Power, he understood that the minister was in consultation with the Minister of Housing and Local Government, Duncan Sandys, with whose department the CPRE had so many dealings. He represented a national body and, Osmond said firmly, 'its intervention in the Inquiry may perhaps serve to underline the point, which was clearly made by Mr Driberg this morning, and has been made by others, that the matters here at stake are of very much more than merely local concern'. At a stroke Osmond had hit the target, and it was largely through the efforts of the CPRE (and no doubt Osmond) that the 'amenity clause' would be formulated as an amendment put down by Lord Lucas in the House of Lords the following year and thereafter become a statutory obligation for applicants, whether they be building new power stations or erecting pylons across the formidable Super Grid, although the latter had already been subject to a couple of public inquiries.[77]

The contest, Osmond continued, had been presented as one between 'a national need for electricity and a number of more or less self-interested local objections; but many of the grounds of objection are themselves of national significance'.[78] So the CPRE, looking at the matter from its wider perspective, 'accepts and endorses the views put before you by this very impressive body of local objectors'. Drily, he added that he was surprised that none of the substantial body of Bradwell residents whom he had been told unreservedly welcomed the power station 'have [sic] been sufficiently interested in this matter to come to this Inquiry to tell you so'.[79] For Osmond, the 'peculiar charm' of the area, so unexpected within a relatively short distance from London, lay in 'its atmosphere of almost primeval remoteness'. Lacking dramatic features, it had an unsophisticated character and a strangely haunting beauty of its own, with the powerful symbol of 'the modest, lonely and ancient chapel of St Peter-on-the-Wall'.[80] It would be a sad day 'when that symbol is superseded by the dominating bulk of the Bradwell Nuclear Power Station'.[81] However unassuming the seventh-century foundation was at first glance, Mervyn Osmond and his sympathetic listeners knew, it conveyed powerful religious and historic essentials, both in its fabric and in its atmosphere. Summarising his organisation's position, Osmond declared that the ministry's intention to build 12 nuclear power stations in *'reasonably remote rural locations'* threatened everything that CPRE stood for.[82] He found it difficult to believe that Essex County Council, 'who normally look after rural Essex so well', could have agreed, 'unless either they had been bemused – as I think sometimes tends to happen in these cases – by the magic talisman of atomic energy or unless they thought that a complete departure from ordinary planning standards was for some reason necessitated by the special requirements of nuclear generation'.[83] His opinion, both in advance of the inquiry and now listening to the evidence, was that no such necessity has been established. 'This, Sir, is for us, and indeed not only for us, but for others, a serious matter with wide implications.'[84] The CPRE only intervened when 'the grounds of objection are really weighty'.[85] But here, he concluded,

> we do feel entitled to ask that neither the Bradwell project nor the policy that it exemplifies should be allowed to go on their way unless it can be clearly shown – and it has not been shown yet, I submit – that there are overriding grounds of public interest to justify the subjection of rural England to this very large-scale industrial invasion.[86]

In the Congregational Chapel in Maldon, where four of the five days of the inquiry took place, Driberg and Betjeman were the most persuasive of the independent witnesses opposing the Bradwell application. The RSPB had fielded their secretary, as did the Youth Hostels Association (YHA), who owned a hostel in the village. The latter brought a letter of objection from the venerable Commons Preservation Society (CPS, founded 1865, later renamed the Open Spaces Society). The YHA and the CPS, the latter of which shared its roots with the National Trust, were concerned about freedom of access, both on land and water.[87] Given the short duration of the inquiry, the opposition needed to collaborate to best effect, so the CPRE would be, at least unofficially, the voice of the Society for the Protection of Ancient Buildings (SPAB), whose concern lay particularly with St Peter-on-the-Wall and its multiple vulnerabilities.

A diversion to St Peter's

In 1907, long in agricultural use, the seventh-century Christian remnant had elbowed its way into the growing caseload of vulnerable buildings coming to the attention of William Morris's SPAB, already 30 years in the field. The secretary of the SPAB, the Arts and Crafts architect Hugh Thackeray Turner, had heard that a Rev. Varney was endeavouring to raise funds for a restoration and had engaged Mr Percy Richard Morley Horder to consider the options. Varney responded adroitly, knowing the SPAB's antipathy to 'restoration' rather than the careful 'repair' the society advocated, and reassured him that he and Horder had 'full sympathy with your Society's principles'.[88] Meanwhile Thackeray Turner had drawn their attention to a scholarly book on Saxon work by Professor Baldwin Brown. As James Bettley explains in the preceding chapter, the 'recent' history of the tiny church was complex and involved matters of liturgy and church history, symbolism and conservation policy, amongst much else. We have no record of Varney and Horder's ideas, but by the 1920s the SPAB was reassured that St Peter's was cared for by the Chelmsford Diocesan Advisory Committee (DAC), which suggested all would be well. They were wrong.

After the war, the SPAB secretary, Monica Dance, received persistent reports about the deteriorating condition of the church. In 1948 the assistant editor of *The Countryman*, Mr Fitter, had been shocked 'to see in how ruinous a condition it was, with a large hole in the roof and a rather pathetic appeal pinned up on the door for a thousand-pound restoration fund'.[89] Mrs Dance told him it was 'a difficult case' which had been before the Society in the past. She wondered if the Ministry of Works might consider scheduling it, 'although unless the building is actually taken into their guardianship this would not ensure its repair'.[90] But when Mrs Dance contacted the Chelmsford DAC, they assured her that the roof, damaged due to a mischance on the nearby missile range, had been mended.[91] Services could now be held there and, further, it was ready 'for a complete restoration when possible in the future – a thing which the Diocese as a whole, including the Bishop himself, so very much desires'.[92] The SPAB and the Chelmsford diocese were, from then on, at loggerheads. The diocesan surveyor Laurence King's proposals were still on the table, though much amended from the conjectural Saxon tower with its 'long and short work' and new arcaded apse (based on Reculver) that he and the bishop had set their hearts on.[93] By now the Council for British Archaeology (CBA) were as outraged as the Royal Fine Art Commission. Mischievously the former observed that 'a new bishop might change things'.[94] As things were, the cement blocks laid over the packed-earth floor looked crude to another sharp-eyed SPAB member, Marc Fitch. He told Mrs Dance that the booklet seeking funds for restoration was still on display in 1952, with its troubling allusions to a 'complete restoration … a phrase sufficient to rouse the suspicions of any member of the SPAB' as he dutifully reported.[95]

Yet in 1955, when the prospect of a nuclear power station reared its head, so close, who was going to step forward to argue for the wider setting of St Peter's in its current unassuming shape? Perhaps the ersatz scheme put forward by Laurence King for the bishop of Chelmsford would have given it greater status at the public inquiry? An anomaly was that the Saxon Shore Fort and even 'the ground beneath all [including modern] structures' had been scheduled in 1924, under ancient monuments legislation set up in 1913, yet the status of the church in terms of statutory protection remained unclear.[96] The SPAB archives contain a thin manila file marked 'Nuclear', with a letter from Anthony Wagner of the College of Arms, whose responsibilities at the Ministry of Town and Country Planning in the war years had given him an important role in driving ahead the upgraded listing of historic buildings in the post-war period. He told Monica Dance that he had spotted an announcement in *The Times* about the two sites identified for the first nuclear power stations. He sent her a copy of his letter of 17 October 1955 to *The Times* drafted from the Athenaeum in which he pointed out that St Peter's drew much of its power from 'the loneliness of the estuary and headland'.[97] Could she round up some suitably influential signatories: for example the two activist peers who were SPAB Trustees, Lord Esher and Lord Euston (the future Duke of Grafton)? John Betjeman and J. M. Richards felt 'as strongly as I do on the subject'.[98] But with scant administrative resources the SPAB had decided to concentrate on Berkeley, since Mrs Dance felt sure that Bradwell was 'CPRE territory'.[99]

The exchange, with its random quality, a consultation based on an 'old boys' network' and letters to *The Times* written in a gentlemen's club, was typical in a period where statutory safeguards were few and the systematic listing of historic buildings in its infancy. St Peter's was to be listed, eventually, at the exceptional level of Grade 1, on the last day of December 1959. By then the power station was nearing completion. In the meantime, links between the CPRE and the SPAB were effective, especially when news reached the former that 'Services Land Requirements' on Dengie Flats were threatening to test explosives close to the church. The response there was that it stood a quarter of a mile outside 'the limit of the danger' and the Air Ministry had given assurances that there would be no damage to the church from blasts and no restriction of public access.[100] But previous accidents (such as that hole in the roof) did not inspire confidence.

Opposition from independent witnesses

Counsel for the CEA painted the inquiry as a clash between those on the Bradwell electoral roll and outsiders who, it was said repeatedly, had been organised, if not coerced. When Willis came to Tom Driberg, he went for him. 'It is you, is it not, who have been instrumental in getting a substantial part of the objections?' Driberg replied that many of his neighbours had been even more active. He denied being the author of a 'stereotyped objection' signed by people from far and near, but he saw no problem in the fact that people in the hall 'had been persuaded and organised and lobbied, as is perfectly legitimate, to come to the meeting'.[101] Willis then suggested that seasonal visitors' opinions were less valid. 'Quite,' responded Driberg, 'but that would be an equal argument for putting this power station in the middle of Brighton front or on Southend Pier, if the summer visitors are of no consequence at all.'[102]

Driberg's long friendship with John Betjeman led to the latter's evidence on the second day of the inquiry, providentially supplying material for more than one entertaining column in the *Spectator*, his own part as a witness unmentioned. Although Betjeman was not appearing in any official capacity, he pointed out that he was both a member of the Royal Fine Art Commission (RFAC) and sat on the committee of the SPAB. He had often bicycled around this area when he was young. 'Essex has always been for me a favourite county.' He had recently been back to make a television film about Bradwell Lodge, Tom Driberg's house.[103] That neat coincidence troubled the CEA's lawyer. But Betjeman used it for copy; in his *Spectator* column the following week he wrote that, if he had known about the inquiry when making the film, 'I could have got a remark or two into the script.'[104] Warming to his topic, he disarmingly asked the inspector, who had described himself as 'only an engineer', if he might 'make a speech?' Permission granted, he continued. 'I came here voluntarily because I regard the siting of power stations as something which is of national importance, and Bradwell power station a test case and a national thing.'[105] He had been delighted to find how much people minded about the proposals and although admittedly an interloper, he stepped forward 'in an attempt to defend Essex, not to exploit it'. Above all, he said, the area spoke of 'unregarded beauty'. As a member of the RFAC he could not recall the Ministry of Fuel and Power ever consulting the body on the site of a power station 'and it does not matter at all what the power station looks like, I mean how excellent it is in architecture, if it is on the wrong site'. Under cross-examination, he argued that this was as much a matter for the Ministry of Housing and Local Government, or that of Agriculture and Fisheries, as for the Ministry of Fuel and Power.

Ten days later, it was the turn of Betjeman's friend and informant Tom Driberg to take the stand. Driberg had been MP for Maldon from 1939 until the previous year and his continued interventions, recorded in Hansard and in the press, reveal his unstinting commitment to the defeat of the power station on this site. He told the inquiry that he had no objection to local industry, such as a local fruit-canning factory, (the jam-makers Wilkin's, at Tiptree) but felt that the seductive promise of new local employment was misleading, since the power station would require highly skilled staff brought from elsewhere. He also argued that a shift from agriculture to more generalised industry might bring 'what the *Architectural Review* in a very interesting publication called a kind of "Subtopia", which is neither true town nor true country'.[106] Driberg argued that the much-mooted short-term benefits to pubs and shops in and around Bradwell would be far outweighed by the realisation that 'something of immense value would have been irretrievably lost'. Two elements stood out, the relatively unspoiled coast so close to London and the 'quite peculiar character' on the Dengie Peninsula, which he evoked in a quote from a local paper: 'a winding sea wall runs for miles with the creeks and saltings on one side, and the flat, dyke-drained fields on the other. One may walk for miles without coming upon another human being amid this half-land of mud and ooze and salted winds.' His objections, he confessed, were 'aesthetic, and I would almost dare to say, spiritual'.[107]

It was Driberg's assumed role in 'active organisation of the opposition' at those village meetings in February and March that concerned Willis, counsel for the CEA, only to rouse the voices of Driberg's supporters in the chapel. But nothing seemed to worry Willis more than the presence of signposts, provided by the Automobile Association (AA), directing people to Bradwell Village Hall. Were some attendees not familiar with the location? It is tempting, if speculative, to imagine that the arrangements were made at the Chelmsford office of the AA, the manager of which was J. A. Baker, the studiedly anonymous author of *The Peregrine*. Few people were more familiar with the back lanes threading out to Bradwell across the Dengie Peninsula. On one bitter day in mid-February 1956, he noticed how the dunlins were using the sea wall close to St Peter's as a sheltered feeding spot, protected from the intense cold and biting wind. Yet, the dispassionate note masking his horror, he also saw and heard how 'aircraft bombed the flats and saltings'.[108]

Harold Willis QC pressed on with his forensic examination of the opposition, moving from the road signs to the stereotyped 'form of objection ... circulated by, no doubt, those dealing with this matter' and signed 'by a number of people' (more than 500, in fact). The level of publicity had drawn in, as Willis put it, 'people right across the [Blackwater] estuary' of whom over 100 objectors attended the full hearing and were 'inclined to cheer when their counsel made a good point'.[109] Looking back 65 years later at this crucial test of public opinion and informed comment, it is shocking that a high volume of concerned response was considered somehow illicit. If the members of the CPRE or of the RSPB, whose secretary had told the room at tedious length about the habits of Brent geese and their liking for flannel weed, to the evident bemusement of the engineers and lawyers, had been encouraged to write and complain, Willis might have been surprised by the volume and strength of opinion.

The decision

The affirmative came in a matter of weeks, arriving hardly two months after the inquiry closed. The CPRE annual report written, presumably, immediately after the inquiry reiterated its strong objection and anxiously waited for the minister's decision.[110] Even before the apparently foregone conclusion had been announced, the overwhelming sense that the opposition case had not been given due weight led to a flood of requests, conveyed in letters to the national press and to every MP, for the inquiry to be reopened.[111] Nobody was listening. With the site now a certainty, and the timetable pressing, consideration turned to how the gigantic structures might be integrated into the landscape. Unlike curvilinear cooling towers, the blocky form of the new generation of power stations did not help them aesthetically, however resourceful the architects (Figure 10.3). Sophisticated landscape design would offer some mitigation and perhaps even complement the lines of the new structures, although it was no easy task. Sylvia Crowe, appointed landscape architect at Bradwell, wrote about the difficulties of settling such immense industrial buildings and their trappings into the countryside and proposed a new term, that of 'landscape counsellor'.[112]

The Landscape of Power was written while Crowe was pondering how to lessen the impact of Bradwell power station on its entirely horizontal landscape. She foresaw, and feared, a crisis triggered by an 'influx of gigantic constructions and power lines' while, more generally, the degree of dependence on nuclear fission, water and oil meant that the 'evolving pattern of power in the landscape is unrelated to the old industrial map'.[113] All of it is a 'challenge, which is so far unanswered but

Figure 10.3 View of the power station from the west in 1969. Kevin Bruce.

rarely recognised'.[114] Discussing Bradwell, she was plainly disquieted about the choice of site as well as the 'element of doubt' on safety grounds. As she would write in *The Landscape of Power*, the situation was unprecedented and 'nothing can humanize [the reactors and turbine houses] or relate them to a small-scale landscape'.[115] Her own hope was that in future such reactors might be set in derelict industrial or mineral-working areas, if the need for immense quantities of water for cooling could be somehow reduced. Her professional standing and expertise gave her the confidence to argue for heavy expenditure on landscape, involving subtle adjustments of level and grading, and to disguise what she termed the 'worried details', which included 'the surrounding 10-ft fence, the sewage works, the 10 acres or so of 45-ft high transformer gear, and the car parks'.[116] Experience had taught her that the extensive degraded surroundings were the problem, and Crowe's strong designs for Bradwell sought to deal with them. Yet her tone suggested a nervousness where nuclear power was concerned, its scale being 'cosmic rather than territorial, and the idea which its appearance should express, [...] the harnessing of universal forces to the service of the earth'.[117]

As had Crowe written in a previous book, *Tomorrow's Landscape* (1956), power stations joined a group of modern functional structures, 'manifestations of the city which find no happy place in either town or country'.[118] New and out of scale, landscape designers must learn to accommodate their potential as 'superhuman landscape'.[119] In 1958 Crowe found a location that exemplified that. She considered the futuristic sphere at Dounreay, perched on the north coast of Scotland, a cosmic, almost visionary structure, far beyond 'human scale'.[120] Perhaps her attempts to settle bulky, boxy Bradwell into a landscape of horizontals, marsh, water and sky had been disillusioning. As David Matless points out, the new 'techno-landscapes' of Crowe and her contemporaries, Brenda Colvin and Geoffrey Jellicoe – the latter moulding waste material into the form of 'barrows' on the nearby downland to help mask the Harwell Research Laboratory – pointed to an energetic reordering of modernism, 'resolving any contradictions between the natural and the new'.[121]

The pair of Magnox stations, Bradwell and Berkeley, began a construction journey that ended with twin official openings on 5 April 1963, although both had been operational since the previous year. Tom Driberg, back in parliament again and representing the inner Essex borough of Barking, had continued to chisel away in the House in 1960 and 1961, raising innumerable points about the schedule, the assessments made on cost (compared with conventionally powered electricity supply) and technology.[122] Public relations drove strategy every step of the roll-out. Pathé News, under the title 'Atom Power Nearer', showed the loading of uranium elements into the reactor at Berkeley and another, almost identical, film was shot at Bradwell. The latter, favoured because of its proximity to London, appeared in countless newscasts, hosting visiting dignitaries such as the prime minister of Japan in 1959 and a major mission from China in 1963. It was also celebrated for record-breaking feats such as towing a 200m girder to the site, as if an entry in the *Guinness Book of Records* would be a cheerful public distraction from the reality of the nuclear enterprise.

The legacy

The 1956 inquiry was told that Bradwell A would be demolished when no longer required. Decommissioning was not part of any future planning. Instead, Bradwell achieved its own peculiar status as the first 'quiescent' Magnox reactor in 2018, 16 years after it closed. As if to echo this level of disinformation, archival material on the early inquiries remains largely inaccessible.[123] Sir Christopher Hinton, the leading nuclear engineer of his generation, did not admit to future difficulties.[124] Decommissioning was not planned for. The parliamentary report by the Public Accounts

Committee (PAC) in November 2020 acknowledges this lack of planning. The Nuclear Decommissioning Agency (NDA) is in charge of 17 nuclear sites, of which 10 were Magnox stations. The NDA is obliged to maintain Bradwell A, in a state of expensive stasis for at least 70 years, over which period it envisages radiation becoming a negligible risk. As the chair of the PAC, Meg Hillier MP, put it: 'the UK went from leading the world in establishing nuclear power to this sorry saga of a perpetual lack of knowledge about the current state of the UK's nuclear sites.'[125]

For all that St Peter's and the surrounding landscape can depend on statutory protection undreamed of in the 1950s, along with other existing nuclear sites it has re-emerged as a preferred location for a new generation of nuclear power station. Far from investigating alternative industrial or derelict zones, as Sylvia Crowe had suggested, the authorities have gone back to reassuringly ready-made infrastructure and existing planning precedent to justify their next steps. As this chapter has shown, however, the original decision to site a nuclear power station at Bradwell, pushed through at speed with little thought given to the natural or historic environments, hardly complies with modern understandings of the importance of assessing the impact of large-scale development. The fragility of the coastal landscape, over which the tiny ancient chapel stands sentinel, offers a subtlest argument against Bradwell B, and thanks to statutory protections the impact of development on the chapel and landscape must be properly considered in the decision-making process.

Notes

1. See below, note 13.
2. Williams 1995, 51–8.
3. Society for the Protection of Ancient Buildings (SPAB) Archive (St Peter's file). A letter dated 12 March 1948 from the assistant editor of *The Countryman*, R. S. R. Fitter, to the secretary of the SPAB, Monica Dance, referred to its 'ruinous condition' and mentioned a large hole in the roof. He had chanced upon its parlous state when out walking. On 25 November, Miss Hackwood of the Ministry of Town and Country Planning wrote to reassure Mervyn Osmond of CPRE, following his letter of 11 November, that 'there will be no danger to the church from blast' and 'there will be no restriction upon public access'. These assurances had been given by the Air Ministry 'to the satisfaction of the Ministry of Works' since the church was a quarter of a mile outside 'the limit of the danger area'. See also Bettley, in this volume.
4. Gascoyne and Medlycott 2014, 36.
5. Gascoyne and Medlycott 2014, 15.
6. Baker 2010 includes Mark Cocker's introduction to Baker's collected writings and the diaries. A useful summary of recent writing on Essex marshland is included in Gascoyne and Medlycott 2014, 33–40.
7. Baker 1971.
8. Hoskins 1955, 231–5.
9. Darley and McKie 2013, chapter 1.
10. Csepely-Knorr et al. 2020.
11. Openshaw 1982, 151.

12 Welsh 2000, 81.
13 Legislation came with the National Parks and Access to the Countryside Act 1949. The Ancient Monuments Protection Act 1882 had designated a few dozen scheduled sites and was much strengthened with the passing of the 1910 Act. Ancient Monument designation long preceded the listing of buildings of architectural and historical significance. Thus the foundations of Othona fort lying partially below St Peter's had been protected since 1914, but it remained (and remains) unclear whether that gave statutory protection to the church until it was given Grade 1 protection as a listed building in late 1959.
14 See, for example, Hussey 1927 and Hebron 2006.
15 A mid-Victorian novel, written by a prolific vicar, the Rev. Sabine Baring-Gould of East Mersea.
16 Morpurgo 2016 (originally published in 2012, with the title *Singing for Mrs Pettigrew)*.
17 Michael Morpurgo vividly catches his childhood memories in his essay 'Let me take you there', which he read on Radio 3 in June 2020: https://www.michaelmorpurgo.com/bbc-radio-3-refuge-in-crisis/ [accessed 14 December 2021]. The builder Murpurgo mentions, Mr Dowsett, was in fact involved in repairing the chapel. See Bettley, in this volume.
18 https://www.theguardian.com/books/2018/oct/06/michael-morpurgo-bradwell-sea-essex-village-home [accessed 14 December 2021].
19 Government white paper, A Programme for Nuclear Power (1955).
20 Welsh 2000, 54–5; see also Welsh 1993.
21 After revisions incorporated in the 1957 white paper, the target of 12 sites was reduced to 11 as some were scaled up. The first-generation nuclear power stations were Bradwell, Berkeley, Oldbury, Dungeness, Hinkley Point, Sizewell, Trawsfynydd, Wylfa, Calder Hall, Chapelcross and Hunterston.
22 Welsh 2000, 46.
23 Welsh 2000, 49.
24 Ross 2021, 93.
25 Ross 2021, 90.
26 Hogg and Brown 2019.
27 Ross 2021, 107.
28 Sheail 1992, 159.
29 Church 2019.
30 Mounfield 1961, 148; see also verbatim record of the public inquiry, https://archive.org/stream/op1265708-1001/op1265708-1001_djvu.txt [accessed 4 April 2021].
31 Sims 2016, 142.
32 Welsh 2000, 78.
33 *The Times* 18 October 1956; see also Welsh 1993.
34 Rough 2011, 37.
35 Rough 2011, 32 (in date order): Bradwell, Hunterston, Hinkley Point, Trawsfynydd, Dungeness, Oldbury, Wylfa.
36 Forgan 2003.
37 Banham and Hillier 1976, 154.
38 Rough 2011, 34.
39 Ross 2021, 96.
40 Rough 2011, 34.
41 Rough 2011, 25.
42 The full extent of the endangered ecology can be seen in a Pathé film clip of December 1958: https://www.britishpathe.com/video/VLVA8LOHH2YG2X3UJHBCDAVMXSL5X-UK-DUNGENESS-NUCLEAR-POWER-STATION-SITE/query/structures [accessed 14 December 2021].
43 A good overview of the discussions and chronology around siting and safety of nuclear facilities is provided in Grimston, Nuttall and Vaughan 2014.
44 ERO A11692 Box 1 transcript. Day 4, 19, para 3.
45 Wall 2019.
46 Betjeman 1955, describing Lloyd as 'unable to stand up to the top-secret mentality of his subordinates'.
47 At Windscale in Westmorland (now Cumbria).
48 ERO A11692 Box 1 transcript. Day 4, 10, para 2, 18, paras 3 and 5, 20, para 6.

49 http://news.bbc.co.uk/onthisday/hi/dates/stories/november/8/newsid_3181000/3181342.stm [accessed 14 December 2021].
50 Welsh 1993, 23–4.
51 Welsh 2000, 80–1.
52 Welsh 1993, 26.
53 Handwritten note inserted at beginning of a scrapbook containing newspaper cuttings (now in the collection of Kevin Bruce), summarising the notice displayed in Bradwell Post Office. It mentioned the turbo-generator, the two reactors and 'associated building and construction works'. There would be no cooling towers 'as at Calder Hall', since water would be used for the purpose 'at the rate of 350,000 gals/min.'. There will be 'no ash, no radioactive waste and no more noise than a normal generator'.
54 *Essex County Standard*, 4 May 1956.
55 Norman Gibson, cited in the *Maldon & Burnham Standard*, 8 March 1956.
56 Rough 2011, 31–2.
57 ERO A11692 Box 1 transcript. Day 1, 26 April, 4–7.
58 https://api.parliament.uk/historic-hansard/commons/1946/may/08/new-towns-bill [accessed 14 December 2021].
59 ERO A11692 Box 1 transcript. Day 1, 26 April, 16–19.
60 ERO A11692 Box 1 transcript. Day 1, 4.
61 ERO A11692 Box 1 transcript. Day 1, 10–11.
62 Welsh 2000, 81.
63 ERO A11692 Box 1 transcript. Day 1, 17.
64 Matters dealt with at length by Willis in his opening remarks to the public inquiry, Day 1, 4–19.
65 Fairbrother 1970, 136. The CPRE Annual Report 1956–7 queried the policy of siting nuclear power stations in 'reasonably remote rural locations'. The inconsistency of the statement, and the speed of the programme, suggested that there would be no opportunity to review the siting policy 'in the light of experience' as promised. In the case of Bradwell, the nearest town, Maldon, was 10 miles away, making it 'a quite *unreasonably* remote rural location'.
66 Sims 2016, 155.
67 House of Commons, Questions, 30 October 1956. Julian Ridsdale, MP for Harwich, asked when the Essex Development Plan was likely to be approved. Rt Hon. Enoch Powell MP, Minister of Housing and Local Government, could not answer, pointing out that many counties were in the same situation of uncertainty.
68 ERO A11692 Box 1 transcript. Day 2, 10–11.
69 Sims 2016, 152–3.
70 ERO A11692 Box 1 transcript. Day 2, 56.
71 ERO A11692 Box 1 transcript. Day 2, 9, paras 13 and 14.
72 Welsh 2000, 81.
73 Now renamed the Campaign to Protect Rural England.
74 Matless 1998, 47–61.
75 Museum of English Rural Life SR DX 151/7. Mervyn Osmond OBE interviewed by Robin Grove-White to mark his retirement after 30 years at the CPRE (CPRE/Shell oral archive).
76 ERO A11692 Box 1 transcript. Day 2, 68.
77 Sheail 1992, 156.
78 ERO A11692 Box 1 transcript. Day 2, 68.
79 ERO A11692 Box 1 transcript. Day 2, 69.
80 ERO A11692 Box 1 transcript. Day 2, 69.
81 ERO A11692 Box 1 transcript. Day 2, 69.
82 ERO A11692 Box 1 transcript. Day 2, 70.
83 ERO A11692 Box 1 transcript. Day 2, 70.
84 ERO A11692 Box 1 transcript. Day 2, 70.
85 ERO A11692 Box 1 transcript. Day 2, 70.
86 ERO A11692 Box 1 transcript. Day 2, 70.
87 ERO A11692 Box 1 transcript. H. Gatcliff represented the YHA on Day 2.
88 SPAB archive (St Peter's file) 28 November 1907.
89 SPAB archive (St Peter's file) 12 March 1948.
90 SPAB archive (St Peter's file) 12 March 1948.
91 SPAB archive (St Peter's file) 12 March 1948.
92 SPAB archive (St Peter's file) 12 March 1948.

93   See Bettley, in this volume.
94   SPAB archive (St Peter's file) minutes of CBA meeting.
95   SPAB archive (St Peter's file) 16 June 1952.
96   See above, note 13.
97   SPAB archive (St Peter's file) 25 October 1955.
98   SPAB archive (St Peter's file) 25 October 1955.
99   SPAB archive (St Peter's file). Despite her confidence in the CPRE arguing against the Bradwell proposals, as they were to do, Mervyn Osmond had written to Monica Dance, on 20 March 1956, urging the SPAB to object to the proposed power station at Berkeley, which, in his opinion after visiting both sites, 'is far more objectionable than the Bradwell proposal which has aroused so many protests'. But those objections had to be confined to letters of concern since there was no public inquiry at Berkeley.
100 SPAB archive (St Peter's file), letter to Mervyn Osmond, CPRE, from Ministry of Town and Country Planning, 25 November 1948.
101 ERO A11692 Box 1 transcript. Day 4, 12, para 3.
102 ERO A11692 Box 1 transcript. Day 4, 13, para 10.
103 ERO A11692 Box 1 transcript. Day 2, 64, paras 7 and 8.
104 Betjeman and Lycett-Green 1997, 330.
105 ERO A11692 Box 1 transcript. Day 2, 64–5.
106 ERO A11692 Box 1 transcript. Day 4, 8.
107 ERO A11692 Box 1 transcript. Day 4, 11, paras 2, 3 and 4. The author of the descriptive passage, 'in an Essex paper', was given as Gordon Strutt.
108 Baker 2010, 331.
109 Welsh 2000, 79.
110 CPRE Annual Report 1955–6, relevant extracts kindly copied by Oliver Hilliam during lockdown.
111 Welsh 2000, 81.
112 Crowe was concurrently the consultant architect at both the Essex New Towns, Harlow and Basildon.
113 Crowe 1958, 9.
114 Crowe 1958, 10.
115 Crowe 1958, 63.
116 Crowe 1958, 66.
117 Crowe 1958, 62 7, 12.
118 Crowe 1956, 151.
119 Crowe 1956, 152.
120 Charlton and Harwood 2020, 108 (entry by Linda Ross).
121 Matless 1998, 223.
122 Exemplified by this: https://api.parliament.uk/historic-hansard/commons/1961/apr/24/nuclear-power-station-bradwell#S5CV0639P0_19610424_HOC_135 [accessed 14 December 2021].
123 Archive material has been transferred from the TNA to the Ministry of Defence, who refused access to TNA AB 16/2227, correspondence regarding the public inquiry, in July 2021.
124 In 1954 Hinton was appointed head of the engineering division of UKAEA, based at Risley. Tensions between his empire and that of Sir John Cockcroft, chairman, who headed the research and development of UKAEA at Harwell, dogged the programme.
125 Hansard, HC 653 published 27 November 2020. https://publications.parliament.uk/pa/cm5801/cmselect/cmpubacc/653/65302.htm [accessed 14 December 2021].

Bibliography

Baker, J. A. 1971. 'On the Essex coast'. *RSPB Birds Magazine* 3: 281–3.
Baker, J. A. 2010. *The Peregrine: The hill of summer & diaries. The complete works of J. A. Baker*. London: HarperCollins.
Banham, M., and B. Hillier (eds). 1976. *A Tonic to the Nation: The Festival of Britain 1951*. London: Thames and Hudson.

Betjeman, J., and C. Lycett-Green. 1997. *Coming Home: An anthology of his prose, 1920–1977*. London: Methuen.
Charlton, S., and E. Harwood (eds). 2020. *100 20th-Century Gardens & Landscapes*. London: Batsford.
Church, F. 2019. 'Amenity as educator: geographies of education, citizenship, and the CPRE in 1930s England'. *Geographical Journal* 185(3): 256–67.
Crowe, S. 1956. *Tomorrow's Landscape*. London: Architectural Press.
Crowe, S. 1958. *The Landscape of Power*. London: Architectural Press.
Csepely-Knorr, L., R. Brooks and L. Coucill. 2020. 'Why the landscapes of post-war infrastructure matter'. *Landscape Journal* 2: 6–8.
Darley, G., and D. McKie. 2013. *Ian Nairn: Words in place*. Nottingham: Five Leaves Publications.
Fairbrother, N. 1970. *New Lives, New Landscapes*. London: Architectural Press.
Forgan, S. 2003. 'Atoms in Wonderland'. *History and Technology* 19(3): 177–96.
Gascoyne, A., and M. Medlycott. 2014. *Essex Historic Grazing Marsh Project*. Chelmsford: Essex County Council.
Grimston, M., W. J. Nuttall and G. Vaughan. 2014. 'The siting of UK nuclear reactors'. *Journal of Radiological Protection* 34(2): 1–24.
Hebron, S. 2006. *The Romantics and the British Landscape*. London: British Library.
Hogg, J., and K. Brown. 2019. 'Introduction: social and cultural histories of British nuclear mobilisation since 1945'. *Contemporary British History* 33(2): 161–9.
Hoskins, W. G. 1955. *The Making of the English Landscape*. London: Hodder and Stoughton.
Hussey, C. 1927. *The Picturesque: Studies in a point of view*. London: Frank Cass & Co.
Luckin, B. 1990. *Questions of Power Electricity and Environment in Interwar Britain*. Manchester and New York: Manchester University Press.
Matless, D. 1998. *Landscape and Englishness* London: Reaktion Books.
Morpurgo, M. 2016. *Homecoming*. London: Walker Books.
Mounfield, P. R. 1961. 'The location of nuclear power stations in the United Kingdom'. *Geography* 46(2), 139–55.
Openshaw, S. 1982. 'The geography of reactor siting policies in the U.K.'. *Transactions of the Institute of British Geographers* 7(2): 150–62.
Ross, L. 2021. 'Dounreay: creating the nuclear north'. *The Scottish Historical Review* C, 1, no. 252: 82–108.
Rough, E. 2011. 'Policy learning through public inquiries? The case of UK nuclear energy policy, 1955–61'. *Environment and Planning C: Government and Policy* 29: 24–45.
Sheail, J. 1992. 'The "amenity" clause: an insight into half a century of environmental protection in the United Kingdom'. *Transactions of the Institute of British Geographers* 17(2): 152–65.
Sims, P. D. 2016. 'The Development of Environmental Politics in Inter-War and Post-War Britain'. Unpublished PhD thesis, Queen Mary University of London.
Wall, C. 2019. '"Nuclear prospects": the siting and construction of Sizewell A power station 1957–1966'. *Contemporary British History* 33(2): 246–73.
Welsh, I. 1993. 'The NIMBY syndrome: its significance in the history of the nuclear debate in Britain'. *British Journal for the History of Science* 26: 15–32.
Welsh, I. 2000. *Mobilising Modernity: The nuclear moment*. London and New York: Routledge.
Williams, G. 1995. *Flying through Fire: FIDO – the fogbuster of World War Two*. Stroud: Alan Sutton.

11
The St Peter's Way:
Leisure, heritage and pilgrimage

Johanna Dale

Although often assumed to be an ancient route, owing to the antiquity of the destination, the St Peter's Way is, in fact, a relatively modern creation. The route was planned and surveyed by members of two leisure walking groups, the Epping Forest Holiday Fellowship and the West Essex Ramblers, in the early 1970s. To members of these groups it was self-evident that the chapel deserved its own long-distance route:

> Since it was built in 654 AD on part of the site of the Roman Fort of Othona, the little chapel of St Peter's-on-the-Wall at Bradwell has fired the imagination of men, and been the inspiration of many pilgrimages. Not surprisingly, therefore, it has also led to thoughts of a footpath route to the chapel.[1]

The route they created was subsequently adopted by Essex County Council, becoming one of the county's promoted leisure paths.[2] The original route runs 41 miles, from Chipping Ongar to the chapel at Bradwell on Sea, after which it is named. Designed with the enjoyment of walking as the driving motivation, the route meanders through rural Essex on footpaths and bridleways, with surprisingly little walking on roads. Recently the British Pilgrimage Trust (formed 2014), a charitable organisation which seeks to 'advance British pilgrimage as a form of cultural heritage that promotes holistic wellbeing, for the public benefit', has publicised the path as a pilgrimage route, extending it less than a mile to start at St Andrew's Church at Greensted.[3] Thanks to this innovation, the Way can now be said to run between the oldest wooden church in the world and the oldest largely intact church in England, providing a compelling heritage narrative for the route. This chapter will argue that considerably greater use could and should be made of the potential of the St Peter's Way to contribute to sustainable rural heritage tourism in Essex.[4] Before doing so it will contextualise the route by investigating its origins and current use and by considering the wider landscape of pilgrimage and medieval heritage in the twenty-first century, exploring ideas of authenticity in the light of a number of pilgrimage–heritage routes that have been created elsewhere in Britain in the last two decades.

Leisure walking and the origins and current uses of the St Peter's Way

In this volume Barbara Yorke suggests that the monastic community at Bradwell would have possessed relics of Cedd and nourished his cult, and no doubt pilgrims would, in this early period, have travelled to Bradwell, either on foot or horseback, or perhaps by boat. They would not, however, have begun their journey at Chipping Ongar, or have favoured a route across the Tillingham marshes (now reclaimed coastal grazing marsh) in preference to an established Roman road.[5] The logic of the route is that not of a medieval pilgrim but of a modern leisure walker. That this might be seen as a strength of the Way, rather than as a hindrance to its promotion as a medieval heritage route, will be discussed below. These examples are invoked here as an entry to appreciating the Way's origins in the context of the growth of walking as a working-class leisure pursuit in the twentieth century, the development of long-distance paths and the relationship between Essex's metropolitan fringe and rural coast. The main author of the Way, Fred Matthews, was involved with the West Essex Group of the Ramblers' Association from its very inception. On Thursday 30 April 1970 a public meeting was held to discuss the formation of a local branch of the Ramblers' Association, with a proposed name of 'N.W. London and the Roding'.[6] On 14 October an inaugural meeting of the group, now known as the 'West Essex' group, was held at Buckhurst Hill Community Association and soon after an initial programme was created, which combined path clearances and surveys with rambles in the Lambridge, Abridge, Epping and Ongar areas.[7] The change of group name is worth remarking on. The historic county of Essex ceded many of its metropolitan areas to Greater London as part of the London Government Act of 1963; however, Lambridge, Abridge, Epping and Ongar remained (and remain) part of Essex. Inaugural members of the group manifestly looked east to rural Essex rather than west to London, whose urban sprawl and new motorways had a huge impact on their local area. An early group walk, part of 'West Essex Footpath Week' in September 1972, was along the planned route of the M11 and was billed as the 'last chance to view the route … in peace'.[8] Members of the group were also active in protesting against the construction of the M25, and Fred Matthews himself was pivotal in the campaign to build Bell Common Tunnel rather than drive London's orbital motorway directly through Epping Forest.[9]

Campaigning to protect Epping Forest, the clearing and surveying of footpaths in West Essex and the development of walking routes were driven by the same motivation: to protect the local countryside and to make it accessible to leisure walkers. This was the *raison d'être* of the Ramblers' Association, which had its origins in the late nineteenth- and early twentieth-century labour movements. During this period, numerous clubs, fellowships and associations were founded, with the aim of promoting constructive, intellectually and morally improving uses of workers' leisure time.[10] Initially mostly based in the industrial cities of the north and midlands, the movement spread across the British Isles, and a National Council of Rambling Federations was set up in 1931, which was superseded by the Ramblers' Association in 1935.[11] The Ramblers' Association, along with other interested bodies, including the Council for

Figure 11.1 First view of the chapel across the Tillingham and Bradwell marshes. Johanna Dale.

the Preservation of Rural England (CPRE, founded in 1926), sought to pressure the government to increase countryside access rights, a campaign in which the mass trespass at Kinder Scout in 1932 has assumed huge symbolic importance, even though in reality it did little to progress access rights, which were only finally enshrined in law in 2000.[12] The struggle for access rights provides the context in which Matthews and his colleague Harry Bitten developed and published guides to *The Three Forests Way* (1977), *The Epping Forest Centenary Walk* (1978), *The Harcamlow Way* (1980) and *The Essex Way* (1984), among others. The Essex Way was conceived after a competition organised by the CPRE. This competition also precipitated the development of the St Peter's Way, which was put forward as an alternative route.[13]

When we consider the possibilities for the Way today, this campaigning background is pertinent. The St Peter's Way was designed to open up rural Essex as a place of low-impact recreation easily accessible from the ever-expanding metropolis. Currently an underutilised resource, this piece of existing and established green infrastructure, which links nationally important heritage sites, could deliver considerably more value to rural businesses along the route and protect rural heritage assets while contributing to changing the negative stereotype that sometimes hampers the county's tourism industry. Recent campaigns by Visit Essex purposefully challenge the modern stereotype of Essex by promoting the county's quiet and peaceful rural areas.[14] Maldon District Council has invested significantly in promotion of its 75-mile coastline (over which St Peter's stands sentinel) as a place of tranquillity within easy reach of the capital.[15] Work on a national coastal path has also drawn attention to the 350 miles of coast in Essex (which is the second longest coastline of any English county), the majority of which is rural in character and much of which is of international importance from an ecological perspective.[16] The landscape of Essex has been much denigrated, thanks to the dominance of an aesthetic that celebrates rugged coasts, open moorlands and mountains over the flatlands and estuaries of the low-lying East Anglian and Essex coasts.[17] This negative appraisal has been challenged in recent years, with authors such as Robert Macfarlane, James Canton, Jules Pretty and Ken Worpole writing of the landscape in appreciative terms.[18] The Way's combination of heritage, landscape and nature fits well within the context of the new emphasis on tourism promotion in Essex and, as will be argued below, within a wider upsurge in interest in medieval-inspired heritage and pilgrimage routes nationally, which has only been accelerated by the COVID-19 pandemic.

On walking the route in autumn 2020 it was found to be mostly well signed, with stiles and bridges along the route in reasonable condition. Several bridges near Chipping Ongar had plaques recording their repair by the Ramblers, and recently installed bridges were encountered on a section of the route between Purleigh and Mundon. Although the route traverses the A12, the main London–Norwich railway line and the A130, these can be safely crossed using a modern underpass, a Victorian foot tunnel and a pedestrian bridge respectively.[19] The longest section of the route on a road is through Steeple on the Dengie Peninsula, where the Way follows the main northern traffic route out towards Bradwell for 1 mile (Matthews noted the unfortunate fact that all footpaths in this area run north–south rather than east–west). Half of this distance is on pavement through the village of Steeple, passing the church and the Star Inn, one of several pubs along the route that could benefit from better promotion of the Way. The remaining half a mile is on the road itself, and as it leaves the village the speed limit increases to 40mph and then 60mph. This is the only section of the route where additional investment in physical infrastructure is urgently needed to ensure the Way can be walked safely at all times of year.

Anecdotal evidence suggests that sections of the Way are walked regularly by local groups of the Ramblers as part of circular routes, and the Way is also walked as a complete linear walk, mainly by Essex-based groups. Every February the Way is used for the St Peter's Way Ultra, a running event organised by Colchester-based Challenge Running, in which the route is covered in a single day of muddy and strenuous activity.[20] As the quotation with which this essay opened makes apparent, the idea of pilgrimage was inherent in the design of the Way, which is named after its destination. The Way has certainly been used for this purpose by local religious groups and leaders, for whom, as James Bettley's chapter in this volume demonstrates, the chapel is of paramount importance. Stephen Cottrell, the recently installed archbishop of York, walked the Way as his last act as bishop of Chelmsford before his promotion to the archiepiscopal see.[21] His successor, Guli Francis-Dehqani, visited the chapel as the culmination of a pilgrimage across her new diocese in the days before her installation as bishop. In June 2012, Cottrell welcomed a group of pilgrims from Canvey Island parish to the chapel at the Chelmsford bishop's residence of Bishopscourt in Margaretting, which is 1 mile off the Way, for morning Eucharist. This group made a pilgrimage along St Peter's Way over four days, stopping at churches along the route for 'worship, fellowship and refreshment'.[22]

The group have made their planning and devotional booklet available on their parish website to help others interested in making the same pilgrimage. Not all pilgrims walked the whole route, with many parishioners joining just for the final day at various points along the path between Steeple and Bradwell. Four years later this same parish embarked on another long-distance pilgrimage. The choice of route was inspired by Bradwell's seventh-century chapel and the Northumbrian connections of St Cedd. The group walked the St Cuthbert's Way, which runs 62½ miles from Melrose in Scotland to Lindisfarne, over six days. In 1973 a pilgrimage from Lindisfarne to Bradwell took place, arriving to coincide with the annual pilgrimage, with the pilgrims travelling the final stretch to Bradwell by boat across the Blackwater from Tollesbury.[23]

Medieval heritage routes, tourism and authenticity

The St Cuthbert's Way is also a modern invention. Unlike the St Peter's Way, which had its origins in grassroots leisure walking, the St Cuthbert's Way was conceived from the beginning as a tourist attraction to bring visitors to the Scottish Borders and Northumberland and was the brainchild of Ron Shaw and Roger Smith, who both worked in the tourism industry in the region. They mapped the route in 1995 and were involved in setting up the infrastructure before it was ceremonially opened in July 1996.[24] Cuthbert, a contemporary of Cedd, whom he must have known, was born *c.* 634 and died in 687. He became a monk at Melrose, where the Way begins, and throughout his life he travelled extensively in the north of England and in Scotland. Shortly after the Synod of Whitby (at which Cedd played a key role), Cuthbert became bishop of Lindisfarne, where he was buried and the route ends. Lindisfarne was not to be Cuthbert's final resting place, however, as Viking raids led to the abandonment of the island in 875. Cuthbert's body was exhumed by the monks and remained on the move until the community finally settled permanently at Durham in 995. Cuthbert's cult was widespread and highly influential in the Middle Ages with numerous miracles attributed to him, and the site of his hermitage on the Farne Islands was a major pilgrimage site.[25] In running from Melrose to Lindisfarne the St Cuthbert's Way purports to reflect the chronology of the saint's life. However, the Way's official website also points to a more pragmatic and practical reason: if you walk from west to east the wind is usually behind you.[26] In any case, the route reflects Cuthbert's trajectory only in the most superficial way and other Cuthbert-related sites on the route do not fit the chronology. For example, St Cuthbert's association with the cave in the Kyloe Hills that is named after him is posthumous. Here the monks of Lindisfarne were said to have sheltered with Cuthbert's body as they fled from the Viking raiders. Carole Cusack has pointed to the fact that the trail provides both real and manufactured encounters with the saint and that, while the official guide mentions a number of sites related to Cuthbert, it also includes sites with no relevance to the saint or medieval Northumbria more broadly, while passing over places with genuine Cuthbert associations.[27]

Cusack has explored what she terms the 'three interlocking discourses that inform the marketing of, and the experience of walking, St Cuthbert's Way'.[28] She identifies these as history, tourism and identity, and her analysis of these three discourses offers a very helpful comparative possibility for the St Peter's Way. She highlights that for many people the appeal of the medieval is the notion that contemporary life is inauthentic and unsatisfying compared with the 'authenticity' of the past, and that this is linked to a contemporary Western desire to be 'spiritual' outside of formal religion, leading to religious practices such as pilgrimage becoming dis-embedded from traditional faith institutions and imbricated with secular travel practices. While strategies of history and heritage thus inform the marketing of St Cuthbert's Way, the narrative surrounding the trail relies on 'genuine fakes'.[29] The starting point of the trail is not Old Melrose, where Cuthbert became a monk, but the ruins of a twelfth-century Cistercian abbey. Likewise, the prominent ecclesiastical ruins on Holy Island at the end of the route date from the high Middle Ages: Lindisfarne was re-colonised by the Durham monks from the late twelfth century, and little evidence of the early medieval monastery survives above ground.[30] Cusack discusses the incongruity of arriving at Holy Island, which she describes as both sharpening and dulling the sense of engagement with early medieval England. It is necessary to cross a major railway line in order to reach the causeway to the island, and most people walk across on the roadway alongside a steady stream of the cars, because the tidal window to walk across the old Pilgrim's Path is so short.

Clare Lees and Gillian Overing have discussed the 'visual paradox' of Lindisfarne, which remains both 'centre and margin'.[31] It 'retains its stunningly distinct geographical identity as a tidal island, and it sits ready to conjure for any visitor, medievalist or otherwise, powerful invocations of solitude, interiority and community'.[32] At the same time it is regularly packed with visitors, whom Lees and Overing see as recalling, but not resembling, the regular passage of royal and clerical guests in the early Middle Ages.[33] In their book on the medieval landscapes of Northumbria,

Lees and Overing argue for the importance of places in enabling us to think within and across centuries. Anyone who has been to the chapel at Bradwell will have experienced the 'pervasive awareness of the presence' of the place and the sense of a connection with the early medieval past (and that of the Roman past beyond it).[34] Bradwell is also something of a 'visual paradox', and many of the characteristics Lees and Overing assign to Lindisfarne also apply here. Although, as the essays by Stephen Rippon and Christopher Thornton and Kevin Bruce demonstrate, the landscape setting of the chapel has been significantly altered by the draining of the surrounding marshes, Bradwell retains a distinct geographical identity and sense of isolation, as do many other early medieval coastal monastic sites, as David Petts's chapter emphasises. The chapel and surrounding landscape conjure for any visitor powerful invocations of solitude, interiority and community. Indeed, as Peter Murphy and Nigel Brown have commented, 'the remoter parts of the Essex coast evoke a sense of timelessness, which belies the profound changes that have formed and transformed the landscape'.[35] Now seen as a peripheral and isolated part of Essex, Bradwell was one of the centres from which Cedd Christianised the early medieval kingdom. In an inversion of Lindisfarne, the chapel is not only a genuine early medieval survival, rather than a high-medieval successor building, but also the site is barely more populated than in the early medieval period, when Bede described *Ythancæstir* as a *civitas*, a term stressing Roman connections rather than designating a large settlement.[36] Unlike on Lindisfarne, there are no noisy pubs here, only the Othona Community, who, with their sustainable and ecological credentials, recall but do not resemble the early medieval monastic community.[37]

To the power of Lindisfarne and Bradwell to invoke connections across millennia can be added the feeling of authenticity occasioned by arriving on foot. St Peter's can only be approached this way, with cars having to be left at the car park at the end of East End Road. Walking is seen as an authentic mode of travel and a leisure pursuit that explicitly rejects modern technologies of rapid, noisy and polluting transportation and which facilitates greater connection to the natural world and self-transformation.[38] Active engagement with the landscape through walking (rather than simply looking on the landscape's scenic qualities) has been shown to be a key factor 'in the complex affective and cognitive process of place experience' in a rural context.[39] Cusack points out that Bede's *vita* paints a portrait of Cuthbert as a man in harmony with nature and that this was an important element for Smith and Shaw in their marketing of the trail.[40] Here discourses of the authenticity of the past and the natural world overlap in compelling ways. Bede tells us much less about Cedd than about Cuthbert, but we know that Cedd too travelled extensively, not least between his two East Saxon foundations at Bradwell and Tilbury and his Northumbrian homeland, on foot, on horseback and presumably by boat.[41] Barbara Yorke has discussed the site of Cedd's monastery at Lastingham and Bede's description of it as being more suitable for 'the haunts of robbers and the dens of wild beasts than for human habitation'.[42] Although scholars are now inclined to see Bede's description as exaggerating the isolation of the setting, it makes apparent the close association between early monastic sites and the natural world. This relationship is immediately apparent at St Peter's, which sits within some of the most highly protected and important habitats in the UK.[43] Thanks to the Essex-based naturalist J. A. Baker and, following in his footsteps, Robert Macfarlane, the coast of the Dengie Peninsula is now recognised and celebrated as a 'wild place'.[44] This wilderness, 'the indefinable essence or spirit that lives in a place, as shadowy as the archetype of a dream, but real, and recognisable', also acts to stimulate powerful feelings of connection across time.[45] Baker writes of the compelling silence on the coast, a very old silence that 'seems to have been sinking slowly down through the sky for numberless centuries, like the slow fall of the chalk through the clear Cretaceous sea'.[46]

The strategies used to promote the St Cuthbert Way are thus highly relevant to the St Peter's Way. The Essex trail is named after a place rather than a person, but likewise offers a combination of natural and historical authenticity, as will be discussed further below. Several modern-day heritage–pilgrimage paths are named after early medieval saints, demonstrating an established interest in these kinds of trails. St Cuthbert's Way is joined near its conclusion by a longer route named after the Northumbrian king Oswald, which opened in 2007 and runs from the site of his victorious battle at Heavenfield, near Hexham, via the Northumbrian royal centre at Bamburgh to Lindisfarne.[47] In 2020 a new complex of trails centred on Durham Cathedral and inspired by Cuthbert, Oswald and other northern saints was inaugurated, aiming to 'portray the region's Saints and their stories, set against a backdrop of the very best of the region's attractions, landscapes, places to eat and drink and visitor accommodation'.[48] The saints Chad (Cedd's brother) and Werburgh, a Mercian princess taught by Chad, are commemorated in the Two Saints Way, which runs from Chester, site of Werburgh's major shrine, to Chad's episcopal seat at Lichfield, and opened in 2012.[49] The proliferation of these trails is part of a wider phenomenon: a fast-growing interest in both historically attested and newly created pilgrimage and heritage routes, both in the UK and worldwide. Inspired by the huge interest in medieval pilgrim routes to the shrine of St James at Santiago de Compostela in north-western Spain, the British Pilgrimage Trust (BPT) was established in 2014 to promote pilgrimage in the UK. One thing the huge popularity of the Camino de Santiago made apparent is that pilgrimage is an attractive proposition not only for people who are active members of Christian churches but also for many who do not partake in formal religion. In the foreword to their recent BPT book *Britain's Pilgrim Places*, Nick Mayhew-Smith and Guy Hayward write of 'meaningful journeys ... [being] ... one of the few universal patterns of human behaviour, seeking out special places where communities share their memories, spill out their hopes and fears'.[50] The introduction to *Britain's Pilgrim Places* is written by Simon Jenkins, a patron of the charity and an atheist. He sees 'a journey with a purpose' as a chance to experience a change of circumstances and escape the pressures of daily living.[51] He equates the comradeship, asceticism and discomfort of the journey to the feelings experienced by ultra-long-distance runners, an observation made manifest in the use of the St Peter's Way by Church of England pilgrim groups, leisure walkers and long-distance runners.[52] For Jenkins pilgrimage is 'an act of homage to history', and the BPT's description of the Way, and of St Peter's Chapel itself, emphasises the historic nature of the route and the chapel.[53]

New developments in medieval pilgrimage and heritage routes

Two recently established routes provide examples of how the St Peter's Way could be repositioned within this new context at the intersection of pilgrimage, history and the natural world. The first is the St Thomas Way, which opened in 2018 and runs from Swansea to Hereford, inspired by an unusual story of medieval pilgrimage. This was developed as part of an Arts and Humanities Research Council-funded project and was a collaboration between academics, creative practitioners, clergy, heritage professionals and local communities. Its creative engagement with a medieval story and innovative form, in terms of both the route itself and its digital presentation, illustrate the potential to engage and attract diverse audiences. The second route is the Old Way, a 250-mile route from Southampton to Canterbury, inspired by a red line linking the two cities on the mid-fourteenth-century Gough Map.[54] Alongside the development of the Old Way, the BPT have launched 'Sanctuary', a project that aims to provide low-cost accommodation for pilgrims while providing income to churches and village halls. The sanctuary model points to the potential of the St Peter's Way to contribute to the sustainability of villages along the route while also securing the future of historic buildings.[55]

Before considering these aspects in relation to the St Peter's Way we return briefly to the idea of authenticity. I suggested above that the fact that the Way was not an authentic medieval pilgrimage route but one developed with the leisure walker in mind was a strength. The fact is that one would not want to walk the majority of ancient pilgrimage routes. The most famous medieval pilgrimage route in England, immortalised in Chaucer's *Canterbury Tales*, was from London to Canterbury to visit the shrine of Thomas Becket and involved travelling along Watling Street (now the A2), hardly a pleasant prospect today. Catherine Clarke discusses this problem with regards to the St Thomas Way. This route is based on a pilgrimage by one William Cragh, a Welsh outlaw who came back to life after being hanged in Swansea and who, in thanks, went on a pilgrimage to Hereford to the tomb of the recently deceased bishop, Thomas de Cantilupe, whose miraculous intervention was credited with bringing William back to life. The medieval road east from Swansea, the most likely route taken by the group, followed the route of the modern A48 (some sections now the M4), and is not an attractive proposition for a walker. Rather than a continuous route, the St Thomas Way is a series of circular walks at 13 different locations across the Welsh Marches. One location that the project team had hoped would be central to the route was Neath, which is home to the remains of a Norman castle and impressive abbey ruins. However, it quickly became apparent that it would 'not be possible to devise a safe, reliable, walking route around Neath' connecting the medieval sites and the river, the treacherous crossing of which was described by Gerald of Wales in the twelfth century, due to the 'transport links and post-industrial infrastructure' that cut across the town and surroundings.[56] The Old Way, likewise, does not take the line of the medieval roads between its 'waypoints', but opts for 'footpaths not roads'. Other considerations in planning the route have been to integrate 'heritage and holy places', as well as 'nature and beauty'. The concerns of the planners of the St Peter's Way in the 1970s to plot the most pleasant walking route thus anticipated contemporary priorities.

Alongside the development of the Old Way, which is a 250-mile route that takes two to three weeks to walk, the BPT have launched their 'Sanctuary' project to provide low-cost accommodation to pilgrims following the route. The sanctuary concept is a simple one, aiming to reinvigorate the ancient tradition of pilgrims taking sanctuary in the communities through which they travel. In return for a donation, a number of churches along the route will, on a pre-booked basis, provide a place to sleep with basic sanitary facilities.[57] This might be within the church itself, in an adjacent building or even a designated camping site within the church grounds. Alice Attlee, the project lead for the BPT, describes how the experience of taking sanctuary in a church is a powerful tool for contemplation and describes how, 'through sleeping within its walls … [she] came to know that church, not simply as a beautiful building of significance, but as a place where … [she] had been welcomed, and made to feel at home'.[58] The BPT's sanctuary project therefore both seeks to enhance the experience of pilgrims but also to generate income and support for rural churches. The problems faced by rural churches, such as dwindling and ageing congregations coupled with often substantial maintenance costs for the upkeep of historically significant buildings, are well known.[59] However, church buildings remain central to the identity of many rural villages.[60] They are also a key attractor of rural tourists, having a significance of place in the rural setting beyond almost anything else other than the landscape itself, so that sustainable development of these cultural and heritage assets is important to the rural economy.[61]

The BPT sanctuary project is not alone in promoting churches as places to sleep. The Churches Conservation Trust (CCT), the charity in which the majority of historically and architecturally important redundant churches are vested, runs an established 'champing' scheme, which began when a group of scouts asked for permission to camp overnight in one of the CCT's churches, and has been running since 2014. Two churches in Essex are available for 'champing': St Nicholas in Berden and St Mary the Virgin in Stansted Mountfitchet. Where possible, the CCT work with local hospitality businesses to provide breakfast and, in time, they intend to provide the option to pre-order additional locally sourced provisions.[62] The BPT website also features a page devoted to helping pilgrims find local food and drink, and it is clear that the consumption of local produce is also coming to be seen as something that is part of the 'authentic' pilgrim or heritage experience.[63] The St Peter's Way, then, could contribute to the sustainability of rural churches in Essex while also supporting local hospitality businesses and food and drink producers, such as New Hall vineyards at Purleigh, through which the Way passes.

The St Thomas Way is particularly innovative in its use of digital technologies. The choice to develop a web-based digital resource for the Way was partly driven by practical considerations, such as the difficulty of providing physical infrastructure across multiple local government jurisdictions and two countries, the problem of maintenance of physical infrastructure that would be vulnerable to vandalism and the issue of the proliferation of interpretation 'clutter' at heritage sites.[64] The web-based format, which is not without sustainability issues, also allows for more immersive and imaginative encounters with medieval pilgrimage practices.[65] The interface is structured around an interactive map, which is not displayed using modern cartographic conventions; instead the locations are depicted as a vertical series. As Clarke explains, this design, which was driven by the practical consideration of being viewable on a smartphone screen, is in dialogue with medieval aesthetic and representational conventions, reflecting the sense of journey as narrative and deliberately echoing the visual language of medieval pilgrimage itinerary maps.[66] The best-known itinerary map was produced by the prolific St Albans monk Matthew Paris in the thirteenth century and depicted the pilgrimage route from London to Jerusalem. Itinerary maps could be for practical use, but also served as prompts for meditative reading and imaginative travel. This meditative/imaginative aspect has significant accessibility implications, opening up the St Thomas Way to people who are unable to walk the physical Way itself, perhaps due to distance, disability or financial circumstances, in the same way that virtual pilgrimages made travel to the Holy Land possible for cloistered nuns in the Middle Ages.[67]

Using a map like Matthew Paris's could also be a dynamic and interactive experience: 'the approach to the holy city is experienced in the turn of the pages, the route can be traced with a fingertip, and flaps showing extra detail for significant places … can be opened up and explored.'[68] Echoing this, the St Thomas Way website offers a range of multimedia content responding to each location on the route. The content is grouped under nine main headings and enables a multilayered approach to the sites, developing a narrative about the route as a whole and the history of individual places on it, while specific features of each location are used to explore aspects of medieval culture. 'Listen and Watch' includes a range of multimedia content, from 3D animations and videos to recordings of ambient sound, medieval music and specially designed medieval soundscapes. The sound element is particularly innovative and responds to an increased interest in aurality in heritage contexts, where the visual has traditionally been prioritised.[69] The soundscapes are key in 'supporting affective and imaginative engagement with the past'.[70] Under the 'Natural World' heading, brief content is provided about some features of the natural environment, with an emphasis on uses in the Middle Ages. Visitors to St Peter's are often struck by the soundscape, by the absence of the sounds of modernity and the dominance of the sounds of the natural world, of the sea breaking on the shell ridges, the calls of birds and the whistling of the wind. These two headings could therefore be particularly fertile in the context of the St Peter's Way.

Repositioning the St Peter's Way

As stated at the beginning of this chapter, in extending the Way to start at Greensted, the BPT have provided a compelling heritage narrative for the route. The short description of the path on their website, despite its misleading suggestion of a medieval origin for the route, hints at how this narrative could be developed further in light of the contexts discussed above.

> **St Peter's Way – 40 miles, 4 days – Greensted to Bradwell, Essex –** This pilgrimage leads you from the heart of the Anglo-Saxon Kingdom of Essex, from the oldest wooden church in the world, St Andrew's, Greensted … all the way to one of Britain's most ancient and remote churches – St Peter's-on-the-Wall, which has attracted pilgrims over the flat expanse of saltmarsh at Bradwell for over a millennium. Follow in their footsteps as you venture through some of the most spectacular countryside in Essex through ancient woodland, over commons and hills, and down to the salt marshes on estuaries and coastline. You will walk across some of Britain's most fertile farmland, weaving your way along the wildlife-rich River Roding, via a C12th church at Blackmore, and from the fragments of the lost Writtle Forest toward the bird-rich waters of Hanningfield Reservoir. Pay your respects to the rescued C14th Mundon Church and the skeletal limbs of the Mundon Oaks will beckon you toward the sea, until you discover Saint Peter's lonely shrine at the edge of the island. Some 1,500 pilgrims make their way here every July, but you can visit this stark, sacred place at any time of year.[71]

The description emphasises the early medieval history of Essex and key early and high medieval heritage sites on the route are mentioned, but it also highlights both historic and contemporary landscapes and encounters with nature. The references to the 'lost Writtle Forest' and 'the skeletal limbs of the Mundon Oaks' provoke thoughts about changing landscapes and the possibility of using the route to explore this aspect of Essex's history, alongside its medieval religious and cultural heritage. The references to the 'wildlife-rich River Roding' and 'bird-rich waters of Hanningfield Reservoir' point to the fact that it is not only on the coast that the route provides opportunities for encounters with the natural world. At the moment, the promotion of the St Peter's Way by Essex County Council, which is predominantly through a freely downloadable PDF guide, lacks a coherent and interwoven narrative and barely mentions early medieval history.[72] The remainder of this chapter will suggest, in light of the examples discussed above, some ways in which the strands identified by the BPT might be brought together and how the route could be presented digitally, both to reach audiences who could not walk the Way and also to act as an impetus to encourage visitors to rural Essex. It does not aim to be comprehensive but seeks to indicate possibilities that could be fruitfully developed.

The modern county of Essex takes its name from the kingdom of the East Saxons, which came into being in the late sixth century before being absorbed into the more powerful kingdom of Wessex in the early ninth century. Relatively little is known about the East Saxon kingdom, compared with other early kingdoms such as Wessex and Northumbria, due to the scarcity of surviving written sources.[73] This means that the chapel at Bradwell and archaeological and landscape evidence are fundamentally important in interpreting Essex's early medieval past. As Stephen Rippon's chapter in this volume explains, the kingdom of the East Saxons was made up of a number of smaller folk territories, with St Peter's being situated in the *regio* of *Deningei*.[74] The Way crosses a number of these territories, and walking through them offers an opportunity to understand their extent and how they were organised, with most people being able to walk to a communal gathering in a day but few able to attend a gathering and return home on the same day.[75] The Way begins in a classic example of a valley-based early folk territory focused on the Roding Valley. Rippon suggests that the site later occupied by Ongar castle was the possible communal meeting place of this folk territory, and that the church at High Ongar was one of two minster churches.[76] Between Chipping Ongar and High Ongar the Way crosses the River Roding and then goes over high ground at Nine Ashes, which is the watershed between the Roding and Wid valleys, with the latter being part of a separate early folk territory focused on the Chelmer Valley.[77] Travelling towards St Peter's, and away from London, the site of Mellitus's episcopal see, also offers the opportunity to consider the stages of conversion to Christianity, from the baptism of King Sæbert in 604 under Kentish influence, through the apostasy of the East Saxons during the plague to the advent of Cedd's Northumbrian mission and his establishment of religious houses at Bradwell and Tilbury. The Prittlewell burial, discovered in 2003 and now the subject of a permanent display at Southend Central Museum, could be used to help tell this story and, in the same way that the Two Saints Way benefited from the increased interest in early medieval history in the region precipitated by the discovery of the Staffordshire Hoard in 2009, the St Peter's Way could draw on, and benefit from interest in, the Prittlewell princely burial, while also increasing visitor numbers to Southend Central Museum.[78]

High and late medieval history could also form part of this narrative and be linked to settlements along the route. Greensted, where King Edmund's body is reputed to have rested in 1013, provides a link to later Anglo-Saxon history, and Ongar, a possible meeting place of an early folk group that became the site of a Norman castle (the motte of which the Way runs alongside), could be used to explain the transitions precipitated by the Norman Conquest. The church at Blackmore, whose architectural importance reflects its pre-Dissolution function as the church of an Augustinian Priory, could be the hook for an exploration of medieval religious communities and the impact of the Reformation on the Essex countryside. A heritage site that lies just off the route, the ruins of the Augustinian priory at Bicknacre, should be integrated into the Way and become part of this narrative. Alongside this story, the River Roding, the fragment of Writtle forest, the Mundon Oaks and coastal grazing marshes and saltmarshes that the route travels through highlight the opportunity to present landscape change and the relationship of people to woodland, marsh and coast in the Middle Ages. Consideration of landscape could be linked to the natural world, with the nature-connectedness of early medieval saints such as Cuthbert being a significant factor in their popular appeal and an important aspect in modern people's encounters with St Peter-on-the-Wall.

Developing a digital interface for the Way would enable this narrative to be presented in a nuanced and multifaceted way. As discussed above, the St Thomas Way website provides an example of the potential of this presentation. The St Peter's Way connects four church buildings of particular heritage interest – St Andrew's at Greensted, St Laurence at Blackmore, St Mary at Mundon and St Peter's – and could be expanded to include the ruins at Bicknacre. The Grade 1 listed church at Mundon is a redundant church cared for by the charity Friends of Friendless Churches (Figure 11.2). They have received significant grant funding to restore this unusual and atmospheric church, and better promotion of the Way would increase the number of beneficiaries of this.[79] During recent

Figure 11.2 St Mary's Mundon before and after coming into the care of the Friends of Friendless Churches. Christopher Dalton/Friends of Friendless Churches.

conservation work a previously unknown medieval wall painting (depicting St Edmund's martyrdom) was uncovered in Mundon, and a 3D tour of the church has recently been created.[80] Three-dimensional tours of the five heritage sites could provide a central backbone for a digital resource while improving access to and knowledge about these important heritage assets, some of which currently have very restricted visiting hours.[81] Three-dimensional presentations of these buildings could also include some reconstructed content or antiquarian maps and drawings, demonstrating, for example, how St Peter's was originally built onto the Roman wall and how the settlement at Bradwell might have looked in the Roman and early medieval periods. Exploring the use of sound would also be particularly fruitful, in terms of both ambient sound at different locations – at St Peter's itself ambient sound recorded at different states of the tide and in different weather conditions – and specially designed soundscapes, evoking, for example, the religious life of the priors at Blackmore or the bustling early medieval settlement at Bradwell.

Conclusion

Thanks to promotion by the BPT, people outside Essex are increasingly aware of the St Peter's Way, and in January 2021 it was the English entry included in a *Guardian* list of '21 places to go in 2021', which covered locations across Europe.[82] This reflects the wider interest in pilgrimage discussed in this essay and the upsurge in walking in England brought about by the COVID-19 pandemic, which led many people to explore their local areas on foot.[83] The St Peter's Way was originally conceived over 50 years ago, developed by the West Essex Ramblers and the Epping Forest Holiday Fellowship before medieval-inspired heritage pilgrim routes were the established phenomenon they are today. This chapter has sought to demonstrate that within the context of interest in walking, pilgrimage and heritage, the St Peter's Way is an under-utilised resource. The physical infrastructure of the route is in place and is cared for by the ECC rights of way team, yet promotion of the Way is now predominantly through the BPT rather than local agencies. Given the significant investment Maldon District Council have made in rural tourism on the Dengie Peninsula and increased promotion of the Essex coast and walking in Essex due to the development of the national coastal path, neglect of the St Peter's Way, which stands at the intersection of national recreational trends and local tourism priorities, is particularly regrettable. In popular consciousness Essex is seldom associated with authenticity, yet the Way offers a unique possibility to attract visitors who might not consider visiting Essex and to introduce them to Essex's rich medieval heritage and beguiling landscape. Fred Matthews, fondly known as the [Alfred] Wainwright of Essex by his friends in the West Essex Ramblers,[84] wrote in the guide to the Way, that 'to arrive [at St Peter's], isolated but not lonely, with the colours which abound on the marsh and the call of the birds, is to appreciate why Essex, although it has not the grandeur of the Pennines, or the Lake District, is such a beautiful county and such a happy place for walking'.[85] Pilgrimage, in its religious and secular manifestations, is a journey in which the destination is key. The attraction of the St Peter's Way and its potential to attract visitors and contribute to sustainable rural tourism across the county rely on the continued tranquillity of the chapel and coastal landscape at Bradwell, on the destination remaining 'isolated but not lonely'.

Notes

1. Matthews and Bitten 1990, 2.
2. Essex County Council 2011, 2.
3. British Pilgrimage Trust, 'The St Peter's Way'. https://britishpilgrimage.org/portfolio/st-peters-way/ [accessed 25 April 2022].
4. Development of rural tourism is a stated aim of the Essex rural strategy. Essex Rural Partnership 2016, 22–3.
5. Chipping Ongar appears to have been chosen for purely practical reasons. At that time the end station on the Central Line, it was a habitual starting place for West Essex walks, although in 1976 complaints about the poor rail service to Ongar led to suggestions that car rambles should start instead at Epping station. Barker 2011, 8. In 1994 London Underground closed the Epping to Ongar section of the Central Line.
6. Barker 2011, 1.
7. Barker 2011, 3.
8. Barker 2011, 5.
9. Whiteley 2018.
10. Prynn 1976, 65; Snape 2004.
11. Prynn 1976, 70.
12. Hey 2011, 199.
13. Matthews and Bitten 1990, 2.
14. The promotion of 'Real Essex' has met with some criticism. See, for example, Hinsliff 2022; Burrows 2022.
15. The Dengie Gateway Project, which aimed to mitigate the economic impact of the closure of the original Bradwell power station by developing tourism on the Dengie Peninsula, was funded through grants from the Coastal Communities Fund (£292,000), the Magnox Socio-Economic fund (£20,000) and match funding from the District Council (£17,000). St Peter's chapel is one of five 'hub' destinations in the District.
16. The Dengie Peninsula is bordered by water on three sides, and much of its coast and intertidal mudflats is designated ecologically important, including Sites of Special Scientific Interest, Special Protection Areas, Special Areas of Conservation and Ramsar wetlands of international importance. The Blackwater, Crouch, Roach and Colne estuaries are also recognised as a Marine Conservation Zone.
17. Nixon 2017, 214.
18. Macfarlane 2007; Worpole and Orton 2005; Pretty 2011; Canton 2013.

19 Fred Matthews also campaigned for the provision of safe road crossing on rights of ways cut by major roads. Whiteley 2018.
20 https://www.challenge-running.co.uk/races/st-peters-way-ultra/ [accessed 25 April 2022].
21 Cottrell, Stephen (@CottrellStephen). 'My first day as Bishop of @chelmsdio began very early on a cold November morning praying the chapel at Bradwell. Not quite my last day today, but lovely to return on foot and pray here one last time'. 2 July 2020, 3:02 pm https://twitter.com/cottrellstephen/status/1278690602025189376 [accessed 25 April 2022]. Cottrell is an enthusiastic pilgrim and published a collection of poems and stories about his pilgrimage to Santiago de Compostela in 2018.
22 http://www.canveycofe.co.uk/pilgrimage.html [accessed 25 April 2022].
23 Kevin Bruce (personal communication).
24 https://www.stcuthbertsway.info/faqs/ [accessed 25 April 2022].
25 A good introduction to Cuthbert's cult is Bonner, Rollason and Stancliffe 1989.
26 https://www.stcuthbertsway.info/long-distance-route/ [accessed 25 April 2022].
27 Cusack 2013, 12.
28 Cusack 2013.
29 Cusack 2013, 4.
30 Tudor 1998, 72; Petts, in this volume.
31 Lees and Overing 2006, 17.
32 Lees and Overing 2006, 10.
33 Lees and Overing 2006, 17.
34 Lees and Overing 2006, 12.
35 Murphy and Brown 1999, 11.
36 Colgrave and Mynors 1969, 282–3 (III, 22).
37 Worpole, in this volume and 2018.
38 Slavin 2003; Edensor 2000.
39 Jepson and Sharpley 2015, 1167.
40 Cusack 2013, 17.
41 As Chris Ferguson's work has shown, using sail power to travel between Bradwell and the Northumbrian coast could have made Bradwell quicker to access from Bamburgh than some sites in the landlocked interior of the Northumbrian kingdom. Ferguson 2011, 295.
42 Yorke, in this volume.
43 See above, note 16.
44 Baker 1967; Macfarlane 2007.
45 Baker 1971.
46 Baker 1971.
47 https://www.stoswaldsway.com [accessed 25 April 2022].
48 http://northernsaints.com [accessed 25 April 2022].
49 https://www.twosaintsway.co.uk [accessed 25 April 2022].
50 Mayhew-Smith and Hayward 2020, 6.
51 Mayhew-Smith and Hayward 2020, 7.
52 Mayhew-Smith and Hayward 2020, 9.
53 Mayhew-Smith and Hayward 2020, 9.
54 https://britishpilgrimage.org/old-way/ [accessed 25 April 2022].
55 As Ian Rotherham argues, rural church tourism is not sustainable if money is only spent in local cafés, pubs or gift shops, with little reinvestment in the presentation or conservation of the church building itself. Rotherham 2007, 69.
56 Clarke 2020b, 66.
57 https://britishpilgrimage.org/sanctuary-project-for-seekers/ [accessed 25 April 2022].
58 https://britishpilgrimage.org/sanctuary-project-for-seekers/ [accessed 25 April 2022].
59 Cooper 2004; Rotherham 2007.
60 Essex Rural Partnership 2016, 24.
61 Essex Rural Partnership 2016, 25. Rotherham 2007, 71.
62 https://champing.co.uk/what-is-champing/faqs/ [accessed 25 April 2022].
63 https://britishpilgrimage.org/discover-local-food/ [accessed 25 April 2022].
64 Clarke 2020a, 12.
65 https://thomasway.ac.uk [accessed 25 April 2022].
66 Clarke 2020a, 13.
67 Rudy 2011.

68 Clarke 2020a, 15.
69 Lopez 2020.
70 Clarke 2020a, 17.
71 https://britishpilgrimage.org/portfolio/st-peters-way/ [accessed 25 April 2022].
72 Essex County Council 2011 downloadable at https://www.essexhighways.org/uploads/files/st_peters_way.pdf [accessed 25 April 2022].
73 For an overview of the written sources see Yorke 1985.
74 Rippon, in this volume.
75 Rippon, in this volume.
76 Rippon 2022.
77 Rippon 2022.
78 Alongside the permanent display at Southend Central Museum there is a website app enabling the presentation of items too fragile and unstable to go on display: https://prittlewellprincelyburial.org [accessed 25 April 2022].
79 In 2009–10 Friends of Friendless Churches received a grant of £138,624 from English Heritage for work on St Mary's Mundon, and they have recently been awarded £50,301.30 from the Culture Recovery Fund. Rachel Morley (personal communication).
80 https://my.matterport.com/show/?m=GwArafFxPh4&fbclid=IwAR3Ci8tq-5E_xuclGM3XastlL9d1ktVYgEtWc9bvKfz_XPw9ILZ3-5vc3Qk [accessed 25 April 2022].
81 For example, the church at Greensted is only open to visitors a couple of days a week.
82 https://www.theguardian.com/travel/2021/jan/02/21-places-for-2021-holidays-were-dreaming-of [accessed 11 February 2021].
83 https://www.theguardian.com/travel/2020/dec/18/how-2020-became-the-year-of-the-walker [accessed 11 February 2021]
84 Barker 2011, 41.
85 Matthews and Bitten 1990, 2.

Bibliography

Baker, J. A. 1967. *The Peregrine*. London: Collins.
Baker, J. A. 1971. 'On the Essex coast'. *RSPB Birds Magazine* 3: 281–3.
Barker, E. C, 2011. *Rambling On and On and On ... The history, life and times of the West Essex group of the Ramblers' Association, 1970–2010* (ERO T/Z 638/1).
Bonner, G., D. Rollason and C. Stancliffe (eds). 1989. *St Cuthbert, His Cult and His Community to AD 1200*. Woodbridge: Boydell Press.
Burrows, T. 2022. 'Out with Towie as Essex tries to shed its brash image'. *The Observer*, 30 January. https://www.theguardian.com/uk-news/2022/jan/30/out-with-towie-as-essex-tries-to-shed-its-brash-image [accessed 25 April 2022].
Canton, J. 2013. *Out of Essex: Re-imagining a literary landscape*. Oxford: Signal Books.
Clarke, C. A. M. 2020a. 'Introduction: remaking medieval pilgrimage: the St Thomas Way'. In *The St Thomas Way and the Medieval March of Wales: Exploring place, heritage, pilgrimage*, edited by C. A. M. Clarke. 1–21. Leeds: Arc Humanities Press.
Clarke, C. A. M. 2020b. 'Place, time, and the St Thomas Way: an experiment in five itineraries'. In *The St Thomas Way and the Medieval March of Wales: Exploring place, heritage, pilgrimage*, edited by C. A. M. Clarke. 57–82. Leeds: Arc Humanities Press.
Colgrave, B., and R. A. B. Mynors (ed. and trans.). 1969. *Bede's Ecclesiastical History of the English People*. Oxford: Clarendon Press.
Cooper, T. 2004. *How Do We Keep Our Parish Churches?* London: The Ecclesiological Society.
Cottrell, S. 2018. *Striking Out: Poems and stories from the Camino*. Norwich: Canterbury Press.
Cusack, C. M. 2013. 'History, authenticity, and tourism: encountering the medieval while walking Saint Cuthbert's Way'. In *Journeys and Destinations: Studies in travel, identity, and meaning*, edited by A. Norman. 1–21. Newcastle upon Tyne: Cambridge Scholars Publishing.
Edensor, T. 2000. 'Walking in the British countryside: reflexivity, embodied practices and ways to escape'. *Body & Society* 6: 81–106.
Essex County Council. 2011. *The St Peter's Way: Surround yourself with wildlife and history*. Chelmsford: Essex County Council.

Essex Rural Partnership. 2016. *Respecting our Past, Embracing our Future: A strategy for rural Essex*. Chelmsford: Essex County Council.

Ferguson, C. 2011. 'Re-evaluating early medieval Northumbrian contacts and the "coastal highway"'. In *Early Medieval Northumbria: Kingdoms and communities, 450–1100*, edited by D. Petts and S. Turner. 283–302. Turnhout: Brepols.

Hey, D. 2011. 'Kinder Scout and the legend of the mass trespass', *Agricultural History Review* 59: 199–216.

Hinsliff, G. 2022. 'Give me the cheeky, rackety Essex I love over a snobby rebrand any day'. *The Guardian*. 28 January. https://www.theguardian.com/commentisfree/2022/jan/28/essex-rebrand-vajazzle-money [accessed 25 April 2022].

Jepson, D., and R. Sharpley. 2015. 'More than sense of place? Exploring the emotional dimension of rural tourism experiences', *Journal of Sustainable Tourism* 23: 1157–78.

Lees, C. A., and G. R. Overing 2006. 'Anglo-Saxon Horizons: places of the mind in the Northumbrian landscape'. In *A Place to Believe In: Locating medieval landscapes*, edited by C. A. Lees and G. R. Overing. 1–26. University Park, PA: The Pennsylvania State University Press.

Lopez, M. 2020. 'Heritage soundscapes: contexts and ethics of curatorial expression'. In *The St. Thomas Way and the Medieval March of Wales: Exploring place, heritage, pilgrimage*, edited by C. A. M. Clarke. 103–20. Leeds: Arc Humanities Press.

Macfarlane, R. 2007. *The Wild Places*. London: Granta.

Matthews, F., and H. Bitten. 1990. *The St Peter's Way*, 3rd edition. Essex: Matthews/Bitten Publications.

Mayhew-Smith, N., and G. Hayward. 2020. *Britain's Pilgrim Places*. London: Lifestyle Press Ltd.

Murphy, P., and N. Brown. 1999. 'Archaeology of the coastal landscape'. In *The Essex Landscape: In search of its history*, edited by L. S. Green. 11–19. Chelmsford: Essex County Council.

Nixon, S. J. 2017. 'Vanishing peregrines: J. A. Baker, environmental crisis and bird-centred cultures of nature, 1954–73'. *Rural History* 28: 205–26.

Pretty, J. 2011. *This Luminous Coast*. Norwich: Full Circle Editions.

Prynn, D. 1976. 'The clarion clubs, rambling and the holiday associations in Britain since the 1890s'. *Journal of Contemporary History* 11: 65–77.

Rippon, S. 2022. *Territoriality and the Early Medieval Landscape: The countryside of the East Saxon kingdom*. Woodbridge: Boydell & Brewer.

Rotherham, I. D. 2007. 'Sustaining tourism infrastructures for religious tourists and pilgrims within the UK'. In *Religious Tourism and Pilgrimage Festivals Management*, edited by R. Raj and N. D. Morpeth. 64–77. Wallingford: CAB International.

Rudy, K. M. 2011. *Virtual Pilgrimages in the Convent: Imagining Jerusalem in the late Middle Ages*. Turnhout: Brepols.

Slavin, S. 2003. 'Walking as spiritual practice: the pilgrimage to Santiago de Compostela'. *Body & Society* 9: 1–18.

Snape, R. 2004. 'The Co-operative Holidays Association and the cultural formation of countryside leisure practice'. *Leisure Studies* 23: 143–58.

Tudor, V. 1998. 'Durham Priory and its hermits in the twelfth century'. In *Anglo-Norman Durham, 1093–1193*, edited by D. Rollason, M. Harvey and M. Prestwich. 67–78. Woodbridge: Boydell and Brewer.

Whiteley, M. 2018. 'Farewell to an Essex stalwart and campaigner'. *South East Walker* 101: 1–2.

Worpole, K. 2018. 'The road to Othona: communitarian settlements in Essex 1880–2018'. In *Radical ESSEX*, edited by H. Dixon and J. Hill. 43–67. Southend-on-Sea: Focal Point Gallery.

Worpole, K., and J. Orton. 2005. *350 Miles: An Essex Journey*. Chelmsford: Essex County Council.

Yorke, B. 1985. 'The East Saxon kingdom', *Anglo-Saxon England* 14: 1–36.

12
Maldon and the Blackwater Estuary: Literature, culture and practice where river meets sea

Beth Whalley

When Cedd first founded the chapel of St Peter-on-the-Wall in the year 654, the edge was where the centre was.[1] The Cotton *mappa mundi*, Cotton MS Tiberius B V (fol. 5v), one of the earliest surviving world maps, shows us that the island of Britain, in the eleventh century, was believed to exist on the furthest edges of the known world. This cartographical marginality did not translate to a position of disempowerment, however. Instead, it became the means by which the myth of English exceptionality was curated and maintained; as Kathy Lavezzo puts it, 'geographical otherness premised both the exaltation and the marginalization of England during the Middle Ages'.[2] Being on the edge of one world meant being on the cusp of the next, and a sense of this God-given otherworldliness would have been experienced keenly at foundations such as St Peter's, located on the north-east tip of the Dengie Peninsula, where the mouth of the River Blackwater meets open ocean. Indeed, many important minsters founded before the eighth century, including St Peter's, succeeded in transforming their 'marginal' estuarine locations into positions of religious, but also social, cultural and economic authority. As David Petts demonstrates in his chapter in this volume, East Saxon foundations such as St Peter's, Tilbury, Barking and Wakering were powerful nodes in a trans-geographic maritime nexus of trade and communication.[3] Minster-in-Thanet, on the Kentish side of the Thames Estuary, even held a small fleet of ships, which made possible its commercial contacts upstream with Mercia and across the Channel to Francia.[4] This network was not limited to ecclesiastical estates either;

Mucking, near Tilbury, is home to the largest early English settlement excavated in England,[5] while in 2003 a late sixth-century elite burial was discovered in the Prittlewell district of Southend-on-Sea, containing a flagon from the eastern Mediterranean, Merovingian coins and garnets from the Indian subcontinent or Sri Lanka.[6] The Sutton Hoo and Snape burials, too, are in close proximity to the estuaries of the Deben and Alde.[7] In short, the character and shape of the early English Christian nation was, to a very large extent, created and preserved not in its physical centre but in its complex, connective estuarine edges.

In modern times, a different distribution of power unfolds, where the metropolis is the centre of authority and the estuary its unruly 'anti-image'.[8] In popular literary culture, estuaries are practically synonymous with the strange and the monstrous: from H. G. Wells's *War of the Worlds* (1898), in which Martians pursue fleeing crowds through Foulness Island and the Dengie Peninsula, to Sarah Perry's *The Essex Serpent* (2016), which tells the story of a Blackwater village tormented by the threat of a mythological sea monster come to life. Importantly for this present chapter, fantasy versions of the Middle Ages often play a role in these modern formulations of estuarine marginality. In the closing pages of his biography of the River Thames, *Thames: Sacred River* (2007), Peter Ackroyd elides the powerful status of the estuary of the past, writing that the 'primeval' Thames Estuary is 'not a human place' and that 'in the poems of the Anglo-Saxons it is a landscape of nightmare'.[9] He continues that estuary towns whose Old English place names still survive, such as Fobbing, Corringham, Mucking and Thurrock, 'seem like some form of atavistic remembrance, some token of an ancient and now forgotten past'.[10] Ackroyd artificially cleaves the river from its estuary; the rhetorical effect is of a nightmarish 'medieval' past that never really finished in the estuary region, in contradiction to the globalising, future-oriented forces which supposedly take place on the River Thames proper. What is more, the fixing of the estuary in an imaginary, temporal and geographical elsewhere has real social, political and economic effects; not just on the Thames, but around the world, river estuaries are filled with the toxic refuse of their neighbouring urban centres.[11] Waste flows from centre to edge, while power and capital flow upstream.

This present chapter turns to the public arts and heritage industries to take a closer look at the 'power geometries' of estuarine place, to borrow the term used by geographer Doreen Massey: that is, the ways in which shifting concepts of space and time are related to power and identity in Maldon and the Blackwater.[12] In their contributions to this volume, Richard Hoggett and David Petts provide insights into the monastic networks of the estuary of the past. Building on their work, I explore the complex relationships between past and present, between exaltation and marginalisation, along the Blackwater. Central to my argument is the fact that it is not St Peter's that comes front and centre in the stories that the Blackwater tells of itself: tellingly, the Maldon District Council Corporate Plan 2019–23 neglects to mention the chapel, instead naming the tenth-century Battle of Maldon battlefield as the 'heritage benchmark' for the region.[13] Anglo-Danish conflict in the Viking age evidently holds a place in the contemporary cultural imaginary that early ecclesiastical history does not. Maldon and the Blackwater, therefore, serve as case studies for understanding how and why particular narratives about the histories of local places are prioritised, and to what ideological ends.

I am by no means the first to consider how and why certain aspects of the medieval past are centred in Western modernity. Indeed, researchers are increasingly understanding the Middle Ages not as an object truth to be excavated but as a shapeshifting projection of the collective desires of any given moment. This has tangible consequences in the present day, as Mary Rambaran-Olm, M. Breann Leake and Micah James Goodrich have pointed out: 'how we engage the past', they write, 'has a palpable (and often dramatic) effect on the lived experiences of our colleagues as well as on the wider communities we inhabit.'[14] My intervention, while modest, takes steps towards showing how these stakes are visible in the present-day Blackwater. By placing the Old English poem *The Battle of Maldon* in dialogue with contemporary public artworks by John Doubleday, Humphrey Spender and Caroline Bergvall, I disclose how collective memories of Blackwater history dramatically affect the experiences of estuary communities today, for better and for worse.

Borders and crossings in *The Battle of Maldon*

In recent decades, there has been a proliferation of scholarship focusing on the 'interplay of water and land' in early English literary culture.[15] Kelley Wickham-Crowley and Catherine A. M. Clarke have both explored how early English writers use fluid landscapes to negotiate the complexities of individual and collective identities; Bede's writings on St Cuthbert recognise the tidal landscapes of Lindisfarne as a mirror to the saint's internal landscape, for instance, while St Guthlac's confrontation with demons in the fens resonates with political power struggles between Britons and Mercians.[16] By functioning as geographical boundaries, bodies of coastal water are important to long-held notions of ownership and territory, yet through their ebbs and flows they simultaneously reveal the precarity of boundary spaces and the impossibility of territorial fixity.[17] As Rebecca Pinner points out in an essay on the East Anglian fens, water functioned as a 'means of defence' and a vehicle for trade and communication, but it was also 'East Anglia's greatest vulnerability' in that it facilitated invasion from outside.[18]

Anxieties about territories and their watery edges are palpable in the anonymous, fragmentary Old English poem *The Battle of Maldon*, which recounts a violent encounter between East Saxons and a band of seafaring invaders. The events documented in the poem are based on a real battle which took place in the year 991, just one of the many Scandinavian incursions along Britain's estuaries in the years preceding Cnut's accession to the throne of England in 1016. In the poem, Vikings ('wicing', 26) arrive on the shores of Essex – near Maldon, just 10 miles west of St Peter's – where they are met by the ealdorman Byrhtnoth and his army.[19] The Vikings demand a payment of tribute ('gafol', 32) in exchange for peace, but Byrhtnoth refuses. In a much-debated act of overconfidence ('ofermod', 89), Byrhtnoth allows his opponents safe passage along an estuarine causeway so that the armies may do battle on an equal footing. The battle is a disaster for the East Saxon troops; Byrhtnoth is killed, some of the warriors flee and the rest of the men die alongside their leader. Byrhtnoth's death was probably of some cultural and political significance, being mentioned not only in the Old English poem, but also in versions A, C, D and E of the *Anglo-Saxon Chronicle*, in Byrhtferth of Ramsey's tenth-century Latin *Vita Oswaldi* and in several twelfth-century Latin sources, including the *Liber Eliensis*. The poem is something of a chance survival; the version we have today was written down in the early eleventh century and had been incorporated into London, British Library, Cotton Otho A XII by the seventeenth century, but those leaves were lost in the Ashburnham fire of 1731. A transcript made by David Casley, deputy keeper of the Cotton Library, and printed by Thomas Hearne in 1726, gives us the version we read today.[20]

The Blackwater – which at the time of the poem's writing was called the Pante – is mentioned twice by name in *The Battle of Maldon*'s 325 lines, a rare instance of topographical precision within the corpus of Old English poetry.[21] The *Maldon* poet describes the turning of the Blackwater's tides at length:

> Then, bearing his shield, [Byrhtnoth] commanded his warriors to advance,
> Those who on the landing-place all stood.

For the water the troop could not go to the other side:
Then came flowing the flood after the ebb-tide.
The water-streams locked together. Too long it seemed to them
Until they together could bear spears.
There they stood in array by the Pante's stream,
The East-Saxon vanguard and the ship-army.
Neither could do harm to the other,
Except one who through the arrow's flight took their fall.
The flood went out, the sailors stood ready,
Many Vikings, eager for battle.

Het þa bord beran,   beornas gangan,
þæt hi on þam easteðe   ealle stodon.
Ne mihte þær for wætere   werod to þam oðrum;
þær com flowende   flod æfter ebban;
lucon lagustreamas.   To lang hit him þuhte
hwænne hi togædere   garas beron.
Hi þær Pantan stream   mid prasse bestodon,
Eastseaxena ord   and se æschere;
ne mihte hyra ænig   oþrum derian
buton hwa þurh flanes flyht   fyl gename.
Se flod ut gewat.   þa flotan stodon gearowe,
wicinga fela,   wiges georne. (62–73)

These lines represent an extraordinary intervention into the narrative of the battle. The 'interplay of water and land' is unquestionably a popular thematic device among early English poets, but it is more unusual in a poem of this genre. The shifting tidal conditions give shape to the battle narrative and defy generic expectations; the 'flod' (65) flows and locks, forcing a 'to lang' (66) pause in the battle's momentum and the narrative flow, which defers the gratification of eager warriors and eager readers. For a full 10 lines, warriors and readers alike are compelled to stand witness to the water. Yet even as the estuary holds bodies apart, everything is in place for its inevitable crossing. Early in the poem, the reader is told that the Viking messenger was 'stod on stæðe' (25) while the Essex vanguard waits on the 'easteðe' (63). Old English *stæþ* translates as 'bank, shore, the land bordered on water', and its cognate in Old Norse is *stǫð*, meaning 'landing-place' or 'harbour' and giving us modern English 'staithe'.[22] Most modern English versions of *Maldon* opt for 'bank' or 'shore' as a translation, foregrounding the idea of the estuary as an edge. Yet understanding the bank as 'staithe' or 'harbour' provokes an imaginative shift, whereby the 'Pantan stream' (68) becomes decidedly navigable space. Notably, this watery mediation of the collision of armies does not appear in any of the other early records of the Battle of Maldon. In the A version of the *Anglo-Saxon Chronicle* we are told only that Byrhtnoth was killed at Maldon by the Danes.[23] The *Vita Oswaldi*, possibly the earliest long account of the battle, emphasises Byrhtnoth's stature and bravery, but makes no mention of the Essex landscape at all;[24] it is only in the twelfth-century *Liber Eliensis* that the 'bridge of water' ('pontem aque') returns to the story.[25]

This powerful, aqueous 'third thing' in the poem – as Julian Yates and Julie Orlemanski put it – has yielded a range of conflicting interpretations.[26] Some early scholars, such as E. D. Laborde, convinced by the poem's verisimilitude, take it as the definitive account of the conflict, and use its precise descriptions of the 'Pantan stream' to locate the battlefield.[27] Laborde places the Viking landing place on Northey Island, identifies the tidal waters as those which flow around the island and into Southey Creek, and suggests that the battle would have taken place on the Essex mainland, east of Maldon and south-west of Northey Island. Drawing conclusions about historical events from literary texts is problematic, however, and several scholars have challenged Laborde's method of inquiry; Daniel Thomas takes the view that Laborde's hypothesis has impeded critical appreciation of the poem as much as it has facilitated it.[28] Thus more recent readers of *Maldon*, including Thomas as well as John D. Niles, Stephen J. Harris and others, have argued that the poem's aqueous interventions are merely mythopoesis or typology: that is, a magnification or wholesale invention of the estuarine setting for the purposes of rhetoric. For Niles, the inclusion of the causeway encounter vividly actualises one of the biggest issues of this period of English history, namely, whether to violently resist or peacefully accommodate incoming Scandinavians through payments of tribute. As Niles puts it, the poet transforms an individual localised incident into a dramatised 'showpiece of contemporary ethics and politics' on a national scale.[29] The Blackwater Estuary becomes the venue for an event of more than local interest, where Byrhtnoth's troops become a microcosm of the English people and the estuarine landscape becomes both a gateway to the nation and a microcosm of England itself.

Harris, meanwhile, argues that the receding tides of the Blackwater, 'flow[ing] from the poet's imagination', typologically correspond to the scriptural parting of the Red Sea.[30] Harris's argument is that the poet deploys Old Testament logic to make sense of the place of the Scandinavian nations in English historical identity at a time when Anglo-Scandinavian power relations were far from settled; after all, Maldon in 991 would have been a mixed community, partly comprised of Scandinavian raiders and their descendants who were now fighting on the side of the East Saxons.[31] Readers familiar with the Old Testament, Harris argues, are invited to compare the 991 Viking arrival in Essex with the Egyptian pursuit of the Israelites through the desert. Here, though, the pursuers are not swallowed by the tide, as the Egyptians are, because their presence in England is understood to be preordained by God; for the poet, 'the Vikings are of the same *ethnie* as the English; they are, like the Anglo-Danes, of Scandinavian ancestry – they, too, are typological Hebrews'.[32] The *Maldon* poet, in other words, invents the shifting estuarine setting as a testing-ground for exploring questions about ethnicity and belonging in a changing world without fixed borders, questions that resonate today as much as they would have done in 991.

Niles and Harris, therefore, compellingly remind us that estuary spaces can be put to powerful symbolic work. I would be inclined to add, though, that we should resist understanding the estuary *only* as symbol. As James L. Smith and Hetta Howes have convincingly argued, water's ability to soak up and reflect its environment, its capacity to act as a mirror for cultural concerns, can be a trap for scholars 'if it means that we perceive the element only as literary fodder, a catalogue of potential representations, and neglect to consider it on its own terms'.[33] However, Smith and Howes add that symbols, like water itself, are 'more of a medium of meaning than a message'.[34] That is, water's material dimensions shape its discursive dimensions, and vice versa; the literal and literary objects exist in dynamic relationship with one another. Building on the readings of Harris, Niles and Laborde, therefore, I would argue that the *Maldon* poet engages so vividly with the real Essex coast precisely because estuaries are not benign backdrops to human experience but powerfully shape the way we interact with the world. Regardless of whether the battle happened at Northey Island or some other estuarine causeway near Maldon, when the poem sees the Viking invaders arrive from across the water unhindered, it attests to the aqueous crossings and connections that were an integral reality of the late tenth-century North Sea region. In so doing, of course, it presents a challenge to Peter Ackroyd's imaginary of a marginal, nightmarish, closed-off estuary region. However, recalling Doreen Massey's notion of power geometries, it also troublingly implies that new arrivals to Essex might only gain access to the 'promised land' of a newly unified Christian nation if they are the correct *ethnie*, according to scriptural precedent and cultural myth: something to which I shall return shortly.

Remembering Byrhtnoth on the Blackwater

Estuarine waters, however we interpret them, clearly hold considerable power in our collective imaginary. While Daniel Thomas is right to caution scholars against taking the topographies of a literary text too literally, his warning has not really changed how texts and landscapes are understood in the popular imagination. Today the events as they unfold in the poem are almost always taken as the events of the battle itself,[35] and the Blackwater Estuary, despite being absent from numerous other accounts of the battle, remains at the core of the narrative as it is recollected and reassembled in Maldon's contemporary heritage. This is the 'excitement of exactitude', in the words of Gillian R. Overing and Marijane Osborn; although the impulse to align a literary text with a particular place is ultimately futile, the sense of being in 'the very place' becomes a powerful – if treacherous – medium for entering into dialogue with the past.[36] Take, for example, the commonly accepted site of the battlefield, the 'heritage benchmark' for Maldon District Council's corporate strategy, which is also notable for being the first battlefield to be entered into Historic England's *Register of Historic Battlefields* in 1995.[37] Historic England, while acknowledging in its battlefield report that early English battlefields are notoriously difficult to locate, draws the boundary of the Maldon battlefield according to Laborde's scholarship on *The Battle of Maldon*.[38] Meanwhile, the National Trust, which owns Northey Island, concedes on its website that 'there has been some debate among historians about the precise location of the battle', but still labels Northey 'the oldest recorded battlefield in Britain'.[39] Neither heritage organisation allows nuance to get in the way of a good story, and the estuarine location becomes an important tool in evoking the mood of the conflict for visitors: 'standing on the causeway', the National Trust website declares, 'it's easy to imagine hearing the clash of swords and whistle of arrows in flight.'[40]

I am sceptical that the Northey Island site is the real location of the battle, but my interest here is not in contesting it. Rather, my argument is that the prioritisation of the battle narrative and its Southey Creek setting in contemporary heritage contexts – over and above the tangible existing fabric of the chapel at Bradwell – deserves closer consideration, regardless of whether it is ultimately historical fact or creative fiction. The remainder of this chapter thus turns to a series of modern and contemporary public monuments, events and artworks which serve to uphold the relationship between Byrhtnoth, the battle and the estuary, often at the exclusion of more nuanced accounts of Maldon's history. It has not always been this way. In a 1993 article Roberta Frank suggests that, although there were

15 editions of *Maldon* and at least as many translations published between 1826 and 1906, there remained a 'public apathy' towards the poem, even in Maldon itself.[41] Popular verses of the nineteenth and early twentieth centuries, including poems by Charles Clark and Rudyard Kipling, do refer to the events of 991, but without disclosing any familiarity with the contents of *The Battle of Maldon*, and without mentioning its topographical context.[42] The first public memorial to Byrhtnoth was a gothic-style sculpture of the ealdorman by Nathaniel Hitch, which was added to a niche on the exterior of All Saints with St Peter Church, Maldon, in 1907, elevated alongside statues of two major figures of the seventh-century conversion period, Mellitus and Cedd, as well as Robert de Mantell, founder of Beeleigh Abbey in 1180, Robert Darcy, MP for Maldon in the fifteenth century, and seventeenth-century cleric and philanthropist Thomas Plume. Frank speculates that in the decade leading up to the First World War, *Maldon*'s themes of heroic idealism and self-sacrifice may have resonated with a wider public.[43] By the 1930s, poets W. H. Auden, John Cornford and David Jones were alluding to *Maldon* in their work. Jones, in his epic 1937 war poem *In Parenthesis*, recognises the fraught character of the Blackwater when he refers to 'the white-tailed eagle at the battle ebb, where the sea wars against the river'.[44] For Jones, human political conflict is complexly caught up with the embattled material conditions of the estuary.

This handful of learned engagements with *Maldon* notwithstanding, it was not until the end of the twentieth century, and the thousand-year anniversary of the battle, that public interest in the poem's estuarine version of the conflict really intensified, an interest whose full impact would not yet have registered with Frank, writing in the early 1990s. This new wave of interest is marked by the formation of Maldon's Millennium Trust, which was tasked with coordinating a programme of events celebrating the anniversary.[45] On 10 and 11 August 1991 major celebrations were held in Maldon, including a battle re-enactment organised by the Norse Film and Pageant Society (complete with falconry and Viking longships loaned from the Jorvik Trust), a recreation of a medieval garden at All Saints with St Peter Church, a torchlit procession, a Viking funeral (Figure 12.1) and a performance of *Homecoming of Beorthnoth, Beorthelm's Son*, J. R. R. Tolkien's alliterative poem set in an imagined aftermath to the battle.[46] These celebrations noticeably cleaved to the version of events as they are articulated in *The Battle of Maldon*; Laborde's suggested topographies were accepted as historical fact for the purposes of the re-enactment, which took place at South House Farm by Southey Creek.

Figure 12.1 Viking longship at the 1991 millennium celebrations. Christine Hancock Archive.

One of the star attractions of the 1991 celebrations was a new commemorative embroidery of the battle which has been displayed at Maldon's Maeldune Heritage Centre since its opening in 1998. The Maldon Embroidery was designed by photographer and designer Humphrey Spender, most famous for his photography of working-class culture in the north-west of England during the 1930s' Mass Observation movement.[47] In the 1950s he turned to painting and textiles, creating work for the Festival of Britain and teaching in the Royal College of Art's textile department, and in 1969 he moved to a house just outside Maldon designed by Su and Richard Rogers, where he spent the rest of his life.[48] Spender's vision for the Maldon Embroidery was realised by 86 local embroiderers under chief embroiderer Lee Cash, over a duration of three years. Approximately 13m long and consisting of seven panels, the display showcases Maldon's history up to 1991, beginning with Essex's conversion to Christianity and the foundation of St Peter's. The first panel (Figure 12.2) features motifs of the chapel and a stone cross alongside battle imagery and figures of Byrhtnoth and Olaf Tryggvason, the king of Norway and leader of the Viking army according to version A of the *Anglo-Saxon Chronicle* (the runic lettering spells out Tryggvason's name). The panel draws particular attention to the mouth of the Blackwater, with the lettering 'Pant' further emphasising that the specific topographies of the Blackwater area matter deeply to these histories. Importantly, too,

Figure 12.2 Panel 1 of the Maldon Embroidery. Maldon District Council.

although the embroidery ostensibly commemorates English resistance against the Vikings, it simultaneously celebrates stylistic commingling of 'Celtic', 'Viking' and 'Saxon' imagery in the panel borders, so the printed guide to the embroidery panels informs us, including interlace, carved figureheads, beasts of battle and Thor's hammer.[49] Moreover, it makes use of both the Latin and the runic alphabet, reminding us, perhaps, that the estuary is not just a boundary but a place where cultures mingle: creatively, violently, complexly.

From a temporal perspective the panels are arranged chronologically, but there is one notable exception; panel 2 confronts the viewer with the intervention of a modern aircraft into the melee of warriors, a German Heinkel bomber which was shot down near Maldon in 1940 (Figure 12.3).[50] This is challenging imagery, an unexpected temporal rift in an otherwise linear sequence, and indeed the printed guide cryptically describes the aircraft as 'controversial', suggesting that its inclusion was intended as a provocation.[51] The plane faces off against silhouettes of two Saxon deserters and, behind these figures, in a dense fusion of imagery, is a shape that takes the form of both a medieval spear and a modern searchlight. Spender's positioning of Byrhtnoth's warriors seems to suggest a continuity of sorts between medieval and modern. Of course, the imaginative collision of medieval and modern warfare is nothing new; Frank writes that *Maldon* is 'always about the latest war' and has often been extrapolated to whichever present day is most in need of it.[52] In the embroidery, the men are conscripted into a trans-temporal border force, undying guardians of Essex's unstable geographic frontiers against Viking and German invaders alike. Alternatively, they might be understood as forebears of Maldon's twentieth-century defenders, therefore implying the existence of a defensive lineage which modern

Figure 12.3 Panel 2 of the Maldon Embroidery. Maldon District Council.

Maldonians, in turn, are invited to sustain. Thus, while the embroidery can to an extent be understood as a celebration of cultural, geographical and temporal crossings, it is also decidedly uneasy about them, because the 'controversial' aircraft is not, after all, invited across the causeway.

That an embroidery was chosen as the commemorative object for the battle's millennium celebrations is significant. In Panel 2 of Spender's embroidery, Byrhtnoth's widow, Ælfflæd, is depicted at work on her own colourful embroidery in a cell at Ely Cathedral. This has some basis in history: according to the *Liber Eliensis*, Ælfflæd donated to Ely, after Byrhtnoth's death, 'a hanging woven upon and embroidered with the deeds of her husband'.[53] This textual record is all that survives of Ælfflæd's textile, and its description has unsurprisingly led to comparisons with another battle which has famously been celebrated in textile: the Battle of Hastings.[54] Spender's 1991 embroidery, with its chronological sequencing and decorative borders, contains clear visual references to the Bayeux Tapestry, the 'ur-template' for modern commemorative community tapestries, in the words of Anna C. Henderson.[55] According to Henderson, the Bayeux Tapestry is an important visual mnemonic which keeps the memory of the Norman Conquest in circulation; Spender's creation does the same work, re-inscribing the Battle of Maldon into public memory and weaving the conflict into a grand origin myth of the Christian nation. This desire to locate events within a broader historical narrative is apparent in the programme for the re-enactment event, too, which links Byrhtnoth's defence of the causeway not only to the battles of Stamford Bridge and Hastings but also to other western narratives of empire-building: specifically, to Horatius' defence of the Pons Sublicius on the River Tiber during the Roman–Etruscan Wars in 508 BC, popularised by Thomas Babington Macaulay's *Lays of Ancient Rome*

(1842).[56] Aqueous spaces, in other words, are shaped by these artworks as sites of national–imperial struggle.

The creation of new material cultures to animate and celebrate distant histories is an important part of what Raphael Samuel calls 'living history', a process of 'improving on the original by installing, in replica and facsimile, what ought to be there but is not', from archaeological replicas and open-air museums to re-enactments and historical walks.[57] As with most historical events from this period of history, the Battle of Maldon has not really left us with anything tangible to grasp: evidence for events is wonderfully fragmentary and contradictory. The embroidery thus serves to create 'flesh-and-blood figures out of fragments', providing a re-imagining of Ælfflæd's textile in order to stabilise 'what otherwise threatens to disintegrate, or to fall into a state of decay'.[58] These kinds of 'living histories' offer an important means of seeing, touching and experiencing a difficult-to-access medieval past. Moreover, by showcasing a series of significant moments in Maldon's history, the embroidery pushes back against modern cultural narratives of a marginal estuary. However, 'living histories' also inevitably participate in a conservative and exclusionary politics. As Joshua Davies has pointed out, when early medieval narratives are used as a means of expressing common bonds and celebrating collective identities in modernity, they can also participate in 'fantasies of wholeness and exclusion' by relying on idealised origin myths and unilinear histories.[59] Spender's work unquestionably deserves recognition for placing a spotlight on Maldon's working-class cultures and local women makers in both past (Ælfflæd) and present (Lee Cash and her team). Yet the embroidery prioritises one sequence of events at the exclusion of others, selecting from a multitude of possible narratives one that reinforces the idea of a unified Christian English nation, beginning with Cedd and the conversion mission and culminating in the present day. Moreover, the Blackwater Estuary is made complicit by serving as the backdrop against which this unilinear history is played out; Panel 1 sets up a spatio-temporal flow from left to right, past to present, river to sea. The embroidery, in other words, is caught between a desire to establish affective contact between past and present and a desire to adhere to early English fantasies of origin.

Similar issues are at stake in Maldon's most public monument to its tenth-century history, a 9ft bronze sculpture of Byrhtnoth (Figure 12.4), which, for all its conspicuousness, has received no critical attention to date. The sculpture was created in 2006 by John Doubleday, who was born in Great Totham, near Maldon, and is a prolific sculptor of historic and fictional figures. The statue, taking Laborde's topographies seriously, is reliant on its spatial context. Installed at the end of Maldon's Promenade

Figure 12.4 *Byrhtnoth*, by John Doubleday, 2006: (top) view from front looking towards Maldon; (bottom) view from rear looking towards Northey Island causeway. Johanna Dale.

Walk, it gazes out across the water towards Northey Island, sword aloft, victorious. As with the embroidery, the sculpture finds itself caught between closure and connectivity, division and unity. On the one hand, the inauguration of the sculpture was an extravagant international affair, attended by John Petre (Lord Lieutenant of Essex) and Bjarne Lindstrøm (Norwegian Ambassador to the United Kingdom) and accompanied by the British and Norwegian national anthems.[60] The event signifies a kind of reconciliation between sides befitting the battle's historical reality; after all, Æthelred II did make *gafol* payments in the aftermath of the battle, securing peace at least temporarily.[61] On the other hand, the sculpture's aggressively defensive posture is unsettling. Byrhtnoth is frozen into a stance of perpetual victory, occluding the nuances surrounding the story of the Battle of Maldon as we know it: Byrhtnoth's defeat, the payment of *gafol*, and the complexity of Anglo-Scandinavian relations both prior to and in the years following the battle.

It is only when visitors look down to Byrhtnoth's feet that the fact of his death in battle comes into focus. It is unmistakably formulated as a good, honourable kind of death. The sculpture's base bears a series of reliefs depicting scenes from the battle alongside scenes of tenth-century daily life, primarily ploughing and other agricultural activities. Tellingly, the sculpture's accompanying information plaque romantically claims that Byrhtnoth 'surrendered his life in defence of the people, religion and way of life represented in the lower relief'. Of course, as we have seen, the 'people' of Maldon prior to the events of 991 were by no means a monolithic unit. Religion, too, was fraught with complexity; the late tenth century was marked by the profound changes brought about by the Benedictine Reform in the English church, while Scandinavia was amid its own long process of Christianisation. The uncomplicated bucolic Christian 'way of life' that Byrhtnoth is assumed to defend is ultimately an imaginary one which does not match up to the realities of the tenth-century Maldon region any more than it does to the realities of the region today. An inscription below the reliefs, meanwhile, reading 'Grant me O Lord thy grace', adapts Byrthnoth's dying prayer in *The Battle of Maldon*: 'Nu ich ah, milde Metod, mæste þearfe þæt þu minum gaste godes geunne þæt min sawul to ðe siðian mote on þin geweald' (175–78a, Now I have, mild creator, the greatest need that you grant goodness to my spirit so that my soul may journey to you, into your power). The phrase, a distinctively archaic and overly romantic take on the Old English, is more reminiscent of a modern grave epitaph than a medieval poem and serves to maintain that tradition, traced by Frank and perceptible in the Maldon Embroidery, of Byrhtnoth as war hero for the twenty-first century.

As with the Maldon Embroidery, the Blackwater Estuary plays a complicated part in all this. As Catherine Clarke has put it, 'tidal spaces complicate easy assumptions about geography, territory, and power, and generate a range of challenging moral, religious, and political implications'.[62] The embroidery and the statue disclose a desire for coherence of both place and time, and yet reaching towards 'easy assumptions about geography', they find something altogether more challenging. In the case of Doubleday's sculpture, the estuary is evoked to shore up nostalgic imaginaries for the battle and for Byrhtnoth, becoming the physical boundary space that separates East Saxon from Viking, here from elsewhere, self from other, territory from non-territory. Yet the fact that Byrhtnoth is asked to remain in situ defending it suggests that it is not so fixed after all, that it needs to be continually reaffirmed in the present if it is to maintain the illusion of stability. By establishing Byrhtnoth's defensive border on land, the sculpture necessarily excludes the waters of the Blackwater from Maldon's territory, quietly reasserting Ackroyd's notion of estuary as nightmarish elsewhere. Indeed, a visitor to the sculpture unfamiliar with the story of the Battle of Maldon might take the figure of Byrhtnoth for his near-contemporary King Cnut, well known in popular discourse – though poorly understood – precisely for his own fraught relationship with aqueous powers.[63] Interpreted this way, the sculpture discloses anxieties about Maldon's vulnerabilities both human and elemental; Byrhtnoth becomes another figure fruitlessly struggling against the inexorable forces of the incoming tide. This becomes a particularly charged message in twenty-first-century coastal Essex, where rising sea levels pose a tangible threat to local futures; some models project that large swathes of Maldon, Heybridge and Northey Island, as well as St Peter's itself, will be below annual flood level by 2050.[64] All this is to say that 'living histories', embroidery and statue alike, deny to an extent the narrative coherence their creators may have sought to reinforce. *In situ*, they rather draw attention to the considerable ambiguities of local space. The statue, part of Maldon's ever-evolving fabric, exists in dynamic conversation with its changing physical surroundings, inevitably becoming enlisted in new conversations and contexts across time.

Maldon in process: spirals, fragments, migrations

Doreen Massey has written at length about the kind of spatial and temporal anxieties discussed above. 'The occasional longing' for coherence, she writes, is 'a sign of the geographical fragmentation, the spatial disruption, of our times'.[65] In the face of the 'ever more powerful and alienating webs' of global capitalism – and the ensuing marginalisation of certain places and spaces, including estuarine regions – local place becomes something to retreat to and defend.[66] The idea of the 'medieval' is inevitably imbricated in all of this; Michel Foucault's insistence that the medieval 'space of emplacement' was 'dissolved' by Galileo and modern science bolsters the myth of a medieval past that is local and knowable.[67] Yet while nurturing an affection for places and their pasts is no bad thing, Massey writes, it all depends on what we mean by place.[68] Ash Amin echoes this in his work on regionalism and territoriality, writing that the 'strong rhetoric of recovering and protecting old regional identities' in the spatial grammar of British politics plays on 'a conservationist regional identity that can be profoundly closed and exclusionary'.[69] This rhetoric is palpable in the brochure for the Maldon battle re-enactment; declaring both that the battle was a 'special landmark in the history of the English race' and that 'our strong Saxon heritage is still apparent and with us in our lives today', it troublingly claims an unbroken and exclusionary continuity of racial identity from past to present.[70] It is at stake, too, in the politics of the UK Conservative Party MP for Maldon, John Whittingdale, who was the patron of Doubleday's Byrhtnoth sculpture. Formerly the Secretary of State for Culture, Media and Sport, Whittingdale is evidently knowledgeable about and invested in the history of his constituency; in his maiden speech in the House of Commons in 1992, he argued that Maldon is 'an area rich in history', specifically referencing the Battle of Maldon, St Peter's and the Bradwell nuclear power station.[71] He is also a former member of the Brexit select committee and was a staunch supporter of the Eurosceptic 'Leave Means Leave' campaign. The imbrication of these local histories in contemporary European politics came into particular focus in November 2017, when Whittingdale tweeted an image of himself wielding a locally discovered Scandinavian sword, captioned: 'Seeing @MichelBarnier with @CommonsEUexit Tempted to take sword from Battle of Maldon. No more Danegeld.'[72] Filtering the narrative of *Maldon* through a selective lens in the service of fiercely nationalist rhetoric, Whittingdale positions the payments made by Britain to the European Union as a kind of twenty-first-century 'Danegeld', figuring the EU as unwanted invaders, while establishing himself as an East Saxon defender of his realm, ready for violence. The spatial politics of *Maldon* are reconfigured, albeit clumsily, for the kind of sentimental and exclusionary politics to which Amin and Massey refer.

This is not to say that the Maldon Embroidery and the Byrhtnoth statue may only invoke exclusionary or nationalist modes of medievalist thinking. However, in smoothing over the complexities of place and in prioritising continuity between past and present, they certainly do not disrupt them; Whittingdale's reactionary nationalism is reliant on the stabilising effect of various forms of 'living history'. Public heritage projects that seek to engage with past local places thus have an ethical responsibility to do so carefully, provisionally and dialogically, treating space, as Massey would put it, as a product of relations which is always in process.[73] Indeed, as Eden Kinkaid has pointed out, while critical–creative interventions can serve to conform to existing power structures and hierarchies, they can also offer new vantage points for thinking about place, challenge dominant institutional epistemologies and unsettle hegemonic identities.[74] I close this chapter, therefore, with two examples of public artworks which, to my mind, continue to challenge the marginalisation of estuarine spaces in modern times, while simultaneously proposing a more expansive politics of place in Essex estuaries. The first is *Colm Cille's Spiral* (2013), a collaborative project by curatorial partnership Difference Exchange and Clare A. Lees with the King's College London (KCL) Centre for Late Antique and Medieval Studies. The 'spiral' reimagined the legacy of the sixth-century Irish monk Colm Cille (St Columba) at six different sites or 'knots' along the coastal networks of the UK and Ireland, beginning in Derry-Londonderry, with the London/Essex 'knot' exploring Colm Cille's influence on Cedd's mission in Essex via the cultural geographies of St Peter-on-the-Wall.[75] The KCL and Difference Exchange team worked with Marc Garrett, from digital arts organisation Furtherfield, on *DISCLOSURE: Old Words Made New*, exploring how Columban modes of knowledge distribution might resonate with a twenty-first-century audience.[76]

One aspect of the programme was *Interruptions: New Ways to Know the Medieval*, a public event developed by Garrett with postgraduate researchers from KCL. Visitors encountered installations around the St Peter's site that encouraged them to reflect on communication networks and cultural distribution in the pre-internet age. Contributions by Francesca Allfrey and Carl Kears invited engagement with Bradwell's estuarine topographical context, via recordings of the Old English poem *The Seafarer* and an image of the Ark from Bodleian Library MS Junius 11. Like the Maldon Embroidery, *Colm Cille's Spiral* thought with and through medieval Christian histories. Yet by encouraging visitors to think in terms of the mobile and the fragmentary, Allfrey and Kears's installations disrupted the sense of medievalist territorial localism inscribed by objects like Doubleday's *Byrhtnoth* statue, instead understanding the Blackwater in terms of its broader cultural resonances. *Interruptions* was complemented by a commission by artist Erica Scourti, a 'video postcard' project which drew inspiration from the Old English poem *The Husband's*

Message, using the medium of Instagram to produce short diaristic reflections on a journey across Europe.[77] The installations did not shy away from difficulty, instead drawing attention to unknowability and to the challenges of communication across space and time.

Another creative–critical intervention that engages with the complexity of place is Caroline Bergvall's *Ragadawn* (2016–). Bergvall, a French-Norwegian cross-disciplinary writer and artist, is no stranger to medieval literary cultures; she is increasingly well known among medievalists for her experimental, trans-geographic and multilingual medievalist works *Meddle English* (2010), *Drift* (2014), *Conference (after Attar)* (2018) and *Alisoun Sings* (2019). *Ragadawn,* part of Bergvall's *Sonic Atlas* series, is a site-specific work influenced by medieval nomadic troubadour love poetry and featuring vocal chorus, field recordings and song sequences. Centring on language exchange and cross-border migration, it has been performed in Berlin, Barcelona, Marseille, Paris, Bodø, Geneva and on the Isle of Skye, picking up recordings of 'fragile' languages as it travels, so that each new performance represents a unique confluence of voices past and present, human and avian: Punjabi, Romanche, Arabic, Berber, Farsi, Andalus-Arabic, Medieval Hebrew, Galician, Ladino, Provençal, Occitan, Old English, Welsh, Scottish Gaelic, Icelandic, Groenlandic and Nightingale. Indeed, multilingualism is at the heart of Bergvall's practice: she cites Gayatri Chakravorty Spivak and Édouard Glissant as particular influences on her relational and trans-historical framework for understanding language.[78] As Áine McMurtry puts it, Bergvall uses the 'polylingual lyric voice' to 'oppose the oppressions of majoritarian discourse' and hold 'forms of language to account for their forced exclusions'.[79]

In 2016 I saw *Ragadawn* performed at Tilbury Docks as part of the inaugural Estuary Festival, which celebrates the Thames Estuary from Thamesmead to Shoeburyness.[80] It was performed at 6.38am by Bergvall and soprano Peyee Chen, overlooking the grey-brown waters of the Thames Estuary, and culminated in a Sikh breakfast of Bombay potatoes and chapatis prepared by the Essex Cultural Diversity Project. In modern consciousness Tilbury is at a slight remove from Bradwell and Maldon – being some 30 miles away from St Peter's – but it is notable for being another node in Colm Cille and Cedd's sprawling estuarine network, as Bede describes it in the *Ecclesiastical History* (III, 22). In bringing *Ragadawn* to Tilbury, Bergvall acknowledges estuaries as places where geographic, cultural and linguistic crossings happen. Yet she doesn't just make visible the estuarine crossings and connections of the powerful. Tilbury is an important node in the medieval Christian estuarine network, but it is also the place where, in 1948, the HMT *Empire Windrush* landed, bringing one of the first groups of post-war Caribbean migrants to Britain, migrants who would later face discrimination under Theresa May's 2012 'hostile environment policy'. It is the place where, in 2014, 35 Afghan Sikh migrants, including 13 children, were found in a shipping container, suffering from hypothermia and dehydration: one man, Meet Singh Kapoor, died.[81] In her work, Massey cautions against the 'over-excited celebration of openness, movement and flight',[82] and indeed Bergvall is careful to attend to the ways in which estuarine flows and mobilities cater to the privileged and uphold unequal power geometries.

Colm Cille's Spiral and *Ragadawn* are two very different projects, but they harbour a shared interest in looking beyond the combative lineages shored up by modern interpretations of *The Battle of Maldon* in order to tell new stories of local places that are transgressive in their trans-temporality and trans-territoriality. As Amin has argued, local advocacy in Britain is often paired with references to 'a common external enemy, to stories of heroism and resistance', and this perhaps goes some way to explaining the continued rhetorical emphasis on Maldon and Byrhtnoth's defence of the estuary in favour of stories about St Peter's.[83] Yet, as *Colm Cille's Spiral* and *Ragadawn* demonstrate, local advocacy does not have to take this form. There are other stories of the Greater Thames Estuary to be told, stories which neither consign the estuary to an imaginary, nightmarish margin (like Ackroyd) nor imbricate it in processes of closure and exclusion (like Whittingdale). Alone, of course, the literary and artistic mappings of the Blackwater that I have explored are not enough to fully overcome the exclusionary forces at work in the modern estuary. In the face of the powerful juggernaut of industrial global capitalism, too, they may seem slight; the issues that confront Essex coastal communities, from life-threatening flooding to toxic nuclear waste disposal, are complex problems requiring multifaceted political, economic and technological solutions. Yet cultural productions do serve as provocative 'interscalar vehicles', as Warren Harper and Nastassja Simensky put it in their own contribution to this volume; by registering aqueous connections across borders and times, they allow us to connect scales and stories that are usually kept apart, in turn opening up possible new futures. If and when the new nuclear power programme – a product of interrelations between the UK, China and France – converges on Bradwell, it will enter into conversation with older stories of international cooperation and conflict, defence and exchange, on the Blackwater. By remaining attuned to the uniqueness of local places while simultaneously registering how those places become entangled in dispersed, complex, trans-temporal and global power geometries, the works I have discussed do make a radical reconfiguration of politics and power seem possible.

Notes

1 Funded by the Deutsche Forschungsgemeinschaft (DFG, German Research Foundation) under Germany's Excellence Strategy in the context of the Cluster of Excellence Temporal Communities: Doing Literature in a Global Perspective – EXC 2020 – Project ID 390608380. I am grateful to Clare A. Lees, Alex Loftus and Joshua Davies for nurturing early ideas, to the CLAMS Early Career Research Forum for reading a nascent version of this work and to Rebecca Pinner, Len Scales and Fran Allfrey for their invaluable comments.
2 Lavezzo 2006, 8.
3 See also Blair 2005, 150.
4 Blair 2005, 257–8.
5 Clark 1993.
6 Blackmore et al. 2019.
7 Petts, in this volume.
8 Platt 2017, 12.
9 Ackroyd 2008, 395, 397.
10 Ackroyd 2008, 397.
11 For many commentators, the now closed landfill site at Mucking Marshes, which received over half a million tonnes of the capital's waste every year at the peak of its operations, is the ultimate signifier of the relationship between London and the Thames Estuary in the twenty-first century. See, for example, Burrows 2016.
12 Massey 1994, 149.
13 Longman 2019, 10.
14 Rambaran-Olm et al. 2020, 361.
15 Wickham-Crowley 2006, 91.
16 Wickham-Crowley 2006; Clarke 2011.
17 Clarke 2011, 100.
18 Pinner 2018, 5.
19 All quoted lines from the Old English poem are from Scragg 1991b. Modern English translations are my own.
20 Scragg 1991a, 15–17.
21 Bede also calls the Blackwater by this name. Colgrave and Mynors 1969, 282–5 (III, 22).
22 Cole 2007, 74.
23 Bately 1986.
24 Lapidge 2009, 156–7.
25 *Liber Eliensis* 1962, II.62.
26 Yates and Orlemanski 2014, 196.
27 Laborde 1925. See also George R. Petty Jr and Susan Petty's 1976 geological survey of Northey Island and the Blackwater.
28 Thomas 2017, 782.
29 Niles 1991, 459.
30 Harris 2003, 175.
31 Neidorf 2012, 463–4.
32 Harris 2003, 183.
33 Smith and Howes 2019, 9.
34 Smith and Howes 2019, 5.
35 Scragg 1993, 21.
36 Overing and Osborn 1994, xvi.
37 Historic England 2017, 5.
38 Historic England 1995.
39 National Trust 2020.
40 National Trust 2020.
41 Frank 1993, 244.
42 Frank 1993, 245–6.
43 Frank 1993, 238. On Nathaniel Hitch's medievalist craft, see Jones 2016.
44 Frank 1993, 238. On David Jones's engagement with early medieval culture, see Brooks 2021.
45 Maeldune Heritage Centre 2019. The Millennium Trust later became the Maeldune Trust, named after the early tenth-century name for Maldon (see Mills 2011).

46 'Battle of Maldon Souvenir Programme', 8. Maldon Millennium Trust, 1991, Christine Hancock personal archive.
47 Frizzell 1997.
48 Hopkinson 2005; Historic England 2012.
49 'The Maldon Embroidery: 991AD–1991', Maldon Millennium Trust, 1991.
50 *Daily Gazette* 1998.
51 'The Maldon Embroidery: 991AD –1991'.
52 Frank 1993, 238.
53 'Cortinam gestis viri sui intertextam atque depictam': *Liber Eliensis* II.63.
54 See Budny 1991, 264.
55 Henderson 2018, 22.
56 'Battle of Maldon Souvenir Programme', 5.
57 Samuel 2012, 172.
58 Samuel 2012, 197, 172.
59 Davies 2018, 149–51.
60 Agombar 2006.
61 See Keynes 1980, 203.
62 Clarke 2011, 101.
63 On Cnut and the tide, see Clarke 2011, 81–2.
64 Climate Central 2019.
65 Massey 1994, 147.
66 Massey 2005, 5.
67 Foucault 1986, 22–3.
68 Massey 1994, 153.
69 Amin 2004, 35.
70 'Battle of Maldon Souvenir Programme', 19.
71 Whittingdale 1992.
72 Whittingdale 2017.
73 Massey 2005, 9.
74 Kinkaid 2019, 1787.
75 *Colm Cille's Spiral* 2013. See also Lees and Overing 2019, 2–4.
76 Allfrey et al. 2015.
77 Scourti 2013.
78 Heisler 2006.
79 McMurtry 2018, 132–3.
80 The Estuary Festival is led by a partnership between Metal (Southend) and Cement Fields (Canterbury) and is funded by Creative Estuary, part of the Thames Estuary Production Corridor project of Sadiq Khan, Mayor of London. The festival's second iteration took place in 2021.
81 See Back and Sinha 2018, 53.
82 Massey 2005, 172–3.
83 Amin 2004, 37.

Bibliography

Ackroyd, P. 2008. *Thames: Sacred River*. London: Vintage.
Agombar, N. 2006. 'Maldon: statue handed over'. *Daily Gazette*, 24 October. https://www.gazette-news.co.uk/news/984075.maldon-statue-handed-over/ [accessed 20 April 2022]
Allfrey, Francesca, Francesca Brooks, Joshua Davies, Rebecca Hardie, Carl Kears, Clare Lees, Kathryn Maude, James Paz, Hana Videen and Victoria Walker. 2015. 'New ways to know the medieval: creativity, pedagogy and public engagement with *Colm Cille's Spiral*', *Old English Newsletter* 46(3).
Amin, A. 2004. 'Regions unbound: towards a new politics of place', *Geografiska Annaler* Series B 86(1): 33–44.
Back, L., and S. Sinha. 2018. *Migrant City*. London: Routledge.
Bately, J. (ed.) 1986. *Anglo-Saxon Chronicle 3 MS A*. Cambridge: D. S. Brewer.
Battle of Maldon Souvenir Programme, 1991. Maldon: Maldon Millennium Trust.

Blackmore, L., I. Blair, S. Hirst and C. Scull. 2019. *The Prittlewell Princely Burial: Excavations at Priory Crescent, Southend-on-Sea, Essex, 2003*. London: Museum of London Archaeology.

Blair, J. 2005. *The Church in Anglo-Saxon Society*. Oxford: Oxford University Press.

Brooks, F. 2021. *Poet of the Medieval Modern: Reading the early medieval library with David Jones*. Oxford: Oxford University Press.

Budny, M. 1991. 'The Byrhtnoth tapestry or embroidery'. In *The Battle of Maldon A.D. 991*, edited by D. J. Scragg. 263–78. Oxford: Basil Blackwell.

Burrows, T. 2016. 'The only grave is Essex: how the county became London's dumping ground'. *The Guardian*, 25 October. https://www.theguardian.com/cities/2016/oct/25/london-dumping-ground-essex-skeleton-crossrail-closet [accessed 20 April 2022].

Clark, A. 1993. *Excavations at Mucking*, vol. 1, *The Site Atlas*. London: English Heritage.

Clarke, C. A. M. 2011. 'Edges and otherworlds: imagining tidal spaces in early medieval Britain'. In *The Sea and Englishness in the Middle Ages: Maritime narratives, identity and culture*, edited by S. I. Sobecki. 81–101. Cambridge: D. S. Brewer.

Climate Central. 2019. 'Land projected to be below annual flood level in 2050'. https://coastal.climatecentral.org/mapview/8/-1.3561/51.6389/4333f7436331d62195d3a5b8e04a97145e6371f630d4b62364c088212f723f9b [accessed 20 April 2022].

Cole, A. 2007. 'The place-name evidence for water transport in early medieval England'. In *Waterways and Canal-Building in Medieval England*, edited by J. Blair. 55–85. Oxford: Oxford University Press.

Colgrave, B., and R. A. B. Mynors (ed. and trans.). 1969. *Bede's Ecclesiastical History of the English People*. Oxford Medieval Texts. Oxford: Clarendon Press.

Colm Cille's Spiral. 2013. https://www.kcl.ac.uk/cultural/projects/archive/2013/colm-cilles-spiral [accessed 20 April 2022].

Daily Gazette. 1998. 'Fred to meet Luftwaffe airman – 58 years on'. 29 September. https://www.gazette-news.co.uk/news/5539122.feature-fred-to-meet-luftwaffe-airman-58-years-on/ [accessed 20 April 2022].

Davies, J. 2018. *Visions and Ruins: Cultural memory and the untimely Middle Ages*. Manchester: Manchester University Press.

Foucault, M., translated by J. Miskowiec. 1986. 'Of other spaces', *Diacritics* 16(1): 22–7.

Frank, R. 1993. 'The Battle of Maldon: its reception, 1726–1906'. *The Battle of Maldon: Fiction and fact*, edited by Janet Cooper. 237–47. London: Hambledon Press.

Frizzell, D. 1997. *Humphrey Spender's Humanist Landscapes: Photo-documents, 1932–1942*. New Haven, CT: Yale University Press.

Harris, S. J. 2003. *Race and Ethnicity in Anglo-Saxon Literature*. New York and London: Routledge.

Heisler, E. 2016. 'Caroline Bergvall: propelled to the edges of a language's freedom, and to the depths of its collective traumas', *Asymptote*. https://www.asymptotejournal.com/visual/eva-heisler-caroline-bergvall-propelled-to-the-edges-of-a-languages-freedom/ [accessed 20 April 2022].

Henderson, Anna C. 2018. *Public History in the Making: Community Tapestry in the British Isles*. Manchester: The University of Manchester ProQuest Dissertations Publishing. https://www.proquest.com/openview/b045db739cb6d4f0d0750badfa050a65/1.pdf?pq-origsite=gscholar&cbl=2026366&diss=y [accessed 11 December 2022].

Historic England. 1995. 'Battle of Maldon 991', Listed 6 June. https://historicengland.org.uk/listing/the-list/list-entry/1000019 [accessed 20 April 2022].

Historic England. 2012. 'The Studio', Listed 3 July. https://historicengland.org.uk/listing/the-list/list-entry/1408257 [accessed 20 April 2022].

Historic England. 2017. 'Battlefields: registration selection guide'. https://historicengland.org.uk/images-books/publications/dsg-battlefields/heag072-battlefields-rsg/ [accessed 20 April 2022].

Hopkinson, A. 2005. 'Humphrey Spender: pioneering photographer who chronicled the state of Britain in the 1930s'. *The Guardian*, 15 March. https://www.theguardian.com/news/2005/mar/15/guardianobituaries.artsobituaries1 [accessed 20 April 2022].

Jones, C. 2016. 'Nathaniel Hitch and the making of church sculpture'. *19: Interdisciplinary Studies in the Long Nineteenth Century* 22. https://doi.org/10.16995/ntn.733 [accessed 11 December 2022].

Keynes, S. 1980. *The Diplomas of King Æthelred 'The Unready', 978–1016: A study in their use as historical evidence*. Cambridge: Cambridge University Press.

Kinkaid, E. 2019. 'At the limits of critical geography: creative interventions into the exclusionary spaces of U.S. geography'. *Gender, Place and Culture* 26(12): 1784–1811.

Laborde, E. D. 1925. 'The site of the Battle of Maldon', *English Historical Review* 158: 161–73.

Lapidge, M. (ed.) 2009. *Byrhtferth of Ramsey: The lives of St Oswald and St Ecgwine*. Oxford: Oxford University Press.
Lavezzo, K. 2006. *Angels on the Edge of the World: Geography, literature, and English community, 1000–1534*. Ithaca, NY, and London: Cornell University Press.
Lees, C. A., and G. R. Overing. 2019. *The Contemporary Medieval in Practice*. London: UCL Press.
Liber Eliensis. 1962. Edited by E. O. Blake. London: Offices of the Royal Historical Society.
Longman, J. 2019. 'Place: Thematic Strategy'. Maldon: Maldon District Council. https://www.maldon.gov.uk/downloads/file/17982/place_-_thematic_strategy [accessed 20 April 2022].
Maeldune Heritage Centre. 2019. 'About us'. Last modified 2 September 2019. http://www.maelduneheritagecentre.org/about/4580898123/ [accessed 20 April 2022].
'The Maldon Embroidery: 991AD–1991'. Maldon Millennium Trust, 1991.
Massey, D. 1994. *Space, Place and Gender*. Minneapolis: University of Minnesota Press.
Massey, D. 2005. *For Space*. London and Thousand Oaks, CA: Sage Publications.
McMurtry, Á. 2018. 'Giving a syntax to the cry: Caroline Bergvall's *Drift* (2014)', *Paragraph: A Journal of Modern Critical Theory* 41(2): 132–48.
Mills, A. D. 2011. 'Maldon'. In *A Dictionary of British Place Names*. Oxford: Oxford University Press. https://www.oxfordreference.com/view/10.1093/acref/9780199609086.001.0001/acref-9780199609086-e-8994 [accessed 20 April 2022].
National Trust. 2020. 'Things to see and do at Northey Island'. Last modified 16 July 2020. https://www.nationaltrust.org.uk/northey-island/features/things-to-see-and-do-at-northey-island. [As of 2022, this wording no longer appears on the National Trust website.]
Neidorf, L. 2012. 'II Æthelred and the Politics of The Battle of Maldon', *Journal of English and Germanic Philology* 111(4): 451–73.
Niles, J. D. 1991. 'Maldon and mythopoesis', *Medievalia* 17: 89–121.
Overing, G., and M. Osborn. 1994. *Landscape of Desire: Partial stories of the medieval Scandinavian world*. Minneapolis: University of Minnesota Press.
Petty, G. R., and S. Petty. 1976. 'Geology and the Battle of Maldon', *Speculum* 51(3): 435–46.
Pinner, R. 2018. 'Thinking wetly: causeways and communities in East Anglian hagiography', *Open Library of Humanities* 4(2), 3: 1–27.
Platt, L. 2017. *Writing London and the Thames Estuary: 1576–2016*. Leiden: Brill.
Rambaran-Olm, M., M. B. Leake and M. J. Goodrich. 2020. 'Medieval studies: the stakes of the field', *postmedieval* 11(4): 356–70.
Samuel, R. 2012 [1994]. *Theatres of Memory*, vol. 1, *Past and Present in Contemporary Culture*. London and New York: Verso.
Scourti, E. 2013. 'The Husband's Message'. *Colm Cille's Spiral*. 4 September. http://www.colmcillespiral.net/the-husbands-message/ [no longer online].
Scragg, D. J. 1991a (ed.). *The Battle of Maldon AD 991*. Oxford: Basil Blackwell.
Scragg, D. J. 1991b (ed.). *The Battle of Maldon*. Manchester: Manchester University Press.
Scragg, D. J. 1993. 'The Battle of Maldon: fact or fiction?' In *The Battle of Maldon: Fiction and fact*, edited by J. Cooper. 19–32. London and Rio Grande, OH: The Hambledon Press.
Smith, J. L., and H. Howes. 2019. 'Medieval water studies: past, present and promise', *Open Library of Humanities* 5(35). https://doi.org/10.16995/olh.443 [accessed 11 December 2022].
Thomas, D. 2017. '*Landes to fela:* geography, topography and place in The Battle of Maldon', *English Studies* 98(8): 781–801.
Whittingdale, J. 1992. 'Maiden speech in the House of Commons'. *Political Speech Archive*. http://www.ukpol.co.uk/john-whittingdale-1992-maiden-speech-in-the-house-of-commons/ [accessed 20 April 2022].
Whittingdale, J. 2017. (@JWhittingdale). 'Seeing @MichelBarnier with @CommonEUexit Tempted to take sword from Battle of Maldon. No more Danegeld.' 7 November 2017, 07:02. https://twitter.com/JWhittingdale/status/928155659803201536 [accessed 20 April 2022].
Wickham-Crowley, K. 2006. 'Living on the *Ecg*: the mutable boundaries of land and water in Anglo-Saxon contexts'. In *A Place to Believe In: Locating medieval landscapes*, edited by C. A. Lees and G. R. Overing. 85–111. University Park, PA: Pennsylvania State University Press.
Yates, J., and J. Orlemanski. 2014. 'Mood change/collective change'. In *Burn after Reading*, edited by E. A. Joy, M. Seaman and J. J. Cohen. 189–201. New York: Punctum Books.

13
The last of Essex: Contemporary architecture and cultural landscape
Charles Holland

In spring 2013 I visited the chapel of St Peter-on-the-Wall for the first time. The building had become a touchstone in conversations with the artist Grayson Perry during the design of *A House for Essex*, and we travelled to the site together.[1] Without knowing a great deal about the history of either the chapel or the Roman site of Othona that proceeded it, I approached the building experientially, as an object within the remarkable landscape of the Dengie Peninsula. Small within the wide-open expanses of the flat marshland but monumental in its simple, emphatic outline, the building left an immediate and powerful impression. Certain formal resonances – an object seen from afar, a building with few conventional signifiers of scale and a chapel conceived as the end of a journey – chimed with the emergent thinking of *A House for Essex* and influenced its development. This chapter explores that influence, placing it within both the historical context of pilgrimage chapels and also the more contemporary cultural landscape of Essex.

In his book charting the history of pilgrimage in the west, James Harpur identifies pilgrimage as associated with both a physical journey and an expression of faith.[2] Pilgrimage requires a journey in which the spatial and physical experience of travel offers a form of spiritual knowledge in itself. The physical effort and level of self-sacrifice involved in pilgrimage is thus an important element. 'Pilgrimage then', he writes, 'may refer to an inner – emotional, mental and spiritual – journey, as well as an outer, physical one.'[3] Beyond physical and emotional effort, pilgrimage predominantly relies on an experience of place that is defined by travel and movement.[4]

Figure 13.1 *A House for Essex*, by FAT/Grayson Perry, external view. Jack Hobhouse.

This chapter is itself a form of pilgrimage, a written journey undertaken with a view to gaining insight and understanding. In it I will explore a contemporary reading of pilgrimage in relationship to the built landscape of Essex. I will focus on a specific building – *A House for Essex* – that has been conceived as the end point of a journey across Essex that takes in a number of other buildings and places, including St Peter-on-the-Wall. *A House for Essex* can be seen as a contemporary reworking of themes present within St Peter's. Formal and historical aspects of the chapel informed both its conceptual and design development. Through exploring these connections alongside those to other buildings and places within Essex this chapter will place St Peter's and *A House for Essex* within a social and cultural reading of Essex and the idea of pilgrimage as a way to explore and read the contemporary landscape.

A House for Essex

A House for Essex is a collaborative architectural project designed by the architecture practice FAT – of which I am a director – and the artist Grayson Perry. FAT and Perry were commissioned by Living Architecture – a company set up by the writer and broadcaster Alain de Botton to build one-off architect-designed houses available as short-term holiday lets – to design the house for a site in Essex, the county in which both Grayson Perry and I grew up.[5] *A House for Essex* was the fifth house to be commissioned by Living Architecture. It was begun in 2012 and completed in 2015.

A House for Essex was conceived as a contemporary form of pilgrimage chapel, and its site in Wrabness in north-east Essex forms the end point of a notional pilgrimage across the county. This journey is based on the life story of a fictional character named Julie Cope. Born in Canvey Island in 1953 – the year of the North Sea flood which left large areas of the Essex coastline under water – Julie Cope's life acts as an armature for the narrative structure of the project. The 'story' of Julie Cope's life, which lasts from 1953 until her death in 2014, can be read as a section through the socio-geographic landscape of Essex. Each of the places in which Julie either lives or works is a location on a journey from the south-east to the north-east of Essex and represents a form of urban or rural settlement.

These include early nineteenth-century 'plotland' settlements, post-war new towns, a mid-century university campus and late twentieth-century suburbia. The route linking these sites stretches from the industrial fringe of London at the southern edge of Essex to its more agricultural north and takes in a number of religious or symbolic buildings, including St Peter-on-the-Wall, St Laurence, Blackmore, and the Black Chapel, North End. The journey reflects the remarkably varied character of Essex and its social demographic build-up. Julie's life acts as a means to reflect on this varied character and the cultural make-up of Essex through the latter half of the twentieth century and the early twenty-first. This journey forms the narrative of Julie Cope's life, but it also informs the design of the house itself. *A House for Essex* refers to the journey through the artworks contained within it, the decorative faience tiles that form its external cladding and its spatial and material composition.

Pilgrimage and wayside chapels

> There were also chapels over and adjoining gates, and chapels at inland ferries, and chapels on the coast and at harbours, some of which, at least, united the interests of the seafarer and the wayfarer, as the ferry led to the road and the road to the ferry.[6]

In his 1897 essay on wayside chapels in England, Alexander Wood details the extraordinarily wide variety of this building type.[7] Often such chapels, which are distinguished by having no adjoining burial ground, are located at sites of transit, places where pilgrims might have to wait before being

Figure 13.2 *A House for Essex* map. Grayson Perry.

able to resume their journey.[8] Wayside chapels are therefore often sites at which pilgrims can offer their devotions along the route to a more significant end point. They might mark sites of significance themselves, but they also perform a strategic role within the composition of the wider pilgrimage journey. For example, the basilica of Our Lady of Walsingham lies on the pilgrim route to Our Lady of Walsingham, a sacred site established in the twelfth century by the noblewoman Richeldis de Faverches and destroyed during the Dissolution of the Monasteries in the sixteenth century.[9] The basilica is informally known as the Slipper Chapel, possibly because pilgrims sometimes remove their shoes there before undertaking the last mile of the journey to Walsingham itself, a section of the journey known as the 'Holy Mile'.[10]

In contrast, pilgrimage chapels represent a destination, the end point of a journey. They might be located by the graves of saints or on the site where miracles are believed to have taken place, as at Walsingham. They might hold objects that are believed to have miraculous properties such as the clothes of a saint or a piece of Jesus' cross. In practice, pilgrimage chapels could also function as staging points on longer journeys or might provide the starting point for other pilgrimages. For instance, Thomas Becket's shrine at Canterbury Cathedral is both the end point of the Pilgrim's Way, which runs from Winchester to Canterbury, and the start of other pilgrimage routes, including from Canterbury to

Rome via the Via Francigena trail and to the cathedral of Santiago de Compostela in Galicia in north-western Spain.[11]

A House for Essex has been conceived as a contemporary pilgrimage chapel. It is dedicated to a secular saint – Julie Cope, or Our Lady of Essex – and contains relics of her life. Its garden includes her gravestone. The pilgrimage journey that leads to the house follows Julie's journey across Essex, and the places where she lived become – in a sense – wayside chapels along a pilgrimage route. Julie Cope is a fictional character, and the journey is part of that fiction. The house therefore acts as a reflection on the fictional aspect of all pilgrimage routes and on the question of what form contemporary pilgrimage could take.

Contemporary pilgrimage

In Powell and Pressburger's 1943 film *A Canterbury Tale*, three strangers meet in a fictional village on the outskirts of Canterbury in Kent.[12] The film consciously evokes Chaucer's *Canterbury Tales*, here reworked as a wartime paean to English values. It begins with medieval pilgrims walking the Pilgrims' Way to Canterbury before the atmosphere is shattered by the arrival of a Second World War fighter plane swooping through the sky.

In the film, Powell and Pressburger's contemporary pilgrims are waylaid by a strange incident, and it is several days before they make their final journey into Canterbury. When they eventually arrive in the city, they witness the destruction of parts of its centre as a result of the Luftwaffe's 'Baedeker raids'. But the cathedral still stands, and each of the three characters makes their way to its precincts and receives a kind of blessing there, a minor miracle which transforms their lives in some way. *A Canterbury Tale* is a story of twentieth-century pilgrims made during the Second World War, partly as a piece of wartime propaganda. Each of the 'pilgrims' is involved in a direct way with the Allied war effort. The fictional village where they stay lies on the North Downs and a place referred to in the film as 'the bend', the point at which travellers on the Pilgrims' Way gain their first view of Canterbury Cathedral.[13] Like the characters, this view is withheld from us until the final section of the film. The structure of the film and the spatial organisation of its narrative thus acts as a form of pilgrimage itself, with the cathedral acting as the pilgrimage site and the village as a wayside chapel – the last wayside chapel in fact – along the pilgrimage route, a place to pause and prepare for the sacred site beyond.

The Pilgrim's Way itself has disputed status. As Emma J. Wells states in her study of British pilgrimage routes, it is reputed to be one of

England's most ancient and infamous trackways, but it is also a Victorian reinterpretation of a medieval route.[14] The Pilgrims' Way starts at the shrine of St Swithun in Winchester Cathedral in Hampshire and ends at the site of St Thomas Becket's shrine at Canterbury Cathedral. The current route, however, was only established in 1978 by the Ramblers' Association, and historic parts of the way have been eradicated over time through development and road-building. The Pilgrims' Way is an imperfect recreation that raises questions regarding the authenticity of route versus the perceived quality of contemporary landscape experience.

The chapel of St Peter-on-the-Wall is the end point of an even more recently established pilgrimage route across Essex. The St Peter's Way runs for just over 40 miles from Greensted to Bradwell. The route includes the twelfth-century churches of St Laurence in Blackmore and St Mary's in Mundon; however, it was only established in the 1970s by members of two leisure walking groups in response to a competition to establish long-distance walking routes in the county.[15] The St Peter's Way, which thanks to its destination quickly attracted religious pilgrims, is thus a modern pilgrimage route and as such is promoted by the British Pilgrimage Trust (BPT), a charity set up to promote contemporary pilgrimage.[16] The BPT's mission is not an explicitly religious one but offers a confluence of contemporary ideas of well-being, spirituality and the appreciation and enjoyment of nature. Consequently, the routes promoted by them depart from older ones in order to plot more picturesque and event-rich experiences than a literal following would allow.[17] This contemporary interpretation of pilgrimage involves a re-reading of the landscape via tourism and leisure. Secular pilgrimage can therefore be seen as a contemporary form that establishes routes via a mix of historical interest and the enjoyment of nature, views and landscape over spiritual or religious connections.

An Essex pilgrimage

In the next section of this chapter, I explore the contemporary pilgrimage journey that underpinned the development of *A House for Essex*, starting with Julie Cope's birthplace in Canvey Island and leading to Wrabness, the site of the house itself.

Canvey Island

> In a newsreel shot from a banking plane
> An archipelago of glorified sheds

> Was all that showed of flooded Canvey Island
> Essex home to bombed-out cockney broods
> Julie May Cope was born early in a loft
> The North Sea pulsing darkly at the stairs
> An Isle of delight, in the mouth of the silvery Thames.[18]

> The air is filled with poison
> The sea is thick with grease
> Somewhere in this hell on earth
> I'll surely get some peace.[19]

Canvey Island is an area of 7 square miles of reclaimed land in the Thames Estuary. The small village centre of the island is just 2 feet above sea level. Though settlement of the area dates back to the Roman period, its most obvious period of development took place during the late Victorian era and early twentieth century.[20] From 1899, Frederick Hester started to develop the area as a seaside resort, selling plots of land, mainly to Londoners who wanted to build their own holiday homes. He built a promenade, pier and what was originally a horse-drawn monorail system. Hester was bankrupted in the process of this, but Canvey continued to develop into a combination of seaside resort and 'plotland' settlement, existing alongside the petrochemical plants at Hole Haven, on the south side of the island.[21]

Grayson Perry's poem *The Ballad of Julie Cope* records that she was born on 1 February 1953, the night of the North Sea flood, which killed 58 people on the island.[22] Many of the small, often fragile holiday bungalows were flooded, with the water reaching ceiling level. The fragility of Canvey's settlement, a combination of self-built bungalows and reclaimed land as well as its bleak, industrial character places Julie's beginnings within the estuarine edge of Essex as it meets London. Perry's tapestry *A Perfect Match* – one of two that that hang in the main Living Room space of *A House for Essex* – includes a depiction of Julie's parents, Norman and June, holding her as they escape their flooded house in a rowing boat manned by a policeman while cars capsize in the water all around. The image is a composite of newspaper photographs and descriptions of the flood as well as images of Canvey itself.

Basildon

> Fleeing the watery blitz the Copes decamp
> And breathe the modern air of Basildon
> All architects' dreams and improving lines.

> Abstract art lectured shoppers buying fags
> Buildings shrieked fair new hopes at old-style folks.[23]

> ... seven parishes living in hair-raising scatters of shacks and gimcrack bungalows: the land in something like 30,000 ownerships and all part of the North Thames-side industrial and commuter region.[24]

Basildon was built as one of the first generation of post-war new towns – one of two in Essex (the other being Harlow).[25] Basildon's existence owes much to the circumstances of post-war Essex and the presence of large areas of 'plotland' developments.[26] During the slump in land prices that resulted from the agricultural depression of the late nineteenth and early twentieth centuries, farmers and landowners explored the possibility of speculative residential development. This manifested itself in a number of settlements formed through the selling off of individual plots. Originally aimed at Londoners looking for an escape at the weekend, the plots were basic and contained no services or infrastructure. Individual plot owners were responsible for building their own dwelling as well as the means to get to their property.

Due to its proximity to London and the comparatively large amounts of agricultural land, Essex developed a number of plotland communities, many in the Laindon and Dunton Hills area later developed into Basildon. The relative success of the plotland communities and the manner in which they grew – the somewhat anarchic, self-built communities described by Norman Scarfe above – was instrumental in the development of the Town and Country Planning Act which came into effect in 1947. The fear of both legitimate but unchecked suburban expansion and of the unchecked expansion of the plotlands resulted directly in the formation of the Metropolitan Green Belt – an area of protected land around London – and the compensatory development of new towns via the New Towns Act of 1946.[27]

Basildon replaced the plotlands in a very direct way, clearing away their haphazard, do-it-yourself ethos in favour of the modernist architecture of municipal social democracy.[28] Julie Cope's family were one of the first generation of Basildon residents, plotlanders from Canvey lured there by the promise of employment and well-built, modern homes. Grayson Perry's poem satirises the paternalistic, cradle-to-grave socialism of the post-war settlement that developed the new towns to provide rational and modern alternatives to the wretched conditions of rural and urban housing. Julie Cope's move from the DIY plotlands of Canvey to the social democratic modernism of Basildon mirrors the transformation of post-war British society more widely. Julie meets and marries her first husband, Dave, in Basildon. They appear together in the second half of the tapestry, *A Perfect Match*, along with the tower of Brooke House – the residential tower built in the centre of the town in the early 1960s – looming over the shopping precincts and neat streets of modernist housing that form the backdrop to Julie Cope's first years of married life.

South Woodham Ferrers

> Then off to their choice of adulthood
> Dave had a road map for contentment, next
> A mortgage on a tick-box starter home
> In a child's drawing of a perfect street.[29]

> South Woodham Ferrers, on a river by the sea. South Woodham Ferrers, a whole new place to be.[30]

South Woodham Ferrers is in many ways the antithesis of the new town modernism of Basildon. It was a product of the Residential Design Guide, an influential document published by Essex County Council in 1973.[31] The Essex Design Guide, as it became commonly known, can be seen as a rejection of modernism enshrined in statutory planning guidance. It became one of the most influential planning documents produced in the UK, ushering in a form of neo-vernacular architecture that has become ubiquitous for new developments across the country. It favoured loose groupings of houses in arrangements that evoked village settlement patterns. It also encouraged the use of traditional Essex building materials such as weatherboarding, brick and plaster.[32]

South Woodham Ferrers was the Essex Design Guide's first significant manifestation. Before it, no one had ever thought of disguising a supermarket as an agricultural barn or a new street of houses as medieval farm cottages. The street names in South Woodham Ferrers provide a literary underpinning for this merry mythmaking, many of them culled from the work of J. R. R. Tolkien, including Gandalf's Ride and Elrond's Rest. While this conceit might feel just about plausible gazing out of your window across the mudflats of the River Crouch Estuary, it becomes trickier when confronting the commercial reality of the town centre. This is predicated around a vast Asda superstore, whose car park effectively forms the town's market square. Meanwhile, the 'actual' square – complete with bandstand – is squeezed behind the Asda with the store's service entrances facing on to it. Asda in fact owns much of the town centre, having bought large chunks of it from Essex County Council. Their dominance is not so much an unfortunate by-product as a fundamental part of South Woodham Ferrers's DNA.

South Woodham Ferrers was opened by Queen Elizabeth II in 1981, a year and a half after Margaret Thatcher's first election victory. Her government ushered in a rejection of the social-democratic project of the post-war era. This radical break from consensus included – perhaps as a compensatory move – a strain of cultural nostalgia for pre-modern social conventions. South Woodham Ferrers could be viewed as the spatial corollary of this combination of social conservatism and economic liberalism. In *The Ballad of Julie Cope*, Julie and her first husband, Dave, move to South Woodham Ferrers in the late 1970s. This move coincides with a shift in the political circumstances of the UK and of Julie's life. Dave – who is later to become a Conservative councillor – shifts jobs from manual to managerial work and moves politically to the right. He joins a band – The Riders of Rohan – in direct acknowledgement of the combination of retrogressive fantasy and economic neo-liberalism that underpins the town's planning.

Maldon

> She feels safe enough to tug her children
> And her tender roots a little further north
> Maldon was an older, shaggier town
> Red-sailed barges, terracotta tiles
> Salt, mud lido, an ancient battlefield.[33]

Following her divorce from Dave, Julie Cope moves to the town of Maldon on the Blackwater Estuary. The older, slower charms of Maldon are contrasted with the new towns of both South Woodham Ferrers and Basildon. In the tapestry *In Its Familiarity, Golden*, Maldon is depicted through the sails of Thames barges on the quay and in the terrace of Victorian cottages in which Julie lives. An important touchstone for Perry's tapestries was the Maldon Embroidery, a 42ft-long series of embroidered panels, which was commissioned to celebrate the 1,000th anniversary of the Battle of Maldon in 991.[34] It was designed by Humphrey Spender, an artist, photographer and textile designer who lived in the village of Ulting, just outside Maldon, from the 1970s until the early years of the twenty-first century. Spender's house – designed in 1968 by Richard and Su Rogers – also forms an oblique stylistic reference point for *A House for Essex* through its vivid colour scheme.[35]

University of Essex, Colchester

> Soon the Essex campus' clunky plazas
> Became her tangible yet dreaming spires
> Though she felt too old for drinking snakebite
> Sporting Converse or nodding out to grunge
> When a sweet IT tech called Robert
> Asked her out to lunch, she took the plunge.[36]

> The English love making things shaggy and softening everything up.
> We decided to do something fierce to let them work within.[37]

The University of Essex was established in 1963, and received its royal charter in 1965. Its campus is just outside Colchester, in Wivenhoe Park, the former landscaped gardens of a country house donated to the university for its use. The University of Essex is a so-called 'plate-glass university', a term referring to the architecture of the new generation of universities founded in the 1960s, which employed a modernist language in contrast to the medieval origins of the UK's oldest universities and the red-brick-based expansion of the university system in the nineteenth century.[38] The university was originally intended to focus on science and technology-based subjects with the ambition of its founding vice-chancellor, Albert Sloman, being to establish a UK rival to the Massachusetts Institute of Technology (MIT) in Boston, USA.[39] As Jess Twyman has argued, however, the later decision to incorporate humanities subjects and in particular sociology into the available subjects shifted the character of the emerging university and was instrumental in radicalising its student population in the late 1960s and early '70s.[40]

The protests and sit-ins that occurred at Essex became both strongly embedded in the public image of the university and linked to the supposed radicalism of its architecture.[41] Its designer Kenneth Capon's description of the architecture as 'something fierce' became strangely prescient. Although the design of the campus makes reference to picturesque precedents such as Italian hill towns, the architecture is uncompromising and also symbolic of post-war social democracy. Julie Cope's decision to return to studying and higher education in the 1980s returns her to some extent to the same architectural impulses that guided Basildon. Here she also meets her second husband, Rob, an IT technician at the university who becomes wealthy as a result of the dotcom boom of the 1990s. Perry's poem describes the marriage of Julie and Rob in bucolic terms. Comfortably off and happy, their life is contrasted to the fractiousness of her marriage to Dave. They marry in a stone circle in Scotland, holiday in India and enjoy birdwatching trips on the Essex and Suffolk coastlines. One of their favourite spots is Wrabness, overlooking the Stour Estuary.

Wrabness

> At the weekend they sought a shrine, a home
> For their love, and they ambled upon it
> A scrappy little house upon a brow
> Squinting north across the Stour to Suffolk.[42]

Wrabness is a small village overlooking the Stour Estuary. It lies 6 miles inland from Harwich and the North Sea. The river is wide and flat at this point, notoriously challenging for sailors as the navigable section is narrow and shallow. To the west the river passes by the small towns of Mistley and Manningtree, after which it is no longer tidal. Wrabness itself has around 400 inhabitants. The housing is mostly post-war and runs along Station Road, which connects the village with Mistley to the west and Ramsey to the east. The landscape here is mostly arable farmland with horse pastures and grazing. Black Boy Lane runs from Station Road down towards the river. It crosses the railway (the Mayflower line between Manningtree and Harwich) and past a number of detached houses before it terminates and a footpath leads down to the banks of the Stour.

A House for Essex is the last house on Black Boy Lane, and its driveway continues the trajectory of the road, leading directly to the front door. The house is aligned with the road so that its succession of roof gables can be seen, one above the other, as you approach it. The footpath deflects to one side of the house and runs within close proximity to it so that the decoration and detail are legible to passers-by. From here the footpath drops down between two copses – East and West Wood – before the wide expanse of river becomes visible. If you turn back to view the house it sits, positioned exactly, between the two banks of trees. The choice of site for the house was important and relates to the idea of pilgrimage chapels due to the proliferation of routes and modes of transport in the vicinity. Lying close to the 80-mile Essex Way, accessible by train, car and – at least theoretically – boat, the house positions itself conceptually and physically in relation to an idea of journey. At the same time, the shift from road to footpath and the presence of the river as the boundary between Essex and Suffolk strongly suggest the idea of the end of a journey and a sense of arrival. Like St Peter-on-the-Wall, the house surveys the banks of the river and forms a highly visible object in the landscape.

The journey described by Julie Cope's life forms a section through the Essex landscape, a physical, cultural and economic journey covering plotland communities, post-war new towns, late twentieth-century suburbia and the rediscovery of historic urbanism and conservation movements. It is one mirrored by wider political shifts, from the social democratic consensus of the post-war settlement through the neo-liberalism ushered in by Margaret Thatcher's Conservative landslide win of 1979 to the expansion of higher education and relative economic prosperity of the New Labour years. Julie Cope's life can be read as a parable of upward mobility and of class tourism. As Perry's poem makes clear, Julie's Indian summer of university and second marriage is a socio-economic shift in class. Signifiers of this include holidays to India and gentle enthusiasms for reading, wine and cooking, which pepper the poem and the artworks. No clear value judgement is made on this shift in her status, though the autobiographical aspects of the story that relate to Perry's own life and that of his mother contain aspects of wish fulfilment.[43] The journey implied by Julie's fictional life allows the house to occupy a physical space that can be perceived as the end point of a possible pilgrimage.

Precedents for *A House for Essex*

If the narrative arc of Julie's life can be seen as a reflection of the journey from Canvey Island to Wrabness, the design of the house itself also draws on a number of precedents in the county. These precedents are combined with wider architectural references to help inform its spatial organisation, formal expression and decorative qualities. The most obvious formal references for the house are the stave churches of Norway and Finland and the wooden Orthodox churches of Russia.[44] These historic types often use self-replicating forms to build large compositions made up of smaller parts. Shed-like shapes are piled up, one on top of the other, increasing in scale. The wooden churches of Russia, in particular, formed a useful touchstone during the early stages of the design process as they combine both monumental form and relatively humble materials. The replication of some elements at various sizes introduces ambiguities of scale that are exploited in the design of *A House for Essex*, where the self-repeating shapes and the lack of windows allow a relatively small object to appear larger than it is. The 'folk' quality of wooden stave churches was also

Figure 13.3 Blackmore Church. Charles Holland.

important in the way that simple construction processes were overlaid with rich painted and applied decoration.

There were also a number of building precedents closer in Essex. St Laurence's Church in Blackmore stands on the site of a medieval priory and its central nave may be twelfth-century and may have been part of the priory itself.[45] The most noticeable feature of the church is its fifteenth-century timber bell tower. Though timber bell towers are not unusual in Essex, the three-stage format of St Laurence's bell tower is.[46] Each stage of the tower becomes smaller, with each separated by a sloping, tiled section of roof like a skirt. The tower of St Laurence has echoes of stave churches and the wooden Russian churches that informed the early design stages of the house and allowed formal resonances between them to develop. The Black Chapel in North End offers both formal and programmatic precedent. This timber-framed building – originally constructed in the fifteenth century – contains both a chapel and a house. The Historic England listing describes it as a 'peculiar' chapel, meaning that it was outside the authority of the diocesan bishop.[47] The central nave leads to the house, which crosses it at right angles, like a transept. Much of the chapel and priest's house was restored in the early nineteenth century, and modifications were made in the twentieth century, which restored the distinctive tie beams that span across the nave. Most fundamentally the house fuses the architectural programmes of chapel and house, drawing little distinction between them in physical terms.

St Peter-on-the-Wall lies on the Roman site of Othona.[48] Most of the site occupied by Othona and the later Anglo-Saxon monastic settlement has been eroded by the sea, leaving St Peter's as an isolated building overlooking the Blackwater Estuary as it meets the North Sea. The building dates from c. 654 and is one of half a dozen seventh-century churches built on Roman sites using largely Roman material.[49] In plan it closely resembled the slightly later Saxon church at Reculver, a structure that also surveys the flat landscape of the Isle of Thanet. In both cases, while the churches appear to stand in remote isolation, they owe their existence to the prominence of their sites and the fact that they once lay at a confluence of routes.[50]

Like the other precedents discussed above, St Peter's exerted an important influence on the development of *A House for Essex*. Much of this influence is again due to the relative lack of detail on the chapel, which contributes to its monumental character. St Peter's has relatively few windows, and they are small compared to its surface area.[51] This increases the sense of scale of the building perceptually within the landscape around it. While the form for *A House for Essex* is more complex than St Peter's, it has similarly been conceived as a singular object in the landscape, one designed to be read as an individual landmark.

The importance of this landmark function in relation to much contemporary architecture is critical. A comparison with the other houses completed as part of the Living Architecture programme helps to clarify this point.[52] In all cases the houses are expressed as horizontal structures, spreading out across the landscape as a series of low sheds or floating masses. To some extent, each of the houses attempts to blend in with the landscape by becoming part of it. *A House for Essex* is vertical in aspect and definitively different to the landscape around it in formal terms. While certain material and colour resonances with the surrounding context are explored, the house itself is designed to stand aloof from context and to form a landmark. Ambiguities of scale are deployed in order to give a relatively small object a presence in its landscape setting, standing apart from it in formal terms. This was the principal lesson learned from St Peter's, while acknowledging the changed circumstances of that building over time. It is hoped that *A House for Essex*'s presence in the landscape links it to pilgrimage and wayside chapels, forming a landmark that aids navigation and establishes a presence that conveys ideas around the completion of a journey.

The house

Figure 13.4 *A House for Essex* exterior and interior sketches. FAT.

Although the house is positioned at the end of both a conceptual and a physical journey, its interior also forms a journey itself. The relationship of the house to the road that leads to it, the axiality of its plan and the formal composition of ascending rooflines suggest movement and coordinate the interior as a spatial sequence. This spatial sequence relates to the narrative sequence of Julie's life as well as a series of formal precedents which I will outline here.

A House for Essex draws on the reference points outlined above to develop a building that refers to both religious and secular architypes and combines symbolic programme with a house. It is relatively small – 170m^2 split over two levels. The main formal compositional device is that of a simple, pitched roof form that repeats four times, each time getting larger. The first of these contains the entry hall, lit from above by two smaller, clerestory dormer windows. Spanning across the middle of this room is the floor of the bathroom above, which appears like a bridge. On the ground floor the next, slightly larger space, contains a staircase, storeroom and shower room. This leads in turn to the kitchen–dining room, which is dominated by a large, recessed fireplace clad in tiles that mimic those of the exterior. The axial route that continues the line of the approach road, the path and then the hallway appears to terminate at the fireplace. Flanking it, though, and also clad in ceramic tiles, are two doors, placed symmetrically either side. These lead to the final and largest volume space, containing the 'chapel'. This space – like the entrance hall – continues all the way to the ceiling, this time an almost triple-height space richly decorated with tapestries, pots and wallpaper featuring depictions of Julie's life.

The first-floor sequence includes a bathroom placed partially over the entrance hall and two bedrooms, which are split by the central line of the roof pitch. The transition from the dining room to the chapel on the ground floor and from the bedrooms to the chapel on the first floor is intentionally dramatic. The hidden doors of the dining room are mirrored above by the doors of two walk-in wardrobes. Entering these leads – via a mirrored space – out onto two balconies that overlook the chapel. The house is thus split between ordinary domestic spaces (kitchen, bathrooms and bedrooms) and a larger symbolic space of the chapel-cum-living room. Separating the two is a wall that refers to medieval rood screens and contains within it a life-size sculpture of Julie Cope.

The chapel room is the dominant space of the house. It also contains most of the major artworks, including the two complex, multiply themed tapestries – *A Perfect Match* and *In Its Familiarity, Golden* – that describe the first and second acts of Julie's life. They hang opposite each other, with the ceramic representation of Julie herself in the middle. Between them hangs a motorbike, an actual reconditioned Honda C90, which in Perry's poem is the instrument of her death. This object is the most obvious 'relic' of her life; but there are others in the CD collection and the books on the bookshelves that comment on the arc of her life in cultural terms and present themselves as objects that she might have owned.

The sequence of rooms and the formal composition of the house play with the idea of journey – the house is a compacted, intense journey towards the chapel space – and with the layouts of chapels and small churches. The central corridor is a nave, with the spaces opening off to its sides as aisles. The living space is the chancel, which is cross-axial, continuing the main front-to-back axis that culminates in a view towards the river as well as a minor axis at right angles that focuses on the two tapestries. The living room leads to a porch that overlooks the river valley. On the floor of this space is another artwork depicting Julie's funeral and containing the following words from Perry's poem:

> He had kissed her and said that if she died
> He would grieve as hard as Shah Jahan
> And build a Taj Mahal upon the Stour.[53]

These words are in effect the origin myth of the house, the ostensible reason why it is built where it is. *A House for Essex* is a Taj Mahal built

Figure 13.5 *A House for Essex* by FAT/ Grayson Perry, interior of living room. Jack Hobhouse.

upon the Stour. It sits on the site of the small farmhouse that Julie and her second husband, Rob, bought to spend their weekends. And yet the house was designed before the full aspects of Julie's life was established. It is a retrospective origin myth, as all origin myths are.

Conclusions

A House for Essex attempts to reflect on a contemporary reading of Essex in built form. Its site at the north-eastern tip of Essex allows a reflection on a journey across the county. This journey takes in the places and buildings explored in this chapter, and the form of the house absorbs many of these influences. The multiple roofs of St Laurence's bell tower inform the concertina of house shapes that make up the main compositional device of *A House for Essex*, while the combination of house and chapel, the two existing in a not fully resolved tension, draws on the precedent of the Black Chapel at North End. Other, more abstracted references can be made to agricultural structures and to St Peter-on-the-Wall, which has acted as both a chapel and a barn in its long history.

The superimposition of forms that make up *A House for Essex* alludes to and develops the idea of journey and personal discovery. The spatial composition also relates to the story of Julie Cope's life in ways that are both direct and allegorical. For instance, the two bedrooms each represent one of her marriages, with a large tapestry acting as a magnified wedding photograph made more vivid. Aspects of the cycles of domestic taste during the period of her life are reflected in the decoration, colours and character of the interior spaces, particularly in the kitchen and bathroom, which form abstracted versions of specific styles. Artworks are incorporated directly into the fabric of the building, including the mosaic that forms the floor of the north entry porch and the tiles that clad the building's exterior. These artworks are framed by the architecture but also contain representations of it, so that the arched structure in which Julie stands on the exterior tiles echoes the arched framing of the dormer windows above. The house is thus both a repository of artworks and relics related to Julie Cope's life and the subject of those works.

Certain repeated motifs – such as the motorcycle wheel – appear in multiple forms. The wheel adorns the roof in the manner of a wind vane, appears on some of the triangular tiles and is literally present in the moped hanging from the living-room roof. Its handlebars appear cast in aluminium as part of the roof sculpture and again on the mosaic floor of the porch, where they also resemble a Viking burial boat carrying her weeping family. The iconography of *A House for Essex* draws on representations of saints such as Our Lady of Walsingham – most obviously in the life-size ceramic sculpture of Julie herself – while the interior contains contemporary relics in the form of books, CDs and ornaments. The statue of Julie is framed within a contemporary reinterpretation of a medieval rood screen, a device that also helps to separate and draw attention to the gap between the secular, domestic parts of the house and the living room, which is coded as chapel. Niches, plinths and shelves form displays spaces for pots and funereal urns. This space is top-lit and immersive, with views turned inwards towards the tapestries and other artworks.

Like St Peter-on-the-Wall, the site for *A House for Essex* is remote while also lying at a busy confluence of routes. In this sense the project also reflects on the nature of contemporary rurality. While relatively unpopulated, the Stour Estuary is a place linked to international trade routes and transport logistics. The house can be seen clearly from the river itself, and its position marks a point where car, train and pedestrian routes come together. As discussed above, its relative visibility is important. It can be seen from the river as well as from across the fields, and its siting allows it to be read as the termination of Black Boy Lane. The form and positioning of the house extenuate its reading as the end point of a journey.

The site is as far north from Canvey Island as it is possible to go without leaving Essex, and yet it is intimately connected to it, not just by the water which loops in and out of Essex's estuarine coast but also by the little houses that populate what is known as Wrabness beach. This row of structures down on the river's edge, a few hundred yards from the house itself, are 'plotland' houses, self-built, 'off-grid' holiday homes that echo the one on Canvey Island where Julie Cope was born. *A House for Essex* is situated at the end of a conceptual journey, a contemporary pilgrimage, that returns us back to the start. It forms a kind of mirror, a reflection on and of the contemporary landscape of Essex and its recent history. The design of the project was a pilgrimage, a journey into that recent past, and the house itself offers a contemporary, secular reading of pilgrimage.

Notes

1. *A House for Essex*, an artistic collaboration between FAT Architecture and Grayson Perry. See Living Architecture: https://www.living-architecture.co.uk/the-houses/a-house-for-essex/overview/ [accessed 25 April 2022].
2. There is a wide literature on pilgrimage, medieval and modern. See, for example, Webb 2002 and Harpur 2016. Wooding 2020 provides a useful introduction to contemporary pilgrimage.
3. Harpur 2016, 7.

4   For those unable to travel other forms of pilgrimage were and are possible. See, for example, Rudy 2011.
5   For a full description of the house and its commissioning refer to Living Architecture's website https://www.living-architecture.co.uk/the-houses/a-house-for-essex/architecture/ [accessed 25 April 2022].
6   Wood 1897, 283
7   Wood 1897, 283.
8   Wood 1897, 28.
9   For the history of Walsingham see McDonald 2012; on the medieval pilgrimage route to Walsingham see Locker 2015, 27–61; on the revival of pilgrimage to Walsingham see Coleman and Elsner 1999.
10 On the name of the Slipper Chapel and the 'Holy Mile' see Locker 2015, 40 and 58–9.
11 On medieval routes to Rome see Birch 1998, 41–52; on contemporary promotion of the Via Francigena and the Camino de Santiago see Lucarno 2016.
12 *A Canterbury Tale*, produced and directed by Michael Powell and Emeric Pressburger, 1943.
13 The hilly spot from which pilgrims first saw their destination was recognised by the topographical moniker 'Mount of Joy' in the Middle Ages: for example, Mons Gaudii on the approach to Rome and Monte do Gozo overlooking Santiago de Compostela.
14 Wells 2016, 155–81.
15 See Dale, in this volume.
16 See Dale, in this volume.
17 See Dale, in this volume
18 Perry 2020 [2015].
19 'Down by the Jetty Blues', 1975, composed by Dr Feelgood/Will Birch. The documentary film *Oil City Confidential* (2010), directed by Julian Temple, provides an account of the relationship between Dr Feelgood and the landscape of Canvey Island.
20 On Roman Canvey see Hedges and Martin 2002.
21 For a background to the history of nineteenth- and twentieth-century Canvey Island see White 2012.
22 For the 1953 flood see Grieve 1959. On Canvey Island's industrial history see Murray 2019.
23 Perry 2015.
24 Scarfe 1968, 48–50.
25 On Harlow's development see Powell et al. 1983, 149–58.
26 See Darley 2018.
27 For a general history of the development of post-war new towns see Alexander 2009.
28 See Darley 2018.
29 Perry 2015.
30 The band Right Hand Man won a competition run by Essex County Council in 1980 to compose the theme song to a promotional advert for South Woodham Ferrers. The promotional video featuring the song was made by the Essex Educational Video Unit and released in 1981.
31 First published in 1973, the Essex Design Guide was an adopted Planning Policy document produced by Essex County Council to guide the design of new residential areas.
32 Holland 2018, 94–7.
33 Perry 2015.
34 On the Maldon Embroidery see Whalley in this volume.
35 Holland 2018, 91–2.
36 Perry 2015.
37 Comment attributed to Kenneth Capon of Architects Co-Partnership, master planners of the University of Essex campus, 1964.
38 On the generation of universities founded in the 1960s see Pellew and Taylor 2021.
39 Lubbock 2018.
40 Twyman 2018.
41 On the Essex protests see also Hoefferle 2021.
42 Perry 2015.
43 For an understanding of Grayson Perry's childhood and early life see Jones 2006.
44 For an overview of wooden church architecture see Opolovnikov and Opolovnikov 1989.
45 Page and Round 1907, 146–8.
46 Bettley and Pevsner 2007, 141–2.

47 List entry 1338494, first listed in 1967: https://historicengland.org.uk/listing/the-list/list-entry/1338494 [accessed 25 April 2022].
48 See Pearson, in this volume.
49 On the fabric of the chapel see Andrews, in this volume.
50 See Hoggett and Petts, in this volume.
51 The windows caused some confusion in the interpretation of the chapel in the nineteenth century. See Bettley, in this volume.
52 There are six other houses in the Living Architecture programme: two on the Suffolk coast, one on the north Norfolk coast, one on the shingle beach at Dungeness (Kent), one in Wales and one in south Devon. For details see https://www.living-architecture.co.uk/default.asp [accessed 25 April 2022].
53 Perry 2015.

Bibliography

Alexander, A. 2009. *Britain's New Towns: Garden cities to sustainable communities*. London and New York: Routledge.
Bettley, J., and N. Pevsner. 2007. *The Buildings of England: Essex*. New Haven, CT, and London: Yale University Press.
Birch, D. J. 1998. *Pilgrimage to Rome in the Middle Ages: Continuity and change*. Woodbridge: The Boydell Press.
Coleman, S., and J. Elsner. 1999. 'Pilgrimage to Walsingham and the re-invention of the Middle Ages'. In *Pilgrimage Explored*, edited by J. Stopford. 189–214. Woodbridge: Boydell & Brewer.
Darley, G. 2018. 'From plotlands to new towns'. In *Radical ESSEX*, edited by H. Dixon and J. Hill. 101–21. Southend-on-Sea: Focal Point Gallery.
Grieve, H. 1959. *The Great Tide: The story of the 1953 flood disaster in Essex*. Chelmsford: Essex County Council.
Harpur, J. 2016. *The Pilgrim Journey: A history of pilgrimage in the western world*. Oxford: Lion Hudson.
Hedges, J., and T. S. Martin. 2002. 'A Roman pottery group from Canvey Island'. *Essex Archaeology and History* 33: 375–8.
Hoefferle, C. 2021. 'Great expectations: Sloman's Essex and student protest in the long sixties'. In *Utopian Universities: A global history of the new campuses of the 1960s*, edited by J. Pellow and M. Taylor. 105–20. London: Bloomsbury Academic.
Holland, C. 2018. 'The rise and fall'. In *Radical ESSEX*, edited by H. Dixon and J. Hill. 69–99. Southend-on-Sea: Focal Point Gallery.
Jones, W. 2006. *Grayson Perry: Portrait of the artist as a young girl*. London: Vintage.
Locker, M. 2015. *Landscapes of Pilgrimage in Medieval Britain*. Oxford: Archaeopress.
Lubbock, J. 2018. 'Planning the University of Essex, 1960–68'. In *Radical ESSEX*, edited by H. Dixon and J. Hill. 123–36. Southend-on-Sea: Focal Point Gallery.
Lucarno, G. 2016. 'The Camino de Santiago de Compostela (Spain) and the Via Francigena (Italy): a comparison between two important historic pilgrimage routes in Europe'. *International Journal of Religious Tourism and Pilgrimage* 4(7): 48–58.
McDonald, T. 2012 (ed.). *Walsingham: Richeldis 950, pilgrimage and history*. Walsingham: R. C. National Shrine.
Murray, S. 2019. 'A history of the oil, gas and petrochemical industries on Canvey Island'. *Essex Archaeology and History* 8: 114–27.
Opolovnikov, A. V., and Y. A. Opolovnikov. 1989. *The Wooden Architecture of Russia: Houses, fortifications, churches*. New York: Harry N. Abrams.
Page, W., and J. H. Round (eds). 1907. *A History of the County of Essex*, vol. 2. London: University of London.
Pellow, J., and M. Taylor (eds). 2021. *Utopian Universities: A global history of the new campuses of the 1960s*. London: Bloomsbury Academic.
Perry, G. 2020 [2015]. The Ballad of Julie Cope. In *Grayson Perry*, by J. Klein. 3rd edition. 312–15. London: Thames and Hudson.

Powell, W. R., B. A. Board, N. Briggs, J. L. Fisher, V. A. Harding, J. Hasler, N. Knight and M. Parsons (eds). 1983. *A History of the County of Essex*, vol. 8. London: University of London.

Rudy, K. M. 2011. *Virtual Pilgrimages in the Convent: Imagining Jerusalem in the late Middle Ages*. Turnhout: Brepols.

Scarfe, N. 1968. *Essex: A Shell guide*. London: Faber and Faber.

Twyman, J. 2018. 'Student uprising at the University of Essex'. In *Radical ESSEX*, edited by H. Dixon and J. Hill. 137–44. Southend-on-Sea: Focal Point Gallery.

Webb, D. 2002. *Medieval European Pilgrimage, c. 700–c. 1500*. Basingstoke: Palgrave.

Wells, E. J. 2016. *Pilgrim Routes of the British Isles*. Marlborough: The Crowood Press.

White, S. 2012. *The History of Canvey Island: Five generations*. Peterborough: Upfront Publishing.

Wood, A. 1897. 'Wayside chapels in England'. *The Downside Review* 16(3): 280–95.

Wooding, J. M. 2020. 'Changing roles of pilgrimage: retreating, remembering, re-enacting'. In *The St Thomas Way and the Medieval March of Wales: Exploring place, heritage, pilgrimage*, edited by C. A. M. Clarke. 25–36. Leeds: Arc Humanities Press.

14
Care and maintenance in perpetuity? The nuclear landscape of the Blackwater Estuary

Warren Harper and Nastassja Simensky

Emerging from the Dengie Peninsula, the Blackwater Estuary in Essex crystallises complex issues around history, heritage, ecology and the geopolitics of energy production. As an estuarine landscape, the Blackwater's interrelationships are planetary. Tides ebb and flow; each winter, birds such as dark-bellied brent geese migrate around 2,500 miles from Siberia to the sucking mud of Essex shores. The chapel of St Peter-on-the-Wall sits atop the remains of a half-submerged Roman fort; in nearby Maldon, the well-known 'Maldon Salt' is panned and processed. The Estuary's involvement in the nuclear military-industrial complex rubs up against the Othona Community. Here the arrangement of humans and non-humans, historical sites and important ecologies, demands consideration, particularly when thinking about and acting on the planning and implementation of the infrastructure of nuclear power production, decommissioning and waste storage.

The context for our co-authored contribution to this volume is our shared academic and pragmatic interest in place-specific art practice and the Blackwater Estuary. Writing as an artist (Simensky) and as a curator (Harper), we consider how the development of place-specific curatorial and artistic methods 'in the field' enables new ways of highlighting current discourses around the nuclear in the region, and the multiplicities of actors and legacies that both run through and inhabit the estuary; Anna Tsing reminds us that 'to listen to and tell a rush of stories is a *method*'.[1]

Throughout this chapter, we will draw on our experience of living and working in Essex and the Blackwater Estuary, as well as on current artistic and curatorial approaches to place and heritage. Although these approaches are not all situated within the Blackwater Estuary itself, they nevertheless shed light on this specific context, to suggest how new artistic and curatorial methods might be developed 'in the field'. We will do this through the consideration of two distinct sections, each of which deploys a specific theoretical device. First, 'Time and Measurement' uses the concept of the *interscalar* to address the varied scales and durations at play within the Estuary and examines how interscalar objects can 'bear witness'. Second, we will respond to the nuclear industry term 'Care and Maintenance' in order to reflect upon how the Othona Community challenges the norms of industrial energy production and ideas of 'care' and custodianship to provide a critical reconsideration of 'heritage' in a time of ecological crisis. Throughout this we will interweave artworks and research projects by international artists who actively articulate the potential of more-than-human perspectives on care, stewardship, temporality, conservation and critical heritage.

Time and measurement

As a product of the dismantling of Bradwell A in 2083, waste materials – including 4,000m² of graphite and sludge from the treatment of radioactive liquid effluents – will join a store of existing low- and intermediate-level waste adjacent to the power station.[2] The graphite currently lies in passive containment within the aluminium-clad reactor buildings, forming the reactor cores from which all fuel rods have been removed. These graphite blocks and their components might be thought to act as a 'material witness' to both the role Bradwell A played in the emerging nuclear energy regime of the 1950s and '60s and the changing face of the Estuary. Artist researcher Susan Schuppli describes the concept of the 'material witnesses' as:

> nonhuman entities and machinic ecologies that archive their complex interactions with the world, producing ontological transformations and informatic dispositions that can be forensically decoded and reassembled back into a history. *Material witnesses* operate as double agents: harboring direct evidence of events as well as providing circumstantial evidence of the interlocutory methods and epistemic frameworks whereby such matter comes to

be consequential. *Material witness* is, in effect, a Möbius-like concept that continually twists between divulging 'evidence of the event' and exposing the 'event of evidence'.[3]

This notion of materials as bearing witness to the events that shape the materials' existence is a productive point of departure. As an example of 'material witness' Schuppli highlights the discovery of radioactive contamination that came from Japan's Fukushima Daiichi nuclear disaster on the shores of Canada five years later. The radioactive signature, which is unique to the accident, made clear the source of the contamination. Taking Schuppli's example as a provocation, we have begun thinking through and speculatively tracing the journeys and stories contained within layers of graphite stored in Bradwell A.

The irradiated graphite in Bradwell A can be used as an anchor and conceptual device to propose an 'interscalar' approach to analysis. In this context, the graphite bears the evidence of the event of nuclear power production in Essex as well as the technologies and materials that made Bradwell A possible. The graphite also enables us to think through this process, to consider the varied and simultaneous timescales and geographic locations at play, as well as their geopolitical implications on this stretch of Essex's coast. For Gabrielle Hecht, contemplating the notion of a specifically African Anthropocene, interscalar vehicles are 'objects and modes of analysis that permit scholars and their subjects to move simultaneously through deep time and human time, through geological space and political space'.[4] The notion of the 'interscalar vehicle' permits us to think about the Estuary and its relations, traversing large swathes of the Earth, while maintaining disparate localities and temporalities within the same conceptual frame. A case in point is the deep time of uranium extracted from countries across the world, such as Australia, which has one of the world's richest deposits, with up to 3,500 tonnes being supplied to the Europe annually, including to the UK.[5] With this in mind, it does not take a leap in imagination to conclude that the mines of Australia provided some uranium for the reactors of Bradwell A, the very same reactors whose radioactive residue still sits with and emanates from the graphite blocks encased on the Blackwater's coast today.

Hecht also proposes the 'interscalar' to consider how scholars (and by extension, artists and curators) might build on the various critiques that have been levelled at the proposition of the Anthropocene as a new epoch, in order to acknowledge and unpack its violently uneven distribution and effects.[6] Hecht argues it is important to understand both that the Anthropocene and its critiques are themselves scalar projects, and that scale can be utilised not just to evoke intimacy and interrelations but also to alienate, discriminate and individuate. With this in mind, Hecht asks how one might use empirical objects as 'interscalar vehicles' in order to connect scales and stories usually kept apart.[7]

Throughout her analysis, Hecht employs uranium-bearing rocks as an interscalar vehicle to engage and incorporate the complexity of the Anthropocene and its politics. Hecht uses these rocks to traverse time and space: from Gabon (in this instance, the location where the uranium was originally mined, and where research has been conducted into the geologic storage of radioactive waste) to France (whose colonial presence and legacy is still felt in the region today). Thus, the interscalar embodies a way to think using matter that bears witness – where time and locality leave their mark – bringing together a rush of apparently disparate but interrelated stories.

The interscalar as a device within art has also been touched upon by Susan Schuppli.[8] She draws on artist and film-maker Harun Farocki's 1969 film *Inextinguishable Fire*, discussing a particular scene where Farocki is seated at a table facing the camera. Farocki reads out testimonies from the Russell Tribunal, describing military violence, chemical warfare and the use of napalm during the Vietnam War.[9] In the film, Farocki aims to present a representation to the viewer that can testify to the extreme heat of a napalm attack, in such a way that does not encourage the viewer to look away or avert their gaze from the screen. Schuppli argues that to do this the artist employs an interscalar device by putting out a lit cigarette on his own forearm in order to convey in some relatable way the intensity of the extreme heat and devastating effects of napalm. Before burning his arm Farocki tells the viewer:

> if we show you pictures of napalm burns, you'll close your eyes. First you'll close your eyes to the pictures. Then you'll close your eyes to the memory. Then you'll close your eyes to the facts. Then you'll close your eyes to the entire context. If we show a person with napalm burns, we will hurt your feelings. If we hurt your feelings you'll feel as if we'd tried napalm out on you, at your expense. We can give you only a hint of an idea of how napalm works.[10]

As Farocki stubs the cigarette out on his arm, a voiceover explains to the viewer that 'a cigarette burns at 400°C. Napalm burns at 3000°C.' As one sees the cigarette hit and burn the flesh of Farocki's arm, the viewer is confronted by the almost eight-fold increase of heat one would have to endure if subjected to napalm. In this moment, the viewer experiences an interscalar shift that propels them to consider the overwhelming ordeal and incredible suffering of a napalm attack.

Schuppli articulates how art can bridge the gap between seemingly incommensurable realities such as between the temperature of napalm and the burning embers of a cigarette, and between chemical weapons and their ethical, moral and legal implications on far-flung geographical locations. Likewise between a radioactive rock from one continent and its transformation into fuel and use in another continent, with all the political, ethical, geological and environmental implications this entails.[11] The interscalar embraces complexity and contradiction. Incommensurate realities are held within the same conceptual frame, whether this is experiential (heat) or geographical (disparate locations geopolitically implicated). In both of the aforementioned instances the objects in question are stand-ins, ways to articulate entangled and complex relations.

In 2002 the decommissioning process began at Bradwell A, and in 2018 the power station entered an eighty-year 'care and maintenance' phase. During this period, an aluminium weather envelope encases and seals the exterior of the site's two reactor buildings until the radioactivity of the infrastructure is sufficiently decayed, at which point the site can be cleared. The graphite sits within the reactor building's aluminium jacket silently emanating the radioactive residues from the uranium rods it housed during Bradwell A's production of nuclear-powered electricity. The graphite used in Bradwell, like other UK Magnox reactors, is a synthetic graphite called Pile Grade A (PGA). PGA was developed in 1950 and is a coarse-grained, impregnated graphite originally manufactured by British Acheson Electrodes Limited and then by Anglo-Great Lakes Limited.[12] The raw materials are filler coke, binder and impregnant. The filler material would have come from petroleum coke from Shell Oil since this had a high degree of crystallinity and purity; however, there may have been some variation in coke due to the prevailing situation in the oil industry. The binder was acquired from North Thames Gas Board and was a 'low ash' pitch manufactured from Ford's coal tar. The impregnant was from a different source, thought to be the Shell Chemical Corporation as this was probably the cheapest suitable impregnant at the time. This demonstrates how it is not only uranium that implicates Bradwell within the geopolitics of industry; if this analysis is applied to other materials and processes within the construction of the nuclear industry's infrastructure, from concrete to glass, links to the extraction and exploitation of places beyond the estuary come into focus.

While it will be at least another 63 years before the graphite is uncoupled from the architecture of the reactor, the depleted uranium rods have already been transported to Sellafield, in Cumbria, in purpose-built storage casks along with other high-level waste. Once at Sellafield, the rods are vitrified in glass to improve stability. The graphite bears witness not only to the neighbouring radioactive rods, but also to the broader infrastructures of nuclear power production, including the mines from which the uranium was extracted. Throughout the next 63 years, the Blackwater Estuary is set to change irrevocably as a result of the impact of climate change and also, should the proposed plans come to fruition, a new nuclear power station. How might one consider the radiological events the graphite has witnessed whilst within the reactor? How might one envision the changes set to occur around the reactor buildings in the years to come? These events comprise an integral part of the UK's nuclear power production, implicating human and non-human others, both within the region and beyond. Artworks that demonstrate the ways contemporary art practice can be rich, complex and inter-disciplinary, developing interscalar approaches, can help answer these questions. In sharing selected examples we seek to demonstrate how such a methodology used within contemporary art can point back and connect to the material culture and specific context of the Estuary. Objects such as the graphite within the reactor buildings are elements of the Estuary's material culture, in a way that is inextricably linked to the landscape while being inaccessible and dangerous to the very surroundings in which it sits.

Artists use various approaches to explore protracted stretches of time, articulate ideas and develop new forms of production that make tangible the scales that operate well beyond the parameters of human life. The place-specific artwork *Temporary Index*, by artists Thomson & Craighead, takes the form of a series of nuclear site markers proposed for nuclear sites and waste storage facilities across the world; these totems signpost to places such as underground disposal facilities while simultaneously counting down the length of time in seconds until the waste in question will become safe for humans (Figure 14.1). The work can be exhibited as a series of counters for multiple sites or as stand-alone totems pointing to nearby radioactive locations counting down second by second the slow half-life decay of the radioactive isotopes they represent.

As part of this ongoing series, Thomson & Craighead were commissioned by Ele Carpenter in partnership with Arts Catalyst to make a physical counter for the Nucleus Archive in Wick, Scotland. The focus of the artwork is Dounreay, situated around 30 miles from the Nucleus Archive, where a counter will tick for approximately 312 years – the length of time the radioactive waste must be stored and isolated from the

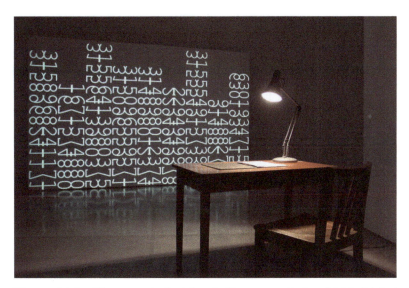

Figure 14.1 Thomson & Craighead, *Temporary Index*, 2016. Digital projection, live information. Image provided courtesy of the artists.

biosphere. This artwork demonstrates how humans measure time through both linguistic and pictorial language, raising pertinent questions about the longevity and effectiveness of human forms of communication, one straightforward but perplexing question being how one might even begin the process of communicating effectively over millennia. Through this process the work seeks to highlight the considerable lengths of time radioactive waste traverses as well as the inter-generational project that confronts humans in terms of its safe storage.[13] For example, it will be at least until the end of the century before the area on the estuary around Bradwell A is opened up to alternative use. Additionally, waste will be stored on site for the foreseeable future if Bradwell B comes to fruition by the late 2030s. When factoring in cooling periods for radioactive waste and the incredibly optimistic projection of a functioning geologic disposal facility in the UK by 2040, waste could be on the Estuary until around 2150, and possibly beyond that. Therefore, if Thomson & Craighead were to produce a counter for the Blackwater Estuary, this could begin at a conservative 130 years, or 4,099,680,000 seconds. If the waste is not removed elsewhere, or if Bradwell B materialises, then this length of time will grow significantly.

The chapel and its predecessor, the Othona fort, however, offer different insights into the chronology of the Estuary, one that looks back rather than forward and raises different questions around time, its measurement and how humans might observe it in different ways. It was in 664, shortly after the chapel's construction, that the founding bishop of the chapel, Cedd, participated in a significant moment in the history of Christianity in Britain: the Synod of Whitby.[14] The Synod established when in the Christian calendar Easter should fall. The impact of preferring the Roman date over the 'Celtic', which caused deep-seated division in the Northumbrian church, highlights the fact that the method of measuring 'time' is often contested and contingent on prevailing ideologies at a given moment.[15]

Examining a specific place through the interscalar – both in terms of material culture and artistic production – it is possible to consider the social, political and geologic implications of different modes of periodisation ascribed to the Estuary: cyclical, recursive and finite. These range from the deep time of uranium deposits and their associated colonial legacies, to the extended timeframes of nuclear energy storage, from radioactive half-lives to the human lifespan of engineers, from the remains of Saxon fish weirs, ongoing fish-breeding and bird migration, to the 'feral' effects of nuclear power production.[16] 'Feral' here describes a situation in which an entity, nurtured and transformed by a human-made infrastructural project, assumes a trajectory beyond human control. Wrapped up in these modes of periodisation are disparate locations, objects, organisms and ecosystems understood across varying scales, which may be complementary or inimical to one another. This reminds us that the movement through scales that the interscalar may facilitate within artistic, curatorial and scholarly work is not necessarily applicable to the specificities of those that inhabit or are implicated within a particular context. The movement through scales should not be fetishised as a frictionless endeavour. The abrasive consequences of these shifts should be examined and understood both in theory and practice, with consideration given to how such movements might not even be possible or desirable; uranium-bearing rocks might allow one to think through time and space, but this should not discount the trauma and damage wrought by the rocks' removal.

The Blackwater Estuary is characterised by saltmarshes and low-lying reclaimed land and is therefore one of the areas that will be impacted by rising sea levels as a result of climate change.[17] This is one of the reasons why the proposed new development of Bradwell B will situate its reactor buildings on islands elevated several metres above the ground. Climate Central, an independent organisation of leading scientists and journalists, predict that by 2050 much of the world's current coastline will be underwater or see increased instances of flooding.[18] This will create new coastal cartographies along the way. When coupled with further inter-generational problems such as nuclear waste storage, the graphite blocks are set to experience two Anthropocenic conflicts, where humans vacillate between waste storage solutions and mitigating risk against rising sea levels. While the graphite blocks at Bradwell A remain enclosed within their aluminium jackets, the estuary outside will face a multitude of changes which will have significant consequences. Such consequences will have lasting effects across deep time, in ways that humans find difficult to measure or easily understand. Many characteristics of nuclear superstructure and management are seemingly unremarkable, like the movement of waste from nuclear site to nuclear site or the passive observation of a decommissioned power station's buildings until they can be dismantled safely. This is the everyday reality of nuclear landscapes that have not succumbed to spectacular disaster. How can contemporary art and curatorial practice make tangible the everyday 'slow violence' of 'nuclearity' characterised by the decommissioning process of a power station, or the labour practices of uranium extraction and other forms of nuclear activity without explicit reference to the spectacular violence of events like Hiroshima, Chernobyl or Fukushima?[19]

Care and maintenance

Fragmented bathymetry surveys, speculative marine archaeology and the unexpected retrieval of objects from the early Holocene period show how the Essex coast 10,000 years ago would be unrecognisable to us today.[20] Large mammalian remains, bone tools and fossilised vegetation dragged into the present by North Sea fishing trawlers provide evidence not only of historic human habitation on Doggerland – a tidal landmass connecting what is currently the UK and Netherlands – but a reminder of low countries' vulnerability to rising sea levels. The coverage and quality of Essex saltmarshes and Bradwell Shell Bank has been declining due to development and an increase in the frequency of storms in recent years with 1,000ha of saltmarsh lost over a 25-year period. The remarkably changeable configuration and composition of the estuarine landscape provides a rich context to consider the impacts that ongoing – and increasingly unpredictable – sea levels and weather have on the often contested interests and relations of human and non-humans. The chapel no longer sits on a peninsula flanked by the sea.[21] Instead of red hills, marsh and grazing sheep, a panorama of alfalfa, winter wheat, yellow oilseed rape and sugar beet fields stretches out, accompanied by the occasional dull thud of munitions testing on Foulness Island some 15 miles away as the crow flies. Industrial production has transformed local populations and labour relations. Looking east from the sea wall, it is possible to see container ships, cruise liners, fishing trawlers and the 48 turbines of Gunfleet Sands offshore wind farm, around 4 miles from Clacton-on-Sea. Turning 180 degrees to face west, North Sea to your back, the aluminium-clad reactors of Bradwell A loom on the horizon. The growth of nuclear energy can be understood as intimately connected with modernist ideas of progress. Resource-thirsty infrastructures and energy can neither be uncoupled from the current climate crisis nor historically and materially isolated from the growth of capitalist modes of production and market-driven economic policy.[22]

The term 'care and maintenance' is a nuclear industry-specific term, to describe the interim period after both of Bradwell A's reactor buildings have been defuelled, decommissioned and covered in weatherproof cladding to create 'safestores' – with all intermediate-level waste packaged for storage on site – and before the remaining structure is dismantled. 'Care and maintenance' serves to foreground the constant attention and monitoring nuclear sites require even in this 'dormant' phase. If Bradwell B comes to fruition, the Blackwater Estuary will be legally, ethically and materially bound to host the nuclear industrial complex in perpetuity, along with the ongoing care and maintenance this entails across future generations. The anthropologist Joseph Masco tells us that 'the bomb is now a multigenerational, national-cultural, economic and environmental mutation, one that has already colonized a deep future',[23] and much the same might be said about nuclear power production. This sentiment is reiterated by Maria Puig de la Bellacasa, who reminds us that to *care* for something is inevitably to create relations.[24] The ongoing care and sustained maintenance of nuclear power and its radioactive residues will need to be maintained for millennia, requiring a present-future-oriented perspective to the relations this creates and how those will change.[25]

While over 60,000 tons of spent nuclear fuel are stored across sites in Europe,[26] these storage sites are not long-term repositories. Unlike the world's first permanent geologic storage facility, Onkalo in Finland, or the proposed and much-contested Yucca Mountain site in the United States, these are merely halfway houses, places where the waste is waiting for its final storage location.[27] Sellafield holds one of the largest inventories of untreated waste, including material from Bradwell A and a stockpile of 140 tonnes of plutonium. Sellafield is also home to the UK's only storage pond for Advanced Gas-cooled Reactor (AGR) fuel, Magnox Swarf Storage

Silos and First-Generation Magnox Storage Pond; now decommissioned, these infrastructures require constant monitoring and security.

Spruce Time, a living artwork by artists Goldin+Senneby, selected from a proposal for a public hospital commission in Malmö, Sweden, is one way of considering the relations of care and maintenance (Figure 14.2). Goldin+Senneby use grafting to create a clone of what is purportedly the oldest tree in the world – 'Old Tjikko', a windswept spruce on Fulufjäll mountain in Dalarna, central Sweden, 400 miles north of Malmö. Researchers have been able to date elements of the tree's root system to at least 9,550 years ago, suggesting it was a sapling during the Ice Age at the start of the Holocene period, 11,700 years ago. The artwork began as soon as the cloning process started in 2019, and from 2025 staff, patients and visitors to the hospital will be able to see the tree inside a custom 'care building', described by Goldin+Senneby as 'a computer-controlled greenhouse attached to the hospital's existing cooling system, where the needs of the tree determine the climate. The greenhouse becomes a customized miniature hospital responsible for the care of this single tree.'[28]

The work is interscalar, conceptually and materially, cutting across geological epochs and the human time of people living in Sweden, to explore varied forms of dependency: technological, economic, human health and planetary. The artwork functions as a time machine drawing on Old Tjikko and the young clone as witness(es) to ongoing and extreme

Figure 14.2 Goldin+Senneby, *Spruce Time*. Henrik Lund Jørgensen/Region Skåne.

climatic changes through which humans and non-humans experience epidemics, starvation and global climate crises. The more extreme global warming becomes, the more the location of the tree in Malmö will contrast with the climate the spruce has experienced on Fulufjäll mountain.

The ambition for *Spruce Time* is that the tree should live for as long as possible – potentially for ever. *Spruce Time* succeeds in going beyond the diagnostic; rather than operating as a diagram or metaphor, the artwork creates new relations that will inevitably shift over time, whether through climatic, social or political pressure and change. Making the world's oldest tree dependent on a hospital and making the hospital's air-conditioning infrastructure part of the tree's ecology as an artwork raise interesting and necessary points of friction. The act of relocating the sapling from an environment that has sustained the tree from which it originated for millennia to a site that requires constant human and technological intervention to ensure the tree's survival troubles several concerns that resonate with the future-oriented nature of heritage practices.[29] In the case of *Spruce Time* these include: the uneven economic stability to sustain a public healthcare system and, in this instance, the infrastructure of the tree, over a prolonged period; the varied forms of human labour and social reproduction necessarily involved in care; and the normative violence of healthcare through the definition of what is biologically healthy, sick or desirable.

Ele Carpenter suggests there has been a shift of responsibility for nuclear storage onto the public sector, and that this in turn would suggest a concern for public health.[30] We can see how works like *Spruce Time* can raise questions about the conditions necessary for ongoing care and maintenance, what such a continuing process might look like and who and what will inherit this responsibility and in what circumstances. Any multigenerational project, whether that is the indefinite care and maintenance of a tree or the safe storage of nuclear waste over millennia, needs mitigating measures in place to ensure such tending is possible. How does one decide on and implement such long-term structures of care and maintenance? How is this continuing process governed in order to safeguard against decisions detrimental to the conditions necessary for commitments extending seemingly infinitely into the future? Answering questions like these becomes increasingly difficult when projecting tens of thousands of years into the future. Inevitable gaps in human understanding of events and activities just a few thousand years in the past only reiterate this.

The Dengie Peninsula is home to rare native oysters and oyster beds that host life support systems for a wide range of diverse species and has been awarded multiple national and international designations: a Marine Conservation Zone, Site of Special and Scientific Interest (SSSI) in 1993,

Recognised Wetland of International Importance (Ramsar) in 1992, Special Protection Area for vulnerable and migratory birds (SPA) and Special Area of Conservation (SAC). These legal designations, highlighting biological diversity and scientific significance, should, in theory, offer some protection during proposed developments. Essex Wildlife Trust volunteers and conservationists have been engaged in maintaining and restoring Essex saltmarsh since the late 1970s to build and preserve critical ecosystems. These include carbon sequestration, bird breeding grounds and fish nurseries of bass and gobies.[31] The open landscape of reedbeds, coastal farmland, shale banks, saltmarsh and mudflats sustains important and much-loved bird species, including waders and wildfowl. Golden and grey plovers, yellow wagtails, curlews, wigeon, knots and bar-tailed godwits are joined in autumn by raucous dark-bellied brent geese. These iconic birds, anticipated by local residents, overwinter in the fields and mudflats, eating eelgrass and winter cereals after their long annual migration across northern Europe from their breeding grounds in Siberia. During winter, it is also possible to glimpse raptors such as hen and marsh harriers, and short-eared owls quartering the grass. Corn bunting can be heard in the wheat and barley, while warblers and shy bearded tits inhabit the borrow dyke. Peregrine falcons nest in boxes atop Bradwell A's cladding, having previously made the reactors their home when the power station still hummed day and night.[32] Water and land are contested from all sides. Both the RSPB and Essex Wildlife Trust issued statements in 2020, in response to the Bradwell B consultation, expressing serious concerns that both migrating and non-migrating species, including shore-nesting birds such as little terns and ringed plovers, will be threatened by the construction and collateral impact of the proposed new nuclear development.[33] What is at stake here goes beyond the immediate threat of large-scale industrial construction. The proposition of a new nuclear plant throws into relief very concrete and unevenly distributed pressures, including energy consumption, access to resources and freedom of movement, severe weather and food sovereignty. These frictions are felt on local, bioregional and intimately personal scales, as well as across collective and social, national-governmental and planetary registers.

In addition to non-human biodiversity and resilience, saltmarshes provide 'soft' solutions to ecosystem preservation, reducing flood risk and the effects of storm surges.[34] Thames lighters have been sunk offshore in an attempt to maintain the saltmarsh, as it is squeezed between the sea wall and the eroding force of the tide. The spectre of Doggerland and the relatively recent storms and severe flooding of 1953 are testament to an unavoidable managed retreat from the sea that will be necessary in coming years.[35] Retreat is not without conflict; South Essex and Suffolk

Shoreline Management is tasked with deciding which areas of the coast, including farmland and even residential areas, may undergo a controlled breach, by opening the sea wall to relieve pressure and reduce the flood risk elsewhere.[36] It is not unusual for areas of land to be compulsorily purchased or, in the case of Foulness Island, annexed by the military. Military research and projects deemed of 'national importance' are prioritised over civic and local authority planning.[37] Bradwell A and the proposal for Bradwell B further complicates this, since the entire site must be protected against sea level rise during all the phases of its operating life and ultimate decommission. The proposal to provide long-term nuclear waste storage at Bradwell requires mitigation against the same threats, stretching even further into the future, and yet controlled retreat inland is a common understanding of midterm shoreline management. On a coast along which sea levels are rising, and which from time to time experiences destructive winds and tides, protection by reinforcing walls is only afforded to urban settlements and valuable or problematic structures, such as the now-redundant Bradwell A power station.

Over the last two decades the language of nuclear industry management has shifted to focus on 'conservation'. Ele Carpenter describes how the nuclear industry's responsibility towards its products is shifting from a 'centralised' state entwined with military interests to private 'decentralised' energy companies and, finally, to a 'distributed public' responsible for waste monitoring.[38] As such, the intergenerational challenge of energy dependency and waste disposal could be considered in terms of an uneasy heritage. This toxic inheritance, however, is very different from what might be more orthodoxly considered 'heritage'. In the context of the Blackwater Estuary, heritage is a term that brings to mind the Grade I listed chapel of St Peter-on-the-Wall. The chapel is part of an inheritance of both the Christian conversion of the seventh-century East Saxon population and subsequent millennia of changing land use, property relations, governance, religion and industry.[39] In more recent history the Blackwater Estuary provided a frontier for the expansion of the nuclear energy industry, as a preferred location for the development of Bradwell A.[40] However when we consider the 100,000 years required to store high-level nuclear waste until it is safe, heritage takes on an uncertain and obligatory context – spatially, temporally and ethically. Issues of dependency, climate change, communication, significant threat to, and preservation of, life collide with the idea of heritage as something chosen, celebrated and gifted to future generations. The latter is often bound up with tourism, ideas of national identity, memory and a type of heritage primarily about preventing loss, as though the past is 'gone' and has no active relation or agency in the present or future.[41] Beth Whalley's chapter in this volume articulates the issues of considering heritage only in terms of the commemorative and the very real impact this has on local politics and identity formation in the present. Currently UNESCO defines heritage as human legacy from the past and what we pass on to future generations.[42] Though this importantly includes sites considered 'dark' heritage, such as the Bikini Atoll nuclear test site and the Hiroshima Peace Memorial (Genbaku Dome), the definition fails to acknowledge the lasting implications of waste as part of the nuclear legacy and very much something we live with now and that future generations will live with, whether they want to or not.[43] Pétursdóttir proposes the terms 'unruly' and 'sticky' heritage to articulate the consequences of living with material legacies that are persistent, leaky and hard to contain both conceptually and physically.[44]

Artist Inas Halabi's single-screen video WE HAVE ALWAYS KNOWN THE WIND'S DIRECTION is a two-pronged inquiry, in which the deadly and invisible isotope Caesium 137 is engaged as a vehicle to simultaneously probe the purported illegal burial of nuclear waste on sites in the south of the West Bank and to render visible the systemic and uneven networks of power and control in the region (Figure 14.3).[45] Combining fragmented footage of the West Bank with performed conversation and interviews

Figure 14.3 Inas Halabi, WE HAVE ALWAYS KNOWN THE WIND'S DIRECTION, 2019–2020. Image provided courtesy of the artist.

with collaborator and physicist Khalil Thabayneh, the film engages nuclear aesthetics by drawing on both scientific discourse and lived, situated knowledge. As an isotope, Caesium 137 represents an example of 'material witness', bringing us closer to what Schuppli describes as not only the 'evidence of event' but also 'the event of evidence'.[46] Within the film Thabayneh and Halabi discuss using colour gel filters to indicate the level of Caesium or Strontium that Thabayneh and his team have measured in soil samples at different locations. The narrative is recounted as a dream by Thabayneh, recalling a village whose inhabitants knew that radiation was dangerous because, while they could not see it, they understood the cumulative effects. In order to 'see' the danger the villagers found a way to dye Caesium 137 and Strontium. The result is a landscape saturated in warm hues of orange to red, the narrator of the dream lamenting that this only serves to remind the villagers that they are going to die. In this way, Halabi uses film-making to account for the unfilmable. Caesium 137 and Strontium for Halabi allow the slowness of geological time to rupture into the present with a disorienting effect, causing us to speculate on uncertain futures. The result is much like Jeffrey Jerome Cohen's observation of stone which, 'conveying within its materiality the thickness of time ... triggers the vertigo of inhuman scale'.[47] *We Have Always Known the Wind's Direction* engages with the sticky heritage of nuclear waste and not only articulates a specific historic and ongoing violence but also challenges the notion of 'contemporary art' as only concerning the here and now to create a present-future temporal position from which individual and collective action can be realised.

Located specifically in Essex, *How to Make a Bomb* is a durational project by artist Gabriella Hirst centred around the propagation and distribution of a nearly extinct rose, *Rosa floribunda* 'Atom Bomb', or the 'Atom Bomb' rose, created and registered by rose breeder Reimer Kordes in 1953 (Figure 14.4).[48] Working with the Old Waterworks in Southend-on-Sea, Hirst plans to bring the plant back into circulation within UK gardens and places associated with the legacy of the nuclear military–industrial complex.[49] Katherine Lawless describes how the 'banality' of processes like nuclear storage, disposal and clean-up are eclipsed by the spectacle of atrocity, while narratives of technological progress are often deployed to mask the ecologically unequal exchange that takes place through the extraction, labour and production of technologies – from which 'clean/green' nuclear is not exempt.[50] Spills, meltdowns and nuclear tests are visual representations of nuclear heritage, which, however, fail to acknowledge the slow violence of contemporary energy regimes – including climate change and the new global enclosures – which

Figure 14.4 *Rosa floribunda* 'Atom Bomb' displayed in Gabriella Hirst's *An English Garden*, 2021. Anna Lukala.

are persistent and not recognised enough within the legacy of nuclear power. *How to Make a Bomb* seeks to make visible these persistent nuclear and military legacies as well as challenging colonial narratives.

The Old Waterworks is near the former Atomic Weapons Research Establishment (AWRE) on Foulness Island, an important part of Britain's nuclear legacy. It was here, in a building called 'X6', that the assembly of the high explosive elements of Britain's first atomic bomb took place, after which the bomb travelled to Australia to be detonated on the Monte Bello Islands in 1952 in a process named *Operation Hurricane*.[51] This marked the beginning of a devastating nuclear testing programme on unceded Indigenous lands across Australia at Emu Field and Maralinga from 1953 to 1963. To this day the Maralinga site forms part of the Woomera Prohibited Area (WPA), which is nearly the size of England. There are several Aboriginal peoples whose land the WPA encompasses: the Maralinga Tjarutja; Anangu Pitjantjatjara Yunkunytjatjara; Antakirinja Matu-Yankunytjatjara; Arabana; Gawler Ranges; and Kokatha.

The rose is the protagonist of a larger project where the artist explores the contradictions in the process of gardening: the care, manipulation and violence inherent within the relationship between plants and humans. The slow process of tending to the roses creates a space for those involved to reflect on historical and ongoing nuclear colonialism, as well as the colonial history of botany and the naming of plants.[52] The gradual redistribution of the 'Atom Bomb' roses and the investment in this are a sobering way to be mindful of the devastating effects of Essex's and, by extension, Britain's nuclear legacy, reclaiming agency against Cold War revivalist fearmongering.[53]

With the right conditions the 'Atom Bomb' rose can live for many years. The ability to meet these conditions highlights challenges for individual carers or host institutions to keep the roses alive. The 'Atom Bomb' rose, redeployed by Hirst in this way as an artwork, can be understood as an interscalar vehicle to conceptually explore global power structures enacted through horticulture, the deep time of the nuclear and the impact of nuclear colonialism.[54]

There have been moments of concern for the land, and Bradwell's involvement with Britain's nuclear legacy. During the 1980s, successful protests prevented proposals for nuclear waste to be stored just below ground level on-site at Bradwell from being realised.[55] However, these historic objections seem to have not been taken up again with regard to the current storage arrangement adjacent to Bradwell A in quite the same way. Not only is the Blackwater Estuary an actual repository for nuclear waste, but all aspects of the nuclear fuel cycle in both the military and civil contexts are implicated within the extraction of matter globally. Alf Hornborg argues that modern and nascent technology is built on the appropriation of labour and land from the peripheries.[56] Bradwell is no different – from the global extraction of uranium in Australia, Canada, the Democratic Republic of the Congo and Namibia, which supply uranium to UK power stations, to the storage of Intermediate Level Radioactive Waste from Dungeness and Sizewell and the 2016 tender for Chinese corporate investment by China General Nuclear (CGN – formerly China Guangdong Nuclear Power Group) in partnership with Électricité de France (EdF), to enter the consultation phase of Bradwell B.[57] The UK's military and civil nuclear industrial complex has effected vast changes to other places and produced considerable waste in the form of mine tailings and other by-products, while impacting people, their communities and the environment. While the effects of the global nuclear industry are seemingly totalising and homogenising, it is crucial to recognise that at the many varied stages of the nuclear cycle these are not evenly distributed. They manifest differently in distinct regions, economies and populations. In order to critique this uneven distribution and slow violence in all its temporal complexity, it is necessary to take up the histories and conditions that generated them, both the visible and invisible. Halabi's work offers an insight into how some artists work against what academic Kathryn Yusoff describes as the universalising effect of Anthropocene discourse.[58]

This universalism obfuscates how exclusionary practices of colonial and capitalist expansion and accumulation are fundamental to current energy and environmental crises and therefore also need to be considered in relation to heritage and the planning and implementation of future governance and infrastructure.[59]

Returning to the Blackwater Estuary, it is possible to see the legacy of collective care and political action engendered by the East London labour movement and Christian socialism in the ongoing work of the Othona Community. The Othona Community, founded by Norman Motley in 1946 as an experiment in 'Christian community', originated in the transformative politics that emerged in response to the violence and exploitation of war and its exacerbating effects of social and ideological divides.[60] After organising 'Answer Back' groups as a chaplain during the war, Motley saw Othona as an open place where discussion about peace and reconciliation was encouraged in order to question how to bring about positive change in the post-war era. Othona was preceded by several communitarian and 'back to the land' movements, in Essex as well as more broadly within the UK, that shared sentiments with the Diggers and Levellers of the seventeenth century.[61] Some of the settlements of the twentieth century, including Frating Hall Farm, near Colchester, provided agricultural and construction training for conscientious objectors and pacifists.[62] Others sought to find new ways of living altogether, such as the communist Purleigh Brotherhood Colony, which lasted from 1896 to 1903 and which, despite being a short-lived experiment, inspired subsequent socialist, feminist and radical publishing movements.

Today the community at Othona is varied and open. The community are regular users and informal custodians of the chapel of St Peter-on-the-Wall, the core of Othona's shared Christian heritage with the Blackwater Estuary. A small team of permanent staff are joined by international volunteers on fixed-term placements, local community members and volunteers who are involved in regular activity and development. Over the decades since Motley's first gatherings, a distributed community of visitors has grown, who return when they can – including engineers, farmers, builders, scientists, musicians, healthcare workers, social workers, authors, conservators, clergy, archaeologists and teachers. As well as providing a space for quiet reflection, study and worship, Othona hosts a regular public programme of talks, work weekends and workshops. This activity responds to both the immediate environment, equality and social and ecological reconciliation, as well as shaping Othona's continued place and ongoing work in a shifting landscape.

Shielded from North Sea winds by a small wooded perimeter, the architecture of the community is low-lying and unassuming. Bordering the legal boundary of the proposed development site for Bradwell B, the off-grid open community produces much of its own electricity and takes care of its own waste through a three-tiered reedbed sewage system and in many ways provides a stark contrast to its industrial neighbour. Bradwell A has become as much part of Othona's past and future heritage as the saltmarshes, chapel, resident badgers and sea wall. The community includes both active and retired nuclear industry workers as well as those involved in both protests against Nirex, a UK body set up to examine safe, economic and environmental aspects of nuclear waste storage, which proposed a low-level waste repository at Bradwell in the 1980s and those involved in campaigns against the proposal for the new nuclear programme and waste storage in the present day. Othona publicly responded to the consultation for Bradwell B, opposing the impact of the initial construction and long-term operations on the environment, the local population and resources of Bradwell on Sea village, and their own continued existence in the Estuary. Whether a new nuclear power programme goes ahead in the near future or not, Othona is already entangled with the legacy of the nuclear industrial complex. In writing about the legacy of collective resistance and community in Essex, Othona could be mis-portrayed as a nail house, heels dug deep in an eroding place and time. However, there is a refusal to turn inwards to build a microcosm and away from critical issues and conditions, some of which we have highlighted in this chapter. Othona's endurance through previous attempts at organised and experimental communities perhaps lies in its active and continued openness in the face of economic and environmental pressures, its model of a distributed rather than closed community and an understanding that 'faith in action' requires imagination, hope and experimentation in equal measure. As a distributed 'community', Othona is both rooted and concretely present in the Blackwater Estuary, but importantly constitutes a geographically dispersed intergenerational group of people.[63] This 'model' alongside the community's public programme resonates with the interscalar analysis of artworks discussed earlier in this chapter. Like Old Tjikko of *Spruce Time*, Othona highlights the potential to reimagine and enact new forms of care, reconciliation, 'useful work' and 'living with' in the face of uncertain futures.

Conclusion

Curatorial and artistic practices are generative ways to begin thinking with multiple scales and temporalities, particularly for place-specific contexts. We argue that the art projects interwoven throughout this chapter operate as interscalar devices, as ways to situate a project spatially and temporally while gesturing towards that which extends far beyond the estuary's shores. This provides a sense, albeit speculatively, of how an art project around the Blackwater Estuary may develop, demonstrating the productive role art can play in pulling together and making connections from things that are perceived or understood to be separate.

Throughout this chapter we have attempted to articulate how art projects can embody interscalar sensibilities, enabling ways to hold complex and incommensurate realities within the same conceptual frame, from varying temporalities to disparate geographies. In Thomson & Craighead's *Temporary Index* or Goldin+Senneby's *Spruce Time* the viewer journeys beyond human timescales. In *We Have Always Known the Wind's Direction*, Halabi employs Caesium 137 to bear witness to purported illicit nuclear waste dumping and the uneven distribution of power and control around the West Bank. Similarly, Harun Farocki's *Inextinguishable Fire* gives the viewer a glimpse, albeit an inevitably inadequate glimpse, into the disturbing intensity of a napalm attack and broader geopolitical violence.

Other geopolitical tensions can be seen in Hirst's *How to Make a Bomb*, which confronts us with the nuclear colonial legacy of Essex, collapsing the geographical locations between Foulness Island and the Monte Bello Islands, Emu Field and Maralinga, where Britain tested its nuclear devices on Indigenous lands. Bringing our attention back to Essex, Hirst's *How to Make a Bomb* project demonstrates a way art can chart the county's nuclear history and the development of Britain's nuclear weapons programme in particular.

We have tried to give a sense of how contemporary art can ask questions about particular contexts, embracing the messiness and leakiness of any given landscape and how its interrelationships extend beyond the arbitrary boundaries one might impose. This opens up more questions than answers. How might a research-led project along these lines operate in the Blackwater Estuary? How might the graphite sitting in Bradwell A's aluminium-clad reactors bear witness to the changes that the Estuary faces? What interscalar stories could it tell us? We have embarked on our own project in relation to the estuary, which is an ongoing process involving regular visits, extensive research and conversations. As a part of this we are asking ourselves how non-human actors that inhabit the Estuary could contribute to these conversations. We suggest that the examples we have brought forward go some way to doing this. These are not necessarily our concluding remarks, then, but rather a provocation, a point of departure searching for the possibilities that art opens up, demonstrating its capacity not merely to illustrate current affairs one dimensionally but also to become a generative and imaginative space that provides new insights into a particular context and its complex local and planetary entanglements, a space that embraces an ecology of knowledges and the different ways of understanding the world that this alludes to.

Notes

1. Tsing 2015, 37.
2. The World Nuclear Waste Report, 2019. https://worldnuclearwastereport.org/ [accessed 26 October 2020].
3. Schuppli 2020, 3.
4. Hecht 2018, 135.
5. On 'deep time' see Ialenti 2020.
6. On the critiques of the Anthropocene see Haraway 2015 and Moore 2016.
7. Hecht 2018, 110–15.
8. Schuppli 2020, 165.
9. The International War Crimes Tribunal for Vietnam was convened by philosopher and anti-war activist Bertrand Russell and aimed to inform public opinion and arouse opposition to the war. For a recent overview see Krever 2017.
10. Farocki 1969.
11. Schuppli 2020, 165.
12. Dr Graham Hall, University of Manchester, personal communication.
13. Carpenter 2020.
14. Two recent analyses of the Synod of Whitby and its impact are Stancliffe 2017 and Dailey 2015.
15. On Cedd's mission see Yorke, in this volume.
16. On the fish weirs see Andrews and Rippon, in this volume.
17. On the inning of marshes around Bradwell see Bruce and Thornton, in this volume.
18. https://www.climatecentral.org/ [accessed 30 November 2020].
19. 'Slow violence' is a term used by Rob Nixon to describe the deferred, gradual and attritional, disproportionate impact of industrial capitalist production on both the environment and poor, disempowered and often involuntarily displaced people, caused by events such as climate change, toxic drift and oil spills: Nixon 2013, 2. We include the slow violence of the processes that bookend the nuclear cycle which are often eclipsed by spectacular events. According to Hecht, 'nuclearity … is a contested technopolitical category. It shifts in time and space. Its parameters depend on history and geography, science and technology, bodies and politics, radiation and race, states and capitalism.' Hecht 2012, 14.
20. For an overview of the archaeology of the Essex coast see Murphy and Brown 1996 and Murphy et al. 2012.
21. For the original landscape setting of St Peter's see Rippon, in this volume.
22. See Darley, in this volume, for the initial choice of Bradwell as a nuclear site and the manner in which the requirements of nuclear power disrupted the existing industrial map.
23. Masco 2006, 38.
24. Puig de la Bellacasa 2012, 198.
25. For further context see the government report on the Nuclear Decommissioning Authority's management of the Magnox contract: https://committees.parliament.uk/publications/3703/documents/36067/default/; and the Department of Energy & Climate Change's Geologic Disposal Facility White Paper: https://assets.publishing.service.gov.uk/government/uploads/system/uploads/attachment_data/file/332890/GDF_White_Paper_FINAL.pdf [accessed 30 January 2022].
26. The World Nuclear Waste Report 2019: https://worldnuclearwastereport.org/ [accessed 25 November 2020].

27 On Onkalo see Foley 2021; on Yucca Mountain see Macfarlane and Ewing 2006.
28 Goldin+Senneby *Spruce Time* project proposal, 2019. www.goldinsenneby.com/sprucetime.pdf [accessed 20 November 2020].
29 On the challenges in conventional thinking on conservation to reconsider the capacity to care, restore, conserve in uncertain and potentially distant futures see DeSilvey 2017.
30 Carpenter 2016, 3.
31 Cooper et al. 2001, 31–40.
32 Bradwell was a favourite haunt of Essex nature writer J. A. Baker, whose most famous book, first published in 1967, recounted his obsessive tracking of peregrine falcons in and around the Blackwater Estuary. In his afterword to the 50th anniversary edition of the book, Robert Macfarlane comments on the nuclear threat that seems to pervade the text and mentions the peregrines nesting on the power station in 2014. Macfarlane 2017, 201, 207.
33 RSPB, https://www.rspb.org.uk/our-work/casework/cases/Bradwell-B/ [accessed 23 September 2021]. Essex Wildlife Trust, https://www.essexwt.org.uk/protecting-wildlife/policies-position-statements/bradwell-b [accessed 23 June 2021].
34 Cooper et al. 2001; see also https://www.essexwt.org.uk/news/restoring-saltmarshes-blackwater-estuary [accessed 26 April 2022].
35 For a detailed history of the 1953 flood in Essex see Grieve 1959.
36 Essex and South Suffolk Shoreline Management Plan 2, 15 October 2010: https://assets.publishing.service.gov.uk/government/uploads/system/uploads/attachment_data/file/289681/gean0310brva-e-e.pdf [accessed 26 April 2022].
37 The Planning Act 2008 (received Royal Assent 26 November 2008) legislation established the legal framework for applying for, examining and determining applications for Nationally Significant Infrastructure Projects.
38 Carpenter 2016, 3.
39 On Cedd's mission see Yorke, in this volume.
40 On the choice of Bradwell for a first-generation nuclear power station see Darley, in this volume.
41 There is rich scholarship across cultural geography, critical heritage and archaeology that articulates the complexity of modern material culture and the management of heritage sites. See, for example: Buchli and Lucas 2001; González-Ruibal 2006; Holtorf and Piccini 2011; McAtackney 2014; DeSilvey 2017.
42 UNESCO currently lists two sites associated with the nuclear industrial complex: Bikini Atoll and the Hiroshima Peace Memorial (Genbaku Dome).
43 For further literature focused on the Hiroshima Peace Memorial see Frost et al. 2019; for the nuclear military context of the Cold War see Hanson 2016; for Bikini Atoll's World Heritage listing see Brown 2013.
44 Olsen and Pétursdóttir 2016, 43.
45 Halabi 2019.
46 Schuppli 2020, 65.
47 Cohen 2015, 78.
48 Hirst and Harper 2020.
49 The Old Waterworks is an artist-led charity of which Warren Harper is the director. It provides studios, facilities and research and development opportunities for artists: https://www.theoldwaterworks.com [accessed 26 April 2022].
50 Lawless 2017, 80.
51 Cocroft and Newsome 2009.
52 On colonial botany see: Schiebinger and Swan 2005; Casid 2004; and Gray and Sheikh 2018.
53 Hirst and Harper 2020.
54 Nuclear colonialism refers to how the entire fuel cycle from uranium mining and refining to nuclear power and weapons development, production and testing, and the subsequent dangers of nuclear waste, disproportionately effects Indigenous peoples and their lands. See Churchill and La Duke 1986; Runyan 2018.
55 'House of Commons – Environment, Food and Rural Affairs – Third Report'. https://publications.parliament.uk/pa/cm200102/cmselect/cmenvfru/407/40703.htm. [accessed 26 January 2022].
56 Hornborg and Martinez-Alier 2016, 328.
57 CGN, http://en.cgnpc.com.cn/encgn/c100080/2016-08/24/content_6bea6747185546458b887848d8c170d7.shtml [accessed 20 November 2021].

58 Yusoff 2018, 53.
59 Yusoff 2018, 53.
60 On Othona and Motley see Worpole, in this volume.
61 On communitarian settlements in Essex see Worpole 2018.
62 On Frating Hall Farm see Worpole 2021.
63 Although the focus of this chapter is primarily located in Essex, Othona is also embedded in West Dorset.

Bibliography

Baker, J. A. 1967. *The Peregrine*. London: Collins.
Brown, S. 2013. 'Poetics and politics: Bikini Atoll and World Heritage listing'. In *Transcending the Culture–Nature Divide in Cultural Heritage*, edited by S. Brockwell, S. O'Connor and D. Byrne. 35–52. Canberra: Australian National University Press.
Buchli, V., and G. Lucas. 2001. 'The absent present: archaeologies of the contemporary past'. In *Archaeologies of the Contemporary Past*, edited by V. Buchli and G. Lucas. 3–18. London: Routledge.
Carpenter, E. 2016. 'The smoke of modernity drifts through the Anthropocene'. In *Power of the Land*, edited by H. Grove-White. Wales: X–10.
Carpenter, E. 2020. *Nuclear Culture & Citizen Participation, Networked and Distributed Art*, Lecture at Arts Catalyst. http://www.modern2020.eu/fileadmin/Final_Conference/Presentations/Day_2/Session_5/3_Ele_Carpenter_Modern2020_2019_FINAL-.pdf [accessed 26 April 2022].
Casid, J. H. 2004. *Sowing Empire: Landscape and colonization*. Minneapolis: University of Minnesota Press.
Churchill, W., and W. LaDuke. 1986. 'Native America: The political economy of radioactive colonialism'. *Insurgent Sociologist* 13(3): 51–78.
Cocroft, W., and S. Newsome. 2009. 'The Atomic Weapons Establishment, Foulness, Essex: Cold War research & development site. Survey report'. Research Department Reports. London: Historic England.
Cohen, J. J. 2015. *Stone: An ecology of the inhuman*. Minneapolis: University of Minnesota Press.
Cooper, N. J., T. Cooper and F. Burd. 2001. '25 years of salt marsh erosion in Essex: implications for coastal defence and nature conservation', *Journal of Coastal Conservation* 7: 31–40.
Dailey, E. T. A. 2015. 'To choose one Easter from three: Oswiu's decision and the Northumbrian synod of AD 644'. *Peritia* 26: 47–64.
DeSilvey, C. 2017. *Curated Decay: Heritage beyond saving*. Minneapolis: University of Minnesota Press.
Essex Wildlife Trust, *Position Statement Bradwell B*: https://www.essexwt.org.uk/protecting-wildlife/policies-position-statements/bradwell-b [accessed 29 September 2021].
Farocki, H. 1969. *Inextinguishable Fire*. Short film.
Foley, T. J. 2021. 'Waiting for waste: nuclear imagination and the politics of distant futures in Finland'. *Energy Research & Social Science* 2: 1–8.
Frost, M. R., D. Schumacher and E. Vickers (eds). 2019. *Remembering Asia's World War Two*. London and New York: Routledge.
Goldin + Senneby, *'Spruce Time' Project Proposal*: www.goldinsenneby.com/sprucetime.pdf [accessed 26 April 2022].
González-Ruibal, A. 2006. 'The past is tomorrow: towards an archaeology of the vanishing present'. *Norwegian Archaeological Review* 39: 110–25.
Gray, R., and S. Sheikh (eds). 2018. 'The wretched Earth: botanical conflicts and artistic interventions'. *Numbers* 32: 151–2.
Grieve, H. E. P. 1959. *The Great Tide: The story of the 1953 flood disaster in Essex*. Chelmsford: Essex County Council.
Halabi, I. 2019. *We Have Always Known the Wind's Direction*. HD film with sound.
Hanson, T. A. 2016. *The Archaeology of the Cold War*. Gainesville, FL: University Press of Florida.
Haraway, D. 2015. 'Anthropocene, Capitalocene, Plantationocene, Chthulucene: making kin'. *Environmental Humanities* 6(1): 159–65.
Hecht, G. 2012. *Being Nuclear: Africans and the global uranium trade*. Johannesburg: Wits University Press.

Hecht, G. 2018. 'Interscalar vehicles for an African Anthropocene: on waste, temporality, and violence', *Cultural Anthropology* 33(1): 109–41.
Hirst, G., and W. Harper. 2020. *An English Garden*. Southend-on-Sea: The Old Waterworks Publishing.
Holtorf, C., and A. Piccini (eds). 2011. *Contemporary Archaeologies: Excavating now*. Frankfurt: Peter Lang.
Hornborg, A., and J. Martinez-Alier (eds). 2016. 'Ecologically unequal exchange and ecological debt', special section of the *Journal of Political Ecology* 23: 328–491.
Ialenti, V. 2020. *Deep Time Reckoning: How future thinking can help Earth now*. Cambridge, MA: The MIT Press.
Krever, T. 2017. 'Remembering the Russell Tribunal'. *London Review of International Law* 5(3): 483–92.
Lawless, K. 2017. 'Mapping the atomic unconscious: postcolonial capital in nuclear glow'. In *Materialism and the Critique of Energy*, edited by B. R. Bellamy and J. Diamanti. 73–94. Chicago, IL: MCM Publishing.
Macfarlane, A., and R. Ewing. 2006. *Uncertainty Underground: Yucca Mountain and the nation's high-level nuclear waste*. Cambridge, MA: The MIT Press.
Macfarlane, R. 2017. 'Afterword'. In *The Peregrine 50th Anniversary Edition*. 193–209. London: Collins.
Masco, J. 2006. *The Nuclear Borderlands*. Princeton, NJ: Princeton University Press.
McAtackney, L. 2014. *An Archaeology of the Troubles: The dark heritage of Long Kesh/Maze prison*. Oxford: Oxford University Press.
Moore, J. W. 2016. *Anthropocene or Capitalocene? Nature, history, and the crisis of capitalism*. Oakland, CA: PM Press.
Motley, N. 1985. *Much Ado about Something: A history of the Othona Community*. Bradwell: The Othona Community.
Murphy, P., and N. Brown. 1996. 'Archaeology of the coastal landscape'. In *The Essex Landscape: In Search of Its History*, edited by L. S. Green. 11–19. Chelmsford: Essex County Council.
Murphy, P., E. Heppell and N. Brown. 2012. 'The archaeology of the Essex coast'. *The Essex Society for Archaeology and History* 3: 141–54.
Nixon, R. 2013. *Slow Violence and Environmentalism of the Poor*. Cambridge, MA: Harvard University Press.
Olsen, B., and Þ. Pétursdóttir. 2016. 'Unruly heritage: tracing legacies in the Anthropocene', *Arkæologisk Forum* 35: 38–45.
Pearson, M., and M. Shanks. 2001. *Theatre/Archaeology*. London and New York: Routledge.
Puig de la Bellacasa, M. 2012. 'Nothing comes without its world: thinking with care'. *The Sociological Review* 60(2): 197–216.
Runyan, A. S. 2018. 'Disposable waste, lands and bodies under Canada's gendered nuclear colonialism'. *International Feminist Journal of Politics* 20(1): 24–38.
Santos, B. de S. 2014. *Epistemologies of the South: Justice against epistemicide*. London and New York: Routledge.
Schiebinger, L., and C. Swan (eds). 2005. *Colonial Botany: Science, commerce, and politics in the early modern world*. Philadelphia, PA: University of Pennsylvania Press.
Schuppli, S. 2020. *Material Witness: Media, forensics, evidence*. Cambridge, MA: The MIT Press.
Stancliffe, C. 2017. 'The Irish tradition in Northumbria after the Synod of Whitby'. In *The Lindisfarne Gospels: New Perspectives*, edited by R. Gameson. 19–42. Leiden: Brill.
Thomson, J., and A. Craighead. n.d. (ongoing). *Temporary Index*.
Tsing, A. L. 2015. *The Mushroom at the End of the World: On the possibility of life in capitalist ruins*. Princeton, NJ: Princeton University Press.
Tsing, A. L., J. Deger, A. K. Saxena and F. Zhou. 2020. *Feral Atlas: The more-than-human Anthropocene*. Stanford, CA: Stanford University Press. http://feralatlas.org [accessed 26 April 2022].
UK Radioactive Waste Inventory. https://ukinventory.nda.gov.uk/wp-content/uploads/2019/11/9B312.pdf [accessed 26 April 2022].
UNESCO. *Hiroshima Peace Memorial (Genbaku Dome)*. https://whc.unesco.org/en/list/775 [accessed 26 April 2022].
World Nuclear Waste Report. 2019. https://worldnuclearwastereport.org/ [accessed 25 November 2020].
Worpole, K. 2018. 'The road to Othona'. In *Radical ESSEX*, edited by H. Dixon and J. Hill. 43–67. Southend-on-Sea: Focal Point Gallery.
Worpole, K. 2021. *No Matter How Many Skies Have Fallen: Back to the land in post-war Britain*. Beaminster: Little Toller Books.
Yusoff, K. 2018. *A Billion Black Anthropocenes or None*. Minneapolis: University of Minnesota Press.

Index

A House for Essex, 17, 332–51
   A Perfect Match, 338, 339–40, 348–9
   appearance, 347–50
   Ballad of Julie Cope, The, 337–8
   Basildon, 338–40, 350–1
   commissioning, 333
   Canvey Island, 337–8, 350–1
   In Its Familiarity, Golden, 341, 348–9
   inspiration, 344–6, 350–1
   landscape setting, 346–7, 350–1
   Maldon, 341, 350–1
   relationship with St Peter-on-the-Wall, 346
   South Woodham Ferrers, 340–1, 350–1
   University of Essex, 342–3, 350–1
   Wrabness, 343, 350–1
   See also Perry, Grayson
Abercrombie, Patrick, 271
Ackroyd, Peter
   Thames: Sacred River, 309, 314, 323, 327
Admiralty, 4–5
Ælfflæd, widow of Byrhtnoth, 319, 320
Æthelbert, king of Kent
   Christian wife, 115, 149
   forged charter, 78, 94, 103
   grant of Tillingham, 94, 103, 116
Æthelburh, sister of Eorcenwald, 124
Æthelred II, king of Northumbria, 322
   coinage of, 97, 100, 169
Æthelwald, king of Deira, 112, 114–15, 117, 118
Æthelwalh, king of the South Saxons, 113–14
Æthelwold, king of East Anglia, 113–14, 135
Æthelwulf, king of Wessex
   coinage of, 97, 100
Allfrey, Francesca, 325
Aidan, bishop of Lindisfarne, 111, 112, 120, 121, 122, 234–5
airport, proposed, 3, 5–8, 19–20, 259
   See also Maplin Sands
Alhflæd, daughter of Oswiu, 113
Alhfrith, son of Oswiu, 123
Ali, Nabil, 18
   Along the Saltmarsh, 18
   The Chapel, 18
Angell, Norman, 240, 255
Anglo-Saxon Chronicle, 144, 311, 313, 317
artistic responses to
   Battle of Maldon, 310–23
   Bradwell A power station, 356–61
   'complexity of place', 325–7
   Essex coastline, 249–51, 355, 362–3

   Essex landscape, 249–51, 289, 309, 332–51
   nuclear landscape, 17–18, 356–60, 369–70, 374–6
   St-Peter-on-the-Wall, 17–18, 18
Arts Council England, 18
Asheldham (Essex), 85, 87, 94, 100, 101–2, 185
Atomic Energy Authority Act, 261
Atomic Weapons Research Establishment, 7, 10, 11, 371
Augustine, missionary and archbishop of Canterbury
   burial in a porticus, 37
   Gregorian mission, 30, 116, 135, 147, 148–9, 150, 152
   Richborough relic, 147
AWRE, see Atomic Weapons Research Establishment

Babingley (Norfolk), 170
Baillie Reynolds, Paul, 231
Baker, J. A., 6–7, 19–20, 277, 294
   The Peregrine, 258–9, 277
Baldwin Brown, G., 232, 274,
Bamburgh (Northumberland), 165, 294
Banyard, James, 251
Barber's Point (Suffolk), 171
Barking (Essex), 93, 280, 308
   bishop of, 221, 226
   monastery, 95, 120, 124, 162, 221, 226
Bassa, priest, 31, 92, 144
Basset, Fulk, bishop of London, 37–8
Bassett, Steven, 82–3
Bataille (Batayl) family, 183, 192, 197–8, 247
   See also Battels
Battels, manor, 177–9, 178, 179, 180–1, 182, 183–4, 185, 187, 191–2, 194, 197–201, 207–8
   See also Effecestrā, La Waule
Battle of Ashingdon, 7
Battle of Maldon (historical event), 7, 315–23
   millennial celebrations, 316–20, 317
   role in modern politics, 324–5
   statue of Byrthnoth, 316, 320–3, 321
   See also Byrthnoth, Maldon Embroidery
Battle of Maldon (poem), 7, 17, 310–14
   symbolism of estuary, 313–14
   symbolism of topography, 313
   symbolism of water, 312–14
   See also Byrthnoth, Maldon Embroidery
Bawsey (Norfolk), 170

Bayeux Tapestry, 319
Beagle, The, 250
Bede, monk of Jarrow
 on Augustine, 37
 on Bertha, 149
 on Bradwell, 19, 117–20
 on Cedd, 19, 27, 78, 81–2, 92, 110–26, 134–5, 161, 179, 219, 294
 on *Cnobheresburg*, 139, 161–2
 on Cuthbert, 293, 310
 on *Dommoc*, 137–8, 161–2
 on Lastingham, 81–2, 117–20, 294
 Letter to Egbert, 170
 on Lichfield, 119
 on Mellitus's church, 81, 94, 116–17
 on Rædwald, 136–7
 on Sigebert, 137–8
 on Tilbury, 19, 81, 326
 on *Ythancæstir*, 27, 78, 81–2, 92, 110, 118–19, 161, 219, 293
Beowulf, 165
Berden (Essex)
 church of St Nicholas, 297
Bergvall, Caroline, 310, 326–7
 Ragadawn, 326–7
Berhtwald, abbot of Reculver, 144–5
Bertha, wife of Æthelbert, 115, 149
Betjeman, John, 259, 260, 265, 273, 275, 276
Bicknacre (Essex), 88
 Augustinian priory, 301
Bigod, Roger, 138
Binchester (County Durham), 71
Bitten, Harry, 289
Blackmore (Essex)
 church of St Laurence, 299, 301, 303, 334, 337, 345, *345*
Blackwater, river, 2, 4, 5, 7, 8, 17, 28, 78, 84, 91, 101, 103, 159, 162, 163, 167, 184, *187*, 194, 201, 204, 217, 239, 240, 242, 255, 258, 260, 265, 266, 270, 278, 291, 308, 309, 310, 311, 313, 315, 316, 317, 319, 320, 323, 325, 327, 341, 346, 355, 356, 357, 360, 361, 362, 362, 368, 372, 373, 374, 375
 Pant(e), old name for, 78, 103, 311–13, 317
Blackwater Estuary, 7, 17, 28, 84, 91, 103, 167, 184, *187*, 194, 201, 204, 206, 239, 240, 242, 258, 266, 278, 308, 313, 315, 320, 323, 341, 346, 355, 356, 360, 361, 362, 364, 368, 372, 373, 374, 375
Blackwater and Dengie Peninsula Protection Association, 267
Blythburgh (Suffolk), 162
Booth, William, 242
Bosham (West Sussex), 161
Botolph, abbot of Iken, 171
Botton, Alain de, 333
BPT, *see* British Pilgrimage Trust
Bradwell A power station
 climate change, 362–3
 decommissioning, 280–1, 356–61, 364–8
 design, 266–7
 development of, 1, 3, 18, 257–64, 359–60, 367–8
 environmental impact, 10–11, 13, 16–17, 280–1
 justification for, 261–5, 270–1
 landscape setting, 258–9, 265, 269–72, 278–80.
 See also Crowe, Sylvia
 opposition to, 259, 267–78, 372–3
 public inquiry, 16–17, 257–60, 263–81
 relationship with Othona, 257, 272
 relationship with St Peter-on-the-Wall, 257, 272, 368
 See also Central Electricity Authority, nuclear power programme
Bradwell B power station, 1–2, 9, 19–20, 257–8, 361–5, 367, 374
Bradwell Bay, RAF airfield, 8–9, *9*, 187, 258, 272
Bradwell Hall (Essex), *86*, 100, *180*, 184, 191–2, 194
Bradwell on Sea (Essex)
 agricultural economy, 193–201, 207, *207*
 Black Death, 192–3, 194–9
 church of St Thomas, 28–9, 37–8
 customs and excise, 204
 dairying, 199–200, 206–8
 Domesday Book, 177–91, *180–1*, *190*, 191–2, *195*
 fishing, 201–3, 207–8
 land drainage, 198–9, 200, 208
 See also 'inning', land reclamation
 manorial history, 177–91, *178*, *179*
 See also Battels, Down Hall, East Hall, *Effecestra*, *La Waule*, Tanyes, Tomlyns Wick, New Wick, Wymarks
 market and fair, 203
 medieval land ownership, 177–91
 military activity, 7–8, 9–10, 56–7, 258
 population figures, 191–3, 197
 population occupations, 200–4
 sheep, 194–7, 208
 shipping, 203–7, *207*
 soils, 193–4
 trade, 203–7, *207*
 wealth, 191–7, 203–7
 wills and probate inventories, 200–1, 202–3, 204–5, *205*
 woodland, *195*, 199
Bradwell Power Generation Company Ltd, 1
Brancaster (Norfolk)
 Roman fort, 56, 60, 67, 70, 72, 131, *132*, 136, 143
Brandon (Suffolk), 169, 170
BRB, *see* Bradwell Power Generation Company Ltd
Brexit, 324
Brinson, Major J., 57, 59
British Archaeological Association, 232
British Pilgrimage Trust, 286, 295–7, 299–300, 303, 337
 Sanctuary project, 296–7
Brittain, Vera, 252
Brooke family, 184–6, 188, 191, 193, 208
 See also Battels, Down Hall, West Wick
Brown, Nigel, 12, 293

Bryan, Guy, 219
Buchanan, Colin, 5–6
Burgh Castle (Norfolk)
　cemetery, 140, 151
　church, 140–1, *140*, 150
　Roman fort, 67, 69, 70, 74, 92, 131–4, *132*, 136, 139–141, *140*, 162
　See also Cnobheresburg; Fursa
burials, Anglo-Saxon
　associated with Roman forts, 55, 57, 61, 101–2, 140–2, 151
　boat burials, 166
　　See also Sutton Hoo; Snape
　in *emporia*, 166–7
　near water, 166–7
Bushe-Fox, J. P., 146–7
Bushnell, G. H. S., 233–4
Butley (Suffolk), 170–2
Byrhtnoth, ealdorman of Essex, 7, 311–23, 327
　statue by John Doubleday, *321*, 324–5
　statue by Nathaniel Hitch, 316
　See also Battle of Maldon

Cælin, brother of Cedd, 111, 114
Caister-on-Sea (Norfolk)
　cemeteries, 141–2, 151
　church, 142, 150
　Roman fort, 60, 69, 70, 72, 131–4, *132*, 136, 141–2, 162
Caistor St Edmund (Norfolk), 101, 139
Calder Hall power station (Cumbria), 261, 263, 264, 266–7, *266*
Camden, William, 53–4, 55, 68
Campaign for Nuclear Disarmament, 264
Canterbury (Kent)
　church of St Mary, 32–3, 149, 220
　church of St Pancras, 30, 32–3, 38, 149, 220
　church of SS Peter and Paul, 30, 32–3, 37, 92, 149
Canute, *see* Cnut
Canvey Island (Essex), 17, 93, 290, 334, 337–9, 344, 351
Capon, Kenneth, 342
Carausius, Roman emperor, 66–9
Carter, H. Malcolm, 30, 32, 232–5
Carter, Henry, 184
　See also Battels
Cash, Lee, 317, 320
Causton (Cawston), John, 182
CBA, *see* Council for British Archaeology
CEA, *see* Central Electricity Authority
Cedd, bishop of the East Saxons
　background, 110–12
　baptism of Swithhelm, 113
　behaviour as bishop, 120–3
　burial at Lastingham, 81–2, 118, 123–5
　conversion of the East Saxons, 14–15, 113–14, 115–20, 124, 135
　conversion of the Middle Angles, 112, 135
　death, 31, 81–2, 111, 118, 123–5
　family, 111–12
　foundation of Lastingham, 114–20
　foundation of *Ythancæstir*, 14, 81–2, 92, 110, 118, 135, 161

　leaving *Ythancæstir*, 95
　Lindisfarne, 111–12
　relationship with Oswiu of Northumbria, 113–15
　relics, 124–6
　role at Synod of Whitby, 111, 115, 122–3
　timeline of life, 111
　translation to Lichfield, 125–6
central places, 90–3
Central Electricity Authority, 261, 265–9, 271, 276–7
Central Electricity Generating Board, 261
CGN, *see* China General Nuclear Power Group
Chad, brother of Cedd and bishop of Lichfield, 111, 115, 118–26, 294
Challenge Running, 290
Chancellor, Frederic, 219–20
Chancellor, Wykeham, 223–4, 227
Chapelle, Count de la, 56–7
Chapman and André's map of Essex (1777), 30, 85, 88, 89–90, 193, 204
charters
　grants to Reculver church, 144–5
　of Æthelbert, king of Kent, 78, 94, 103
　of Offa, king of the East Saxons, 82
　of Swæfred, king of the East Saxons, 78, 82, 83, *86–7*, 94, 103
Chelmsford, diocese of, 16, 41, 220–1, 235, 274, 290
Chertsey (Surrey), 124
Chillingworth, John, *57*
China General Nuclear Power Group, 1, 372
Chipping Ongar (Essex), 17, 286, 287, 290, 300
Christian Pacifist Forestry and Land Units, 252
Christianisation
　of the East Angles, 136–42, 150–1
　of the East Saxons, 81–2, 115–17, 124
　of Kent, 149–50
　of the Middle Angles, 112, 135,
　as reclamation of *Britannia*, 116, 148, 152
　reuse of Roman buildings, 15, 92, 102–3, 116, 119, 130–1, 147–51, 152
Christmas family, 185–6, 188, 208
　See also Down Hall, New Wick
Churches Conservation Trust, 297
Clark, Douglas, 265, 267, 270–1
Clarke, Polly, 240
coastal erosion, 12, 54, 58, 59, 63, 79, 131–2, 134, 143, 146, 161, 163, 250–1
coastal landscapes, 163–5, 239–42, 247–51, 254–5, 257–9, 362–3
Coenwulf, king of Mercia, 99, 145
　coinage of, 97, 100
Colchester (Essex), 3–4, 17, 35, 101, 193, 204, 207, 221, 229, 290, 342–3
Coleman, John, 186, 188, 200
　See also Down Hall, New Wick
Columba, bishop of Iona, 112, 118, 120, 122–3, 160, 161, 325
　Colm Cille's Spiral, 325, 327
　See also Iona
Colvin, Brenda, 280
Common Ground, 239
Commons Preservation Society, 271–2, 273
conversion, *see* Christianisation

Council for British Archaeology, 231–2, 274
Council for the Preservation of Rural England, 262, 264, 271–3, 275, 278
Countryside Stewardship scheme, 12–13
Cnobheresburg, 92, 139, 161–2
  See also Burgh Castle
Cnut, king of England, 7, 311, 323
Colchester Museum, 72, 95, 97, 100, 103
Cope, Julie, 17, 334, 336, 337–9, 341–2, 344, 348, 350–1
  See also A House for Essex
Corpus of Early Medieval Coin Finds, 97–100, *98–9*
Cottrell, Stephen, archbishop of York, 290
Council of *Clovesho*, 138
COVID-19 pandemic, 2, 289, 303
Cox, J. Charles, 220
CPRE, *see* Council for the Preservation of Rural England
Crawford, Lord, 232–3
Crouch, river, 2, 4–5, 7–8, 84, 103, 159, 163, 167, 225, 250, 258, 340
Crowe, Sylvia, 259, 278–81
  The Landscape of Power, 278–9
Crowland (Lincolnshire), 165–6
Cublington (Buckinghamshire), 5, 19
Cultural Engine, 18
Cuthbert, bishop of Lindisfarne, 165, 291–2, 293–4, 301, 310
Cynebill, brother of Cedd, 111, 114, 118

Danbury (Essex), 84–5, 88–9, 103
Danbury Hills (Essex), 14, 85, 88, 89–90, 102
Dance, Moira, 274–5
Darwin, Charles, 250
Defence Evaluation and Research Agency, 8
Defenders of Essex, 6
Dengie Flats (Essex), 8–9, 258, 275
Dengie Peninsula, 2, 3, 5, 14, 15, 19, 20, 242, 245, 250, 259–60, 277, 294, 309, 335
  Anglo-Saxon settlement of, 101–2
  documentary history, 15
  ecological designations, 366–7
  medieval occupation, 82–90, *84*, 94–103, 159, 167, 199, 251, 258, 308, 332
  military use of, 8–10, 257
  Roman occupation, 53–4, 58, 63, 65–6, 69–70
  See also Deningei
Deningei, folk territory
  Anglo-Saxon settlement of, 101–2
  central places, 90–3, 103
  Domesday survey, 85
  extent of, 78, 82–90, *84*, 103
  field / parish boundaries, 85, 88–9
  medieval landholdings, 90–4
  royal vills, 90–4, 103
  woodland, 85, 88–9
  See also Dengie Peninsula, Tillingham, Ythancæstir
DERA, *see* Defence Evaluation and Research Agency
Dicul, Irish monk, 161
Difference Exchange, 325
  Colm Cille's Spiral, 325, 327
  DISCLOSURE: Old Words Made New, 325

Doggerland, 363, 367
Dommoc, diocese of, 92, 137–8, 150, 161–2
  See also Dunwich, Walton Castle
Doune (Downe) family, 184–5, 187, 198–9
  See also Down Hall, Taynes
Dounreay power station (Caithness), 262, 263–4, 280, 360
Dover (Kent)
  Roman fort, 54, 131, *132*, 142–3
Down Hall, manor, 8, 38, *86*, 100, 177–9, *178*, *179*, 184–7, *187*, 193–4, 198–200, 202, 204, 207–8
Dowsett, H. W., 225, 227, 260
Driberg, Tom, 240, 265–6, 268, 270–3, 276–7, 280
Dungeness power station (Kent), 264, 372
Dunwich (Suffolk), 138, 161–2, 163
Durham (County Durham), 291–2, 294

Eadbald, king of Kent, 116
Eadred, king of the English, 145
Ealhmund, king of Kent, 145
Eardwulf, king of west Kent, 145
EAS, *see* Essex Archaeological Society
East Hall, manor, 81, *87*, 100, 177–83, *178*, *179*, *180*, *183*, 184, 188, 191–2, 194–8, 201, 202, 204, 207–8.
  See also Effecestrā, La Waule
East Saxon kingdom
  Anglo-Saxon migration, 101, 300
  boundaries of, 82–3,
  central places, 90–3
  conversion of, 81–2, 115–17, 300–1
  folk territories, 82–90, 300
Eastlands Farm, 80, *86*, *180*, 185, 191, 196–7, 225
EDF, *see* Électricité de France
Edmund Ironside, 7
Edward the Elder, 91
Edwin, king of Northumbria, 137
Effecestrā, manor, 28, 179–82, *180*, *190*, 194, *195*
  See also East Hall, *La Waule*
Egbert, king of Kent
  granting of Reculver, 31, 92, 144
Électricité de France, 1, 372
Elmham (Norfolk), 137–8, 150
Ely (Cambridgeshire), 164, 319
emporia, trading ports, 93, 166–8, 172
Eorcenwald, bishop of London, 124
Eorpwald, king of East Anglia, 137
Epping Forest Holiday Fellowship, 286, 303
Essex Archaeological Society, 217, 219
Essex Cultural Diversity Project, 18, 326
Essex Design Guide, 340–1
Essex Way, 343–4
Evetts, L. C., 234

Fairbrother, Nan, 269
Farocki, Harun, 358–9, 375
FAT Architecture, 333
Felix, bishop of East Anglia, 92, 123, 136–8, 161
Finán, bishop of Lindisfarne, *111*, 112, 113
Finch, Alan, 7–8
fish traps, 28–29, *80*, *96*, 96–7, 201–3
Fitch, Marc, 274
Fletcher, Eric, 231–2

INDEX   383

Flintham, Matthew, 10
Flixborough (Lincolnshire), 169
Foulness Island, 2–3, 5, 7–8, 259, 309
    military use of, 2–3, 7–8, 10–11, 364, 368, 371, 375
    See also Maplin Sands
Francis-Dehqani, Guli, bishop of Chelmsford, 290
Fry, T. M., 259, 269
Furnee, Bettina, 250–1
    Lines of Defence, 251
Fursa, Irish missionary, 92, 139–41, 161
    See also Burgh Castle; Cnobheresburg

Galpin, F. W., 225
Garrett, Marc, 325
Goldin + Senneby, 365–6, 375
    Spruce Time, 365–6, *365*, 375
Gordon, Eric, 233
Gordon, Lewis, 4–5
Great Chesterford (Cambridgeshire), 69
Great Wakering (Essex), 93
Green, Charles, 139, 141
Greensted (Essex)
    St Andrew's church, 286, 299, 301, 337
Gregory the Great, pope, 116, 148, 152
    letter to Augustine, 148
Grimmitt, H. W., 268
Guthlac of Crowland, 165–6, 310–11
    Life of Saint Guthlac, 165–6

Halabi, Inas, 369–70, 372, 375
    We Have Always Known the Wind's Direction, 369–70, *369*, 375
Harden, D. B., 231
Harrison, B., 270
Heasman, Arthur, 222
Hecht, Gabrielle, 357–8
Herbert, J. B., 270–1
Higham family, 184, 191
    See also Battels
Hillier, Meg, 281
Hinton, Christopher, 262, 281
Hirst, Gabriella, 370–2, 375
    'Atom Bomb' rose, 370–1, *371*
    How to Make a Bomb, 370–2, 375
Hlothhere, king of Kent, 144–5
HMT Empire Windrush, 326–7
Hoggeston (Buckinghamshire), 19
Honorius, emperor of Rome, 67, 132
Honorius, archbishop of Canterbury, 137
Hoskins, W. G., 259

Iken (Suffolk), 162, *162*, 171, 172
Ingelric, chaplain of Edward the Confessor, 91
Ingwald, bishop of London, 78, 83, 94, *95*, 103
'Inning', 3, 11, 194, 200, 208
    See also land reclamation
Iona (Argyll and Bute), 112, 115, 118, 120, 122–3, 126, 160, 234–5, 242
    See also Columba
Ipswich Ware, pottery, 35, 91, 95, 168–9

Jellicoe, Geoffrey, 280
Jenkins, Simon, 295
Johnson, Stephen, 68, 139

Kears, Carl, 325
'Kentish' churches, 30–1, 32–3, 36–37, 38, 135–6, 149–50, 300–1
King, H. W., 219
King, Laurence, 41, 225–35, *230*, 274–5
    See also St Peter-on-the-Wall restoration (proposed)
Knapp, W. T., 223

Lake, H. A., 221
land reclamation, 2–3, 4–5, 11, 15, 55, 80, 163–5, 177, 194, 200, 208, 258
    See also 'inning'
Land Settlement Association, 253–4
Lansbury, George, 242–3
Lastingham (North Yorkshire)
    burial of Cedd, 124–5
    carved stone, 125, *125*
    foundation of, 81–2, 95, 110, 114–20, *114*, *119*, 119–20, 165, 235, 294
La Waule/Walle, manor, 28, 179–82, 183
    See also East Hall, Effecestra
Lees, Clare, 292–3, 325
Leland, John, 144
Lewin, Thomas, 39, 55–6, 61, 67–8, 70, 217, 219–20, 230
Lichfield (Staffordshire), 119, 120, 122, 124–6, 294
liminality, 159, 240–2, 247–50, 259–60, 292–3, 308–9
Lindisfarne (Northumberland), 100, 110, 112, *112*, 115, 123, 126, 161, 242, 291–4, 310
Lindstrøm, Bjarne, 322
Linnets Cottage, 7, 241
literary responses, see artistic responses
Liudhard, Frankish bishop, 115
Living Architecture, 333–4, 346
Lloyd, G., 265
Loftus, E. A., 231
long-distance walking routes, 17, 286–304, 336–7
    See also Old Way, St Chad's Way, St Cuthbert's Way, St Peter's Way, St Thomas Way
Luckin, Bill, 263
Luckin, William, 184
    See also Battels
Lyminge (Kent), 168–9, 220
Lympne (Kent)
    Roman fort, 54–5, 64, 72, 131–4, *132*, 142–3

Macfarlane, Robert, 249, 289, 294
Magnox, 259, 261, 265, 266, 270, 280–1
Malcolm Carter, H., 232, 234
Maldon (Essex)
    A House for Essex, 341–2
    archaeological excavations, 91, 95
    as central place, 91, 103, 192–3, 314
    Congregational Chapel, 269, 273
    port, 202, 205–7
    salt production, 355
    See also Battle of Maldon

Maldon District Council, 17, 289, 303, 310, 315
Maldon Embroidery, 317–20, *318*, *319*, 323, 341
  See also Byrhtnoth, Battle of Maldon
Maplin Sands Airport, 3, 5, 7, 19, 259
mappa mundi, 308
Mare, John de la, 100, 196, 198, 203
Marshall, Richard, 243–4
Martello towers, 7
Matthews, Fred, 287–90, 304
May, Theresa, 327
McLeod, George, 242
Mellitus, bishop of London, 78, 81, 92, 94, 103, 116–17, 148, 300, 316
Melrose (Scottish Borders), 291–2
Metropolis Sewage and Essex Reclamation Company, 5
Micklethwaite, J. T., 220–1
Middleton Murry, John, 252
Mildmay family, 186, 188, 200, 208.
  See also Down Hall
Ministry of Public Buildings and Works, 30, 40, 42, 57, 221–2, 224, 227, 229, 231–3, 274
Ministry of Works, *see* Ministry of Public Buildings and Works
Minster-in-Sheppey (Kent), 162
Minster-in-Thanet (Kent), 162, 308
Mirrington, Alexander, 95, 97, *98–9*, 100
Misler, Andrea-Reneé, 242, 243
mission stations, 15, 110, 151
missionaries, 2, 14–15, 100, 110–12, 120, 123, 147–8, 151–2, 270
  See also Augustine, Christianisation, Romanitas
Moll, Herman, 54
monasteries, Anglo-Saxon
  archaeological character, 163, 168–70
  association with Roman sites, 15, 92, 102–3, 116, 119, 147–51
  coastal locations of, 159–72
  hermitages, 165–6
  isolated locations, 165–6, 171–2
  landscape setting of, 159–72
  liminality, 159, 171–2
  See also Cnobheresburg, Ely, Iken, Iona, Lastingham, Lindisfarne, *Romanitas*, Saxon Shore Forts, Tilbury, Ythancæstir
Morant, Philip, 30, 40, 177–8, 217, 219, 230
Morpurgo, Michael, 11–12, 260–1
Mortimer, Cromwell, 54
Motley, Norman, 16, 240, 242–5, 251, 255, 373
  Much Ado About Something, 242
Mucking (Essex), 308–9
Mundon (Essex), 191, 290
  church of St Mary, 299, 301–3, *302*, 337
'My Bradwell' website, 1

Nairn, Ian, 259
National Farmers' Union, 270
Nature Conservancy, 264
NDA, *see* Nuclear Decommissioning Agency
Newport (Essex), 90, 93

New Wick, estate, 7–8, 177–9, 178, *179*, 186, 188, 200, 207
Nicholson, Charles, 225–6
Nicholson, Max, 264
Nirex, 374
Northey Island (Essex), 313–15, 322–3
Notitia Dignitatum, 54, 67–8, 131–4, *133*, 136
Nuclear Decommissioning Agency, 281
nuclear power programme, 1–3, 9–11, 16–20, 261–7, 270, 278–81, 368, 372–3
  See also Bradwell A power station
Nucleus Archive (Highland), 360–1
Nursling (Hampshire), 162
Nuthampstead (Hertfordshire), 5

Oda, archbishop of Canterbury, 145
Offa, king of the East Saxons, 82
Offa, king of Mercia, 126
Office of Works, *see* Ministry of Public Buildings and Works
Old St Peter's (Rome), 92
Old Way, 295–7
Oldbury power station (South Gloucestershire), 270
Oliver, Stuart, 240
O'Neil, Bryan, 231
Orford Ness (Suffolk), 11
  See also Atomic Weapons Research Establishment
Osmond, Mervyn, 271–3
Oswald, king of Northumbria, 114, 160, 294, 311, 313
Oswine, king of Deira, 122
Oswiu, king of Northumbria, 112, 113–15, 123
Othona, Roman fort
  abandonment, 71–2, 134–5
  Anglo-Saxon re-occupation, 13, 15, 55, 101–2
  aerial photographic assessment, 57–8, 61–2
  approach road, 63
  archaeological excavations, 27–28, 54–7, *56*, 60–2, *62*, 64–5, 73, 80–1, 95–6, 101–2
  brooches, 72–3, *73*
  burials, 55, 57, 61, 101–2
  coin sequence, 66–7, 71–2
  construction, 66, 70, 134–5
  Countryside Stewardship scheme, 12–13
  date, 66, 70–2
  discovery and identification, 5, 54–56, 68, 217
  economic role, 69–72
  erosion of ruins, 54, 58–9
  evidence for animal butchery, 69–71
  external ditch, 57, 59
  extramural settlement, 14, 57–8, 61–5, 73
  field-walking, 57–8, 61–2, *62*, 63–5, 73
  First World War activity, 56–7, 252
  form and layout, 58–61, *62*, 63–4
  function, 14, 67–72
  garrison, 67
  geophysical survey, 57–8, 60–2, *62*, 63–5, 73
  heritage designations, 275

INDEX   **385**

landscape context, 58, *58*, 78–83, *79*, *80*
perimeter walls, 57, 58–61
ramparts, 57, 59
reconstruction, *60*
relationship with Bradwell A power station, 257
relationship with other Saxon Shore Forts, 59, 60, 67, 69–72, 130–4
research potential, 72–3
Roman occupation, 13–14, 66–72
Second World War activity, 58, 64, 79–80, 252
as source of stone, 34, 54, 71, 130–1
types of stone used, 59–60, 71
See also Bradwell on Sea, Saxon Shore Forts, St-Peter-on-the-Wall, *Ythancæstir*
Othona Community
archaeological excavations, 57, 64–5, 67, 70–2, 95–6
Burton Bradstock (Dorset), 243
ethos, 239–44, 247–55, 355, 373–4
expansion, 243–5
farming, 252–4
foundation, 16, 240–4, 251, 373
infrastructure, 245–7, 373–4
landscape setting, 239–42, 247–8, 254–5
Nissen huts, 239, 243, *244*, 245
pacifism, 252–3
relationship with Bradwell A power station, 246, 374
relationship with St Peter-on-the-Wall, 240–1, 247, 255
'spirit of place', 239–41, 247–51, 269–70
See also Bradwell on Sea, Motley, Norman, Othona, St Peter-on-the-Wall
Our Lady of Walsingham (Norfolk), 335, 351
Owen, J. R. B., 221, 225
Owens, Susan, 249

pacifism, 251–3
Pant(e), river, *see* Blackwater
Paris, Matthew, 298
Parker, Christopher William, 220–1, 222, 226
Parker, Clement W., 224
Parker, Dorcas, 225
Parker, Dorothy, 201
Parker, John Oxley, 55–6, 60–1, 72, 80, 95, 97, 100–2, 217, 221, 226–7
Parker, Oxley Durant, 224–5
PAS, *see* Portable Antiquities Scheme
Peace Pledge Union, 252
Peada, king of the Middle Angles, 113, 135
Peculiar People, 251–2
Peers, Charles, 30, 40–1, 57, 220–5, 230, 233, 235
Penda, king of Mercia, 114
Perry, Grayson, 17, 332–3, 338–9
See also A House for Essex
Perry, Sarah, 249, 309
The Essex Serpent, 309
Petre, John, 322
Pevensey (Sussex)
Roman fort, 60, 69, 131–4, *132*
Peverel, Ranulf de, 38, *180*, 184–5

See also Down Hall
Pewet Island, 28, 200, 204
fish traps, 28–9
pilgrimage, 290–8, 303–4, 332–3
contemporary, 336–7
maps, 298
Santiago de Compostela, 295, 335
wayside chapels, 334–6
See also British Pilgrimage Trust
Pilgrim's Way, 335–6
Pincheon (Pynchon) family, 182, 184, 189–91, *189*, 199, 208
See also Battels, East Hall, *Effecestra*, *La Waule*, Wymarks
Plowden, E., 261
Portable Antiquities Scheme, 97, 100–2
Portchester (Hampshire)
Roman fort, 56, 61, 67, 72, 131, *132*, 133–4
Portmahomack (Highlands), 169
Prittlewell, Southend (Essex)
church of St Mary, 167
princely burial, 115, 167, 301, 309
royal vill, 93

Qinetiq, 8
Quakers, *see* Society of Friends

Rædwald, king of East Anglia, 136–7
railway, proposed, 1, 3–4
Ramblers' Association, 287–8, 337
Raymant, Alan, 1
Reculver (Kent)
archaeological excavations, 143–4
carved cross, 144
Chapel House, 145
church of St Mary, 30, 31–2, *32*, 37, 143–5, *144*, 162, 232–3, 274, 346
demolition, 143–4, *144*, 145
fort gifted to Bassa, 31, 92, 144–5
Roman fort, 72, 131–4, *132*, 142–5
Reedham (Norfolk), 69
Rendlesham (Suffolk), 113, 135, 138, 166
Richborough (Kent)
archaeological excavations, 145–6
burials, 147
chapel of St Augustine, 146–7
religious reuse, 146–7, 162
Roman church, 146
Roman fort, 61, 69, 72, 131–4, *132*, 145–6
Ricule, sister of Æthelbert, 115–16
Rigold, Stuart, 134, 138, 142–3, 147
Roach Smith, Charles, 55–6, 61, 68, 70, 217
Rochester (Kent), 138, 162, 220
Rodings (Essex), 82–3, 88
Rogers, Richard and Su, 317
Rogibus, 12
Romanitas, 15, 92, 102–3, 116, 119, 147–51
Roskill Commission, 5
Royal Commission on the Historical Monuments of England, 223–4
Royal Fine Art Commission, 232, 274, 276
Royal Society for the Protection of Birds, 6, 258, 259, 273, 278, 369

RSPB, *see* Royal Society for the Protection of Birds
Ruskin, John, 248

Sæbbi, sub-king of the East Saxons, 124
Sæbert, king of the East Saxons, 81, 116, 300–1
St Cuthbert's Way
  creation, 291–2
  relationship with Cuthbert, 291–3
St Mary's Stadium, Southampton (Hampshire), 166–7, 168
St Osyth (Essex), 7, 188, 204, 205
St Peter-on-the-Wall,
  altar, 223–4, 233–5, *234*
  approach road, 293
  apse, 28, 37
  archaeological excavations, 35–6, 38, 39, 57, 168–9, 230
  bell tower/belfry, 29, 38, 230
  burials, 55, 57, 61, 101–2, 135
  chancel arches, 32, *33*, 36, 39, 42, 232–3
  coastal location, 15, 159–72
  coin sequence, 97–100, *98–9*, 169
  construction phases, 34–7, 41–2, 135
  Countryside Stewardship scheme, 12–13
  date, 35–6, 55
  entrance door, 38, 41–2, 227
  fire, 29–30
  floor, 228–9
  foundation by Cedd, 13, 14, 27, 78, 81–2, 92, 110, 118–19, 124, 126, 152, 219
  furniture, 224–5, 229, 233–4
  groundplan, *31*, 32, 135
  heritage designations, 275
  landscape setting, 2, 14, 15, 27, 28–29, *29*, 159–60, 178–91, 221, 293–4, 332
  medieval decline, 13, 15
  medieval landholdings, 28–9, 179–84, *see also* Battels, East Hall, *Effecestra*, *La Waule/Walle*
  military use of, 8, 227, 235, 275
  mortar, 35, 37, 41–2
  nave, 32, 37, 230
  ownership, 220–1, 226–7
  pilgrimage (annual), 16, 224–5, 229, 233, 235
  pilgrimage (Brentwood), 225
  place of worship, 16
  porch, 28, 32, 38, 41–2, 230
  porticus, 28, 37, 42, 230
  recognition of, 14, 15, 217–24, 235
  rededication service, 14, 15, 224, 235
  relationship with Bradwell A power station, 257
  relationship with church of St Thomas, Bradwell on Sea, 28–9, 37–8, 100, 217
  relationship with Kentish churches; 30–1, 32–3, 36–37, 38, 135–6, 220, 231
  relationship with Roman fort, 27–8, 34–6, 130, 135
  restoration (carried out), 14, 15, 29–30, *40*, 40–2, 220–3, 225–9

restoration (proposed by King), 228–35, *230*, 274–5
reused Roman masonry, 34, 54, 59, 71, 135
rood (crucifix), 229–31, 234, *234*, *see also* Stephens, Francis
roof, 38–9, 41, 225–6, 227–9
second-generation church, 30–1, 119–20, 124, 126, 135–6
Second World War damage, 41, 227, 235, 275
soundscape, 298–9
stone-by-stone survey, 14, 30, 32, *33*, 41–2, *43*, *45*, *47*, *49*
structural history, 30–8, 41–2
tower, 38, 230
trustees, 220–1, 226–7
types of stone used, 33–5, 37, 38, 39–40, 42, 71, 223
use as barn, 13–14, 30, 35, 37, 39–40, 42, 218
vestry, 233
windows, 36, 37, 41–2, 227
See also Cedd, Othona, Othona Community, Saxon Shore Forts, *Romanitas*, *Ythancæstir*
St Peter's Way, 17, 291, 337
  creation, 286–9, 299
  ethos, 287–9
  ideas for improvement, 299–300, 303–4
  infrastructure, 290, 299
  pilgrimage, 290–1
  usage, 290, 295
St Thomas Way, 295–6, 297–8, 301
St Valery-sur-Somme (Somme), *180*, 182–3, 194, 195–6
St Werburgh, 294
Sales Point (Essex), 7
  fish traps, 28–9, *80*, 95–7, *96*, 201–2, 208
salt production, 59, 69–71, 81, 200, 206, 242, 258, 277, 355
saltmarsh, 20, 78, 81, 194, 198–200, 208, 241–2, 249, 260, 301, 362–3, 367, 374
Sanders, Henry, 224
Sandys, Duncan, 272
Saxon Shore Forts, 7, 14, 15, 55, 130–52
  as sites for later churches, 130–52
  See also Brancaster, Burgh Castle, Caister-on-Sea, Dover, Lympne, *Notitia Dignitatum*, Othona, Pevensey, Portchester, Reculver, Richborough, Walton Castle
Schuppli, Susan, 356–9, 370
Scourti, Erica, 325–6
Seafarer, The, 325
Seaxbald, king of the East Saxons, 135
Selsey (West Sussex), 161–2
Seven Years Association, 225
Shaw, Ron, 291
Shenstone, Gerald, 234–5, *234*
Sheppard, Dick, 252
Shoreline Management Plan, 3, 19, 367–8

INDEX **387**

Sigebert, king of East Anglia, 92, 137, 139, 161
Sigebert 'Sanctus', king of the East Saxons, 81, *111*, 113, 121–2, 125, 135, 161
Sigehere, sub-king of East Saxons, 124
Sizewell power station (Suffolk), 11, 265, 372
Sledd, king of the East Saxons, 115
Sloman, Albert, 342
Smith, J. R., 8
Smith, Roger, 291
Snape (Suffolk)
  boat burials, 166–7, 171, 309
  Snape Maltings, 251
Society for the Protection of Ancient Buildings, 273–6
Society of Friends, 252–3
Society of Friends of St Peter and St Cedd, 225
South Elmham (Suffolk)
  Old Minster, 220
South Essex Estuary and Reclamation Act (1852), 4
South Essex Estuary and Reclamation Company, 4–5, 9, 54, 217
Southminster (Essex), 85, 90, 93, 94, *98–9*, 100, 192–3, 203, 206, 223, 260
SPAB, *see* Society for the Protection of Ancient Buildings
Spender, Humphrey, 317, 341
Spurrell, Frederick, 55, 218–19
Staffordshire Hoard, 301
Stansted Mountfitchet (Essex)
  church of St Mary, 297
Steadman, George, 225
Steeple (Essex), 85, *87*, 94, 251, 290–1
Stephens, Francis, 229, *234*
Stoke Quay, Ipswich (Suffolk), 166–8
Strood Channel, 4
Strutt & Parker, 12
Stukeley, William, 54
Stutton (Suffolk), 162
Sutton Hoo (Suffolk), 135, 137–8, 166–7, 171, 309
Swæfred, king of the East Saxons, 78, 82, 83, *86–7*, 94, 103
Swithhelm, king of the East Saxons, 113–14, 135
Synod of Whitby, 30–1, *111*, 115, 122–3, 124, 291, 362

Tanyes, manor, 177–9, *178, 179*, 185–6, 187–9, 191, 194, 198–200
  See also New Wick
Thabayneh, Khalil, 369–70
Thackeray Turner, Hugh, 274
Thanet (Kent), 143, 147, 346
Thatcher, Margaret, 341, 344
Theodore, archbishop of Canterbury, 124, 136, 137
Theodred, bishop of London, 94, 116
Thomson & Craighead, 360–1, 375
  Temporary Index, 360, *361*, 375
Thurleigh (Bedfordshire), 5

Tilbury (Essex), 19, 81, 92–3, 95, 110, 117–18, 161, 231, 267, 294, 301, 308, 326–7
  See also Bede, Cedd
Tillingham (Essex)
  forged charter of Æthelbert, 78, 94, 103, 116–17
  fragmentation of estate, *86–7*, 94
  placename, 117
  possible royal vill, *86–7*, 93–4, 103
  reconstruction of estate, *86–7*, 94, *95*, 116–17, 159, 184–5, 192, 201, 204, 206, 251, 287
  See also Mellitus
Tolkien, J. R. R., 316, 340
Tomlyns Wick, manor, 177–9, *178, 179*, 185–6, 187–8, 199–200
  See also New Wick
Trawsfynydd power station (Gwynedd), 262
Tredsall family, 205–6
Two Saints' Way, 294, 301

UK Atomic Energy Authority, 261–5, 267, 269
UKAEA, *see* UK Atomic Energy Authority
Underwood, Eric, 269

Via Francigena Trail, 335
Viking raids, 2, 7, 138, 145, 150, 291–2, 310–14, 317–18

Wade, Robert, 186, 188, 191.
  See also Down Hall, New Wick
Wadham, Jane, 14, 30, 32, 38, 41–2, 43, 45, 47, 49
Wakering (Essex), 93, 162, 308
Walsham, Alexandra, 239–40, 251
Walton Castle (Suffolk)
  church, 138–9, 150
  Roman fort, 92, 131–4, *132, 137*, 136–8, 142, 149, 162, 163
  See also Dommoc
WARA, *see* Wing Airport Resistance Association
Warner, John, 219
Wealdhere, bishop of London, 82
Wells, H. G., 309
  War of the Worlds, 309
Wentworth Day, J., 270
West Essex Ramblers, 286, 303–4
Whithorn (Wigtownshire), 169
Whittingdale, John, 324–5, 327
Wicken Bonhunt (Essex), 90, 93, 95
Wilfrid, bishop of York, 161–2
Willis, Harold, QC, 268–71, 276–8
Wine, bishop of London, 117, 124
Wing Airport Resistance Association, 19
Winwæd, battle of, 114
Woodcock, George, 253
Wormegay (Norfolk), 168, 170
Wrabness (Essex), 17, 334, 337, 343–4, 351
Wulfhere, king of Mercia, 113, 117, 124
Wulfred, archbishop of Canterbury, 145

Wymarks, estate, 7, 8, 177–9, *178*, *179*, 182, 184, 188–91, *189*, 199–200, 204
Wynfrith (Boniface), archbishop of Mainz, 162

Youth Hostels Association, 273
Ythancæstir
    abandonment, 81–2, 95, 103
    Domesday survey, 28
    fish traps, 96–7
    foundation by Cedd, 14, 27, 78, 81–2, 92, 110, 118–19, 135, 219, 224, 293
    identification of, 53–4
    landscape context, 78–83, *79*, *80*, 83–93, 94, 100, 102–3, 179
    placename, 81, 135, 179
    possible royal vill, 91–2
    relationship with church of St Thomas, Bradwell on Sea, 100
    relationship with Lastingham, 117–18
    trade networks, 167–9
    See also Bradwell on Sea, Othona, St Peter-on-the-Wall

www.ingramcontent.com/pod-product-compliance
Lightning Source LLC
Chambersburg PA
CBHW040712140425
25064CB00008B/152